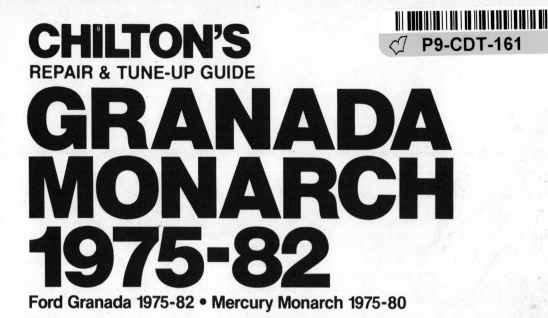

# CHILTON'S
## REPAIR & TUNE-UP GUIDE

# GRANADA MONARCH 1975-82

Ford Granada 1975-82 • Mercury Monarch 1975-80

Vice President and General Manager JOHN P. KUSHNER
Managing Editor KERRY A. FREEMAN, S.A.E.
Senior Editor RICHARD J. RIVELE, S.A.E.
Editor RON WEBB

CHILTON BOOK COMPANY
Radnor, Pennsylvania
19089

## SAFETY NOTICE

Proper service and repair procedures are vital to the safe, reliable operation of all motor vehicles, as well as the personal safety of those performing repairs. This book outlines procedures for servicing and repairing vehicles using safe, effective methods. The procedures contain many NOTES, CAUTIONS and WARNINGS which should be followed along with standard safety procedures to eliminate the possibility of personal injury or improper service which could damage the vehicle or compromise its safety.

It is important to note that repair procedures and techniques, tools and parts for servicing motor vehicles, as well as the skill and experience of the individual performing the work vary widely. It is not possible to anticipate all of the conceivable ways or conditions under which vehicles may be serviced, or to provide cautions as to all of the possible hazards that may result. Standard and accepted safety precautions and equipment should be used when handling toxic or flammable fluids, and safety goggles or other protection should be used during cutting, grinding, chiseling, prying, or any other process that can cause material removal or projectiles.

Some procedures require the use of tools specially designed for a specific purpose. Before substituting another tool or procedure, you must be completely satisfied that neither your personal safety, nor the performance of the vehicle will be endangered.

Although information in this guide is based on industry sources and is as complete as possible at the time of publication, the possibility exists that the manufacturer made later changes which could not be included here. While striving for total accuracy, Chilton Book Company cannot assume responsibility for any errors, changes, or omissions that may occur in the compilation of this data.

## PART NUMBERS

Part numbers listed in this reference are not recommendations by Chilton for any product by brand name. They are references that can be used with interchange manuals and aftermarket supplier catalogs to locate each brand supplier's discrete part number.

## ACKNOWLEDGMENTS

The Chilton Book Company expresses its appreciation to the Ford Motor Company for the technical information and illustrations contained within this manual.

Ford special tools mentioned in some procedures can be ordered through your Ford dealer or directly from the Owatonna Tool Company, Owatonna, Minnesota 55060.

Manufactured in the United States of America
1234567890      2109876543

Chilton's Repair & Tune-Up Guide: Granada and Monarch 1975–82
ISBN 0-8019-7311-2 pbk.
Library of Congress Catalog Card No. 82-72933

# CONTENTS

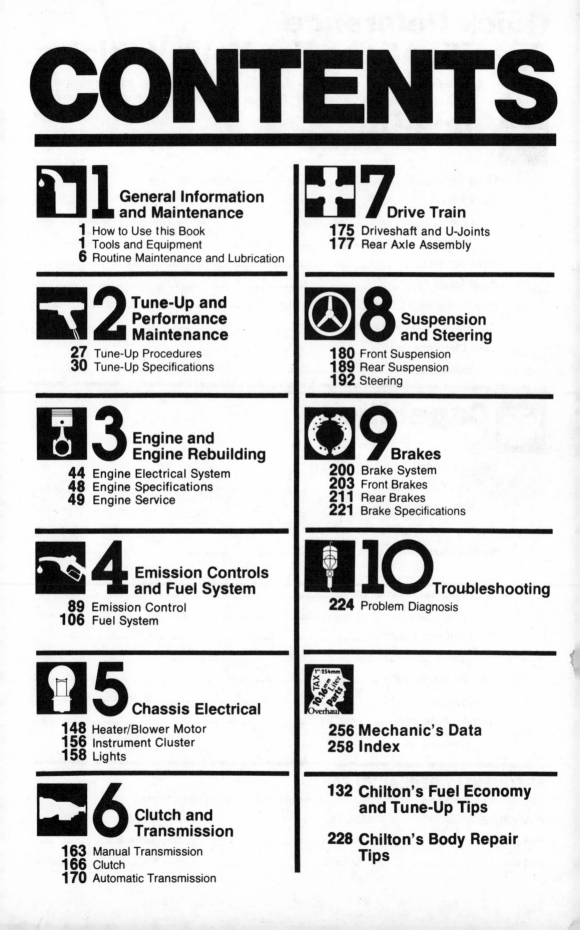

# Quick Reference Specifications For Your Vehicle

Fill in this chart with the most commonly used specifications for your vehicle. Specifications can be found in Chapters 1 through 3 or on the tune-up decal under the hood of the vehicle.

## Tune-Up

Firing Order_____

Spark Plugs:

    Type_____

    Gap (in.)_____

Point Gap (in.)_____

Dwell Angle (°)_____

Ignition Timing (°)_____

    Vacuum (Connected/Disconnected)_____

Valve Clearance (in.)

    Intake_____       Exhaust_____

## Capacities

Engine Oil (qts)

    With Filter Change_____

    Without Filter Change_____

Cooling System (qts)_____

Manual Transmission (pts)_____

    Type_____

Automatic Transmission (pts)_____

    Type_____

Front Differential (pts)_____

    Type_____

Rear Differential (pts)_____

    Type_____

Transfer Case (pts)_____

    Type_____

## FREQUENTLY REPLACED PARTS

Use these spaces to record the part numbers of frequently replaced parts.

| PCV VALVE | OIL FILTER | AIR FILTER |
|---|---|---|
| Manufacturer_____ | Manufacturer_____ | Manufacturer_____ |
| Part No._____ | Part No._____ | Part No._____ |

# General Information and Maintenance

## HOW TO USE THIS BOOK

Chilton's Repair & Tune-Up Guide for the Granada/Monarch is intended to teach you about the inner workings of your car and save you money on its upkeep. The first two chapters contain maintenance and tune-up information and procedures. The following chapters concern themselves with the more complex systems of your car. Operating systems from engine through brakes are covered to the extent that we feel the average do-it-yourselfer should get involved. This book will not explain such things as rebuilding the differential for the simple reason that the expertise required and the investment in special tools make this task uneconomical.

We will tell you how to do many jobs (using available tools) that can save you money, give you personal satisfaction and help you avoid problems.

This book will also serve as a reference for owners who want to understand their car and/or their mechanics better. In this case, no tools at all are required.

Before removing any parts, read through the entire procedure. This will give you the overall view of what tools and supplies will be required.

The sections begin with a brief discussion of the system and what it involves, followed by adjustments, maintenance, removal and installation procedures, and repair or overhaul procedures. When repair is not considered feasible, we tell you how to remove the part and then how to install the new or rebuilt replacement. In this way, you at least save the labor costs. Backyard repair of such components as the alternator is just not practical.

Two basic mechanic's rules should be mentioned here. One, whenever the left side of the car or engine is referred to, it is meant to specify the driver's side. Conversely, the right side of the car means the passenger's side.

Secondly, most screws and bolts are removed by turning counterclockwise, and tightened by turning clockwise. Safety is always the most important rule. Constantly be aware of the dangers involved in working on an automobile and take the proper precautions. Use jackstands when working under a raised vehicle. Don't smoke or allow an exposed flame to come near the battery or any part of the fuel system. Always use the proper tool and use it correctly; bruised knuckles and skinned fingers aren't a mechanic's standard equipment. Always take your time and have patience; Once you have some experience, working on your car will become an enjoyable hobby.

## TOOLS AND EQUIPMENT

It would be impossible to catalog each and every tool that you may need to perform all the operations included in this book. It would also not be wise for the amateur to rush out and buy an expensive set of tools on the theory that he may need one of them at some time. The best approach is to proceed slowly, gathering together a good quality set of those tools that are used most frequently. Don't be misled by the low cost of bargain tools. It is far better to spend a little more for quality, name brand tools. Forged wrenches, 6 or 12 point sockets and fine-tooth ratchets are by far preferable to their less expensive counterparts. As any good mechanic can tell you, there are few worse experiences than trying to work on a car or truck with bad tools. Your monetary savings will be far outweighed by frustration and mangled knuckles.

Begin accumulating those tools that are used most frequently; those associated with routine maintenance and tune-up. In addition to the normal assortment of screwdrivers and pliers, you should have the following tools for routine maintenance jobs:

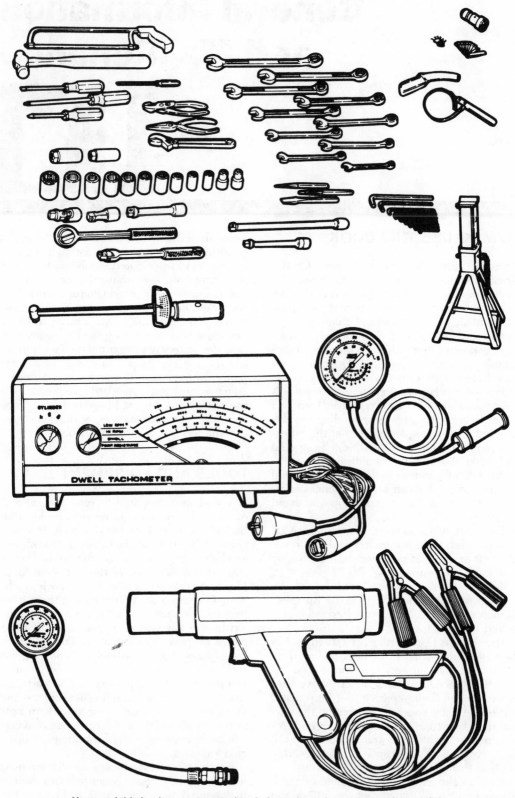

**You need this basic assortment of tools for most maintenance and repair jobs**

1. SAE and metric wrenches, sockets and combination open end/box end wrenches.
2. Jackstands—for support;
3. Oil filter wrench;
4. Oil filler spout or funnel;
5. Grease gun—for chassis lubrication;
6. Hydrometer—for checking the battery;
7. A low flat pan for draining oil;
8. Lots of rags for wiping up the inevitable mess.

In addition to the above items, there are several others that are not absolutely necessary, but are handy to have around. These include oil drying compound, a transmission funnel, and the usual supply of lubricants, antifreeze and fluids, although these can be purchased as needed. This is a basic list for routine maintenance, but only your personal needs can accurately determine your list of tools.

The second list of tools is for tune-ups. While the tools involved here are slightly more sophisticated, they need not be outrageously expensive. There are several inexpensive tachometers on the market that are every bit as good for the average mechanic as an expensive professional model. Just be sure that it works on 4, 6, and 8 cylinder engines. A basic list of tune-up equipment could include:

1. Tachometer;
2. Spark plug wrench;
3. Timing light (preferably a DC high voltage light that works from the car's battery);
4. A set of flat feeler gauges;
5. A set of round wire spark plug gauges.

In addition to these basic tools, there are several other tools and gauges you may find useful. These include:

1. A compression gauge. The screw-in type is slower to use, but eliminates the possibility of a faulty reading due to escaping pressure;
2. A manifold vacuum gauge;
3. A test light;
4. An induction meter. This is used for determining whether or not there is current in a wire. These are handy for use if a wire is broken somewhere in a wiring harness.

As a final note, you will probably find a torque wrench necessary for all but the most basic work. The beam type models are perfectly adequate, although the newer click type are more precise.

## Special Tools

Normally, the use of special factory tools is avoided for repair procedures, since these are not readily available for the do-it-yourself mechanic. When it is possible to perform the job with more commonly available tools, it will be pointed out, but occasionally, a special tool was designed to perform a specific function and should be used. Before substituting another tool, you should be convinced that neither your safety nor the performance of the vehicle will be compromised.

Some special tools are available commercially from major tool manufacturers. Others for your car can be purchased from your dealer or from Owatonna Tool Co., Owatonna, Minnesota 55060.

## SERVICING YOUR VEHICLE SAFELY

It is virtually impossible to anticipate all of the hazards involved with automotive maintenance and service but care and common sense will prevent most accidents.

The rules of safety for mechanics range from "don't smoke around gasoline," to "use the proper tool for the job." The trick to avoiding injuries is to develop safe work habits and take every possible precaution.

### Do's

• Do keep a fire extinguisher and first aid kit within easy reach.

• Do wear safety glasses or goggles when cutting, drilling, grinding or prying. If you wear glasses for the sake of vision, then they should be made of hardened glass that can serve also as safety glasses, or wear safety goggles over your regular glasses.

• Do shield your eyes whenever you work around the battery. Batteries contain sulphuric acid; in case of contact with the eyes or skin, flush the area with water or a mixture of water and baking soda and get medical attention immediately.

• Do use safety stands for any under-car service. Jacks are for raising vehicles; safety stands are for making sure the vehicle stays raised until you want it to come down. Whenever the vehicle is raised, block the wheels remaining on the ground and set the parking brake.

• Do use adequate ventilation when working with any chemicals. Asbestos dust resulting from brake lining wear could cause cancer.

• Do disconnect the negative battery cable when working on the electrical system.

• Do follow manufacturer's directions whenever working with potentially hazardous materials. Both brake fluid and antifreeze are poisonous if taken internally.

• Do properly maintain your tools. Loose hammerheads, mushroomed punches and chisels, frayed or poorly grounded electrical cords, excessively worn screwdrivers, spread wrenches (open end), cracked sockets, slipping ratchets, or faulty droplight sockets can cause accidents.

• Do use the proper size and type of tool for the job being done.

• Do when possible, pull on a wrench handle rather than push on it, and adjust your stance to prevent a fall.

• Do be sure that adjustable wrenches are tightly adjusted on the nut or bolt and pulled so that the face is on the side of the fixed jaw.

• Do select a wrench or socket that fits the nut or bolt. The wrench or socket should sit straight, not cocked.

• Do strike squarely with a hammer; avoid glancing blows.

• Do set the parking brake and block the wheels if the work requires that the engine be running.

## Don't's

• Don't run an engine in a garage or anywhere else without proper ventilation—EVER! Carbon monoxide is poisonous; it is absorbed by the body 400 times faster than oxygen; it takes a long time to leave the human body and you can build up a deadly supply of it in your system by simply breathing in a little every day. You may not realize you are slowly poisoning yourself. Always use power vents, windows, fans or open the garage doors.

• Don't work around moving parts while wearing a necktie or other loose clothing. Short sleeves are much safer than long, loose sleeves. Hard-toed shoes with neoprene soles protect your toes and give a better grip on slippery surfaces. Jewelry such as watches, fancy belt buckles, beads or body adornment of any kind is not safe while working around a car. Long hair should be hidden under a hat or cap.

• Don't use pockets for toolboxes. A fall or bump can drive a screwdriver deep into your body. Even a wiping cloth hanging from the back pocket can wrap around a spinning shaft or fan.

• Don't smoke when working around gasoline, cleaning solvent or other flammable material.

• Don't smoke when working around the battery. When the battery is being charged, it gives off explosive hydrogen gas.

• Don't use gasoline to wash your hands; there are excellent soaps available. Gasoline may contain lead, and lead can enter the body through a cut, accumulating in the body until you are very ill. Gasoline also removes all the natural oils from the skin so that bone dry hands will suck up oil and grease.

• Don't service the air conditioning system unless you are equipped with the necessary tools and training. The refrigerant, R-12, is extremely cold and when exposed to the air, will instantly freeze any surface it comes in contact with, including your eyes. Although the refrigerant is normally non-toxic, R-12 becomes a deadly poisonous gas in the presence of an open flame. One good whiff of the vapors from burning refrigerant can be fatal.

## SERIAL NUMBER IDENTIFICATION

### Vehicle Identification Number (VIN)

The (VIN) Vehicle Identification Number for title and registration purposes is stamped on a metal tab attached to the instrument panel close to the lower windshield frame on the driver's side of the car.

A thirteen digit number is used through 1980. The first digit identifies the model year, and the fifth digit identifies the installed engine.

A seventeen digit number is used from 1981. The tenth digit identifies the model year, and the eighth digit identifies the installed engine.

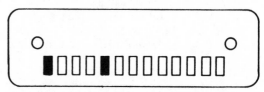

A thirteen digit VIN number is used through 1980

A seventeen digit VIN number is used from 1981

### Vehicle Certification Label

The Vehicle Certification Label is attached to the left front door lock face panel or door pillar.

### Engine Identification

Identification of the engine can be made by finding the letter code in the Vehicle Identification Number than referring to the engine identification chart to determine the engine type and size. An engine identification label is also attached to the engine, usually to the valve cover. The symbol codes on the identification

### Engine Codes

| Year | Code | Cyl. | Liters | Cubic Ins. | Carb |
|------|------|------|--------|-----------|------|
| 1975–77 | T | 6 | 3.3 | 200 | 1 bbl. |
| | L | 6 | 4.1 | 250 | 1 bbl. |
| | F | 8 | 5.0 | 302 | 2 bbl. |
| | H | 8 | 5.8 | 351W | 2 bbl. |
| 1978–79 | L | 6 | 4.1 | 250 | 1 bbl. |
| | F | 8 | 5.0 | 302 | 2 bbl. |
| 1980 | C | 6 | 4.1 | 250 | 1 bbl. |
| | D | 8 | 4.2 | 255 | 2 bbl. |
| | F | 8 | 5.0 | 302 | 2 bbl. |
| 1981 | A | 4 | 2.3 | 140 | 2 bbl. |
| | B | 6 | 3.3 | 200 | 1 bbl. |
| | D | 8 | 4.2 | 255 | 2 bbl. |
| 1982 | A | 4 | 2.3 | 140 | 2 bbl. |
| | B | 6 | 3.3 | 200 | 1 bbl. |
| | 3 | 6 | 3.8 | 232 | 2 bbl. |

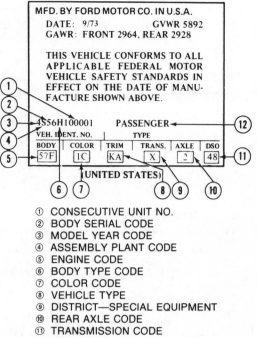

① CONSECUTIVE UNIT NO.
② BODY SERIAL CODE
③ MODEL YEAR CODE
④ ASSEMBLY PLANT CODE
⑤ ENGINE CODE
⑥ BODY TYPE CODE
⑦ COLOR CODE
⑧ VEHICLE TYPE
⑨ DISTRICT—SPECIAL EQUIPMENT
⑩ REAR AXLE CODE
⑪ TRANSMISSION CODE
⑫ TRIM CODE

**Vehicle certification label through 1980**

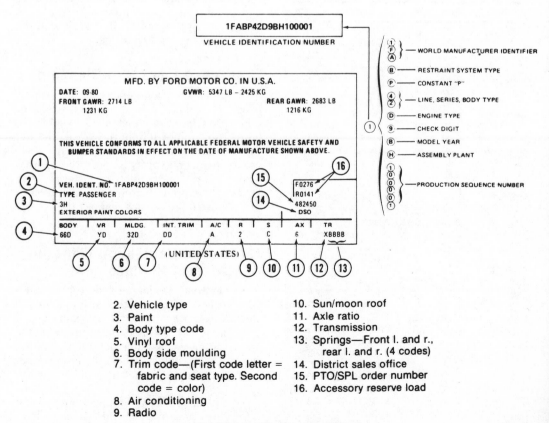

2. Vehicle type
3. Paint
4. Body type code
5. Vinyl roof
6. Body side moulding
7. Trim code—(First code letter = fabric and seat type. Second code = color)
8. Air conditioning
9. Radio
10. Sun/moon roof
11. Axle ratio
12. Transmission
13. Springs—Front l. and r., rear l. and r. (4 codes)
14. District sales office
15. PTO/SPL order number
16. Accessory reserve load

**Vehicle identification from 1981**

tag not only identify the engine but are used for determining parts usage. The codes are shown in the dealer's master parts catalog to designate unique parts.

## Transmission & Rear Axle Identification

The transmission or rear axle can be identified by finding the rear axle code which appears on the bottom of the Vehicle Certification Label and referring to the identification chart. There is also an identification tag attached to the transmission or rear axle.

### Transmission Codes

| Code | Model | Manufacturer |
|---|---|---|
| 1 | 3 Speed | Ford |
| 6 | 4 Speed OD | Borg-Warner |
| 7 | 4 Speed | Hummer |
| C | C5 Auto | Ford |
| S | JATCO Auto | * |
| V | C3 Auto | Ford |
| W | C4 Auto | Ford |

* Japan Automatic Transmission Co.

### Rear Axle Ratio Codes

| Year | Ratio | I.D. | Code | Size |
|---|---|---|---|---|
| 1975–76 | 2.75 | 2 | WDX-A | 9″ |
| | 3.00 | 6 | WDX-B | 9″ |
| | 3.00 | 0 | WFB-F | 9″ Lok |
| | 3.07 | 5 | WER-T | 8.7″ |
| 1976 | 3.00 | 0 | WFD-R | 8″ Lok |
| 1977 | 2.50 | J | WFG-B | 9″ Lok |
| | 3.40 | 7 | WDW-AD | 8″ |
| 1975–78 | 2.79 | 3 | WDW-AB | 8″ |
| | 2.75 | 2 | WER-V | 8.7″ |
| | 3.00 | 0 | WFB-E | 9″ Lok |
| 1975–79 | 3.00 | 6 | WDW-Z | 8″ |
| 1977–78 | 2.47 | B | WER-AC | 8.7″ |
| | 2.50 | J | WFB-G,G1 | 9″ Lok |
| | 2.50 | J | WFB-K | 9″ Lok |
| 1978–79 | 2.47 | C | WFB-G | 9″ Lok |
| 1979 | 2.79 | 3 | WDW-AF | 8″ |
| 1980 | 3.00 | 6 | WDW-Z | 8″ |
| | 2.79 | 3 | WDW-AF | 8″ |
| | 2.47 | B | WDX-L | 9″ |
| | 2.75 | K | WDX-R | 9″ |
| 1980–82 | 2.73 | 8 | WGX-S | 7.5″ |
| 1981 | 3.08 | Y | WFC-A | 7.5″ Lok |
| 1982 | 2.73 | M | WFC-E | 7.5″ Lok |
| | 3.45 | R | WFC-F | 7.5″ Lok |
| | 3.08 | Z | WFC-G | 7.5″ Lok |
| | 3.45 | R | WFC-H | 7.5″ Lok |
| | 3.08 | Z | WFC-J | 7.5″ Lok |
| | 2.47 | B | WGX-D | 7.5″ |
| | 3.08 | Y | WGX-Y | 7.5″ |
| | 2.73 | 8 | WGX-Z | 7.5″ |
| | 2.47 | B | WGX-AB | 7.5″ |
| | 3.45 | F | WGX-AC | 7.5″ |
| | 2.47 | B | WGX-AD | 7.5″ |
| | 3.45 | F | WGX-AE | 7.5″ |
| | 3.08 | Y | WGX-AF | 7.5″ |

## ROUTINE MAINTENANCE

Routine maintenance is preventive medicine. It is the single most important process that can be taken in avoiding repairs and extending the life of any automobile. By taking only a minute or so each day to check such things as the oil level, tire pressures and the coolant level, you'll be able to stop any developing problems (such as a small leak in the radiator) before they become difficult and expensive repairs. You'll save time and money in the long run.

### Air Filter Replacement

At the intervals recommended in the maintenance chart, the air filter element must be replaced. If the vehicle is operated under severely dusty conditions, the element should be changed sooner. The air filter cover is retained with a single wing nut or wing nuts and clips. To replace the element, remove the cover and discard the old element. While the air cleaner is removed, check the choke plate and external linkage for freedom of movement. Brush away all dirt and spray the plate corners and linkage with a small amount of penetrating cleaner/lubricant. Wipe the airfilter housing clean with a solvent-moistened rag and install the new element with the word "front" facing the front of the car. Install the cover and wing nut finger tight.

### Crankcase Filler Cap Cleaning

At the intervals recommended in the maintenance chart, the oil filler cap must be cleaned. Disconnect the positive crankcase ventilation hose (if so equipped) from the cap and lift the cap from the rocker cover. Soak the cap in kerosene or mineral spirits to clean the internal element of sludge and blow-by material. After agitating the cap in the solution, shake the cap dry. Reinstall the cap and connect the hose, if so equipped.

### Crankcase Ventilation Filter (in Air Cleaner) Replacement

At the intervals recommended in the maintenance chart, or sooner if the car is operated in dusty areas, at low rpm, for trailer towing, or if the car is used for short runs preventing the engine from reaching operating temperature, the crankcase ventilation filter in the air cleaner must be replaced. Do not attempt to clean this filter.

To replace the filter, simply remove the air filter cover and pull the old crankcase filter out of its housing. Push a new crankcase filter into the housing and install the air filter cover.

## Preventive Maintenance Schedule

Occasionally maintenance schedules differ from car to car. Check the schedule in your owner's manual or on the glove box door. If the maintenance intervals differ, follow the intervals given by the manufacturer.

| Interval | Item | Service |
|---|---|---|
| **1975–76** | | |
| Every 5 months or 5,000 miles | Brakes | inspect |
| | Crankcase | change oil & filter |
| | Differential | check level |
| | Chassis fittings | lubricate |
| | Transmission, automatic | check level |
| | Transmission, manual | check level |
| | Power steering | check level |
| | Idle speed | adjust |
| | Throttle kickdown | check |
| | Throttle solenoid-off speed | check |
| Every 6 months | Cooling system | inspect |
| Every 15 months or 15,000 miles | Brake master cylinder | check level |
| | Parking brake linkage | oil with 10W |
| | Air cleaner element | replace |
| | Air cleaner temperature valve | check |
| | Choke system | inspect |
| | Distributor cap and rotor | inspect |
| | Distributor wick | oil with 10W |
| | Drive belts | check & adjust |
| | EGR system | clean and inspect |
| | Fuel filter | replace |
| | Ignition timing | adjust |
| | Manifold heat riser | inspect |
| | PCV system | inspect |
| | Spark plug wires | inspect |
| | Thermactor system | inspect |
| | Cooling system | change coolant |
| Every 22,500 miles | Spark plugs | replace |
| Every 25 months or 25,000 miles | Transmission | change lubricant |
| Every 30 months or 30,000 miles | Air cleaner crankcase filter | replace |
| | EEC canister | inspect |
| | Fuel vapor system | inspect |
| | PCV valve | replace |
| **1977–80** | | |
| Every 6 months or 6,000 miles | Crankcase | change oil & filter |
| | Idle speed | check |
| | Ignition timing | check |
| | Decel throttle control system | check |
| | Chassis fittings | lubricate |
| | Clutch linkage | inspect and oil |
| | Exhaust system heat shields | inspect |
| | Transmission | check level |
| Every 15 months or 15,000 miles | Exhaust control valve | check & lubricate |
| | Drive belts | check and adjust |
| | Air cleaner temperature control | check |
| | Choke system | check |
| | Thermactor system | check |
| | Crankcase breather cap | clean |
| | EGR system | clean and inspect |
| | PCV system | clean and inspect |
| | Cooling system | change coolant |
| Every 22,500 miles | Spark plugs | replace |
| Every 30 months or 30,000 miles | PCV valve | replace |
| | Air cleaner element | replace |
| | Air cleaner crankcase filter | replace |

## Preventive Maintenance Schedule (cont.)

Occasionally maintenance schedules differ from car to car. Check the schedule in your owner's manual or on the glove box door. If the maintenance intervals differ, follow the intervals given by the manufacturer.

| Interval | Item | Service |
|---|---|---|
| **1977–80** | | |
| Every 30 months or 30,000 miles | Fuel vapor system<br>Brake master cylinder<br>Brake | inspect<br>check<br>inspect |
| **1981–82** | | |
| Every 12 months or 7,500 miles | Crankcase<br>Idle speed<br>Drive belts<br>Transmission & rear axle<br>Cooling system | change oil and filter<br>check<br>check and adjust<br>check fluid level<br>check coolant level, hose condition |
| Every 22,500 miles | Spark plugs | replace |
| Every 30 months or 30,000 miles | Air cleaner<br>Crankcase filter<br>PCV valve<br>Cooling system<br>Fuel vapor system<br>Brake master cylinder<br>Brakes<br>Linkage and steering<br>Suspension<br>Front wheel bearings | replace element<br>replace<br>replace<br>change coolant<br>inspect<br>check<br>inspect<br>lubricate<br>lubricate<br>repack |

The crankcase ventilation filter will pull right out of its housing. It cannot be cleaned it must be replaced

Pulling out the PCV valve

## PCV Valve Replacement

At recommended intervals, the PCV valve should be replaced. It cannot be cleaned. The PCV valve is located in the valve cover.

## Fuel Filter Replacement

At recommended intervals, the fuel filter must be replaced. The filter is located inline at the carburetor inlet. The procedure for replacing the fuel filter is as follows:

The fuel filter is located at the carburetor inlet

Factory clamps can be removed with pliers. You may want to replace them with small hose clamps

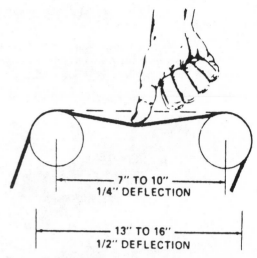

7" TO 10"
1/4" DEFLECTION

13" TO 16"
1/2" DEFLECTION

**Proper belt deflection**

### EXCEPT VV CARBURETORS

1. Remove the air filter.
2. Loosen the retaining clamp(s) securing the fuel inlet hose to the fuel filter. If the hose has crimped retaining clamps, these must be cut off and replaced.
3. Pull the hose off the fuel filter.
4. Unscrew the fuel filter from the carburetor and discard the gasket, if so equipped.
5. Install a new gasket, if so equipped, and screw the filter into the carburetor.
6. Install a new retaining clamp onto the fuel hose. Push the hose onto the fuel filter and tighten the clamp.
7. Start the engine and check for leaks.
8. Install the air filter.

### VARIABLE VENTURI CARBURETORS

1. Remove the air cleaner.
2. Unscrew the fuel line nut from the carburetor inlet nut using a flare nut wrench.
   NOTE: *To prevent kinking of the fuel line and for ease of installation loosen the fuel line nut at the fuel pump.*
3. Unscrew the inlet fitting from the carburetor and remove the fuel filter gasket and spring.
4. Install the spring, new filter, new gasket and inlet fitting into the carburetor.
5. Tighten the fuel line at the carburetor and then at the fuel pump.
6. Start the engine and check for leaks.
7. Install the air cleaner.

**Alternator adjusting bolt (arrow)**

## Drive Belt Adjustment

Check the drive belts every 5,000 miles for signs of wear such as cracking and fraying. Check to see that the belt is dry on all sides, and check for incorrect tension. Determine the belt tension at a point halfway between the pulleys by pressing on the belt with moderate thumb pressure. There should be about ¼ inch

**Power steering pump mounting bolts**

of "give" on belts up to 10 inch length and ½ inch give on belts longer than 10 inches at this point. If the movement is too much or too little, loosen the mounting bolts of whichever

## HOW TO SPOT WORN V-BELTS

V-Belts are vital to efficient engine operation—they drive the fan, water pump and other accessories. They require little maintenance (occasional tightening) but they will not last forever. Slipping or failure of the V-belt will lead to overheating. If your V-belt looks like any of these, it should be replaced.

**Cracking or weathering**

This belt has deep cracks, which cause it to flex. Too much flexing leads to heat build-up and premature failure. These cracks can be caused by using the belt on a pulley that is too small. Notched belts are available for small diameter pulleys.

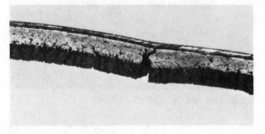

**Softening (grease and oil)**

Oil and grease on a belt can cause the belt's rubber compounds to soften and separate from the reinforcing cords that hold the belt together. The belt will first slip, then finally fail altogether.

**Glazing**

Glazing is caused by a belt that is slipping. A slipping belt can cause a run-down battery, erratic power steering, overheating or poor accessory performance. The more the belt slips, the more glazing will be built up on the surface of the belt. The more the belt is glazed, the more it will slip. If the glazing is light, tighten the belt.

**Worn cover**

The cover of this belt is worn off and is peeling away. The reinforcing cords will begin to wear and the belt will shortly break. When the belt cover wears in spots or has a rough jagged appearance, check the pulley grooves for roughness.

**Separation**

This belt is on the verge of breaking and leaving you stranded. The layers of the belt are separating and the reinforcing cords are exposed. It's just a matter of time before it breaks completely.

accessory the belt in question is driving (alternator, power steering, etc.) and remove or increase the slack by pulling or pushing the accessory accordingly. Tighten the mounting bolts and recheck tension.

### SERPENTINE DRIVE BELT

Some late models feature a single, wide, ribbed V-belt that drives the water pump, alternator and power steering. To install a new belt, simply retract the belt tensioner with a pry bar and slide the old belt off of the pulleys. Slip on a new belt and release the tensioner. The spring powered tensioner eliminates the need for periodic adjustments.

## Battery Care

Loose, dirty, or corroded battery terminals are a major cause of "no-start". Keep an eye on the terminals; inspect them each time you check your oil, which should be frequently.

When a white powder or crystals (acid build-up) accumulates on the terminals, it is time to clean them. Inexpensive battery terminal cleaning tools are available at auto parts stores and automotive departments, and they work very well. First, clean all surface corrosion off the terminals with an old toothbrush and a so-

**Power steering pump adjusting nut**

lution of baking soda and water. Unbolt the terminal wire clamps from the battery posts and use a puller to remove the cable.

Use the "female" end of the cleaning tool on the battery post; rotate the tool around on the post until the post is shiny. Remove the cap from the tool, revealing the wire brush.

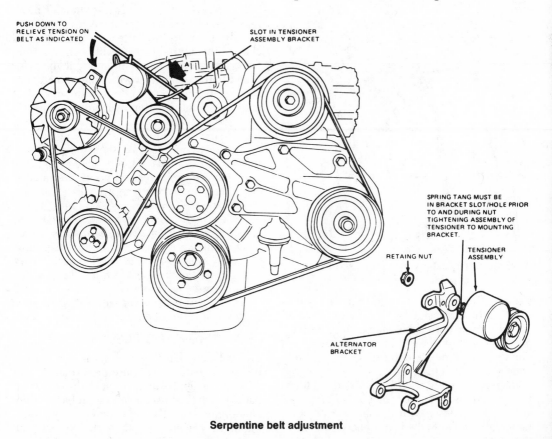

**Serpentine belt adjustment**

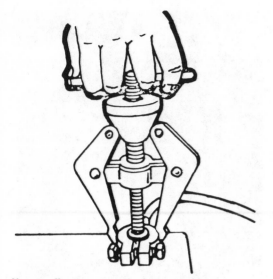

**Use a puller to remove the battery cable**

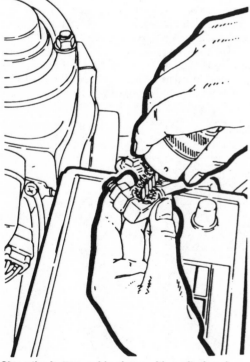

**Clean the battery cable clamp with a wire brush**

Ream out each battery cable clamp with the brush until the inside of the clamp is shiny (the sheen on both cable clamps and battery posts, along with the tightness of the connection between the two, determines how good a connection you'll have).

Inspect the battery cables for signs of fraying, peeled insulation, or chafing, and replace any cable that looks marginal. Install and tighten the cables to the battery posts, and give both terminals a light coating of petroleum jelly. This will help retard corrosion. Batteries with side terminals require a different cleaning tool, but the same maintenance steps should be followed.

Finally, check the electrolyte level and the specific gravity of each cell. Hold each cell cap up to a light and check for blockage—the holes allow the hydrogen gas, produced by the chemical reaction in the battery, to escape safely.

It is not possible to check the specific gravity or fluid level on sealed ("maintenance free") batteries. Instead, the indicator built into the top of the case must be relied on to display any signs of battery deterioration. If the indicator is dark, the battery can be assumed to be OK. If the indicator is light, the specific gravity is low, and the battery should be charged or replaced.

There are two rules-of-thumb to follow when assessing the specific gravity test on your battery. If all cells read "poor" on your hydrometer, the car's charging system may not be doing its job, unless the battery is just plain old and is due for replacement. Check alternator belt tension; a slipping belt may not be spinning the alternator fast enough to keep the battery charged.

If, however, three cells are OK and three read "poor" (or four and two), the problem usually points to the battery. If the battery is close to the last months of its lifespan, it is time for a replacement; you'll undoubtedly be in for "dead battery before work", stalling and "no-start" at traffic lights, and other dreaded situations. When the battery will only spin the engine slowly (or not at all), and when there is such a marked difference in the amount of charge between cells, take the battery to a service station and have it put on charge for a few hours. If the problems still occur after a good charging, the battery simply will not hold a charge and has "had it."

NOTE: *When you install a new battery, make sure you jot down the date of installation in the front of this book. Also, most batteries have a decal attached that has small perforated dots marked on it. The dots are numbered and correspond to months and years. Pop out the dots according to your purchase date, as a future reference.*

## REPLACING BATTERIES

The cold cranking power rating of a battery measures battery starting performance and provides an approximate relationship between battery size (and usually expected battery life) and engine size. The cold cranking power rating of a replacement battery should *match or*

## HOW TO SPOT BAD HOSES

Both the upper and lower radiator hoses are called upon to perform difficult jobs in an inhospitable environment. They are subject to nearly 18 psi at under hood temperatures often over 280°F., and must circulate nearly 7500 gallons of coolant an hour—3 good reasons to have good hoses.

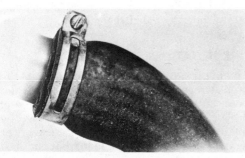

**Swollen hose**

A good test for any hose is to feel it for soft or spongy spots. Frequently these will appear as swollen areas of the hose. The most likely cause is oil soaking. This hose could burst at any time, when hot or under pressure.

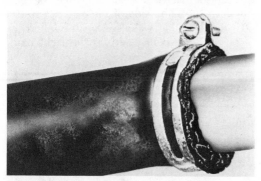

**Cracked hose**

Cracked hoses can usually be seen but feel the hoses to be sure they have not hardened; a prime cause of cracking. This hose has cracked down to the reinforcing cords and could split at any of the cracks.

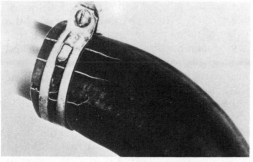

**Frayed hose end (due to weak clamp)**

Weakened clamps frequently are the cause of hose and cooling system failure. The connection between the pipe and hose has deteriorated enough to allow coolant to escape when the engine is hot.

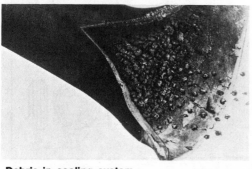

**Debris in cooling system**

Debris, rust and scale in the cooling system can cause the inside of a hose to weaken. This can usually be felt on the outside of the hose as soft or thinner areas.

*exceed* the cubic-inch displacement of your engine.

## Tires

The tread wear of the tires should be checked about twice a year. Tread wear should be even across the tire. Excessive wear in the center of the tread indicates overinflation. Excessive wear on the outer corners of the tread indicates underinflation. An irregular wear pattern is usually an indication of improper front wheel alignment or incorrect wheel balance. On a vehicle with improper front wheel alignment, the car will tend to pull to one side of a flat road if the steering wheel is released while driving the car. Incorrect wheel balance will usually produce vibrations at high speeds. When the front wheels are out of balance, they will produce vibration in the steering wheel, while rear wheels out of balance will produce vibration in the floor pan of the car.

### TIRE PRESSURE

One way to prolong tire life is to maintain proper pressure in the tires. This should be checked at least once a month and should be done with the tires cold (not driven for one hour). If you check the tire pressure when the tires are warm, you will obtain a falsely high reading. Refer to the accompanying tire inflation chart, or to the sticker attached to the rear face of the right-hand door pillar (two-door models) or attached to the right rear hinge face (four-door models). Snow tires require a 4 psi cold increase in the rear tire pressure above

that listed in the chart. For example, a 6.45 x 14 snow tire will require 30 psi to be properly inflated. Under no circumstances must the maximum inflation pressure, which is stamped on the sidewall of the tire, be exceeded. If you plan to do any trailer towing, it is recommended that the tire pressure (cold) be increased by 6 psi on the rear wheels, again being careful not to exceed the maximum inflation pressure.

### TIRE ROTATION

Another way to prolong tire life is to rotate the tires at regular intervals. These intervals depend on the type of tire and on the type of driving you do, but generally they should be rotated every 6,000 miles or twice a year, or sooner if abnormal wear due to front end misalignment is apparent. Follow the accompanying tire rotation diagram for the type of tires your car is equipped with: conventional (bias-ply or bias-belted) or redial-ply. Because of the design of radial-ply tires, it is imperative that they remain on the same side of the car and travel in the same direction. Therefore, in a four-tire rotational sequence, the front and rear radial tires of the same side are merely swapped.

Studded snow tires, radial or conventional, are just as choosy about the direction they travel in. If you equip your car with studded snow tires, mark them "LR" or "RR" prior to removal so that next year they may be installed on the same side of the car. If a studded snow tire that was used on the left rear wheel one year is installed on the right rear

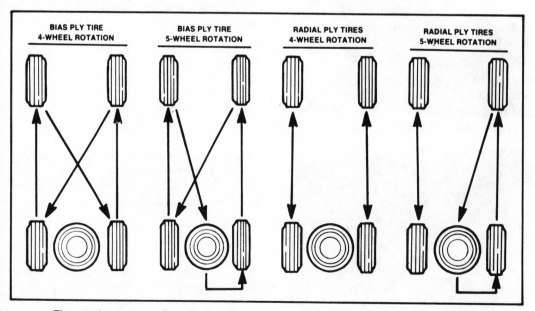

Tire rotation patterns. Do not use a temporary–use only spare in the five wheel pattern

wheel the next year, the result will be a dangerous condition where the studs pull out of the tire and are flung to the rear. Remember, never mix radial, belted, and/or conventional types tires on your car. Always make sure that all tires and wheels are of the same size, type and load-carrying capacity.

NOTE: *If your Granada or Monarch is equipped with an optional "Space Saver Tire," do not include it during rotation of the other four tires.*

## Windshield Wipers

Intense heat from the sun, snow and ice, road oils and the chemicals used in windshield washer solvents combine to deteriorate the rubber wiper refills. The refills should be replaced whenever the blades begin to streak or chatter.

### WIPER REFILL REPLACEMENT

Normally, if the wipers are not cleaning the windshield properly, only the refill has to be replaced. The blade and arm usually require replacement only in the event of damage. It is not necessary (except on new Tridon refills) to remove the arm or the blade to replace the refill (rubber part), though you may have to position the arm higher on the glass. You can do this by turning the ignition switch on and operating the wipers. When they are positioned where they are accessible, turn the ignition switch off.

There are several types of refills and your vehicle could have any kind, since aftermarket blades and arms may not use exactly the same type refill as the original equipment.

Most Anco styles use a release button that is pushed down to allow the refill to slide out of the yoke jaws. The new refill slides in and locks in place. Some refills are removed by locating where the metal backing strip or the refill is wider. Insert a small screwdriver blade between the frame and metal backing strip. Press down to release the refill from the retaining tab.

The Trico style is unlocked at one end by squeezing 2 metal tabs, and the refill is slid out of the frame jaws. When the new refill is installed, the tabs will click into place, locking the refill.

The polycarbonate type is held in place by a locking lever that is pushed downward out of the groove in the arm to free the refill. When the new refill is installed, it will lock in place automatically.

The Tridon refill has a plastic backing strip with a notch about an inch from the end. Hold the blade (frame) on a hard surface so that the frame is tightly bowed. Grip the tip of the backing strip and pull up while twisting counterclockwise. The backing strip will snap out of the retaining tab. Do this for the remaining tabs until the refill is free of the arm. The length of these refills is molded into the end and they should be replaced with identical types.

No matter which type of refill you use, be sure that all of the frame claws engage the refill. *Before operating the wipers, be sure that no part of the metal frame is contacting the windshield.*

## Fluid Level Checks

### ENGINE OIL

The oil level in the engine should be checked at fuel stops. The check should be made with the engine warm and switched off for a period of about one minute so that the oil has time to drain down into the crankcase. Pull out the dipstick, wipe it clean and reinsert it. The level of the oil must be kept within the "safe" area, above the "add 1" mark on the dipstick. If the oil level is kept above the "safe" area, heavy oil consumption will result. If the level remains below the "add 1" mark, severe engine damage may result. The "add 1" and "add 2" refer to U.S. measure quarts. Remember that in Canada, the Imperial measure quart is used and it is equal to $5/4$ of a U.S. quart. When topping up, make sure that the oil is the same type and viscosity rating as the oil already in the crankcase.

### MANUAL TRANSMISSION FLUID

At the intervals recommended in the maintenance schedule, the fluid level in the manual transmission should be checked. With the car standing perfectly level, apply the parking brake, set the transmission in neutral, stop the engine and block all four wheels. Wipe all dirt and grease from the upper filler plug on the side of the transmission. Using a sliding T-bar handle or an adjustable wrench, remove the filler plug. The lubricant should be level with the bottom of the filler hole. If required, add SAE 90 manual transmission fluid to the proper level, using a syringe. Install the filler plug.

### AUTOMATIC TRANSMISSION FLUID

At the intervals recommended in the maintenance schedule, the automatic transmission fluid level should be checked. The level should also be checked if abnormal shifting behavior is noted. With the car standing on a level surface, firmly apply the parking brake. Run the engine at idle until normal operating temperature is reached. Then, with the right foot

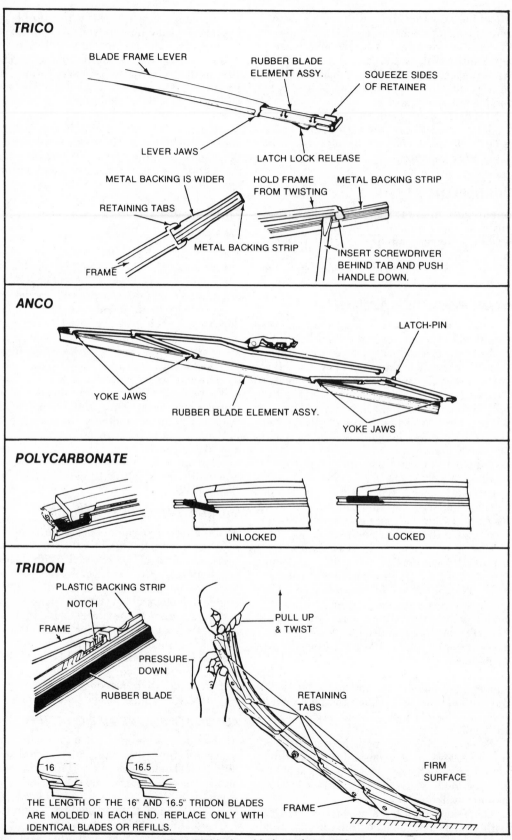

*TRICO*

BLADE FRAME LEVER

RUBBER BLADE ELEMENT ASSY.

SQUEEZE SIDES OF RETAINER

LEVER JAWS

LATCH LOCK RELEASE

METAL BACKING IS WIDER

RETAINING TABS

METAL BACKING STRIP

FRAME

HOLD FRAME FROM TWISTING

METAL BACKING STRIP

INSERT SCREWDRIVER BEHIND TAB AND PUSH HANDLE DOWN.

*ANCO*

LATCH-PIN

YOKE JAWS

RUBBER BLADE ELEMENT ASSY.

YOKE JAWS

*POLYCARBONATE*

UNLOCKED

LOCKED

*TRIDON*

PLASTIC BACKING STRIP

NOTCH

FRAME

PULL UP & TWIST

PRESSURE DOWN

RUBBER BLADE

RETAINING TABS

16

16.5

THE LENGTH OF THE 16″ AND 16.5″ TRIDON BLADES ARE MOLDED IN EACH END. REPLACE ONLY WITH IDENTICAL BLADES OR REFILLS.

FRAME

FIRM SURFACE

**Windshield wiper blade replacement**

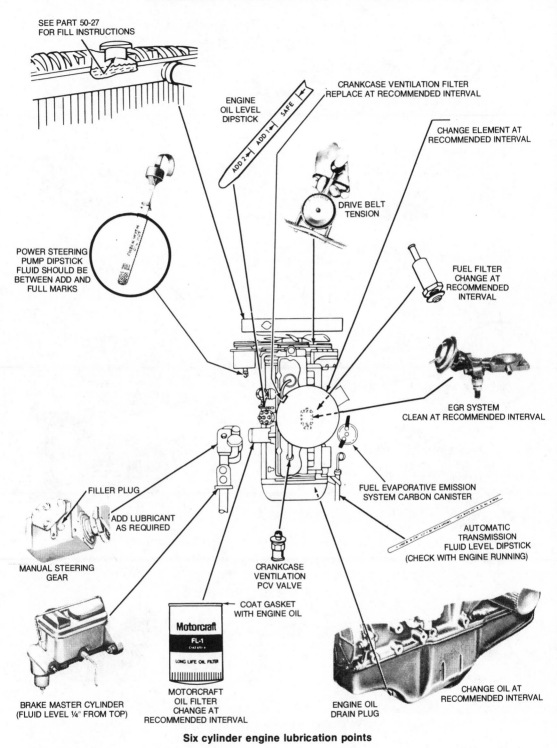

SEE PART 50-27
FOR FILL INSTRUCTIONS

ENGINE
OIL LEVEL
DIPSTICK

SAFE
ADD 1
ADD 2

CRANKCASE VENTILATION FILTER
REPLACE AT RECOMMENDED INTERVAL

CHANGE ELEMENT AT
RECOMMENDED INTERVAL

DRIVE BELT
TENSION

POWER STEERING
PUMP DIPSTICK
FLUID SHOULD BE
BETWEEN ADD AND
FULL MARKS

FUEL FILTER
CHANGE AT
RECOMMENDED
INTERVAL

EGR SYSTEM
CLEAN AT RECOMMENDED INTERVAL

FILLER PLUG

ADD LUBRICANT
AS REQUIRED

FUEL EVAPORATIVE EMISSION
SYSTEM CARBON CANISTER

AUTOMATIC
TRANSMISSION
FLUID LEVEL DIPSTICK
(CHECK WITH ENGINE RUNNING)

MANUAL STEERING
GEAR

CRANKCASE
VENTILATION
PCV VALVE

COAT GASKET
WITH ENGINE OIL

**Motorcraft**
FL-1
LONG LIFE OIL FILTER

CHANGE OIL AT
RECOMMENDED INTERVAL

BRAKE MASTER CYLINDER
(FLUID LEVEL ¼" FROM TOP)

MOTORCRAFT
OIL FILTER
CHANGE AT
RECOMMENDED INTERVAL

ENGINE OIL
DRAIN PLUG

**Six cylinder engine lubrication points**

firmly planted on the brake pedal, shift the transmission selector through all the positions, allowing sufficient time in each range to engage the transmission. Shift the selector into park (P). With the engine still running, pull out the transmission dipstick, located at the rear of the engine compartment. Wipe it clean and reinsert it, pushing it down until it seats in the tube. Pull it out and check the level. The level should be between the "add" and "full" marks.

CAUTION: *Do not overfill the transmis-*

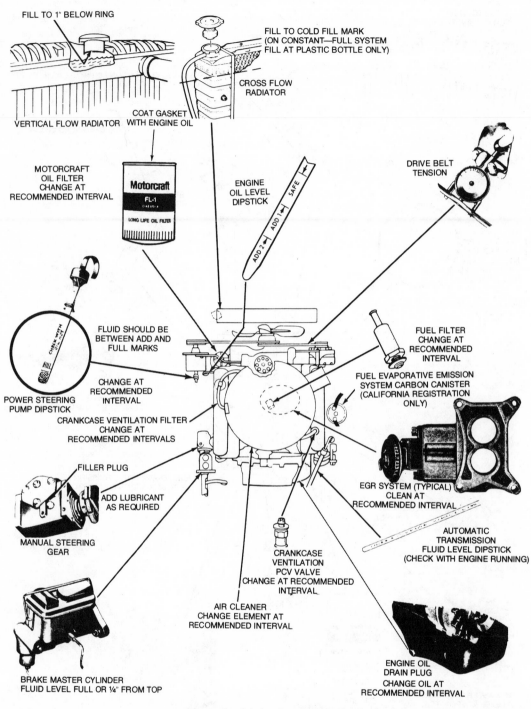

FILL TO 1" BELOW RING

FILL TO COLD FILL MARK
(ON CONSTANT—FULL SYSTEM
FILL AT PLASTIC BOTTLE ONLY)

CROSS FLOW
RADIATOR

VERTICAL FLOW RADIATOR

COAT GASKET
WITH ENGINE OIL

MOTORCRAFT
OIL FILTER
CHANGE AT
RECOMMENDED INTERVAL

Motorcraft
FL-1
LONG LIFE OIL FILTER

ENGINE
OIL LEVEL
DIPSTICK

SAFE
ADD 1
ADD 2

DRIVE BELT
TENSION

FLUID SHOULD BE
BETWEEN ADD AND
FULL MARKS

CHECK WITH HOT
FILL

POWER STEERING
PUMP DIPSTICK

CHANGE AT
RECOMMENDED
INTERVAL

CRANKCASE VENTILATION FILTER
CHANGE AT
RECOMMENDED INTERVALS

FILLER PLUG

ADD LUBRICANT
AS REQUIRED

MANUAL STEERING
GEAR

FUEL FILTER
CHANGE AT
RECOMMENDED
INTERVAL

FUEL EVAPORATIVE EMISSION
SYSTEM CARBON CANISTER
(CALIFORNIA REGISTRATION
ONLY)

EGR SYSTEM (TYPICAL)
CLEAN AT
RECOMMENDED INTERVAL

AUTOMATIC
TRANSMISSION
FLUID LEVEL DIPSTICK
(CHECK WITH ENGINE RUNNING)

CRANKCASE
VENTILATION
PCV VALVE
CHANGE AT RECOMMENDED
INTERVAL

AIR CLEANER
CHANGE ELEMENT AT
RECOMMENDED INTERVAL

BRAKE MASTER CYLINDER
FLUID LEVEL FULL OR ¼" FROM TOP

ENGINE OIL
DRAIN PLUG
CHANGE OIL AT
RECOMMENDED INTERVAL

**V8 engine lubrication points**

*sion, as foaming and loss of fluid through the vent may cause the transmission to malfunction*

## MASTER CYLINDER BRAKE FLUID

At the intervals recommended in the maintenance schedule, the fluid in the master cylinder should be checked. Before checking the level, carefully wipe off the master cylinder cover to remove any dirt or water that would fall into the fluid reservoir. Then push the retaining clip to one side and remove the cover and seal. The fluid level should be maintained at ¼ inch from the top of the reservoir. Top up as necessary with heavy-duty brake fluid meeting DOT 3 or 4 specifications.

## COOLANT

The coolant level in the radiator should be checked on a monthly basis, preferably when the engine is cold. On a cold engine, the coolant level should be maintained at one inch below the filler neck on vertical flow radiators, and 2½ inches below the filler neck at the "cold fill" mark on cross-flow radiators. Top up as necessary with a mixture of 50% water and 50% ethylene glycol antifreeze, to ensure proper rust, freezing and boiling protection. If you have to add coolant more often than once a month or if you have to add more than one quart at a time, check the cooling system for leaks. Also check for water in the crankcase oil, indicating a blown cylinder head gasket.

CAUTION: *Exercise extreme care when re-* moving the cap from a hot radiator. Wait a few minutes until the engine has time to cool somewhat, then wrap a thick towel around the radiator cap and slowly turn it counterclockwise to the first stop. Step back and allow the pressure to release from the cooling system. Then, when the steam has stopped venting, press down on the cap, turn it one more stop counterclockwise and remove the cap.

## REAR AXLE FLUID

At the intervals recommended in the maintenance schedule, the rear axle fluid level should be checked. With the car standing perfectly level, apply the parking brake, set the transmission in park or first gear, stop the engine

## Capacities

| Year | Engine | Engine Crankcase (add 1 qt for filter) | Transmission ( pts) 3 speed manual | 4 speed manual | Automatic | Drive Axle (pts) | Fuel Tank (gal) | Cooling System (qts) w/o AC | with AC |
|------|--------|------|------|------|------|------|------|------|------|
| 1975 | 6-200 | 4 | 3.5 | — | 17.5 | 5 | 19.2 | 9.9 | — |
|      | 6-250 | 4 | 3.5 | — | 17.5 | 5 | 19.2 | 10.5 | 10.7 |
|      | 8-302 | 3.5① | 3.5 | — | 17.5 | 5 | 19.2 | 14.4 | 14.6 |
|      | 8-351 | 3.5① | — | — | 20.5 | 5 | 19.2 | 15.7 | 16.7 |
| 1976 | 6-200 | 4 | 3.5 | — | 17.5 | 5② | 19.2③ | 9.9 | — |
|      | 6-250 | 4 | 3.5 | — | 17.5 | 5② | 19.2③ | 10.5 | 10.7 |
|      | 8-302 | 4 | 3.5 | — | 17.5 | 5② | 19.2③ | 14.4 | 14.6 |
|      | 8-351 | 4 | — | — | 20.5 | 5② | 19.2③ | 15.7 | 16.7 |
| 1977 | 6-200 | 4 | — | 5⑤ | 16.5 | ④ | 19.2③ | 9.9 | — |
|      | 6-250 | 4 | — | 5⑤ | 16.5 | ④ | 19.2③ | 10.5 | 10.7 |
|      | 8-302 | 4 | — | 5⑤ | 16.5 | ④ | 19.2③ | 14.4 | 14.6 |
|      | 8-351 | 4 | — | — | 20.5 | ④ | 19.2③ | 15.7 | 16.7 |
| 1978 | 6-250 | 4 | — | 5 | 16.5 | 5⑥ | 18 | 10.5 | 10.6 |
|      | 8-302 | 4 | — | 5 | 16.5 | 5⑥ | 18 | 14.2 | 14.3 |
| 1979 | 6-250 | 4 | — | 4.5 | ⑦ | 4.5 | 18 | 10.5 | 10.7 |
|      | 8-302 | 4 | — | 4.5 | ⑦ | 4.5 | 18 | 14.2 | 14.3 |
| 1980 | 6-250 | 4 | — | 4.5 | ⑧ | ④ | 18 | 10.6 | 10.8 |
|      | 8-255 | 4 | — | 4.5 | ⑧ | ④ | 18 | 14.6 | 14.7 |
|      | 8-302 | 4 | — | 4.5 | ⑧ | ④ | 18 | 14.2 | 14.3 |
| 1981 | 4-140 | 4 | — | 2.8 | ⑨ | 3.5 | 16 | 8.4 | 8.5 |
|      | 6-200 | 4 | — | — | ⑨ | 3.5 | 16 | 8.4 | 8.5 |
|      | 8-255 | 4 | — | — | ⑨ | 3.5 | 16 | 14.8 | 15.2 |
| 1982 | 4-140 | 4 | — | 2.8 | ⑩ | 3.2 | 16⑪ | 8.4 | 8.5 |
|      | 6-200 | 4 | — | — | ⑩ | 3.2 | 16⑪ | 8.4 | ·8.5 |
|      | 6-232 | 4 | — | — | ⑩ | 3.2 | 16⑪ | 14.8 | 15.2 |

① Add ½ qt with filter change
② With rear disc brakes—4
③ 18.1 on certain models
④ 8 in. gear—4.5
  8.75 in. gear (1977 only)—4.0
  9 in. gear—5.0
⑤ Fill to the bottom of the filler hole
⑥ Codes 6 and 0—4.5; code B—4.0
⑦ JATCO—17; C4—20
⑧ JATCO—17; C4—19.2

⑨ 4-140; C-4—13.6
  6-200; C-3—16.0
  6-200; C-4 w/10¼" converter—14.4
  6-200; C-4 w/12" converter—19.2
  8-255; C-4—19.2
⑩ 4-140; C-3—16.0
  6-200; C-5—22.0
  6-232; C-5—22.0
⑪ Extended range option; 20 gal.

and block all four wheels. Wipe all dirt and grease from the filler plug. Using a sliding T-bar handle (⅜ inch) or an adjustable wrench, remove the filler plug. The proper level is ⅜ inch from the bottom of the filler plug hole. To check the fluid level in the axle, bend a clean, straight piece of wire to a 90-degree angle and insert the bent end of the wire into the axle while resting it on the lower edge of the filler hole. Top up as necessary with SAE 90 hypoid gear lube, using a syringe. Install the filler plug.

### STEERING GEAR LUBRICANT

#### Except Rack and Pinion

If there is binding in the steering gear or if the wheels do not return to a straight-ahead position after a turn, the lubricant level of the steering gear should be checked. Remove the filler plug, using an ¹¹/₁₆-inch open-end wrench, and remove the lower cover bolt, using a ⁹/₁₆-inch wrench, to expose both holes. Slowly turn the steering wheel to the left until it stops. At this point, lubricant should be rising in the lower cover bolt hole. Then slowly turn the steering wheel to the right until it stops. At this point, lubricant should be rising in the filler plug hole. If the lubricant does not rise when the wheel is turned, add a small amount of SAE 90 steering gear lubricant until it does. Replace the cover bolt and the filler plug when finished.

### POWER STEERING RESERVOIR FLUID

At the intervals recommended in the maintenance schedule, the fluid level in the power steering reservoir (if so equipped) should be checked. Run the engine until the fluid reaches operating temperature. Turn the steering wheel from lock-to-lock several times to relieve the system of any trapped air. Turn off the engine. Unscrew the cap and dipstick assembly from the reservoir. The level must be maintained between the "full" mark and the end of the dipstick. Top up as necessary with ATF Type F.

### AIR CONDITIONING REFRIGERANT

Granadas and Monarchs equipped with air conditioning do not have a sight glass located in the refrigerant lines. Therefore, without specialized equipment and training, it is not possible to check the refrigerant level. This is not an oversight on Ford's part. They took the sight glass out of the system in an effort to discourage home mechanics from fooling with the air conditioning system. If you suspect a problem in your air conditioner, take it to a Ford dealer or other competent garage.

# LUBRICATION

## Oil and Fuel Recommendations

When adding oil to the crankcase or changing the oil or filter, it is important that oil of an equal quality to the original be used in your car. The use of inferior oils may void your warranty. Generally speaking, oil that has been rated "SE (thru 1980) or "SF" (from 1981), heavyduty detergent" by the American Petroleum Institute will prove satisfactory.

Oil of the SE/SF variety performs a multitude of functions in addition to its basic job of reducing friction of the engine's moving parts. Through a balanced formula of polymeric dispersants and metallic detergents, the oil prevents high temperature and low temperature deposits and also keeps sludge and dirt particles in suspension. Acids, particularly sulphuric acid, as well as other byproducts of combustion of sulphur fuels, are neutralized by the oil. These acids, if permitted to concentrate, may cause corrosion and rapid wear of the internal parts of the engine.

It is important to choose an oil of the proper viscosity for climatic and operational conditions. Viscosity is an index of the oil's thickness at different temperatures. A thicker oil (higher numerical rating) is needed for high temperature operation, whereas thinner oil (lower numerical rating) is required for cold weather operation. Due to the need for an oil that embodies both these characteristics in parts of the country where there is wide temperature variation within a small period of time, multigrade oils have been developed. Basically, a multigrade oil is thinner at low temperatures and thicker at high temperatures. For example, a 20W-40 oil exhibits the characteristics of a 20 weight oil when the car is first started and the oil is cold. Its lighter

## Oil Recommendations Chart

| Multi-Viscosity Oils | | |
|---|---|---|
| When Outside Temperature Is Consistently | | Use SAE Viscosity Number |
| Fahrenheit | Celsius | |
| Below +32°F | Below 0°C | 5W-30* |
| −10°F to +90°F | −23°C to 32°C | 10W-30 |
| −10°F to +90°F | −23°C to 32°C | |
| (or above) | (or above) | 10W-40 |
| Above +10°F | Above −12°C | 20W-40 |
| | | 20W-50 |
| Single Viscosity Oils | | |
| −10°F to +32°F | −23°C to 0°C | 10W |
| +10°F to +60°F | −12°C to 16°C | 20W-20 |
| +32°F to +90°F | 0°C to 32°C | 30 |
| Above +60°F | Above 32°C | 40 |

weight allows it to travel to the lubricating surfaces quicker and offer less resistance to starter motor cranking than, let's say, a straight 30 weight oil. But after the engine reaches operating temperature, the 20W-40 oil begins acting like a straight 40 weight oil, its heavier weight providing greater lubricating protection and less susceptibility to foaming than a straight 30 weight oil. Whatever your driving needs, the oil-viscosity temperature chart should prove useful in selecting the proper grade. The SAE viscosity rating is printed or stamped on the top of every oil container.

NOTE: *Oil rated "SF" can be used in any engine.*

Most 1975 and all '76 and later Monarchs and Granadas are equipped with catalytic converters, making the use of unleaded fuel mandatory. The use of leaded fuel in these cars will damage the converter.

## Changing Engine Oil and Filter

At the intervals recommended in the maintenance schedule, the oil and filter should be changed. After the engine has reached operating temperature, shut it off, firmly block the wheels, apply the parking brake, place a drip pan beneath the engine and remove the drain plug. Allow the engine to drain thoroughly before replacing the drain plug. Place the drip pan beneath the oil filter. To remove the filter, turn it counterclockwise, using a strap wrench. Wip the contact surface of the new filter clean and coat the rubber gasket with clean engine oil. Wipe off the mating surface of the adapter on the block. To install, hand turn the new filter clockwise until the gasket just contacts the cylinder block. Do not use a strap wrench to tighten the filter. Hand turn

On the V8 engines, you can reach the oil filter only from underneath

the filter another half turn to tighten it. Remove the filler cap on the valve cover and fill the crankcase with the proper amount of oil. Start the engine and check the oil filter and drain plug for leaks.

CAUTION: *Prolonged and repeated skin contact with used engine oil, with no effort to remove the oil, may be harmful. Follow these simple precautions when handling used motor oil:*

• *Avoid prolonged skin contact with used motor oil.*

• *Remove oil from skin by washing thoroughly with soap and water or waterless hand cleaner. Do not use gasoline, thinners or solvents.*

• *Avoid prolonged skin contact with oil-soaked clothing.*

Certain operating conditions may warrant more frequent oil changes. If the vehicle is used for short trips, where the engine does not have a chance to fully warm up before it is shut off, water condensation and low temperature deposits may make it necessary to change the oil sooner. Driving in dusty areas or pulling a trailer may also make more frequent oil changes necessary.

## Coolant Draining and Flushing

CAUTION: *The V6-232 (3.8L) engine is equipped with aluminum cylinder heads. If a radiator flushing compound is required, use only a brand that is safe for use in aluminum components. Use a permanent type coolant that meets Ford Specifications ESE-*

Removing the engine oil drain plug

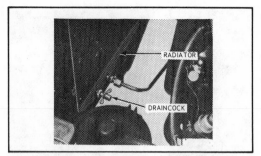

The petcock is on the bottom of the radiator, but it sometimes is not as easy to find as this one

Six cylinder engine block drain plug

M97B43A *or* ESE-M97B44A *such as Prestone II when adding to, or changing the contents of the cooling system.*

At two-year intervals or if the coolant is rusty or dirty in appearance, the cooling system must be drained and flushed. To drain the system, place a catch pan beneath the petcock (drain cock) at the bottom of the radiator and open the petcock by rotating it counterclockwise. Then, using a ⅜-inch wrench or socket, remove the cylinder block drain plug(s), taking care to catch the old coolant. On four and six-cylinder models, the drain plug is located at the right rear of the block, in front of the starter. On V6 and V8 models, there are two drain plugs, one on each side of the block.

To remove rust, sludge and other foreign matter from the cooling system, a cooling system cleaner should be used in the engine prior to flushing. Flushing may be accomplished either by inserting a garden hose into the radiator cap opening, or by using special pressure flushing equipment available at many service stations. In either case, the flushing should be done with the thermostat removed. When using the pressure flushing method, it is advisable to make sure that the cylinder head bolts are tightened to specifications to prevent possible coolant leakage into the cylinders.

The procedure for flushing is as follows: run the engine at operating temperature for sev-

eral minutes to circulate the cooling system cleaner. Using a towel, carefully remove the radiator cap in two stages, allowing the pressure to be released before fully removing the cap. Insert a garden hose or the pressure flushing fitting into the radiator. Open the radiator petcock and remove the engine drain plug(s). Run the engine at fast idle until the water is coming out clear. Shut off the engine and then remove the garden hose or the pressure flusher. Close the petcock and install the drain plug(s). Inspect the radiator and heater hoses for cracks, bulges or soft spots and replace as required. Replace the thermostat. Consult the capacities chart and fill the cooling system to within one inch of the filler neck or to the cold-fill mark on sealed systems with a mixture of 50% water and 50% ethylene glycol antifreeze. Install the radiator cap, turning it only to the first position (off pressure), thereby allowing the system to bleed off all trapped air bubbles. Start the engine and allow it to reach operating temperature. Recheck the coolant level and add as required. Check the system for leakage.

## Chassis Greasing
### FRONT SUSPENSION BALL JOINTS

At recommended intervals, the lower ball joints must be lubricated. The upper ball joints on Granadas and Monarchs have polyethylene liners and do not require lubrication. Since Monarchs and Granadas are not equipped with grease fittings at the ball joints, it is necessary to remove the plugs on the bottom of the ball joints prior to greasing.

If you are using a jack to raise the front of the car, be sure to install jack stands, block the rear wheels and fully apply the parking brake. If the car has been parked in a temperature below 20°F for any length of time, park it in a heated garage for half an hour or so until the ball joints loosen up enough to accept the grease. Wipe all accumulated dirt from around the ball joint lubrication plugs. Remove the plugs with a ³⁄₁₆-inch socket wrench. Using a hand-operated, low pressure grease gun fitted with a rubber tip and loaded with a suitable chassis grease, force lubricant into the joint only until the joint rubber boot begins to swell.

NOTE: *Do not force lubricant out of the rubber boot, as this destroys the weathertight seal.*

Install the grease plugs.

### STEERING ARM STOPS

At the intervals recommended in the maintenance schedule, the steering arm stops must be cleaned and lubricated. The stops are lo-

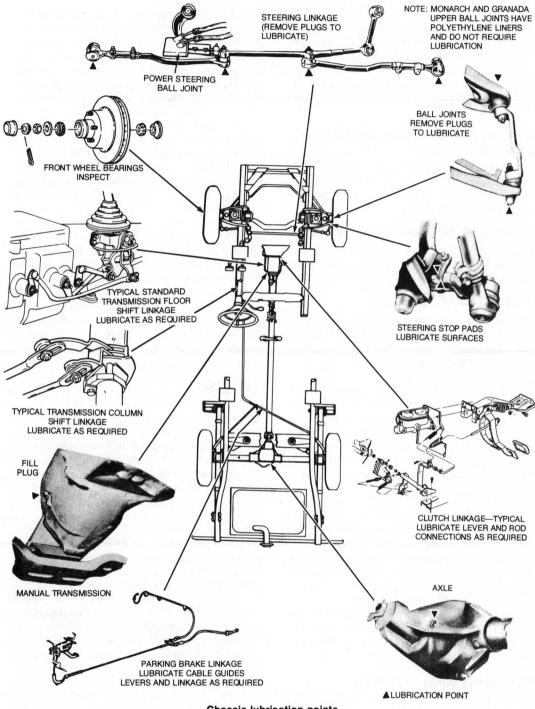

STEERING LINKAGE
(REMOVE PLUGS TO
LUBRICATE)

NOTE: MONARCH AND GRANADA
UPPER BALL JOINTS HAVE
POLYETHYLENE LINERS
AND DO NOT REQUIRE
LUBRICATION

POWER STEERING
BALL JOINT

BALL JOINTS
REMOVE PLUGS
TO LUBRICATE

FRONT WHEEL BEARINGS
INSPECT

TYPICAL STANDARD
TRANSMISSION FLOOR
SHIFT LINKAGE
LUBRICATE AS REQUIRED

STEERING STOP PADS
LUBRICATE SURFACES

TYPICAL TRANSMISSION COLUMN
SHIFT LINKAGE
LUBRICATE AS REQUIRED

FILL
PLUG

CLUTCH LINKAGE—TYPICAL
LUBRICATE LEVER AND ROD
CONNECTIONS AS REQUIRED

MANUAL TRANSMISSION

AXLE

PARKING BRAKE LINKAGE
LUBRICATE CABLE GUIDES
LEVERS AND LINKAGE AS REQUIRED

▲LUBRICATION POINT

**Chassis lubrication points**

cated on the inside of the steering arm and the upturned end of the suspension strut where the strut is attached to the lower control arm. Clean all friction points and apply a suitable chassis grease as per the chassis lubrication diagram.

## POWER STEERING CONTROL VALVE BALL STUD

On models equipped with power steering, the control valve ball stud (joint) must be lubricated every three years or 36,000 miles. Wipe the area around the grease plug clean of all dirt and foreign material. Remove the grease plug and install a grease fitting. Using a low pressure grease gun, apply a suitable chassis grease to the joint until the rubber boot begins to bulge. Any further lubrication will destroy the weathertight seal. Remove the grease fitting and install the plug.

### MANUAL TRANSMISSION AND CLUTCH LINKAGE

On models so equipped, apply a small amount of chassis grease to the pivot points of the transmission and clutch linkage as per the chassis lubrication diagram.

### AUTOMATIC TRANSMISSION LINKAGE

On models so equipped, apply a small amount of 10W engine oil to the kickdown and shift linkage at the pivot points.

### PARKING BRAKE LINKAGE

At yearly intervals or whenever binding is noticeable in the parking brake linkage, lubricate the cable guides, levers and linkages with a suitable chassis grease.

### BODY LUBRICATION

At the intervals recommended in the maintenance schedule, door, hood and trunk hinges, checks and latches should be greased with a white grease such as Lubriplate®. Also, the lock cylinders should be lubricated with a few drops of graphite lubricant.

### DRAIN HOLE CLEANING

The doors and rocker panels of your car are equipped with drain holes to allow water to drain out of the inside of the body panels. If the drain holes become clogged with dirt, leaves, pine needles, etc., the water will remain inside the panels, causing rust. To prevent this, open the drain holes with a screwdriver. If your car is equipped with rubber dust valves instead, simply open the dust valve with your finger.

## PUSHING AND TOWING

NOTE: *Push starting is not recommended for cars equipped with a catalytic converter. Raw gas collecting in the converter may cause damage. Jump starting is recommended.*

To push start your manual transmission equipped car (automatic transmission models cannot be push started), make sure of bumper alignment. If the bumper of the car pushing does not match with your car's bumper, it

would be wise to tie an old tire either on the back of your car, or on the front of the pushing car. Switch the ignition to "ON" and depress the clutch pedal. Shift the transmission to third gear and hold the accelerator pedal about halfway down. Signal the push car to proceed, when the car speed reaches about 10 mph, gradually release the clutch pedal. The car engine should start, if not have the car towed.

If the transmission and rear axle are in proper working order, the car can be towed with the rear wheels on the ground for distances under 15 miles at speeds no greater than 30 mph. If the transmission or rear is known to be damaged or if the car has to be towed over 15 miles or over 30 mph the car must be dollied or towed with the rear wheels raised and the steering wheel secured so that the front wheels remain in the straight-ahead position. Never use the key controlled steering wheel lock to hold the front wheels in position. The steering wheel must be clamped with a special clamping device designed for towing service. If the key controlled lock is used damage to the lock and steering column may occur.

## JACKING

Your car is equipped with a scissors type jack which is placed under the side of the car so that it fits into the notch in the vertical rocker panel flange nearest the wheel to be changed. These jacking notches are located approximately 8 inches from the wheel opening on the rocker panel flanges.

When raising the car with the scissors jack follow these precautions: Park the car on a level spot, put the selector in P (PARK) with an automatic transmission or in reverse if your car has a manual transmission, apply the parking brake and block the front and the back of the wheel that is diagonally opposite the wheel being changed. These jacks are fine for changing a tire, but never crawl under the car when it is supported only by the scissors jack.

CAUTION: *If you're going to work beneath*

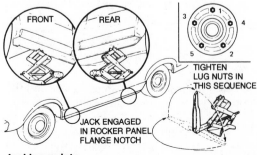

**Jacking points**

## JUMP STARTING A DEAD BATTERY

The chemical reaction in a battery produces explosive hydrogen gas. This is the safe way to jump start a dead battery, reducing the chances of an accidental spark that could cause an explosion.

### Jump Starting Precautions

1. Be sure both batteries are of the same voltage.
2. Be sure both batteries are of the same polarity (have the same grounded terminal).
3. Be sure the vehicles are not touching.
4. Be sure the vent cap holes are not obstructed.
5. Do not smoke or allow sparks around the battery.
6. In cold weather, check for frozen electrolyte in the battery.
7. Do not allow electrolyte on your skin or clothing.
8. Be sure the electrolyte is not frozen.

### Jump Starting Procedure

1. Determine voltages of the two batteries; they must be the same.
2. Bring the starting vehicle close (they must not touch) so that the batteries can be reached easily.
3. Turn off all accessories and both engines. Put both cars in Neutral or Park and set the handbrake.
4. Cover the cell caps with a rag—do not cover terminals.
5. If the terminals on the run-down battery are heavily corroded, clean them.
6. Identify the positive and negative posts on both batteries and connect the cables in the order shown.
7. Start the engine of the starting vehicle and run it at fast idle. Try to start the car with the dead battery. Crank it for no more than 10 seconds at a time and let it cool off for 20 seconds in between tries.
8. If it doesn't start in 3 tries, there is something else wrong.
9. Disconnect the cables in the reverse order.
10. Replace the cell covers and dispose of the rags.

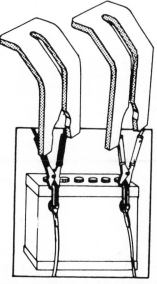

**Side terminal batteries occasionally pose a problem when connecting jumper cables. There frequently isn't enough room to clamp the cables without touching sheet metal. Side terminal adaptors are available to alleviate this problem and should be removed after use.**

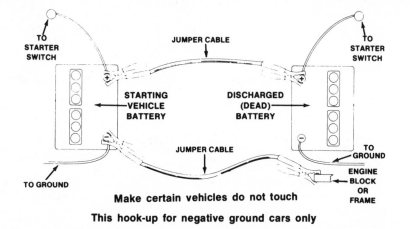

TO STARTER SWITCH

JUMPER CABLE

TO STARTER SWITCH

STARTING VEHICLE BATTERY

DISCHARGED (DEAD) BATTERY

JUMPER CABLE

TO GROUND

ENGINE BLOCK OR FRAME

TO GROUND

**Make certain vehicles do not touch**

**This hook-up for negative ground cars only**

*the car, always support it with jackstands.*

When using a floor jack the car may be listed by positioning the jack under the center of the number two crossmember. The front, as well as either side of the rear end, may be lifted by positioning the floor jack under the rocker flange at the contact points used for the scissor jack supplied with the vehicle. To lift both sides of the rear at once, position the floor jack under the differential housing.

# Tune-Up and Performance Maintenance

## TUNE-UP PROCEDURES

The tune-up is a routine maintenance operation which is essential for the efficient and economical operation, as well as the long life of your car's engine. The interval between tune-ups is a variable factor which depends upon the way you drive your car, the conditions under which you drive it (weather, road type, etc.), and the type of engine installed in your car.

CAUTION: *When working with a running engine, make sure that there is proper ventilation. Also make usre that the transmission is in Neutral (unless otherwise specified) the parking brake is fully applied and the wheels blocked. Always keep hands, long hair, clothing, neckties and tools well clear of the hot exhaust manifold(s) and radiator. When the ignition is running, do not grasp the ignition wires, distributor cap, or coil wire, as a shock in excess of 40,000 volts may result.*

## Spark Plugs

A typical spark plug consists of a metal shell surrounding a ceramic insulator. A metal electrode extends downward through the center of the insulator and protrudes a small distance. Located at the end of the plug and attached to the side of the outer metal shell is the side electrode. The side electrode bends in at a 90° angle so that its tip is even with, and parallel to, the tip of the center electrode. The distance between these two electrodes (measured in thousandths of an inch) is called the spark plug gap. The spark plug in no way produces a spark but merely provides a gap across which the current can arc. The coil produces anywhere from 20,000 to 40,000 volts which travels to the distributor where it is distributed through the spark plug wires to the spark plugs. The current passes along the center electrode and jumps the gap to the side electrode, and, in so doing, ignites the air/fuel mixture in the combustion chamber.

### SPARK PLUG HEAT RANGE

Spark plug heat range is the ability of the plug to dissipate heat. The longer the insulator (or the farther it extends into the engine), the hotter the plug will operate; the shorter the insulator the cooler it will operate. A plug that absorbs little heat and remains too cool will quickly accumulate deposits of oil and carbon since it is not hot enough to burn them off. This leads to plug fouling and consequently to misfiring. A plug that absorbs too much heat will have no deposits, but, due to the excessive heat, the electrodes will burn away quickly and in some instances, preignition may result. Preignition takes place when plug tips get so hot that they glow sufficiently to ignite the fuel/air mixture before the actual spark occurs. This early ignition will usually cause a pinging during low speeds and heavy loads.

The general rule of thumb for choosing the correct heat range when picking a spark plug is: if most of your driving is long distance, high speed travel, use a colder plug; if most of your driving is stop and go, use a hotter plug. Original equipment plugs are compromise plugs, but most people never have occasion to change their plugs from the factory-recommended heat range.

### REPLACING SPARK PLUGS

A set of spark plugs usually requires replacement after about 20,000 to 30,000 miles on cars with electronic ignition, depending on your style of driving. In normal operation, plug gap increases about 0.001 in. for every 1,000–2,500 miles. As the gap increases, the plug's voltage requirement also increases. It requires a greater voltage to jump the wider gap and about two to three times as much voltage to fire a plug at high speeds than at idle.

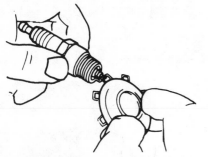

**Checking spark plug gap**

When you're removing spark plugs, you should work on one at a time. Don't start by removing the plug wires all at once, because unless you number them, they may become mixed up. Take a minute before you begin and number the wires with tape. The best location for numbering is near where the wires come out of the cap.

1. Twist the spark plug boot and remove the boot and wire from the plug. Do not pull on the wire itself as this will ruin the wire.

2. If possible, use a brush or rag to clean the area around the spark plug. Make sure that all the dirt is removed so that none will enter the cylinder after the plug is removed.

3. Remove the spark plug using the proper size socket. (Use a $^{13}/_{16}$ in. for BRF plugs or $^5/_8$ in. for AWSF and ASF plugs.) Turn the socket counterclockwise to remove the plug. Be sure to hold the socket straight on the plug to avoid breaking the plug, or rounding off the hex on the plug.

4. Once the plug is out, check it against the plugs shown in the four page color insert, "Fuel Economy & Tune Up Tips" to determine engine condition. This is crucial since plug readings are vital signs of engine condition.

5. Use a round wire feeler gauge to check the plug gap. The correct size gauge should pass through the electrode gap with a slight drag. If you're in doubt; try one size smaller and one larger. The smaller gauge should go through easily while the larger one shouldn't go through at all. If the gap is incorrect, use the electrode bending tool on the end of the gauge to adjust the gap. When adjusting the gap, always bend the side electrode. The center electrode is non-adjustable.

6. Squirt a drop of penetrating oil on the threads of the new plug and install it. Don't oil the threads too heavily. Turn the plug in clockwise by hand until it is snug.

7. When the plug is finger tight, tighten it with a wrench. If you don't have a torque wrench, tighten the plug as shown.

8. Install the plug boot firmly over the plug. Proceed to the next plug.

NOTE: *Coat the inside of each spark plug boot with silicone grease. (Motorcraft WA-10-D7AZ-19A331A, Dow Corning No. 111 or General Electric G627 are acceptable.) Failure to do so could result in a misfired plug.*

## CHECKING AND REPLACING SPARK PLUG CABLES

Visually inspect the spark plug cables for burns, cuts, or breaks in the insulation. Check the spark plug boots and the nipples on the distributor cap and coil. Replace any damaged wiring. If no physical damage is obvious, the wires can be checked with an ohmmeter for excessive resistance. Nominal resistance is 5 K-ohms or less per inch of cable.

When installing a new set of spark plug cables, replace the cables one at a time so there will be no mixup. Start by replacing the longest cable first. Install the boot firmly over the spark plug. Route the wire exactly the same as the original. Insert the nipple firmly into the tower on the distributor cap. Repeat the process for each cable.

NOTE: *Coat the inside of each spark plug boot with silicone grease before reinstalling the plug wire.*

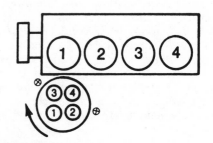

**4-140 (2300cc)**
**Engine Firing Order: 1-3-4-2**
**Distributor Rotation: clockwise**

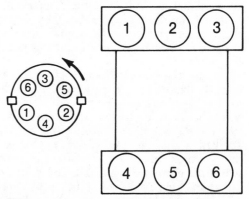

**V6-232**
**Engine Firing Order: 1-4-2-5-3-6**
**Distributor Rotation: counterclockwise**

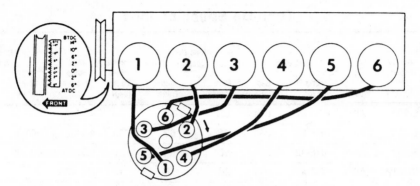

**6-200, 250**
**Engine Firing Order: 1-5-3-6-2-4**
**Distributor Rotation: clockwise**

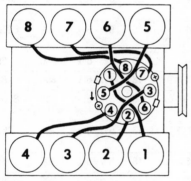

**V8-255, 302**
**Distributor Rotation: counterclockwise**

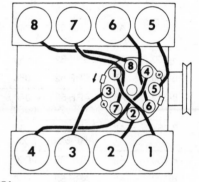

**V8-351**
**Distributor Rotation: counterclockwise**

## Solid-State Ingition

Breakerless or solid-state ignition has been standard on Granada/Monarchs since their introduction. The transistorized ignition system eliminates the breaker points and condenser, thereby eliminating a major part of a conventional tune-up.

For 1975–76, the system is referred to simply as breakerless. In 1977, an improved system with greater spark output called Dura Spark was introduced. The Dura Spark ignition can be identified by the larger distributor cap and thicker (from 7mm to 8mm) spark plug wires. The Dura Spark system utilizes higher voltages—up to 42,000 plus volts—to allow wider spark plug gaps necessary to fire required leaner fuel-air mixtures.

### TROUBLESHOOTING THE BREAKERLESS IGNITION SYSTEM (1975–76)

The system, which at first appears to be extremely complicated, is, in actuality, extremely simple to diagnose and repair. Diagnosis does, however, require the use of a voltmeter and an ohmmeter. You will also need several jumper wires with both blade ends and alligator clips.

The symptoms of a defective component within the solid-state system are exactly the same as those you would encounter in a conventional system. Some of these symptoms are:

• Hard or no starting;
• Rough idle;
• Poor fuel economy;
• Engine misses under load or while accelerating;
• Excessive hydrocarbons (emissions).

If you suspect a problem in your ignition system, there are certain preliminary checks which you should carry out before you begin to check the electronic portions of the system.

First, it is extremely important to make sure that the vehicle battery is in a good state of charge. A defective or poorly charged battery will cause the various components of the ignition system to read incorrectly when they are being tested. Second, check and make sure all wiring connections are clean and tight, not only at the battery, but also at the distributor cap, ignition coil and electronic control module.

NOTE: *The location of the module varies*

## Tune-Up Specifications

| Year | No. Cyl Displacement (cu in.) | Model | Spark Plugs Orig Type | Gap (in.) | Ignition Timing (deg) ▲ Man Trans | Auto Trans | Valves Intake Opens (deg) ∎ | Fuel Pump Pressure (psi) | Idle Speed (rpm) ▲ Man Trans ● | Auto Trans ● |
|---|---|---|---|---|---|---|---|---|---|---|
| '75 | 6-200 | All | BRF-82 | .044 | 6B | 6B | 20 | 4½–5½ | 750/500 | 600/500 ② |
| | 6-250 | All | BRF-82 | .044 | 6B | 6B | 26 | 4½–5½ | 850/500 | 600/500 ② |
| | 8-302 | All | ARF-42 | .044 | 6B | 8B | 20 | 5½–6½ | 900/500 | 650/500 ② |
| | 8-351W | All | ARF-42 | .044 | — | 4B | 15 | 5½–6½ | — | 700/500 ② |
| '76 | 6-200 | All | BRF-82 | .044 | 10B ① @ 600 | — | 20 | 4½–5½ | 800 | 620 ② |
| | 6-250 | All | BRF-82 | .044 | ④ | ⑤ | 26 | 4½–5½ | 850 | 600 ② |
| | 8-302 | All | ARF-42/52 ① | .044 | 12B ① @ 500 | ③ | 20 | 5½–6½ | 750 | 650(700) ② |
| | 8-351W | All | ARF-52 | .044 | — | 8(10B) ② @ 625(650) | 15 | 5½–6½ | — | 625(650) ② |
| '77 | 6-200 | All | BRF-82 | .050 | 6B ① | — | 20 | 5½–6½ | 800 | 650 ② |
| | 6-250 | All | BRF-82 | .050 | 4B ① | 6B(8B) ① | 18 | 5½–6½ | 850 | 600 ② |
| | 8-302 | All | ARF-52 (ARF-52-6) | .050 (.060) | 6B ① | 6B(12B) ① | 16 | 5½–6½ | 750 | 650(700) ② |
| | 8-351 | All | ARF-52 (ARF-52-6) | .050 (.060) | — | 4B ① | 23 | 5½–6½ | — | 625 ② |
| '78 | 6-250 | All | BRF-82 | .050 | 4B ① | 14B(6B) ① | 18 | 5½–6½ | 800 | 600 ② |
| | 8-302 | All | ARF-52 (ARF-52-6) | .050 (.060) | TDC ① | TDC ① | 16 | 5½–6½ | 500 | 600 ② |
| '79 | 6-250 | All | BSF-82 | .050 | 4B ① | 10B(6B) ① | 18 | 5½–6½ | 800 | 600 ② |
| | 8-302 | All | ASF-52 (ASF-52-6) | .050 (.060) | 12B ① | 8B(12B) ① | 16 | 4–6 | 500 | 550 ② |
| '80 | 6-250 | All | BSF-82 | .050 | 4B ① | 10B ① | 18 | 5½–6½ | 700 | 550 ② |
| | 8-255 | All | ASF-42 | .050 | — | 6B ① | 16 | 4–6 | — | 550 |
| | 8-302 | All | ASF-52 | .050 | — | 6B(8B) | 16 | 4–6 | — | 500 |
| '81 | 4-140 | All | AWSF-42 | .034 | 6B ① | 6B ① | 22 | 5½–6½ | 850 ① | 750 ① |
| | 6-200 | All | BSF-92 | .050 | — | 10B ① | 20 | 5½–6½ | — | 700 ① |
| | 8-255 | All | ASF-42 | .050 | — | 10B ① | 16 | 4–6 | — | 700 ① |
| '82 | 4-140 | All | AWSF-42 | .034 | 6B ① | 6B ① | 22 | 5½–6½ | 850 ① | 750 ① |
| | 6-200 | All | BSF-92 | .050 | — | 10B ① | 20 | 5½–6½ | — | 700 ① |
| | 6-232 | All | AGSP-52 | .044 | — | ① | 13 | 6–8 | — | ① |

▲ See text for procedure
∎ All figures Before Top Dead Center
● Where two idle speed figures are separated by a slash, the first figure is for idle speed with solenoid energized and automatic transmission in Drive, while the second is for idle speed with solenoid disconnected and automatic transmission in Neutral.
Figures in parentheses are for California
B Before Top Dead Center
— Not applicable
① Depends on emission equipment; check underhood specifications sticker. See the NOTE.

② In Drive
③ 49 state—8B @ 650 rpm
　Calif.—4B @ 700 rpm
④ w/o AC—6B @ 750 rpm
　with AC—8B @ 750 rpm
⑤ w/o AC—14B @ 500
　California with AC—8B @ 750 rpm
NOTE: *The underhood specifications sticker often reflects tune-up specification changes made in production. Sticker figures must be used if they disagree with those in this chart.*

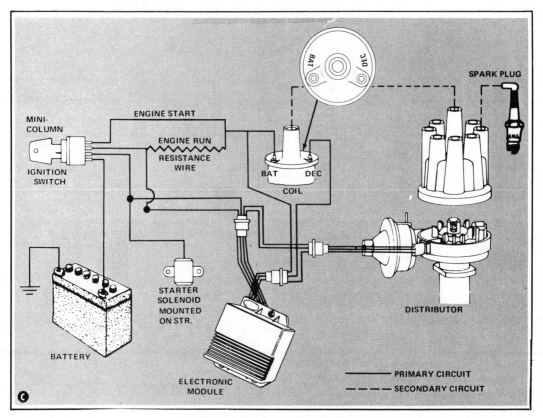

**Solid state ignition system circuitry**

*with engine installation, but it can be easily found by tracing the distributor wires.*

Since the only change between electronic and conventional ignition systems is in the distributor component area, it is a good idea to check the secondary ignition circuit first. If the secondary circuit checks out properly, then the engine condition is not the fault of the ignition system. Secondary ignition system tests can be made following the directions and sequences in the standard troubleshooting section.

NOTE: *Do not short out individual cylinders by removing the plug wires (or by any other method) on cars equipped with catalytic converters. You will damage the converter and possibly start a fire.*

If the secondary ignition circuit is fine, then your problem is not in the ignition system. However, if the engine is still not functioning properly, then the primary ignition circuit must be examined.

Check the distributor cap for cracks, chips, carbon tracks, pitting on the rotor contacts or any other high voltage leaks or failures. Replace the cap if defective.

If the cap appears all right, then visually inspect the armature. Ensure that the armature pin is in place, and that the armature is on tight and rotates when the engine is cranked.

Make sure there are no cracks, chips or rounded edges on the armature. If everything appears to be all right, check the stator next.

To test the stator (also known as the magnetic pickup assembly), you will need an ohmmeter. Run the engine until it reaches operating temperature, then turn the ignition switch to the "off" position. Disconnect the wire harness from the distributor. Connect the ohmmeter between the orange and purple wires. Resistance should be between 400 and 800 ohms. Next, connect the ohmmeter between the black wire and a good ground on the engine. Operate the vacuum advance, either by hand or with an external vacuum source. Resistance should be zero ohms. Finally, connect the ohmmeter between the orange wire and ground, and then the purple wire and ground. Resistance should be over 70,000 ohms in both cases. If any of your ohmmeter readings differ from the above specifications, then the stator is defective and must be replaced as a unit. Removal and installation is as follows:

1. Unplug the distributor wire harness. Remove the distributor cap and rotor.

2. Noting the relative position of the roll pin to the drive shaft, remove the armature and pin from the shaft by prying up with a pair of

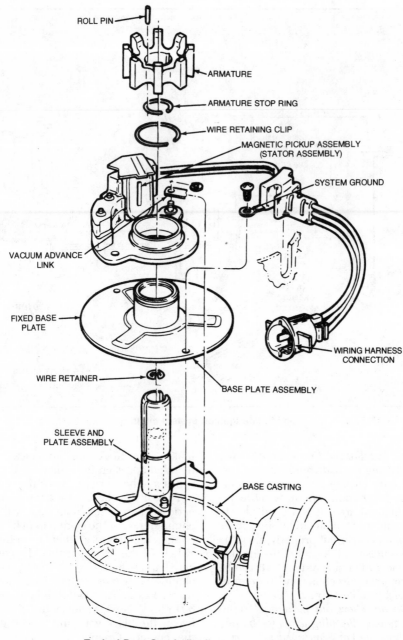

ROLL PIN

ARMATURE

ARMATURE STOP RING

WIRE RETAINING CLIP

MAGNETIC PICKUP ASSEMBLY
(STATOR ASSEMBLY)

SYSTEM GROUND

VACUUM ADVANCE
LINK

FIXED BASE
PLATE

WIRING HARNESS
CONNECTION

WIRE RETAINER

BASE PLATE ASSEMBLY

SLEEVE AND
PLATE ASSEMBLY

BASE CASTING

**Typical Dura-Spark distributor—exploded view**

**IMPORTANT PREPARATION NEEDS**
- AN ACCURATE VOLTMETER AND OHMMETER.
- VEHICLE BATTERY IN A GOOD STATE OF CHARGE.
- THREE JUMPER WIRES (SEE BELOW).

**MAKE TWO JUMPER WIRES/APPROXIMATELY 6 INCHES LONG/BLADE ENDS**

**MAKE ONE JUMPER WIRE/APPROXIMATELY 12 INCHES LONG/ALLIGATOR CLIPS**

**These are the jumper wires you'll need**

screwdrivers or using a small gear puller. Make sure the roll pin doesn't fall inside the distributor.

3. Remove the wire retaining clip from the base plate. Remove the stator ground screw which connects the wire harness to the base plate.

4. Remove the snap ring which secures the vacuum advance link to the stator assembly.

5. Remove the stator.

**Check for any obvious defects in the distributor**

6. Installation is in reverse order.

If the stator is good, then either the electronic module or the wiring connections must be checked next. Because of its complicated electronic nature, the electronic module itself cannot be checked, except by substitution. If you have access to a module which you know to be good (perhaps a friend or relative with a '75 or later model Ford), then perform a substitution test at this time. If this alleviates the problem, then the original module is faulty and must be replaced. If this substitution does not solve the problem or if you cannot locate a spare module which you know to be good, then disconnect the two wiring harnesses from the module and, using a voltmeter, check the circuits listed.

**Unplug the module connectors here. Leave the module end alone or you'll short the module out**

NOTE: *Make no tests at the module side of the connectors.*

1. Starting Circuit—Connect the voltmeter leads to ground and to the corresponding female socket of the white male from the module (you will need a jumper wire with a blade end). Crank the engine over. The voltage should be between 8 and 12 volts.

2. Running Circuit—Turn the ignition switch to the "on" position. Connect the voltmeter leads to ground and the corresponding female socket of the red male lead from the module. Voltage should be battery voltage plus or minus 0.1 volts.

3. Coil Circuit—Leave the ignition switch on. Connect the voltmeter leads to ground and to the corresponding female socket of the green male lead from the module. Voltage should be battery voltage plus or minus 0.1 volts.

If any of these readings are incorrect, inspect and repair any broken, loose, frayed or dirty connections. If this doesn't solve the problem, perform a battery source test.

To make this test, *do not* disconnect the coil. Connect the voltmeter leads to the battery (BAT) terminal at the coil and a good ground. Connect a jumper wire from the DEC terminal at the coil to a good ground. Make sure all lights and accessories are off. Turn the ignition switch on. Check the voltage. If the voltage is below 4.9 volts, then check the primary wiring for broken strands, cracked or frayed wires, or loose or dirty terminals. Repair or replace any wires you find defective. If the voltage is *above* 7.9, then you have a problem in the resistance wiring and it must be replaced. Replace the wire with one of the same resistance value and length.

It should be noted here that if you do have a problem in your electronic ignition circuit, most of the time it will be a case of loose, dirty or frayed wires. The electronic module itself, being completely solid state, is not ordinarily subject to failure. It is possible for the unit to fail, of course, but as a general rule, the source of an ignition system problem will be somewhere else in the circuit.

### TROUBLESHOOTING DURA-SPARK IGNITION

NOTE: *Troubleshooting of the Dura Spark III system is not given because of the great complexity of the system. Service of the Dura Spark III system should be referred to a qualified, professional technician.*

The symptoms of a defective component within the Dura-Spark system are exactly the same as those you would encounter in a conventional ignition system. Some of the symptoms are:

## 1975 Test Sequence

| | Test Voltage Between | Should Be | If Not, Conduct |
|---|---|---|---|
| Key On | Socket #4 and Engine Ground | Battery Voltage ±0.1 Volt | Module Bias Test |
| | Socket #1 and Engine Ground | Battery Voltage ±0.1 Volt | Battery Source Test |
| Cranking | Socket #5 and Engine Ground | 8 to 12 volts | Cranking Test |
| | Jumper #1 and #8 Read #6 | more than 6 volts | Starting Circuit Test |
| | Pin #7 and Pin #8 | ½ volt minimum AC or any DC volt wiggle | Distributor Hardware Test |
| | **Test Voltage Between** | **Should Be** | **If Not, Conduct** |
| Key Off | Socket #7 and #3 Socket #8 and Engine Ground Socket #7 and Engine Ground Socket #3 and Engine Ground | 400 to 800 ohms 0 ohms more than 70,000 ohms | Magnetic Pick-up (Stator) Test |
| | Socket #4 and Coil Tower Socket #1 and Pin #6 | 7,000 to 13,000 ohms 1.0 to 2.0 ohms | Coil Test |
| | Socket #1 and Engine Ground | more than 4.0 ohms | Short Test |
| | Socket #4 and Pin #6 | 1.0 to 2.0 ohms | Resistance Wire Test |

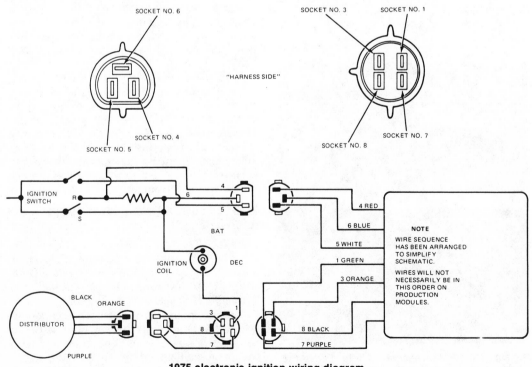

**1975 electronic ignition wiring diagram**

## 1976 Test Sequence

| | Test Voltage Between | Should Be | If Not, Conduct |
|---|---|---|---|
| Key On | Socket #4 and Engine Ground | Battery Voltage ±0.1 Volt | Battery Source Test |
| | Socket #1 and Engine Ground | Battery Voltage ±0.1 Volt | Battery Source Test |
| Cranking | Socket #5 and Engine Ground | 8 to 12 volts | Check Supply Circuit (starting) through Ignition Switch |
| | Jumper #1 to #8 Read #6 | more than 6 volts | Starting Circuit Test |
| | Pin #3 and Pin #8 | ½ volt minimum AC or any DC volt wiggle | Distributor Hardware Test |

| | Test Voltage Between | Should Be | If Not, Conduct |
|---|---|---|---|
| Key Off | Socket #8 and #3 | 400 to 800 ohms | Magnetic Pick-up (Stator) Test |
| | Socket #7 and Engine Ground | 0 ohms | |
| | Socket #8 and Engine Ground | more than 70,000 ohms | |
| | Socket #3 and Engine Ground | more than 70,000 ohms | |
| | Socket #4 and Coil Tower | 7,000 and 13,000 ohms | Coil Test |
| | Socket #1 and Engine Ground | more than 4.0 ohms | Short Test |

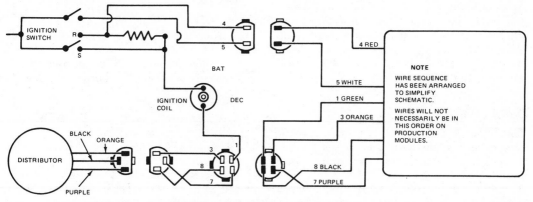

1976 electronic ignition wiring diagram

- Hard or no starting
- Rough idle
- Poor fuel economy
- Engine misses while under load or while accelerating.

NOTE: *Due to the sensitive nature of the Dura-Spark system and the complexity of the test procedures, it is recommended that you refer to your dealer if you suspect a problem in your electronic ignition system. The system can, of course, be tested by substituting known good components (module, stator, etc.)*

CAUTION: *If you wish to do your own troubleshooting read the next pages carefully, be sure you understand the procedures before you attempt any ignition system tests.*

## OPERATION

With the ignition switch "on," the primary circuit is on the ignition coil is energized. When the armature "spokes" approach the magnetic pickup coil assembly, they induce a voltage which tells the amplifier to turn the coil primary current off. A timing circuit in the amplifier module will turn the current on again after the coil field has collapsed. When the current is "on," it flows from the battery through the ignition switch, the primary windings of the ignition coil, and through the amplifier module circuits to ground. When the current is off, the magnetic field built up in the ignition coil is allowed to collapse, inducing a high voltage into the secondary windings of the coil. High voltage is produced each time the field is thus built up and collapsed. When Dura Spark is used in conjunction with EEC, and EEC computer tells the Dura Spark module when to turn the coil primary current off or on. In this case, the armature position is only a reference signal of engine timing, used by reference signal of engine timing, used by the EEC computer in combination with other reference signals to determine optimum ignition spark timing.

The high voltage flows through the coil high tension lead to the distributor cap where the rotor distributes it to one of the spark plug terminals in the distributor cap. This process is repeated for every power stroke of the engine.

Ignition system troubles are caused by a failure in the primary and/or the secondary circuit; incorrect ignition timing; or incorrect distributor advance. Circuit failures may be caused by shorts, corroded or dirty terminals, loose connections, defective wire insulation, cracked distributor cap or rotor, defective pick-up coil assembly or amplifier module, defective distributor points or fouled spark plugs.

If an engine starting or operating trouble is attributed to the ignition system, start the engine and verify the complaint. On engines that will not start, be sure that there is gasoline in the fuel tank and that fuel is reaching the carburetor. Then locate the ignition system problem using the following procedures.

### DURA SPARK I

The following Dura Spark II troubleshooting procedures may be used on Dura Spark I systems with a few variations. The Dura Spark I module has internal connections which shut off the primary circuit in the run mode when the engine stalls. To perform the above troubleshooting procedures, it is necessary to by-pass these connections. However, with these connections by-passed, the current flow in the primary becomes so great that it will damage both the ignition coil and module unles a ballast resistor is installed in series with the primary circuit at the BAT terminal of the ignition coil. Such a resistor is available from Ford (Motorcraft part number DY-36). A 1.3 ohm, 100 watt wire-wound power resistor can also be used.

To install the resistor, proceed as follows.
NOTE: *The resistor will become very hot during testing.*
1. Release the BAT terminal lead from the coil by inserting a paper clip through the hole in the rear of the horseshoe coil connector and manipulating it against the locking tab in the connector until the lead comes free.
2. Insert a paper clip in the BAT terminal

of the connector on the coil. Using jumper leads, connect the ballast resistor.
3. Using a straight pin, pierce both the red and white leads of the module to short these two together. This will by-pass the internal connections of the module which turn off the ignition circuit when the engine is not running.
CAUTION: *Pierce the wires only AFTER the ballast resistor is in place or you could damage the ignition coil and module.*
4. With the ballast resistor and by-pass in place, proceed with the Dura Spark II troubleshooting procedures.

### DURA SPARK II

NOTE: *Troubleshooting procedures are not given for the EEC systems because of their great complexity.*
The following procedures can be used to determine whether the ignition system is working or not. If these procedures fail to correct the problem, a full troubleshooting procedure should be performed by a qualified service department.

#### Preliminary Checks

1. Check the battery's state of charge and connections.
2. Inspect all wires and connections for—breaks, cuts, abrasions, or burn spots. Repair as necessary.
3. Unplug all connectors one at a time and inspect for corroded or burned contacts. Repair and plug connectors back together. DO NOT remove the silicone compound in the connectors.
4. Check for loose or damaged spark plug or coil wires. A wire resistance check is given at the end of this section. If the boots or nipples are removed on 8mm ignition wires, re-line the inside of each with new silicone dielectric compound (Motorcraft WA 10).

#### Special Tools

To perform the following tests, two special tools are needed; the ignition test jumper shown in

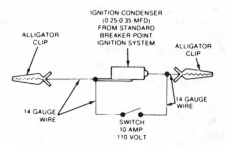

**Test jumper switch used for troubleshooting the Dura Spark ignition system**

the illustration and a modified spark plug. Use the illustration to assemble the ignition test jumper. The test jumper must be used when performing the following tests. The modified spark plug is basically a spark plug with the side electrode removed. Ford makes a special tool called a Spark Tester for this purpose, which besides not having a side electrode is equipped with a spring clip so that it can be grounded to engine metal. It is recommended that the Spark Tester be used as there is less chance of being shocked.

## Run Mode Spark Test

NOTE: *The wire colors given here are the main colors of the wires, not the dots or hashmarks.*

*STEP 1*

1. Remove the distributor cap and rotor from the distributor.
2. With the ignition off, turn the engine over by hand until one of the teeth on the distributor armature aligns with the magnet in the pick-up coil.
3. Remove the coil wire from the distributor cap. Install the modified spark plug (see Special Tools, above) in the coil wire terminal and using heavy gloves and insulated pliers, hold the spark plug shell against the engine block.
4. Turn the ignition to RUN (not START) and tap the distributor body with a screwdriver handle. There should be a spark at the modified spark plug.
5. If a good spark is evident, the primary circuit is OK: perform Start Mode Spark Test. If there is no spark, proceed to Step 2.

*STEP 2*

1. Unplug the module connector(s) which contain(s) the green and black module leads.
2. In the harness side of the connector(s), connect the special test jumper (see Special Tools, above) between the leads which connect to the green and black leads of the module pig tails. Use paper clips on connector socket holes to make contact. Do not allow clips to ground.
3. Turn the ignition switch to RUN (not START) and close the test jumper switch. Leave closed for about 1 second, then open. Repeat several times. There should be a spark each time the switch is opened. On Dura Spark I systems, close the test switch for 10 seconds on the first cycle. After that, 1 second is adequate.
4. If there is no spark, the problem is probably in the primary circuit through the ignition switch, the coil, the green lead or the black

lead, or the ground connection in the distributor: perform Step 3. If there is a spark, the primary circuit wiring and coil are probably OK. The problem is probably in the distributor pick-up, the module red wire, or the module: perform Step 6.

*STEP 3*

1. Disconnect the test jumper lead from the black lead and connect it to a good ground. Turn the test jumper switch on and off several times as in Step 2.
2. If there is no spark, the problem is probably in the green lead, the coil, or the coil feed circuit: perform Step 5.
3. If there is spark, the problem is probably in the black lead or the distributor ground connection: perform Step 4.

*STEP 4*

1. Connect an ohmmeter between the black lead and ground. With the meter on its lowest scale, there should be no measurable resistance in the circuit. If there is resistance, check the distributor ground connection and the black lead from the module. Repair as necessary, remove the ohmmeter, plug in all connections and repeat Step 1.

If there is no resistance, the primary ground wiring is OK: perform Step 6.

*STEP 5*

1. Disconnect the test jumper from the green lead and ground and connect it between the TACH-TEST terminal of the coil and a good ground on the engine.
2. With the ignition switch in the RUN position, turn the jumper switch on. Hold it on for about 1 second then turn it off as in Step 2. Repeat several times. There should be a spark each time the switch is turned off. If there is no spark, the problem is probably in the primary circuit running through the ignition switch to the coil BAT terminal, or in the coil itself. Check coil resistance (test given later in this section), and check the coil for internal shorts or opens. Check the coil feed circuit for opens, shorts or high resistance. Repair as necessary, reconnect all connectors and repeat Step 1. If there is spark, the coil and its feed circuit are OK. The problem could be in the green lead between the coil and the module. Check for open or short, repair as necessary, reconnect all connectors and repeat Step 1.

*STEP 6*

To perform this step, a voltmeter which is not combined with a dwell meter is needed. The slight needle oscillations (½ V) you'll be looking for may not be detectable on the combined voltmeter/dwell meter unit.

1. Connect a voltmeter between the orange and purple leads on the harness side of the module connectors.

CAUTION: *On catalytic converter equipped cars, disconnect the air supply line between the Thermactor by-pass valve and the manifold before cranking the engine with the ignition off. This will prevent damage to the catalytic converter. After testing, run the engine for at least 3 minutes before reconnecting the by-pass valve, to clear excess fuel from the exhaust system.*

2. Set the voltmeter on its lowest scale and crank the engine. The meter needle should oscillate slightly (about ½ volt). If the meter does not oscillate, check the circuit through the magnetic pick-up in the distributor for open, shorts, shorts to ground and resistance. Resistance between the orange and purple leads should be 400–1000 ohms, and between each lead and ground should be more than 70,000 ohms. Repair as necessary, reconnect all connectors and repeat Step 1.

If the meter oscillates, the problem is probably in the power feed to the module (red wire) or in the module itself: proceed to Step 7.

*STEP 7*

1. Remove all meters and jumpers and plug in all connectors.

2. Turn the ignition switch to the RUN position and measure voltage between the battery positive terminal and engine ground. It should be 12 volts.

3. Next, measure voltage between the red lead of the module and engine ground. To make this measurement, it will be necessary to pierce the red wire with a straight pin and connect the voltmeter to the straight pin and to ground. DO NOT ALLOW THE STRAIGHT PIN TO GROUND ITSELF.

4. The two readings should be within one volt of each other. If not within one volt, the problem is in the power feed to the red lead. Check for shorts, open, or high resistance and correct as necessary. After repairs, repeat Step 1.

If the readings are within one volt, the problem is probably in the module. Replace with a good module and repeat Step 1. If this corrects the problem, reconnect the old module and repeat Step 1. If problem returns, permanently install the new module.

**Start Mode Spark Test**

NOTE: *The wire colors given here are the main colors of the wires, not the dots or hashmarks.*

1. Remove the coil wire from the distributor cap. Install the modified spark plug mentioned under "Special Tools", in the coil wire and ground it to engine metal either by its spring clip (Spark Tester) or by holding the spark plug shell against the engine block with insulated pliers.

NOTE: *See "CAUTION" under Step 6 of "Run Mode Spark Test".*

2. Have an assistant crank the engine using the ignition switch and check for spark. If there is good spark, the problem is probably in the distributor cap, rotor, ignition cables or spark plugs. If there is no spark, proceed to Step 3.

3. Measure the battery voltage. Next, measure the voltage at the white wire of the module while cranking the engine. To make this measurement, it will be necessary to pierce the white wire with a straight pin and connect the voltmeter to the straight pin and to ground. DO NOT ALLOW THE STRAIGHT PIN TO GROUND ITSELF. The battery voltage and the voltage at the white wire should be within 1 volt of each other. If the readings are not within 1 volt of each other, check and repair the feed through the ignition switch to the white wire. Recheck for spark (Step 1). If the readings are within 1 volt of each other, or if there is still no spark after power feed to white wire is repaired, proceed to Step 4.

4. Measure the coil BATT terminal voltage while cranking the engine. The reading should be within 1 volt of battery voltage. If the readings are not within 1 volt of each other, check and repair the feed through the ignition switch to the coil. If the readings are within 1 volt of each other, the problem is probably in the ignition module. Substitute another module and repeat test for spark (Step 1).

## SYSTEM COMPONENT TESTING

### Ignition Coil Tests

The ignition coil must be diagnosed separately from the rest of the ignition system.

1. Primary resistance is measured between the two outer coil terminals. Disconnect the coil harness connector. Make sure the ignition switch is OFF. Connect an ohmmeter between the two coil terminals. Primary resistance for Dura Spark I systems should measure 0.71–0.77 ohms. Dura Spark II system should measure 1.13–1.23 ohms.

2. Secondary resistance is measured between the BATT and center (coil wire) terminals of the coil. Disconnect the coil harness connector and the center coil wire. Make sure the ignition switch is OFF. Connect an ohmmeter between the two coil terminals. Secondary resistance should measure; 7350–

8250 ohms for Dura Spark I systems and 7700–11,500 ohms for Dura Spark II.

If resistance tests are alright, but the coil is still suspected have the ignition coil tested on a coil tester. If the reading on the coil tester differs from the original testing, check for a defective wiring harness. If significantly different replace the ignition coil.

### Resistance Wire Test

Replace the resistance wire if it doesn't show a resistance of 1.05–1.15 ohms. The resistance wire isn't used on Dura Spark I.

### Spark Plug Wire Resistance

Resistance on these wires must not exceed 5,000 ohms per inch. To properly measure this, remove the wires from the plugs, and remove the distributor cap. Measure the resistance through the distributor cap at that end. Do not pierce any ignition wire for any reason. Measure only from the two ends. Do not pull on the wires. Grasp and twist the boot to remove the wire.

Whenever the high tension wires are removed from the plugs, coil, or distributor, silicone grease must be applied inside the boot before reconnection. Use a clean small screwdriver blade to coat the entire interior surface with Ford silicone grease D7AZ-19A331-A, Dow Corning #111, or General Electric G-627.

### Adjustments

The air gap between the armature and magnetic pick-up coil in the distributor is not adjustable, nor are there any adjustments for the amplifier module. Inoperative components are simply replaced. Any attempt to connect components outside the vehicle may result in component failure.

## PICK-UP REPLACEMENT

### Except EEC

1. Remove the distributor cap and rotor, disconnect the distributor harness plug.

NOTE: *To remove the two-piece Dura Spark distributor cap, take off the top portion, then the rotor, then the bottom adaptor.*

2. Using a small gear puller or two screwdrivers, lift or pry the armature from the advance plate sleeve. Remove the roll pin.

3. Remove the large wire retaining cip from the base plate annular groove.

For 1976–81 models:

4. Remove the snap-ring which secures the vacuum advance link to the pick-up assembly.

5. Remove the magnetic pick-up assem-

bly ground screw and lift the assembly from the distributor.

6. Lift the vacuum advance arm off the post on the pick-up assembly and move it out against the distributor housing.

For 1982 models:

7. Remove the ground screw which retains the ground strap.

8. Pull upward on the lead wires to remove the rubber grommet from the distributor base.

9. Remove the E-clip which retains the vacuum advance pull rod to the stator assembly.

10. Lift the pull rod off of the stator post and move the rod out against the distributor housing.

11. Remove the stator assembly.

Installation—all models:

12. Place the new pick-up assembly in position over the fixed base plate and slide the wiring in position through the slot in the side of the distributor housing.

13. Install the wire snap-ring securing the pick-up assembly to the fixed base plate.

14. Position the vacuum advance arm over the post on the pick-up assembly and install the snap-ring.

15. Install the grounding screw through the tab on the wiring harness and into the fixed base plate.

16. Install the armature on the advance plate sleeve making sure that the roll pin is engaged in the matching slots.

17. Install the distributor rotor cap.

18. Connect the distributor wiring plug to the vehicle harness.

## BREAKERLESS IGNITION SYSTEM TACH HOOKUP

A terminal on the coil is provided for connecting a tachometer. The terminal is labeled "Tach-Test" and has a small arrowhead pointing to the proper terminal. Connect the red lead (positive) to this terminal and connect the

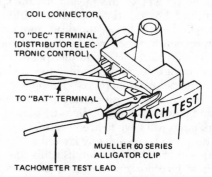

COIL CONNECTOR

TO "DEC" TERMINAL (DISTRIBUTOR ELECTRONIC CONTROL)

TO "BAT" TERMINAL

TACH TEST

MUELLER 60 SERIES ALLIGATOR CLIP

TACHOMETER TEST LEAD

**Attaching dwell/tachometer lead to coil connector**

black ground lead (negative) of the dwell-tach to a good ground on the engine (e.g., thermostat housing bolt).

## Ignition Timing

Regular ignition timing adjustments are not, strictly speaking, necessary. However, it is always a good idea to check timing occasionally and a basic understanding of ignition timing is essential.

> CAUTION: *On models equipped with EEC III, all ignition timing is controlled by the EEC module. Initial ignition timing is not adjustable and no attempt at adjustment should be made.*
>
> NOTE: *Ford recommends that only timing lights of the inductive pickup variety be used; conventional timing lights may give a false reading due to the higher coil-charging currents.*

Ignition timing is the measurement in degrees of crankshaft rotation of the instant the spark plugs in the cylinders fire, in relation to the location of the piston, while the piston is on its compression stroke.

Ideally, the air-fuel mixture in the cylinder will be ignited (by the spark plug) and just beginning its rapid expansion as the piston passes top dead center (TDC) of the compression stroke. If this happens, the piston will be beginning the power stroke just as the compressed (by the movement of the piston) and ignited (by the spark plug) air-fuel mixture starts to expand. The expansion of the air-fuel mixture will then force the piston down on the power stroke and turn the crankshaft.

It takes a fraction of a second for the spark from the plug to completely ignite the mixture in the cylinder. Because of this, the spark plug must fire before the piston reaches TDC, if the mixture is to be completely ignited as the piston passes TDC. This measurement is given in degrees (of crankshaft rotation) *before* the piston reaches *top dead center* (BTDC). If the ignition timing setting for your engine is six degrees (6°) BTDC, this means that the spark plug must fire at a time when the piston for that cylinder is 6° before top dead center of its compression stroke. However, this only holds true while your engine is at idle speed.

As you accelerate from idle, the speed of your engine (rpm) increases. The increase in rpm means that the pistons are now traveling up and down much faster. Because of this, the spark plugs will have to fire even sooner if the mixture is to be completely ignited as the piston passes TDC. To accomplish this, the distributor incorporates means to advance the timing of the spark as engine speed increases.

The distributor in your car has two means of advancing the ignition timing. One is called centrifugal advance and is actuated by weights in the distributor. The other is called vacuum advance and is controlled by that large circular housing on the side of the distributor.

In addition, some distributors have a vacuum-retard mechanism which is contained in the same housing on the side of the distributor as the vacuum advance. The function of the mechanism is to retard the timing of the ignition spark under certain engine conditions. This causes more complete burning of the air-fuel mixture in the cylinder and consequently lowers exhaust emissions.

Because these mechanisms change ignition timing, it is necessary to disconnect and plug the one or two vacuum lines from the distributor when setting the basic ignition timing.

If ignition timing is set too far advanced (BTDC), the ignition and expansion of the air-fuel mixture in the cylinder will try to force the piston down the cylinder while it is still traveling upward. This causes engine "ping," a sound which resembles marbles being dropped into an empty tin can. If the ignition timing is too far retarded (after, or ATDC), the piston will have already started down on the power stroke when the air-fuel mixture ignites and expands. This will cause the piston to be forced down only a portion of its travel. This will result in poor engine performance and lack of power.

Ignition timing adjustment is checked with a timing light. This instrument is connected to the number one (no. 1) spark plug of the engine. The timing light flashes every time an electrical current is sent from the distributor, through the no. 1 spark plug wire, to the spark plug. The crankshaft pulley and the front cover of the engine are marked with a timing pointer and a timing scale. When the timing pointer is aligned with the "0" mark on the timing scale, the piston in no. 1 cylinder is at TDC of its compression stroke. With the engine running and the timing light aimed at the timing pointer and timing scale, the stroboscopic flashes from the timing light will allow you to check the ignition timing setting of the engine. The timing light flashes every time the spark plug in the no. 1 cylinder of the engine fires. Since the flash from the timing light makes the crankshaft pulley seem stationary for a moment, you will be able to read the exact position of the piston in the no. 1 cylinder on the timing scale on the front of the engine.

### IGNITION TIMING ADJUSTMENT

Clean the crankshaft damper/pulley and timing pointer on the water pump housing with a

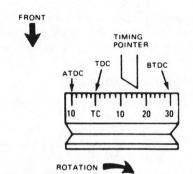

**4-140 timing marks**

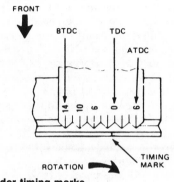

**6 cylinder timing marks**

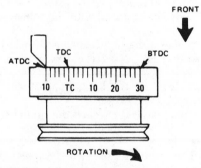

**V8 timing marks**

solvent-soaked rag or a wire brush so that the marks can be seen. Connect a stroboscopic timing light to the no. 1 cylinder spark plug (see firing order illustration) and to the battery, according to the manufacturer's instructions. Scribe a mark on the crankshaft damper/pulley and on the pointer with chalk or luminescent (day glo) paint to highlight the correct timing setting. Disconnect the vacuum hose(s) at the distributor vacuum capsule and plug it (them) with a pencil, golf tee, or some other small pointed object.

Connect one lead to the "Tach Test" connection atop the ignition coil and the other wire to a good ground. Make sure all wires clear the fan. Set the idle speed to specifications. With the engine running, aim the timing light

at the pointer and the marks on the damper/pulley. If the marks made with the chalk or paint coincide when the timing light flashes, the engine is timed correctly. If the marks do not coincide, stop the engine. Loosen the distributor locknut and start the engine again. While observing the timing light flashes on the markers, grasp the distributor vacuum capsule—not the distributor cap—and rotate the distributor until the marks do coincide. Stop the engine and tighten the distributor locknut, taking care not to disturb the setting. As a final check, start the engine once more to make sure that the timing marks align.

NOTE: *If necessary, readjust idle speed to specifications. The timing setting is correct only at idle speed.*

Reconnect the vacuum hose(s) to the distributor. Readjust the curb idle speed to specifications as outlined under "Idle Speed and Mixture Adjustment." Remove the timing light and tachometer from the engine.

## Valve Adjustment

All engines are equipped with hydraulic valve lifters or lash adjusters. Valve systems with hydraulic lifters operate with zero clearance in the valve train. There is no need of scheduled valve adjustment because of the hydraulic valve lifters ability to compensate for slack. All components of the valve train should be checked for wear if there is excessive play. If the valve train has been disassembled for any reason a preliminary valve adjustment may be necessary. Refer to the engine chapter (Chapter 3) for instruction on preliminary valve adjustment.

## Carburetor

This section contains only carburetor adjustments as they normally apply to engine tune-up.

When the engine in your car is running, air-fuel mixture from the carburetor is being drawn into the engine by a partial vacuum that is created by the downward movement of the piston on the intake stroke of the four-stroke cycle of the engine. The amount of air-fuel mixture that enters the engine is controlled by throttle plate(s) in the bottom of the carburetor. When the engine is not running, the throttle plate(s) is (are) closed, completely blocking off the bottom of the carburetor from the inside of the engine. The throttle plates are connected, through the throttle linkage, to the gas pedal in the passenger compartment of the car. After you start the engine and put the transmission in gear, you depress the gas pedal to start the car moving. What you actually are doing when you depress the gas pedal is opening the throttle plate in the carburetor to admit more of the air-fuel mixture to the engine. The further you open the throttle plates in the carburetor, the higher the engine speed becomes.

As previously stated, when the engine is not running, the throttle plates in the carburetor are closed. When the engine is idling, it is necessary to open the throttle plates slightly. To prevent having to keep your foot on the gas pedal when the engine is idling, an idle speed adjusting screw was added to the carburetor. This screw has the same effect as keeping your foot slightly depressed on the gas pedal. The idle speed adjusting screw contacts a lever (the throttle lever) on the outside of the carburetor. When the screw is turned in, it opens the throttle plate on the carburetor, raising the idle speed of the engine. This screw is called the curb idle adjusting screw, and the procedures in this section will tell you how to adjust it.

In addition to the carb idle adjusting screw, most engines have a throttle solenoid. When the key is turned to "off," the engine normally stops running. However, if an engine has a high operating temperature and a high idle speed, it is possible for the temperature of the cylinder instead of the spark plug to ignite the air-fuel mixture. When this happens, the engine continues to run after the key is turned off. To solve this problem, a throttle solenoid was added to the carburetor. The solenoid is a cylinder with an adjustable plunger and an electrical lead. When the ignition key is turned to "on," the solenoid plunger extends to contact the carburetor throttle lever and raise the idle speed of the engine. When the ignition key is turned to "off," the solenoid is deenergized and the solenoid plunger falls back from the throttle lever. This allows the throttle lever to fall back and rest on the curb idle adjusting screw. This drops the engine idle speed back far enough that the engine will not run on.

Since it is difficult for the engine to draw the air-fuel mixture from the carburetor with the small amount of throttle plate opening that is present when the engine is idling, an idle mixture passage is provided in the carburetor. This passage delivers air-fuel mixture to the engine from a hole which is located in the bottom of the carburetor below the throttle plates. This idle mixture passage contains an adjusting screw which restricts the amount of air-fuel mixture that enters the engine at idle.

NOTE: *With the electric solenoid disengaged, the carburetor idle speed adjusting screw must make contact with the throttle lever to prevent the throttle plates from jamming in the throttle bore when the engine is turned off.*

## IDLE SPEED AND MIXTURE ADJUSTMENTS

Due to higher emission standards, idle systems have become so complex it is recommended that any idle speed adjustments be done at a qualified shop.

NOTE: *In order to limit exhaust emissions, plastic caps have been installed on the idle fuel mixture screw(s) that prevent the carburetor from being adjusted to an overly rich fuel mixture. Under no circumstances should these limiters be modified or removed. Not only is it illegal, you probably won't improve your car's performance and may even hurt it. A satisfactory idle may be obtained within the range of the limiters.*

If the idle speed must be adjusted and you are not able to take your car to a qualified garage;

1. Start the engine and allow it to reach operating temperatures.

2. Make sure the parking brake is on and the wheels are firmly chocked. This is important since automatic transmission cars have their high idle adjusted with the transmission in drive.

3. Remove the air cleaner and make sure the choke is fully open (choke plate in vertical position). Put the air cleaner back on. Check to see that the air conditioner and other accessories are turned off.

4. If you haven't checked the timing at this point, do it now. Attach a tachometer to the engine.

5. The carburetor has two idle speeds: high idle and low idle. On automatic transmission cars, the high idle is adjusted with the transmission in drive. On V8s, the high idle speed is adjusted with the throttle solenoid activated (plugged in). The solenoid adjustment is made by turning the solenoid adjusting screw in or out, then tightening the locknut. On other models, simply turn the adjusting screw in or out. There is no locknut.

6. The low idle speed is adjusted with the throttle solenoid deactivated (unplugged). Disconnect the solenoid lead at the connector near the harness, not at the carburetor. When adjusting the low idle, the transmission should be in neutral. The adjustment is made with the curb idle adjusting screw on the carburetor. After adjusting the lower idle speed, reconnect the solenoid lead at the harness connector and open the throttle slightly by hand, allowing the solenoid plunger to extend.

NOTE: *Sometimes it is difficult to adjust the idle speed with the air cleaner installed. If you have problems, take the air cleaner off and make an approximate adjustment, keeping in mind that the reinstallation of the air cleaner will cause the idle to drop. Continue with this trial and error method until the proper idle speed is attained.*

## Catalytic Converter Precautions

Most models are equipped with catalytic converters to clean up exhaust emissions after they leave the engine. Naturally, lead-free fuel must be used in order to avoid contaminating the converter and rendering it useless. However, there are other precautions which should be taken to prevent a large amount of unburned hydrocarbon from reaching the converter. Should a sufficient amount of HC reach the converter, the unit could overheat, possibly damaging the converter or nearby mechanical components. There is even the possibility that a fire could be started. Therefore, when working on your car, the following conditions should be avoided:

1. The use of fuel system cleaning agents and additives.

2. Operating the car with a closed choke or a submerged carburetor float.

3. Extended periods of engine run-on (dieseling).

4. Turning off the ignition with the car in motion.

5. Ignition or charging system failure.

6. Misfiring of one or more spark plugs.

7. Disconnecting a spark plug wire while testing for a bad wire or plug, or poor compression in one cylinder.

8. Push starting the car, especially when hot.

9. Pumping the gas pedal when attempting to start a hot engine.

10. Using leaded gasoline.

# Engine and Engine Rebuilding

# 3

## ENGINE ELECTRICAL

### Ignition System

Refer to Chapter 2 for a description of, and troubleshooting procedures for, the ignition system.

### Distributor

CAUTION: *On models equipped with EEC III ignition system. The distributor is locked into place and adjustment is never required because all timing control is handled by the EEC III module. Rotor alignment is critical with this system and any servicing should be done only by qualified mechanics.*

### REMOVAL

1. Remove the air cleaner on the V6 and V8 engines.
2. On the 4-cylinder and 6-cylinder in-line engines, remove one thermactor pump mounting bolt, and the drive belt; then swing the pump to one side to allow access to the distributor. If necessary disconnect the thermactor air filter and lines.
3. Disconnect the distributor wiring connector from the vehicle wiring hanress.
4. Disconnect the vacuum line(s) from the distributor.
5. Remove the distributor cap and wires and lay to one side.
6. Scribe a mark on the distributor body and the cylinder block indicating the position of the rotor. These remaks will be used as guides during installation of the distributor.
7. Remove the distributor hold down bolt and clamp and lift the distributor out of the block.
NOTE: *Do not rotate the engine while the distributor is out of the block, or it will be necessary to time the engine.*

### INSTALLATION

1a. If the engine was cranked (disturbed) with the distributor removed, it will now be necessary to retime the engine. If the distributor has been installed incorrectly and the engine will not start, remove the distributor from the engine and start over again. Hold the distributor close to the engine and install the cap on the distributor in its normal position. Locate the No. 1 spark plug tower on the distributor cap. Scribe a mark on the body of the distributor directly below the No. 1 spark plug wire tower on the distributor cap. Remove the distributor cap from the distributor and move the distributor and cap to one side. Remove the No. 1 spark plug and crank the engine over until the No. 1 cylinder is on its compression stroke. To accomplish this, place a wrench on the lower engine pulley and turn the engine slowly in a clockwise direction until the TDC mark on the crankshaft damper aligns with the timing pointer. If you place your finger over (cold engine) the No. 1 spark plug hole, you will feel air escaping as the piston rises in the combustion chamber. One of the armature segments must be aligned with the stator as to properly install the distributor. Make sure that the oil pump intermediate shaft

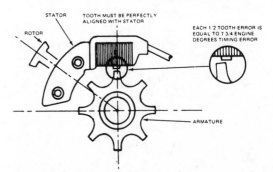

**Electronic distributor static timing position (6 cylinder similiar)**

properly engages the distributor shaft. It may be necessary to turn (with crankshaft pulley nut using socket and breaker bar) the engine after the distributor drive gear is partially engaged, in order to engage the oil pump intermediate shaft. Install, but do not tighten the retaining clamp and bolt. Rotate the distributor to a point where the armature tooth is aligned properly. Tighten the clamp.

1b. If the engine was not cranked (disturbed) when the distributor was removed, position the distributor in the block with the rotor aligned with the mark previously scribed on the distributor body and cylinder block. Install the distributor hold-down bolt and clamp fingertight.

2. Install the vacuum hoses and connect the ignition wire to the wiring harness.

3. Install the rotor adapter and distributor cap.

4. Install the thermactor pump and belt on the four and in-line six cylinder engines. Adjust the belt tension so that there is a ¼ inch deflection at its longest point.

5. Connect the thermactor hoses and the filter.

6. Install the air cleaner and check the ignition timing.

## Alternator

### ALTERNATOR PRECAUTIONS

To prevent damage to the alternator and regulator, the following precautions should be taken when working with the electrical system.

1. Never reverse the battery connections.

2. Booster batteries for starting must be connected properly. See Chapter 1.

3. Disconnect the battery cables before using a fast charger; the charger has a tendency to force current through the diodes in the opposite direction for which they are designed. This burns out the diodes.

4. Never use a fast charger as a booster for starting the vehicle.

5. Never disconnect the voltage regulator while the engine is running.

6. Avoid long soldering times when replacing diodes or transistors. Prolonged heat is damaging to AC generators.

7. Do not use test lamps of more than 12 volts (V) for checking diode continuity.

8. Do not short across or ground any of the terminals on the AC generator.

9. The polarity of the battery, generator, and regulator must be matched and considered before making any electrical connections within the system.

10. Never operate the alternator on an open circuit. Make sure that all connections within the circuit are clean and tight.

11. Disconnect the battery terminals when performing any service on the electrical system. This will eliminate the possibility of accidental reversal of polarity.

12. Disconnect the battery ground cable if arc welding is to be done on any part of the car.

### SIDE TERMINAL ALTERNATOR

#### Removal

1. Disconnect the ground cable at the battery.

2. Loosen the alternator attaching bolt and remove the adjustment arm attaching bolt. Remove the drive bolt from the pulley.

3. Remove the electrical connectors from the alternator. To remove the stator and field connectors depress the lock tab and pull the connector straight off the terminals.

4. Remove the alternator attaching bolt and remove the alternator.

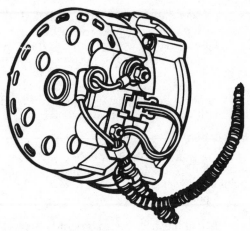

Side terminal alternator

#### Installation

1. Position the alternator to the engine, and install the spacer (if used) and the alternator attaching bolt. Tighten the bolt to a snug position.

2. Install the adjustment arm attaching bolt.

3. Install the drive belt on the pulley and adjust the belt tension. Apply pressure on the alternator front housing adjusting ear and tighten the adjusting arm bolt and the alternator mounting bolt. Test the tightness of the belt by pressing it firmly with your thumb at its longest run. The deflection should be about a ¼ inch.

4. Connect the electrical connectors to the alternator.

5. Connect the battery ground cable.

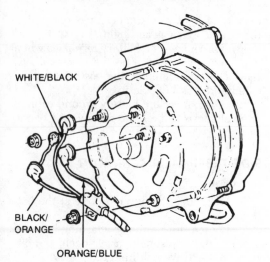

WHITE/BLACK

BLACK/ ORANGE

ORANGE/BLUE

**Rear terminal alternator**

## Alternator/Regulator Identification

| Color Code | Amps. | Type | Regulator |
|---|---|---|---|
| Orange | 40 | RT | Electronic ① |
| Green | 60 | RT | Electronic ① |
| Black | 65 | RT | Electronic |
| Black | 70 | ST | Electronic ① |
| Red | 100 | ST | Electronic |

RT-Rear Terminal    ST-Side Terminal
Field Current at 12V should be 4.0 on electronic regulators
① Electro-mechanical regulators were used in 1975 and 76 on all models, and on various models in 1977–78. Electro-mechanical regulators are not interchangeable with eletronic models.

## REAR TERMINAL ALTERNATOR

### Removal

1. Disconnect the ground cable from the battery.
2. Loosen the alternator pivot bolt and adjuster bolt and remove the drive belt.
3. Disconnect the wiring terminals from the back of the alternator. The push on type terminals should be pulled straight off the terminal to prevent damage to the terminal.
4. Remove the alternator adjuster bolt and pivot bolt and remove the alternator.

### Installation

1. Position the alternator on the engine and install the pivot bolt and the adjuster bolt and tighten until snug.
2. Connect the wiring terminals to the back of the alternator.
3. Install the drive belt and tighten the tension until there is a ¼ inch deflection at its longest span. Apply pressure on the front housing only.
4. Tighten the adjuster bolt and connect the ground cable to the battery.

## Regulator

Most of the voltage regulators used are 100 percent solid state, consisting of transistors, diodes, and resistors. The regulators are preset and calibrated by the manufacturer. No readjustment is required or possible on these units.

### REMOVAL AND INSTALLATION

1. Remove the battery ground cable.
2. Disconnect the regulator from the wiring harness.

3. Remove the regulator mounting screws and remove the regulator.
4. Installation is the reverse of removal.

## Starting System

The function of a starting system is to crank the engine at a speed fast enough to permit the engine to start. Heavy cables, connectors, and switches are used in the starting system because of the large current required by the starter while it is cranking the engine. The amount of the resistance in the starting circuit must be kept to an absolute minimum to provide maximum current for starter operation. A discharged or damaged battery, loose or corroded connections or partially broken cables will result in slower than normal cranking speeds, and may even prevent the starter from cranking the engine.

The starting system includes an integral positive-engagement drive, battery, a remote control starter switch (part of the ignition switch), the neutral-start switch, (automatic transmission with floor shift only), the starter relay, and heavy circuit wiring.

When the ignition key is turned to the start position it actuates the starter relay, through the starter control circuit. The starter relay then connects the battery to the starter.

## Starter

### REMOVAL AND INSTALLATION

1. Disconnect the negative battery cable from the battery.
2. Raise the front of the car and support on jackstands.
3. Disconnect the electrical cable from the starter motor.
4. Remove the starter motor mounting bolts and the starter.
NOTE: *Depending on year and engine, it*

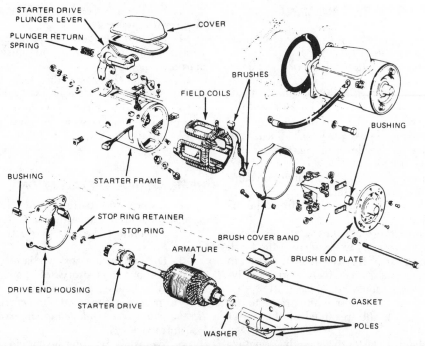

**Exploded view of a typical starter motor**

*may be necessary to disconnect the (starter side) motor mount and jack up the engine slightly or turn the wheels to gain enough room to dismount the motor or clear the steering linkage.*

5. Installation is in the reverse order of removal. Mounting bolts should be tighten to 15–20 ft. lbs.

### STARTER BRUSH REPLACEMENT

Replace the starter brushes when they are worn to ¼ in. Always install a complete set of new brushes.

1. Loosen and remove the brush cover band, gasket, and starter drive plunger lever cover. Remove the brushes from their holders.

2. Remove the two through-bolts from the starter frame.

3. Remove the drive end housing and the plunger lever return spring.

4. Remove the starter drive plunger lever pivot pin and lever, and remove the armature.

5. Remove the brush end plate.

6. Remove the ground brush retaining screws from the frame and remove the brushes.

7. Cut the insulated brush leads from the field coils, as close to the field connection point as possible.

8. Clean and inspect the starter motor.

9. Replace the brush end plate if the insulator between the field brush holder and the end plate is cracked or broken.

10. Position the new insulated field brushes lead on the field coil connection. Position and crimp the clip provided with the brushes to hold the brush lead to the connection. Solder the lead, clip, and connections together using rosin core solder. Use a 300-watt soldering iron.

11. Install the ground brush leads to the frame with the retaining screws.

12. Clean the commutator with 00 or 000 sandpaper.

13. Position the brush end plate to the starter frame, with the end plate boss in the frame slot.

14. Install the armature in the starter frame.

15. Install the starter drive gear plunger lever to the frame and starter drive assembly, and install the pivot pin.

16. Partially fill the drive end housing bearing bore with grease (approximately ¼ full). Position the return spring on the plunger lever, and the drive end housing to the starter frame. Install the through-bolts and tighten to specified torque (55 to 75 in. lbs). Be sure that the stop ring retainer is seated properly in the drive end housing.

17. Install the commutator brushes in the brush holders. Center the brush springs on the brushes.

18. Position the plunger lever cover and brush cover band, with its gasket, on the starter. Tighten the band retaining screw.

19. Connect the starter to a battery to check its operation.

## STARTER DRIVE REPLACEMENT

1. Remove the starter from the engine.
2. Remove the brush cover band.
3. Remove the starter drive plunger lever cover.
4. Loosen the thru-bolts just enough to allow removal of the drive end housing and the starter drive plunger lever return spring.
5. Remove the pivot pin which attaches the starter drive plunger lever to the starter frame and remove the lever.
6. Remove the stop ring retainer and stop-ring from the armature shaft.
7. Remove the starter drive from the armature shaft.
8. Inspect the teeth on the starter drive. If they are excessively worn, inspect the teeth on the ring gear of the flywheel. If the teeth on the flywheel are excessively worn, the flywheel ring gear should be replaced.
9. Apply a thin coat of white grease to the armature shaft, in the area in which the starter drive operates.
10. Install the starter drive on the armature shaft and install a new stop-ring.
11. Position the starter drive plunger lever on the starter frame and install the pivot pin. *Make sure the plunger lever is properly engaged with the starter drive.*
12. Install a new stop ring retainer on the armature shaft.

13. Fill the drive end housing bearing fore ¼ full with grease.
14. Position the starter drive plunger lever return spring and the drive end housing to the starter frame.
15. Tighten the starter thru-bolts to 55–75 in. lbs.
16. Install the starter drive plunger lever cover and the brush cover band on the starter.
17. Install the starter.

## Battery

### REMOVAL AND INSTALLATION

1. Loosen the battery cable bolts and spread the ends of the battery cable terminals.
2. Disconnect the negative battery cable first.
3. Disconnect the positive battery cable.
4. Remove the battery hold-down.
5. Wearing heavy gloves, remove the battery from under the hood. *Be careful not to tip the battery and spill acid on yourself or the car during removal.*
6. To install, wearing heavy gloves, place the battery in its holder under the hood. *Use care not to spill the acid.*
7. Install the battery hold-down.
8. Install the positive battery cable first.
9. Install the negative battery cable.
10. Apply a *light* coating of grease to the cable ends.

## General Engine Specifications

| Year | Engine Displacement (cu in.) | Carburetor Type | Horsepower @ rpm | Torque @ rpm (ft. lb.) | Bore x Stroke (in.) | Advertised Compression Ratio | Oil Pressure @ 2000 rpm |
|------|------|------|------|------|------|------|------|
| '75 | 6-200 MT | 1 bbl | 75 @ 3200 | 145 @ 2000 | 3.680 x 3.130 | 8.3:1 | 30–50 |
| | 6-200 AT | 1 bbl | 74 @ 3400 | 132 @ 2400 | 3.680 x 3.130 | 8.3:1 | 30–50 |
| | 6-250 MT | 1 bbl | 85 @ 2900 | 180 @ 2000 | 3.680 x 3.910 | 8.0:1 | 40–50 |
| | 6-250 AT | 1 bbl | 72 @ 2900 | 180 @ 1400 | 3.680 x 3.910 | 8.0:1 | 40–60 |
| | 6-250 MT Cal | 1 bbl | 79 @ 2800 | 177 @ 1600 | 3.680 x 3.910 | 8.0:1 | 40–60 |
| | 6-250 AT Cal | 1 bbl | 70 @ 2800 | 175 @ 1400 | 3.680 x 3.910 | 8.0:1 | 40–60 |
| | 8-302 | 2 bbl | 129 @ 3800 | 220 @ 1800 | 4.000 x 3.000 | 8.0:1 | 40–60 |
| | 8-302 Cal | 2 bbl | 115 @ 3600 | 203 @ 1800 | 4.000 x 3.000 | 8.0:1 | 40–60 |
| | 8-351W | 2 bbl | 143 @ 3600 | 255 @ 2200 | 4.000 x 3.500 | 8.2:1 | 40–65 |
| | 8-351W Cal | 2 bbl | 153 @ 3400 | 270 @ 2400 | 4.000 x 3.500 | 8.2:1 | 40–65 |
| '76 | 6-200 MT | 1 bbl | 81 @ 3400 | 151 @ 1700 | 3.682 x 3.126 | 8.3:1 | 30–50 |
| | 6-250 MT | 1 bbl | 87 @ 3000 | 187 @ 1900 | 3.682 x 3.910 | 8.0:1 | 40–60 |
| | 6-250 AT | 1 bbl | 78 @ 3000 | 187 @ 1900 | 3.682 x 3.910 | 8.0:1 | 40–60 |
| | 6-250 AT Cal | 1 bbl | 76 @ 3000 | 179 @ 1300 | 3.682 x 3.910 | 8.0:1 | 40–60 |
| | 8-302 MT | 2 bbl | 134 @ 3600 | 242 @ 2000 | 4.000 x 3.000 | 8.0:1 | 40–60 |

## General Engine Specifications (cont.)

| Year | Engine Displacement (cu in.) | Carburetor Type | Horsepower @ rpm | Torque @ rpm (ft. lb.) | Bore x Stroke (in.) | Advertised Compression Ratio | Oil Pressure @ 2000 rpm |
|------|------|------|------|------|------|------|------|
| '76 | 8-302 AT | 2 bbl | 133 @ 3600 | 243 @ 1800 | 4.000 x 3.000 | 8.0:1 | 40–60 |
| | 8-302 AT Cal | 2 bbl | 130 @ 3600 | 238 @ 1600 | 4.000 x 3.000 | 8.0:1 | 40–60 |
| | 8-351 AT | 2 bbl | 143 @ 3200 | 285 @ 1600 | 4.000 x 3.500 | 8.0:1 | 45–65 |
| | 8-351 AT Cal | 2 bbl | 140 @ 3400 | 276 @ 1600 | 4.000 x 3.500 | 8.0:1 | 45–65 |
| '77 | 6-200 MT | 1 bbl | 98 @ 4400 | 151 @ 2000 | 3.682 x 3.126 | 8.5:1 | 30–50 |
| | 6-250 MT | 1 bbl | 98 @ 3400 | 182 @ 1800 | 3.682 x 3.910 | 8.1:1 | 40–60 |
| | 6-250 AT | 1 bbl | 98 @ 3600 | 190 @ 1400 | 3.682 x 3.910 | 8.1:1 | 40–60 |
| | 6-250 AT Cal | 1 bbl | 86 @ 3000 | 185 @ 1800 | 3.682 x 3.910 | 8.1:1 | 40–60 |
| | 8-302 MT | 2 bbl | 122 @ 3200 | 237 @ 1600 | 4.000 x 3.000 | 8.4:1 | 40–60 |
| | 8-302 AT | 2 bbl | 134 @ 3600 | 245 @ 1600 | 4.000 x 3.000 | 8.4:1 | 40–60 |
| | 8-302 AT Cal | VV | 122 @ 3400 | 222 @ 1400 | 4.000 x 3.000 | 8.1:1 | 40–60 |
| | 8-351 AT | 2 bbl | 135 @ 3200 | 275 @ 1600 | 4.000 x 3.500 | 8.3:1 | 40–60 |
| '78 | 6-250 | 1 bbl | 97 @ 3200 | 210 @ 1400 | 3.682 x 3.910 | 8.5:1 | 40–60 |
| | 8-302 | 2 bbl | 139 @ 3600 | 250 @ 1600 | 4.000 x 3.000 | 8.4:1 | 40–60 |
| | 8-302 Cal | VV | 133 @ 3600 | 243 @ 1600 | 4.000 x 3.000 | 8.1:1 | 40–60 |
| '79 | 6-250 | 1 bbl | 97 @ 3200 | 210 @ 1400 | 3.682 x 3.910 | 8.6:1 | 40–60 |
| | 8-302 | 2 bbl | 137 @ 3600 | 243 @ 2000 | 4.000 x 3.000 | 8.4:1 | 40–60 |
| | 8-302 Cal | VV | 138 @ 3800 | 239 @ 2000 | 4.000 x 3.000 | 8.4:1 | 40–60 |
| '80 | 6-250 | 1 bbl | 90 @ 3200 | 194 @ 1660 | 3.682 x 3.910 | 8.6:1 | 40–60 |
| | 8-255 | 2 bbl | 117 @ 3800 | 193 @ 2000 | 3.680 x 3.000 | 8.8:1 | 40–60 |
| | 8-302 | 2 bbl | 134 @ 3600 | 232 @ 1600 | 4.000 x 3.000 | 8.4:1 | 40–60 |
| '81 | 4-140 | 2 bbl | 88 @ 4600 | 118 @ 2600 | 3.781 x 3.126 | 9.0:1 | 40–60 |
| | 6-200 | 1 bbl | 88 @ 3200 | 154 @ 1400 | 3.683 x 3.126 | 8.6:1 | 30–50 |
| | 8-255 | 2 bbl | 115 @ 3400 | 205 @ 2200 | 3.680 x 3.000 | 8.2:1 | 40–60 |
| '82 | 4-140 | 2 bbl | 88 @ 4600 | 118 @ 2600 | 3.781 x 3.126 | 9.0:1 | 40–60 |
| | 6-200 | 1 bbl | 88 @ 3200 | 154 @ 1400 | 3.683 x 3.126 | 8.6:1 | 30–50 |
| | 6-232 | 2 bbl | 112 @ 4000 | 175 @ 2600 | 3.814 x 3.388 | 8.8:1 | 40–60 |

All horsepower and torque figures are SAE net figures
W—Windsor
AT—Automatic transmission

MT—Manual transmission
Cal—California
VV—Variable Venturi

## ENGINE MECHANICAL

### Engine

#### REMOVAL AND INSTALLATION

NOTE: *During the process of engine removal you will come across a number of steps which call for the removal of a separate component or system. In all of these instances, a detailed removal procedure can be found elsewhere in the chapter, or in some cases, in another chapter which deals with the specific component in question.*

NOTE: *Tag all wires and vacuum hoses for identification to prevent confusion during installation.*

1. Scribe the hood hinge outline on the under-hood surface for reinstallation alignment. Have a helper support the front of the hood, remove the mounting bolts and the hood.

2. Position the car under the engine lifting device. Drain the coolant into a suitable container.

3. Disconnect the battery, negative cable

## Valve Specifications
(All measurements in inches)

| Engine No. Cyls. Displacement (cu. in.) (L,) | Year | Seat Angle (deg.) | Face Angle (deg.) | Spring Test Pressure (lbs. @ in.) | Spring Installed Height (in.) | Stem to Guide Clearance (in.) | | Stem Diameter (in.) | |
|---|---|---|---|---|---|---|---|---|---|
| | | | | | | Intake | Exhaust | Intake | Exhaust |
| 4-140 (2.3L) | 1981–82 | 45 | 44 | 159–175 @ 1.16 | 1.5312–1.5938 | .0010– .0027 | .0015– .0032 | .3416 | .3411 |
| 6-200 (3.3L) | 1975–77 | 45 | 44 | 150 @ 1.18 (intake) 150 @ 1.22 (exhaust) | $1^{19}/_{32}$ | .0008– .0025 | .0010– .0027 | .3104 | .3102 |
| | 1981–82 | 45 | 44 | 142–158 @ 1.22 | 1.5625–1.5938 | .0008– .0025 | .0010– .0027 | .3100 | .3098 |
| 6-232 (3.8L) | 1982 | 44°30'– 45° | 45°30'– 45°45' | 202 @ 1.27 | $1^{11}/_{16}$ (intake) $1^{19}/_{32}$ (exhaust) | .0010– .0027 | .0015– .0032 | .3420 | .3415 |
| 6-250 (4.1L) | 1975–80 | 45 | 44 | 150 @ 1.22 | $1^{19}/_{32}$ | .0008– .0025 | .0010– .0027 | .3104 | .3102 |
| 8-255 (4.2L) | 1980–81 | 45 | 44 | Intake 190–214 @ 1.36 Exhaust 190–215 @ 1.18 | Intake 1.6719–1.7031 Exhaust 1.5781–1.6094 | .0010– .0027 | .0015– .0032 | .3416 | .3411 |
| 8-302 (5.0L) | 1975–80 | 45 | 44 | Intake 190–210 @ 1.36 Exhaust 190–210 @ 1.20 | Intake 1.6719–1.7031 Exhaust 1.5781–1.6094 | .0010– .0027 | .0015– .0032 | .3416 | .3411 |
| 8-351 (5.8L) | 1975–77 | 45 | 44 | Intake 200 @ 1.34 Exhaust 200 @ 1.20 | Intake $1^{25}/_{32}$ Exhaust $1^{5}/_{8}$ | .0010– .0027 | .0015– .0032 | .3420 | .3415 |

## Torque Specifications
(All readings in ft. lb.)

| Year | Engine Cu in. Displacement | Cylinder Head Bolts | Rod Bearing Bolts | Main Bearing Bolts | Crankshaft Pulley Bolt | Flywheel-To-Crankshaft Bolts | Manifold | | Oil Pan | Valve Cover |
|---|---|---|---|---|---|---|---|---|---|---|
| | | | | | | | Intake | Exhaust | | |
| 1981–82 | 140 | 80–90 | 30–36 | 80–90 | 100–120 | 54–64 | 14–21 | 16–23 | 7–9 | 3–5 |
| 1975–80 | 200, 250 | ① | 21–26 | 60–70 | 85–100 | 75–85 | — | 18–24 | 7–9 | 3–5 |
| 1982 | 232 | 65–81⑥ | 30–36⑥ | 62–81⑥ | 85–100 | 75–85 | 17–19 | 15–22 | 7–9 | 3–5 |
| 1975–80 | 255, 302 | ② | 19–24 | 60–70 | 70–90 | 75–85 | 23–25④ | 18–24 | 7–9 | 3–5 |
| 1975–76 | 351 | ③ | 19–24 | 60–70⑤ | 70–90 | 75–85 | 23–25④ | 18–24 | 7–9 | 3–5 |
| 1977 | 351 | ③ | 40–45 | 95–105⑤ | 70–90 | 75–85 | 23–25④ | 18–24 | 7–9 | 3–5 |

① Torque bolts in three steps: 1—50–55; 2—60–65; 3—70–75
② Torque bolts in two steps: 1—55–65; 2—65–72
③ Torque bolts in two steps: 1—95–105; 2—105–112
④ After assembly retorque while the engine is hot
⑤ ½ in. bolts, 95–105: ⅜ in. bolts, 35–45
⑥ Tighten to listed torque, loosen 2 complete turns, retighten to listed torque. Fasteners must be oil-coated.

## Crankshaft and Connecting Rod Specifications
(All measurements in inches)

| Engine Displacement (cu in.) | Crankshaft | | | | Connecting Rod | | |
| | Main Bearing Journal Diameter | Main Bearing Oil Clearance | Shaft End-Play | Thrust on No. | Journal Diameter | Oil Clearance | Side Clearance |
|---|---|---|---|---|---|---|---|
| 4-140 | 2.3982–2.3990 | .0008–.0015 ③ | .004–.008 | 3 | 2.0464–2.0472 | .0008–.0015 ④ | .0035–.0105 |
| 6-200 | 2.2482–2.2490 | .0008–.0024 | .004–.008 | 5 | 2.1232–2.1240 | .0008–.0024 | .003–.010 |
| 6-232 | 2.5185–2.5195 | .0005–.0023 | .004–.008 | 3 | 2.1228–2.1236 | .0008–.0026 | .010–.020 |
| 6-250 | 2.3982–2.3990 | .0008–.0024 | .004–.008 | 5 | 2.1232–2.1240 | .0008–.0024 | .003–.010 |
| 8-255 | 2.2482–2.2490 | ② | .004–.008 | 3 | 2.1236–2.1328 | .0008–.0024 | .010–.020 |
| 8-302 | 2.2482–2.2490 | .0005–.0024 ① | .004–.008 | 3 | 2.1228–2.1236 | .0008–.0024 | .010–.020 |
| 8-351 | 2.9994–3.0002 | .0008–.0026 | .004–.008 | 3 | 2.3103–2.3111 | .0008–.0026 | .010–.020 |

① 1975–78: No. 1—.0001–.0020
  1979 and later: No. 1—.0001–.0017
② No. 1—.0001–.0017
  All others—.0004–.0021
③ 1982: .0008–.0026
④ 1982: .0008–.0024

## Piston and Ring Specifications
(All measurements in inches)

| Engine Displacement (cu in.) | Piston Clearance | Ring Gap | | | Ring Side Clearance | | | Wear Limit |
| | | Top Compression | Bottom Compression | Oil Control | Top Compression | Bottom Compression | Oil Control | |
|---|---|---|---|---|---|---|---|---|
| 6-200, 250 | 0.0013–0.0021 | 0.0008–0.016 | 0.008–0.016 | 0.015–0.055 | 0.002–0.004 | 0.002–0.004 | snug | 0.006 |
| 4-140, 6-232, 8-255, 302 351 | 0.0018 ① 0.0026 | 0.010–0.020 | 0.010–0.020 | 0.015–0.055 | 0.002–0.004 | 0.002–0.004 | snug | 0.006 |

① 4-140: .0014–.0022: 6-232: .0014–.0028

## Camshaft Specifications
(All measurements in inches)

| Engine | Journal Diameter | | | | | Bearing Clearance | Lobe Lift | | Endplay |
| | 1 | 2 | 3 | 4 | 5 | | Intake | Exhaust | |
|---|---|---|---|---|---|---|---|---|---|
| 4-140 (2.3L) | 1.7713–1.7720 | 1.7713–1.7720 | 1.7713–1.7720 | 1.7713–1.7720 | — | .001–.003 | .2437 | .2437 | .001–.007 |
| 6-200 (3.3L) | 1.8095–1.8105 | 1.8095–1.8105 | 1.8095–1.8105 | 1.8095–1.8105 | — | .001–.003 | .245 | .245 | .001–.007 |
| 6-232 (3.8L) | 2.0505–2.0515 | 2.0505–2.0515 | 2.0505–2.0515 | 2.0505–2.0515 | — | .001–.003 | .240 | .241 | ① |
| 6-250 (4.1L) | 1.8095–1.8105 | 1.8095–1.8105 | 1.8095–1.8105 | 1.8095–1.8105 | — | .001–.003 | .245 | .245 | .001–.007 |
| 8-255 (4.2L) | 2.0805–2.0815 | 2.0655–2.0665 | 2.0505–2.0515 | 2.0355–2.0365 | 2.0205–2.0215 | .001–.003 | .2375 | .2375 | .001–.007 |
| 8-302 (5.0L) | 2.0805–2.0815 | 2.0655–2.0665 | 2.0505–2.0515 | 2.0355–2.0365 | 2.0205–2.0215 | .001–.003 | .2375 | .2474 | .001–.003 |
| 8-351 (5.8L) | 2.0805–2.0815 | 2.0655–2.0665 | 2.0505–2.0515 | 2.0355–2.0365 | 2.0205–2.0215 | .001–.003 | .260 | .260 | .001–.007 |

① Endplay controlled by button and spring mounted on end of camshaft.

first. Remove the battery to avoid accidental damage.

4. Disconnect all hoses to the air cleaner. Remove the air cleaner assembly and mounting brackets.

5. On four cylinder models, disconnect and remove the exhaust manifold shroud. On all engines, remove or disconnect any thermactor (air pump) parts that will interfere with the engine removal.

6. Remove the upper and lower radiator hoses. Remove all drive belts.

7. Unbolt and remove, or unbolt and move the radiator shroud back over the water pump. If your car is equipped with an automatic transmission, disconnect the two cooler lines from the radiator tank.

8. Remove the fan blades, fan spacer, pulley, radiator shroud and radiator.

9. Disconnect the heater hoses from the water pump and cylinder head/block/manifold fitting. On four cylinder models, disconnect the heater hoses from the water pump and carburetor choke fitting.

10. Disconnect the wiring to the alternator, oil pressure switch, ignition coil, temperature switch and starter motor. On

NOTE: *The starter motor wiring might be easier to disconnect after the car has been jacked up and supported on jackstands.*

11. Disconnect the accelerator linkage, vacuum modulator line (automatic transmission equipped models), transmission downshift rod (automatic transmission models), vacuum brake booster line (models equipped), EGR valve, speed control cables and connectors (if equipped).

12. Unbolt the power steering pump and air conditioner compressor with hoses connected, position out of the way and secure.

CAUTION: *If there is not enough slack in the refrigerant lines to position compressor out of the way, the refrigerant in the system must be evacuated before the lines can be disconnected. See Chapter 1 for warning. Unless you are familiar with air conditioning and have the proper equipment have the system evacuated by a professional.*

13. Disconnect the flexible fuel line (from the gas tank) at the fuel pump and plug the line.

14. Remove the flywheel/converter housing to engine upper mounting bolts.

NOTE: *On four cylinder engines, two 10mm x ⅜ in. studs are used to attach the upper housing to the engine. If the studs are removed, make sure thay are reinstalled with the metric threads in the engine block.*

15. Raise the front of the car and safely support with jackstands. Drain the engine oil.

Drain from both oil pan, plugs, if equipped, on V8 engines.

16. Disconnect the starter motor wiring, if not already disconnected. Remove the starter motor.

17. Disconnect the exhaust pipe/converter from the exhaust manifold(s). Wire the pipe(s) out of the way.

18. On cars equipped with a manual transmission, disconnect the clutch retracting spring. Disconnect the clutch equalizer shaft and arm bracket at the frame rail. Remove the clutch shaft and bracket.

19. Remove the flywheel/converter housing lower inspection cover.

20. On models equipped with an automatic transmission, disconnect the torque converter from the flywheel. It will be necessary to rotate the engine to gain access to the four converter mounting nuts. Use a socket on a breaker bar or ratchet to turn the engine via the crankshaft pulley center bold. Always turn the engine in a clockwise direction.

21. Mark a converter mounting stud and the flywheel to insure balance alignment for reinstallation.

22. Disconnect the right and left front motor mount insulators at the number 2 crossmember. Remove the lower flywheel/converter housing to engine mounting bolts.

23. On automatic transmission equipped models, pry the converter slightly away from the flywheel and secure the converter to the transmission with a piece of wire or small "C" clamp on housing.

24. Lower the car from the jackstands. Support the front of the transmission on a piece of wood with a hydraulic jack.

25. Attach a lifting sling to the engine removal brackets. Connect a chain hoist and raise the engine slightly to clear the front motor mounts.

26. Carefully pull the engine forward to disengage the converter or front transmission shaft. Slowly raise the engine out of the engine compartment. Avoid bending the rear cover plate or damaging any components.

27. Secure the transmission and move the car from under hoist. Lower engine to workbench, ground or install on engine stand.

28. Installation Tips: On cars equipped with an automatic transmission, start the converter pilot into the crankshaft while aligning the marks that are made previously. Make sure the studs engage the holes in the flywheel. On manual transmission equipped cars, start the transmission mainshaft into the clutch disc. While installing the engine an adjustment of the transmission position with relation to the

engine may be required. Raise transmission with the jack or lower the engine as necessary. If the converter mounting stud alignment is off, or the transmission mainshaft fails to enter the clutch disc, turn the engine in a clockwise direction (manual transmission in gear). Install the upper engine to transmission mounting bolts after the engine and transmission mate firmly together. Align engine mounting insulators with mount brackets, remove the jack from under the transmission and lower the engine into place.

29. Complete the rest of the engine installation in the reverse order of removal.

## Engine/Transmission Mounts
### REMOVAL AND INSTALLATION

NOTE: *Whenever self-locking nuts/bolts are used they must be replaced with new self-locking nuts/bolts.*

**Front Mounts**

1. Disconnect the negative battery cable at the battery. Jack up the front of the car and safely support with stands.
2. Remove the nut and washer that attach the front insulators to the crossmember pedestals.

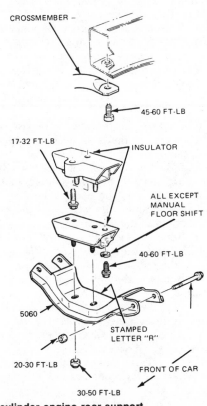

**Six cylinder engine rear support**

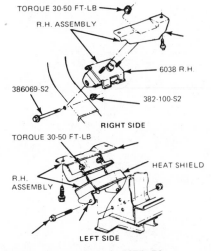

**V8 engine front support—1975–76**

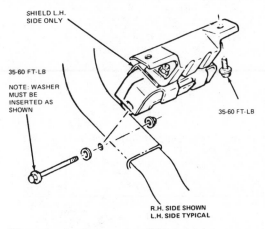

R.H. SIDE SHOWN
L.H. SIDE TYPICAL

**V8 engine front supports—1977 and later**

NOTE: *In some cases removal of a heat shield will aid in gaining necessary clearance.*

3. Remove the fan shroud mounting screws. Raise the front of the engine using a block of wood and a hydraulic jack under the front of the oil pan.
4. When the insulator studs have cleared the mounting pedestals, remove the insulator from the engine by unbolting.
5. Install new insulator(s) and reverse the removal sequence for installation.

**Transmission Mount**

1. Disconnect the negative battery cable at the battery. Raise the front of the car and safely support on jackstands.
2. Place a block of wood and a hydraulic jack under the transmission.
3. On automatic transmission models; Remove the two nuts attaching the insulator to the crossmember. Raise the transmission with

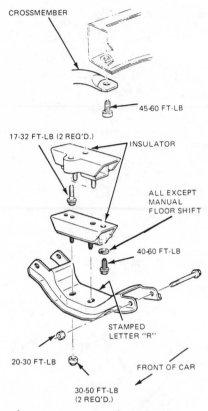

CROSSMEMBER

45-60 FT-LB

17-32 FT-LB (2 REQ'D.)

INSULATOR

ALL EXCEPT
MANUAL
FLOOR SHIFT

40-60 FT-LB

STAMPED
LETTER "R"

20-30 FT-LB

FRONT OF CAR

30-50 FT-LB
(2 REQ'D.)

**V8 engine rear supports—through 1977**

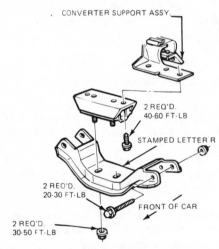

CONVERTER SUPPORT ASSY.

2 REQ'D.
40-60 FT-LB

STAMPED LETTER R

2 REQ'D.
20-30 FT-LB

FRONT OF CAR

2 REQ'D.
30-50 FT-LB

**V8 engine rear supports—1978 and later**

the jack high enough to clear the crossmember. Unbolt the insulator from the transmission.

4. On manual transmission models; Raise the jack slightly and remove the two bolts and nuts attaching the crossmember to the frame side rails. Unbolt the insulator from the crossmember and transmission.

5. Install a new insulator in the reverse order of removal.

# Rocker Arm (Valve) Cover
## *REMOVAL AND INSTALLATION*
### Four Cylinder 140 Cu In. Engine
### Six Cylinder 200 and 250 Cu In. Engines

1. Remove the air cleaner assumbly and mounting brackets.

2. Label for identification and remove all wires and vacuum hoses interfering with valve cover removal. Remove the PCV valve with hose. Remove the accelerator control cable bracket if necessary.

3. Remove the valve cover retaining bolts. On four cylinder models, the front bolts equipped with rubber sealing washers must be installed in the same location to prevent oil leakage.

4. Remove the valve cover. Clean all old gasket material from the valve cover and cylinder head gasket surfaces.

5. Install in reverse order of removal. Use oil resistant sealing compound and a new valve cover gasket. When installing the valve cover gasket, make sure all the gasket locating tangs are engaged into the cover notches provided.

### V6 and V8 Engines

NOTE: *When disconnecting wires and vacuum lines, label them for reinstallation identification.*

1. Remove the air cleaner assembly.

2. On the right side;

a. Disconnect the automatic choke heat chamber hose from the inlet tube near the right valve cover if equipped.

b. Remove the automatic choke heat tube if equipped and remove the PCV valve and hose from the valve cover. Disconnect EGR valve hoses.

c. Remove the thermactor bypass valve and air supply hoses as necessary to gain clearance.

d. Disconnect the spark plug wires from the plugs with a twisting pulling motion; twist and pull on the boots only, never on the wire; position the wires and mounting bracket out of the way.

e. Remove the valve cover mounting bolts; remove the valve cover.

3. On the left side;

a. Remove the spark plug wires and bracket.

b. Remove the wiring harness and any vacuum hoses from the bracket.

c. Remove the valve cover mounting bolts and valve cover.

4. Clean all old gasket material from the valve cover and cylinder head mounting surfaces.

NOTE: *V6 engines do not use valve cover*

*gaskets. Scrap away old RTV sealant and clean covers. Spread an even bead ³/₁₆″ wide of RTV sealant on the valve covers and reinstall.*

5. Installation is in reverse order of removal. Use oil resistant sealing compound and a new vlave cover gasket. When installing the valve cover gasket, make sure all the gasket tangs are engaged into the cover notches provided.

## Rocker Arm (Cam Follower) and Hydraulic Lash Adjuster
### REMOVAL AND INSTALLATION
#### Four Cylinder 140 Cu In. Engine

NOTE: *A special tool is required to compress the lash adjuster.*

Valve lash adjusting tool used to collapse the hydraulic cam follower—4-140

1. Remove the valve cover and associated parts as required.

2. Rotate the camshaft so that the base circle of the cam is against the cam follower you intend to remove.

3. Remove the retaining spring from the cam follower, if so equipped.

4. Using special tool T74P-6565-B or a valve spring compressor tool, collapse the lash adjuster and/or depress the valve spring, as necessary, and slide the cam follower over the lash adjuster and out from under the camshaft.

5. Install the cam follower in the reverse order of removal. Make sure that the lash adjuster is collapsed and released before rotating the camshaft.

## Rocker Arm Shaft/Rocker Arms
### REMOVAL AND INSTALLATION
#### 6 Cylinder In-Line Engines

1. Remove the rocker arm (valve) cover (see previous section).

2. Remove the rocker arm shaft mounting bolts, two turns at a time for each bolt. Start at the ends of the rocker shaft and work toward the middle.

3. Lift the rocker arm shaft assembly from the engine. Remove the pin and washer from each end of the shaft. Slide the rocker arms, springs and supports off the shaft. Keep all parts in order or label them for position.

4. Clean and inspect all parts, replace as necessary.

5. Assemble the rocker shaft parts in reverse order of removal. Be sure the oil holes in the shaft are pointed downward. Reinstall the rocker shaft assembly on the engine.

NOTE: *Lubricate all parts with motor oil before installation.*

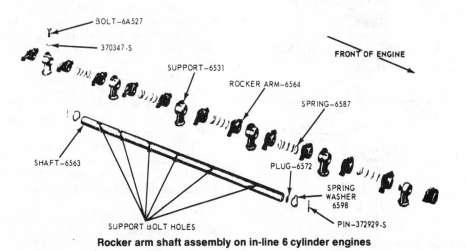

Rocker arm shaft assembly on in-line 6 cylinder engines

Clean all mounting surfaces, use a new valve cover gasket and install the valve cover.

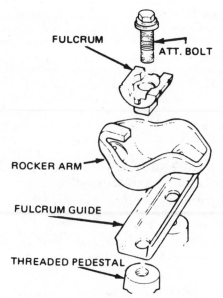

**Late V8 engine rocker arm assembly**

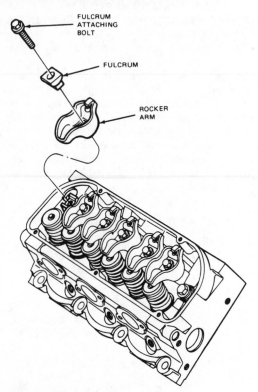

**V6 rocker arm assembly**

### V6 and V8 Engines

1. Remove the rocker arm (valve) covers (see previous section).

2. Remove the rocker arm mounting bolt, fulcrum, rocker arm and fulcrum guide (V8 engines). (The fulcrum guide is retained by two rocker arm assemblies, both must be removed to free the guide).

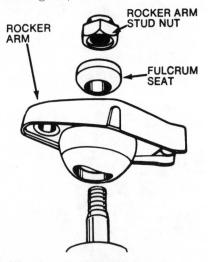

**Early V8 rocker arm assembly**

3. Clean and inspect all parts, replace as necessary.

4. Lubricate all parts with motor oil and reinstall on engine.

5. Clean all mounting surfaces, use new valve cover gaskets (V8 engines) or RTV sealant and install the valve covers.

## Intake Manifold

### REMOVAL AND INSTALLATION

**Four Cylinder 140 Cu In. Engine**

1. Drain the cooling system.

2. Remove the air cleaner and disconnect the throttle linkage from the carburetor.

3. Disconnect the fuel and vacuum lines from the carburetor.

4. Disconnect the carburetor solenoid wire at the quick-disconnect.

5. Remove the choke water housing and thermostatic spring from the carburetor.

6. Disconnect the water outlet and crankcase ventilation hoses from the intake manifold.

7. Disconnect the deceleration valve-to-carburetor hose at the carburetor.

8. Start from each end; work toward the middle; remove the intake manifold attaching bolts and remove the manifold.

9. Clean all old gasket material from the manifold and cylinder head.

10. Apply water-resistant sealer to the intake manifold gasket and position it on the cylinder head.

11. Install the intake manifold attaching nuts. Follow the sequence given in the illustrations.

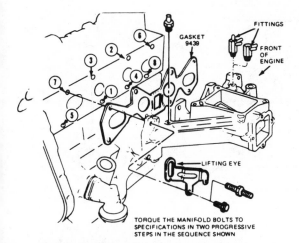

**4-140 intake manifold installation**

12. Connect the water and crankcase ventilation hoses to the intake manifold.

13. Connect the deceleration valve-to-carburetor hose to the carburetor.

14. Position the choke water housing and thermostatic spring on the carburetor and engage the end of the spring coil in the slot and the choke adjusting lever. Align the tab on the spring housing. Tighten the choke water housing attaching screws.

15. Connect the carburetor solenoid wire.

16. Connect the fuel and vacuum lines to the carburetor.

17. Connect the throttle linkage to the carburetor.

18. Install the air cleaner and fill the cooling system.

### Six Cylinder In-Line Engines

On six cylinder in-line engines, the intake manifold is integral with the cylinder head and cannot be removed.

### V6 and V8 Engines

1. Drain the cooling system and disconnect the negative battery cable. Remove the air cleaner assembly.

2. Disconnect the upper radiator hose and water pump by-pass hose from the thermostat housing and/or intake manifold. Disconnect the temperature sending unit wire connector. Remove the heater hose from the choke housing bracket and disconnect the hose from the intake manifold.

3. Disconnect the automatic choke heat chamber air inlet tube and electric wiring connector from the carburetor. Remove the crankcase ventilation hose, vacuum hoses and EGR hose. Label the various hoses and wiring for reinstallation identification.

4. Disconnect the Thermactor air supply hose at the check valve. Loosen the hose clamp at the check valve bracket and remove the air by-pass valve from the bracket and position to one side.

5. Remove all carburetor and automatic transmission linkage attached to the carburetor or intake manifold. Remove the speed control servo and bracket, if equipped. Disconnect the fuel line and any remaining vacuum hoses or wiring from the carburetor or intake manifold.

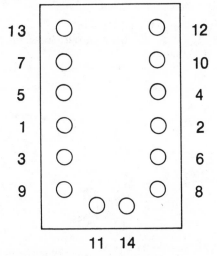

**V6 intake manifold torque sequence**

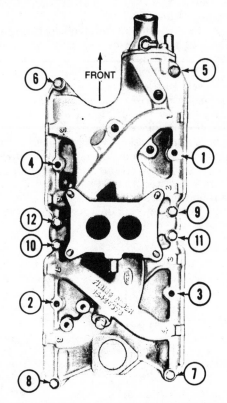

**Intake manifold torque sequence on the V8-255 and 302**

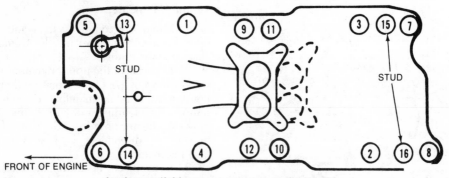

Intake manifold torque sequence on the V8-351

6. On V8 engines, disconnect the distributor vacuum hoses from the distributor. Remove the distributor cap and mark the relative position of the rotor on the distributor housing. Disconnect the spark plug wires at the spark plugs and the wiring connector at the distributor. Remove the distributor hold-down bolt and remove the distributor.

NOTE: *Distributor removal is not necessary on V6 engines.*

7. If your car is equipped with air conditioning and the compressor or mounting brackets interfere with manifold removal; remove the brackets and compressor and position out of the way. Do not disconnect any compressor lines.

8. Remove the intake manifold mounting bolts. Lift off the intake manifold and carburetor as an assembly.

NOTE: *The manifold on V6 engines is sealed at each end with an RTV type sealer. If prying at the front of the manifold is necessary to break the seal, take care not to damage the machined surfaces.*

9. Clean all gasket mounting surfaces. V6 engines have aluminum cylinder heads and intake manifold; exercise care when cleaning the old gasket material or RTV sealant from the machined surfaces.

10. Installation is in the reverse order of removal.

11. End seals are not used on V6 engines. Apply a ⅛ inch bead of RTV sealant at each end of the engine where the intake manifold seats. Install the intake gaskets and the manifold.

12. On V8 engines, make sure the intake gaskets interlock with the end seals. Use nonhardening gaskets seals on the end seals.

13. After installing the intake manifold, run a finger along the manifold ends to spread the RTV sealer or to make sure the end seals have not slipped out of place.

14. Torque the manifold mounting bolts to the required specifications in the proper sequence. Recheck the torque after the engine has reached normal operating temperature.

## Exhaust Manifold

NOTE: *Although, in most cases, the engine does not have exhaust manifold gaskets installed by the factory, aftermarket gaskets are available from parts stores.*

### REMOVAL AND INSTALLATION

#### Four Cylinder 140 Cu In. Engine

1. Remove the air cleaner.

2. Remove the heat shroud from the exhaust manifold.

3. Place a block of wood under the exhaust

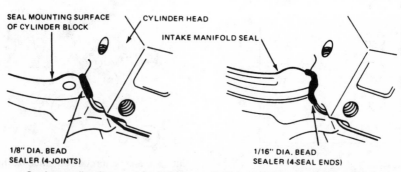

Sealer application area for intake manifold installation on all V8 engines

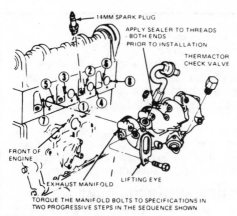

**4-140 exhaust manifold torque sequence**

pipe and disconnect the exhaust pipe from the exhuast manifold.

4. Remove the exhaust manifold attaching nuts and remove the manfiold.

5. Install a light coat of graphite grease on the exhaust manifold mating surface and position the manifold on the cylinder head.

6. Install the exhaust manifold attaching nuts and tighten them in the sequence shown in the illustration to 12–15 ft. lbs.

7. Connect the exhaust pipe to the exhaust manifold and remove the wood support from under the pipe.

8. Install the air cleaner.

### Six Cylinder In-Line Engines

1. Remove the air cleaner and heat duct body.

2. Disconnect the muffler inlet pipe and remove the choke hot air tube from the manifold.

3. Remove the EGR tube and any other emission components which will interfere with manifold removal.

4. Bend the exhaust manifold attaching bolt lock tabs back, remove the bolts and the manifold.

5. Clean all manifold mating surfaces and place a new gasket on the muffler inlet pipe.

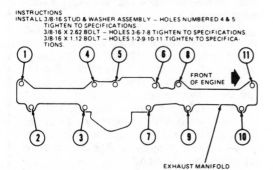

INSTRUCTIONS
INSTALL 3/8-16 STUD & WASHER ASSEMBLY – HOLES NUMBERED 4 & 5 TIGHTEN TO SPECIFICATIONS
3/8-16 X 2.62 BOLT – HOLES 3-6-7-8 TIGHTEN TO SPECIFICATIONS
3/8-16 X 1.12 BOLT – HOLES 1-2-9-10-11 TIGHTEN TO SPECIFICATIONS.

**6-200, 250 exhaust manifold torque sequence**

6. Reinstall manifold by reversing the procedure. Torque attaching bolts in sequence shown. After installation, warm the engine to operating temperature and re-torque to specifications.

### V8 Engines

1. Remove the air cleaner and intake duct assembly.

2. Disconnect the automatic choke heat chamber air inlet hose from the inlet tube near the right valve cover. Remove the automatic choke heat tube.

3. Remove the nuts or bolts retaining the heat stove to the exhaust manifold and remove the stove.

4. Disconnect the exhaust manifold(s) from the muffler or converter inlet pipe(s).

5. Remove the manifold retaining bolts and washers and the manifold(s).

6. Reverse the above procedure to install, using new inlet pipe gaskets. Torque the exhaust manifold retaining bolts to specifications, in sequence from the centermost bolt outward. Start the engine and check for exhaust leaks.

## Cylinder Head
### REMOVAL AND INSTALLATION
#### 4 Cylinder 140 Engine

1. Drain the cooling system.
2. Remove the air cleaner.
3. Remove the valve cover.

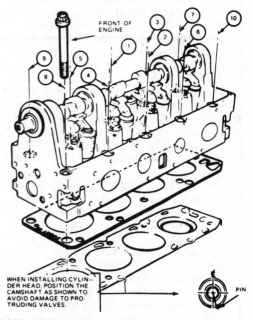

**4-140 cylinder head installation**

## ENGINE OVERHAUL

Most engine overhaul procedures are fairly standard. In addition to specific parts replacement procedures and complete specifications for your individual engine, this chapter also is a guide to accepted rebuilding procedures. Examples of standard rebuilding practice are shown and should be used along with specific details concerning your particular engine.

Competent and accurate machine shop services will ensure maximum performance, reliability and engine life. Procedures marked with the symbol shown above should be performed by a competent machine shop, and are provided so that you will be familiar with the procedures necessary to a successful overhaul.

In most instances it is more profitable for the do-it-yourself mechanic to remove, clean and inspect the component, buy the necessary parts and deliver these to a shop for actual machine work.

On the other hand, much of the rebuilding work (crankshaft, block, bearings, pistons, rods, and other components) is well within the scope of the do-it-yourself mechanic.

### Tools

The tools required for an engine overhaul or parts replacement will depend on the depth of your involvement. With a few exceptions, they will be the tools found in a mechanic's tool kit (see Chapter 1). More in-depth work will require any or all of the following:
• a dial indicator (reading in thousandths) mounted on a universal base
• micrometers and telescope gauges
• jaw and screw-type pullers
• scraper
• valve spring compressor
• ring groove cleaner
• piston ring expander and compressor
• ridge reamer
• cylinder hone or glaze breaker

• Plastigage®
• engine stand

Use of most of these tools is illustrated in this chapter. Many can be rented for a one-time use from a local parts jobber or tool supply house specializing in automotive work.

Occasionally, the use of special tools is called for. See the information on Special Tools and the Safety Notice in the front of this book before substituting another tool.

### Inspection Techniques

Procedures and specifications are given in this chapter for inspecting, cleaning and assessing the wear limits of most major components. Other procedures such as Magnaflux and Zyglo can be used to locate material flaws and stress cracks. Magnaflux is a magnetic process applicable only to ferrous materials. The Zyglo process coats the material with a flourescent dye penetrant and can be used on any material. Check for suspected surface cracks can be more readily made using spot check dye. The dye is sprayed onto the suspected area, wiped off and the area sprayed with a developer. Cracks will show up brightly.

### Overhaul Tips

Aluminum has become extremely popular for use in engines, due to its low weight. Observe the following precautions when handling aluminum parts:
• Never hot tank aluminum parts (the caustic hot-tank solution will eat the aluminum)
• Remove all aluminum parts (identification tag, etc.) from engine parts prior to hot-tanking.
• Always coat threads lightly with engine oil or anti-seize compounds before installation, to prevent seizure.
• Never over-torque bolts or spark plugs, especially in aluminum threads.

Stripped threads in any component can be repaired using any of several commercial repair kits (Heli-Coil, Microdot, Keenserts, etc.)

When assembling the engine, any parts that will be in frictional contact must be prelubed to provide lubrication at initial start-up. Any product specifically formulated for this purpose can be used, but engine oil is not recommended as a pre-lube.

When semi-permanent (locked, but removable) installation of bolts or nuts is desired, threads should be cleaned and coated with Loctite® or other similar, commercial non-hardening sealant.

## Repairing Damaged Threads

Several methods of repairing damaged threads are available. Heli-Coil® (shown here), Keenserts® and Microdot® are among the most widely used. All involve basically the same principle—drilling out stripped threads, tapping the hole and installing a prewound insert—making welding, plugging and oversize fasteners unnecessary.

Two types of thread repair inserts are usually supplied—a standard type for most Inch Coarse, Inch Fine, Metric Coarse and Metric Fine thread sizes and a spark plug type to fit most spark plug port sizes. Consult the individual manufacturer's catalog to determine exact applications. Typical thread repair kits will contain a selection of prewound threaded inserts, a tap (corresponding to the outside diameter threads of the insert) and an installation tool. Spark plug inserts usually differ because they require a tap equipped with pilot threads and a combined reamer/tap section. Most manufacturers also supply blister-packed thread repair inserts separately in addition to a master kit containing a variety of taps and inserts plus installation tools.

Before effecting a repair to a threaded hole, remove any snapped, broken or damaged bolts or studs. Penetrating oil can be used to free frozen threads; the offending item can be removed with locking pliers or with a screw or stud extractor. After the hole is clear, the thread can be repaired, as follows:

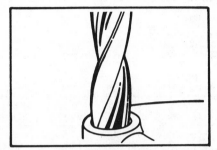

Drill out the damaged threads with specified drill. Drill completely through the hole or to the bottom of a blind hole

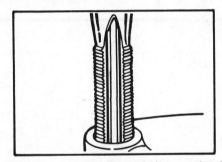

With the tap supplied, tap the hole to receive the thread insert. Keep the tap well oiled and back it out frequently to avoid clogging the threads

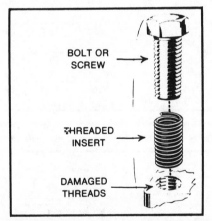

Damaged bolt holes can be repaired with thread repair inserts

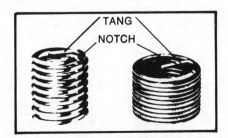

Standard thread repair insert (left) and spark plug thread insert (right)

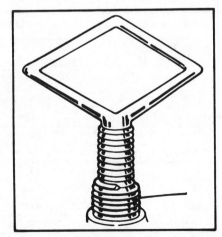

Screw the threaded insert onto the installation tool until the tang engages the slot. Screw the insert into the tapped hole until it is ¼–½ turn below the top surface, After installation break off the tang with a hammer and punch

## Standard Torque Specifications and Fastener Markings

In the absence of specific torques, the following chart can be used as a guide to the maximum safe torque of a particular size/grade of fastener.
- There is no torque difference for fine or coarse threads.
- Torque values are based on clean, dry threads. Reduce the value by 10% if threads are oiled prior to assembly.
- The torque required for aluminum components or fasteners is considerably less.

### U.S. Bolts

| SAE Grade Number | 1 or 2 | | | 5 | | | 6 or 7 | | |
|---|---|---|---|---|---|---|---|---|---|
| Number of lines always 2 less than the grade number. |  | | |  | | |  | | |
| | Maximum Torque | | | Maximum Torque | | | Maximum Torque | | |
| Bolt Size (Inches)—(Thread) | Ft./Lbs. | Kgm | Nm | Ft./Lbs. | Kgm | Nm | Ft./Lbs. | Kgm | Nm |
| ¼—20 | 5 | 0.7 | 6.8 | 8 | 1.1 | 10.8 | 10 | 1.4 | 13.5 |
| —28 | 6 | 0.8 | 8.1 | 10 | 1.4 | 13.6 | | | |
| 5/16—18 | 11 | 1.5 | 14.9 | 17 | 2.3 | 23.0 | 19 | 2.6 | 25.8 |
| —24 | 13 | 1.8 | 17.6 | 19 | 2.6 | 25.7 | | | |
| 3/8—16 | 18 | 2.5 | 24.4 | 31 | 4.3 | 42.0 | 34 | 4.7 | 46.0 |
| —24 | 20 | 2.75 | 27.1 | 35 | 4.8 | 47.5 | | | |
| 7/16—14 | 28 | 3.8 | 37.0 | 49 | 6.8 | 66.4 | 55 | 7.6 | 74.5 |
| —20 | 30 | 4.2 | 40.7 | 55 | 7.6 | 74.5 | | | |
| ½—13 | 39 | 5.4 | 52.8 | 75 | 10.4 | 101.7 | 85 | 11.75 | 115.2 |
| —20 | 41 | 5.7 | 55.6 | 85 | 11.7 | 115.2 | | | |
| 9/16—12 | 51 | 7.0 | 69.2 | 110 | 15.2 | 149.1 | 120 | 16.6 | 162.7 |
| —18 | 55 | 7.6 | 74.5 | 120 | 16.6 | 162.7 | | | |
| 5/8—11 | 83 | 11.5 | 112.5 | 150 | 20.7 | 203.3 | 167 | 23.0 | 226.5 |
| —18 | 95 | 13.1 | 128.8 | 170 | 23.5 | 230.5 | | | |
| ¾—10 | 105 | 14.5 | 142.3 | 270 | 37.3 | 366.0 | 280 | 38.7 | 379.6 |
| —16 | 115 | 15.9 | 155.9 | 295 | 40.8 | 400.0 | | | |
| 7/8— 9 | 160 | 22.1 | 216.9 | 395 | 54.6 | 535.5 | 440 | 60.9 | 596.5 |
| —14 | 175 | 24.2 | 237.2 | 435 | 60.1 | 589.7 | | | |
| 1— 8 | 236 | 32.5 | 318.6 | 590 | 81.6 | 799.9 | 660 | 91.3 | 894.8 |
| —14 | 250 | 34.6 | 338.9 | 660 | 91.3 | 849.8 | | | |

### Metric Bolts

| Relative Strength Marking | 4.6, 4.8 | | | 8.8 | | |
|---|---|---|---|---|---|---|
| Bolt Markings |  | | |  | | |
| | Maximum Torque | | | Maximum Torque | | |
| Bolt Size Thread Size x Pitch (mm) | Ft./Lbs. | Kgm | Nm | Ft./Lbs. | Kgm | Nm |
| 6 x 1.0 | 2–3 | .2–.4 | 3–4 | 3–6 | .4–.8 | 5–8 |
| 8 x 1.25 | 6–8 | .8–1 | 8–12 | 9–14 | 1.2–1.9 | 13–19 |
| 10 x 1.25 | 12–17 | 1.5–2.3 | 16–23 | 20–29 | 2.7–4.0 | 27–39 |
| 12 x 1.25 | 21–32 | 2.9–4.4 | 29–43 | 35–53 | 4.8–7.3 | 47–72 |
| 14 x 1.5 | 35–52 | 4.8–7.1 | 48–70 | 57–85 | 7.8-11.7 | 77–110 |
| 16 x 1.5 | 51–77 | 7.0–10.6 | 67–100 | 90–120 | 12.4–16.5 | 130–160 |
| 18 x 1.5 | 74–110 | 10.2–15.1 | 100–150 | 130–170 | 17.9–23.4 | 180–230 |
| 20 x 1.5 | 110–140 | 15.1–19.3 | 150–190 | 190–240 | 26.2–46.9 | 160–320 |
| 22 x 1.5 | 150–190 | 22.0–26.2 | 200–260 | 250–320 | 34.5–44.1 | 340–430 |
| 24 x 1.5 | 190–240 | 26.2–46.9 | 260–320 | 310–410 | 42.7–56.5 | 420–550 |

NOTE: *On cars with air conditioning, remove the mounting bolts and the drive belt, and position the compressor out of the way. Remove the compressor upper mounting bracket from the cylinder head.*

CAUTION: *If the compressor refrigerant lines do not have enough slack to permit repositioning of the compressor without first disconnecting the refrigerant lines, the air conditioning system will have to be evacuated by a trained air conditioning serviceman. Under no cricumstances should an untrained person attempt to disconnect the air conditioning refrigerant lines.*

4. Remove the intake and exhaust manifolds from the head.

5. Remove the camshaft drive belt cover. Note the location of the belt cover attaching screws that have rubber grommets.

6. Loosen the drive belt tensioner and remove the belt.

7. Remove the water outlet elbow from the cylinder head with the hose attached.

8. Remove the cylinder head attaching bolts.

9. Remove the cylinder head from the engine.

10. Clean all gasket material and carbon from the top of the cylinder block and pistons and from the bottom of the cylinder head.

11. Position a new cylinder head gasket on the engine and place the head on the engine.

NOTE: *If you encounter difficulty in positioning the cylinder head on the engine block, it may be necessary to install guide studs in the block to correctly align the head and the block. To fabricate guide studs, obtain two new cylinder head bolts and cut their heads off with a hack saw. Install the bolts in the holes in the engine block which correspond with cylinder head bolt holes nos. 3 and 4, as identified in the cylinder head bolt tightening sequence illustration. Then, install the head gasket and head over the bolts. Install the cylinder head attaching bolts, replacing the studs with the original head bolts.*

12. Using a torque wrench, tighten the head bolts in the sequence shown in the illustration.

13. Install the camshaft drive belt.

14. Install the camshaft drive belt cover and its attaching bolts. Make sure the rubber grommets are installed on the bolts. Tighten the bolts to 6–13 ft. lbs.

15. Install the water outlet elbow and a new gasket on the engine and tighten the attaching bolts to 12–15 ft. lbs.

16. Install the intake and exhaust manifolds. See the procedures for intake and exhaust manifold installation.

17. Assemble the rest of the components in reverse order of removal.

### 6 Cylinder In-Line Engines

1. Drain cooling system, remove the air cleaner and disconnect the negative battery cable.

NOTE: *On cars with air conditioning, remove the mounting bolts and the drive belt, and position the compressor out of the way of the left cylinder head. Remove the compressor upper mounting bracket from the cylinder head.*

CAUTION: *If the compressor refrigerant lines do not have enough slack to permit repositioning of the compressor without first disconnecting the refrigerant lines, the air conditioning system will have to be evacuated by a trained air conditioning serviceman. Under no circumstances should an untrained person attempt to disconnect the air conditioning refrigerant lines.*

2. Disconnect exhaust pipe at the manifold end, spring the exhaust pipe down and remove the flange gasket.

3. Disconnect the fuel and vacuum lines from the carburetor. Disconnect the intake manifold line at the intake manifold.

4. Disconnect the accelerator and retracting spring at the carburetor. Disconnect the transmission kick-down linkage, if equipped.

5. Disconnect the carburetor spacer outlet line at the spacer. Disconnect the radiator upper hose and the heater hose at the water outlet elbow. Disconnect the radiator lower hose and the heater hose at the water pump.

6. Disconnect the distributor vacuum control line at the distributor. Disconnect the gas filter line on the inlet side of the filter.

7. Disconnect and label the spark plug wires and remove the plugs. Disconnect the temperature sending unit wire.

8. Remove the rocker arm cover.

9. Remove the rocker arm shaft attaching bolts and the rocker arm and shaft assembly. Remove the valve pushrods, keep them in order for installation in their original positions.

10. Remove the remaining cylinder head bolts and lift off the cylinder head. Do not pry under the cylinder head as damage to the mating surfaces can easily occur.

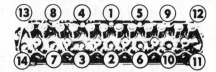

**Cylinder head torque sequence for 6-200, 250**

To help in installation of cylinder head, two 6 in. x $7/16$–14 bolts with heads cut off and the head end slightly tapered and slotted, for installation and removal with a screwdriver, will reduce the possibility of damage during head replacement.

11. Clean the cylinder head and block surfaces. Be sure of flatness and no surface damage.

12. Apply cylinder head gasket sealer to both sides of the new gasket and slide the gasket down over the two guide studs in the cylinder block.

NOTE: *Apply gasket sealer only to steel shim head gaskets. Steel/asbestos composite head gaskets are to be installed without any sealer.*

13. Carefully lower the cylinder head over the guide studs. Place the exhaust pipe flange on the manifold studs (new gasket).

14. Coat the threads of the end bolts for the right side of the cylinder head with a small amount of water-resistant sealer. Install, but do not tighten, two head bolts at opposite ends to hold the head gasket in place. Remove the guide studs and install the remaining bolts.

15. Cylinder head torquing should proceed in three steps and in prescribed order. Tighten to 55 ft. lbs., then give them a second tightening to 65 ft. lbs. The final step is to 75 ft. lbs., at which they should remain undisturbed.

16. Lubricate both ends of the pushrods and install them in their original locations.

17. Apply lubricant to the rocker arm pads and the valve stem tips and position the rocker arm shaft assembly on the head. Be sure the oil holes in the shaft are in a down position.

18. Tighten all the rocker shaft retaining bolts to 30–35 ft. lbs. and do a preliminary valve adjustment (make sure there are no tight valve adjustments).

19. Hook up the exhaust pipe.

20. Reconnect the heater and radiator hoses.

21. Reposition the distributor vacuum line, the carburetor gas line and the intake manifold vacuum line on the engine. Hook them up to their respective connections and reconnect the battery cable to the cylinder head.

22. Connect the accelerator rod and retracting spring. Connect the choke control cable and adjust the choke. Connect the transmission kickdown linkage.

23. Reconnect the vacuum line at the distributor. Connect the fuel inlet line at the fuel filter and the intake manifold vacuum line at the vacuum pump.

24. Lightly lubricate the spark plug threads and install them. Connect spark plug wires and be sure the wires are all the way down in their

sockets. Connect the temperature sending unit wire.

25. Fill the cooling system. Run the engine to stabilize all engine part temperatures.

26. Adjust engine idle speed and idle fuel-air adjustment.

27. Coat one side of a new rocker cover gasket with oil-resistant sealer. Lay the treated side of the gasket on the cover and install the cover. Be sure the gasket seals evenly all around the cylinder head.

### V6 Engine

1. Drain the cooling system.

2. Disconnect the cable from the battery negative terminal.

3. Remove the air cleaner assembly including air intake duct and heat tube.

4. Loosen the accessory drive belt idler. Remove the drive belt.

5. If the left cylinder head is being removed:

    a. If equipped with power steering, remove the pump mounting brackets' attaching bolts, leaving the hoses connected, place the pump/bracket assembly aside in a position to prevent the fluid from leaking out.

    b. If equipped with air conditioning, remove the mounting brackets' attaching bolts, leaving the hoses connected, position the compressor aside.

6. If the right cylinder head is being removed:

    a. Disconnect the thermactor diverter valve and hose assembly at the by-pass valve and downstream air tube.

    b. Remove the assembly.

    c. Remove the accessory drive idler.

    d. Remove the alternator.

    e. Remove the thermactor pump pulley. Remove the thermactor pump.

    f. Remove the alternator bracket.

    g. Remove the PCV valve.

7. Remove the intake manifold.

8. Remove the valve rocker arm cover attaching screws. Loosen the silicone rubber

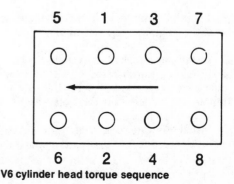

**V6 cylinder head torque sequence**

gasketing material by inserting a putty knife under the cover flange. Work the cover loose and remove. The plastic rocker arm covers will break if excessive prying is applied.

9. Remove the exhaust manifold(s).

10. Loose the rocker arm fulcrum attaching bolts enough to allow the rocker arm to be lifted off the pushroad and rotated to one side.

11. Remove the pushrods. Label the pushrods, they should be installed in the original position during assembly.

12. Remove the cylinder head attaching bolts. Remove the cylinder head(s).

13. Remove and discard the old cylinder head gasket(s). Discard the cylinder head bolts.

14. Lightly oil all bolt and stud bolt threads before installation except those specifying special sealant.

15. Clean the cylinder head, intake manifold, valve rocker arm cover and cylinder head gasket surfaces. If the cylinder head was removed for a cylinder head gasket replacement, check the flatness of the cylinder head and block gasket surfaces.

16. Position new head gasket(s) on the cylinder block using the dowels for alignment.

17. Position the cylinder heads to the block.

18. Apply a thin coating of pipe sealant or equivalent to the threads of the short cylinder head bolts (nearest to the exhaust manifold). Do not apply sealant to the long bolts. Lightly oil the cylinder head bolt flat washers. Install the flat washers and cylinder head bolts (Eight each side).

CAUTION: *Always use new cylinder head bolts to assure a leak tight assembly. Torque retention with used bolts can vary, which may result in coolant or compression leakage at the cylinder head mating surface area.*

19. Tighten the attaching bolts in sequence. Back-off the attaching bolts 2–3 turns. Repeat tightening sequence.

NOTE: *When the cylinder head attaching bolts have been tightened using the above sequential procedure, it is not necessary to retighten the bolts after extended engine operation. However, the bolts can be checked for tightness if desired.*

20. Dip each pushrod end in heavy engine oil. Install the push rods in their original porsition. For each valve rotate the crankshaft until the tappet rests on the heel (base circle) of the camshaft lobe.

21. Position the rocker arms over the push rods, install the fulcrums, and tighten the fulcrum attaching bolts to 61–132 in. lbs.

CAUTION: *Fulcrums must be fully seated in cylinder head and pushrods must be seated in rocker arm sockets prior to final tightening.*

22. Lubricate all rocker arm assemblies with heavy engine oil. Finally tighten the fulcrum bolts to 19–25 ft. lbs. For final tightening, the camshaft may be in any position.

NOTE: *If the original valve train components are being installed, a valve clearance check is not required. If a component has been replaced, perform a valve clearance check.*

23. Install the exhaust manifold(s).

24. Apply a 1/8–3/16 inch bead of RTV silicone sealant to the rocker arm cover flange. Make sure the sealer fills the channel in the cover flange. The rocker arm cover must be installed within 15 minutes after the silicone sealer application. After this time, the sealer may start to set-up, and its sealing effectiveness may be reduced.

25. Position the cover on the cylinder head and install the attaching bolts. Note the location of the wiring harness routing clips and spark plug wire routing clip stud bolts. Tighten the attaching bolts to 36–60 in. lbs. torque.

26. Install the intake manifold.

27. Install the spark plugs, if necessary.

28. Connect the secondary wires to the spark plugs.

29. Install the oil fill cap. If equipped with air conditioning, install the compressor mounting and support brackets.

30. On the right cylinder head:

   a. Install the PCV valve.

   b. Install the alternator bracket. Tighten attaching nuts to 30–40 ft. lbs.

   c. Install the thermactor pump and pump pulley.

   d. Install the alternator.

   e. Install the accessory drive idler.

   f. Install the thermactor diverter valve and hose assembly. Tighten the clamps securely.

31. Install the accessory drive belt and tighten to the specified tension.

32. Connect the cable to the battery negative terminal.

33. Fill the cooling system with the specified coolant.

CAUTION: *This engine has an aluminum cylinder head and requires a special unique corrosion inhibited coolant formulation to aovid radiator damage.*

34. Start the engine and check for coolant, fuel, and oil leaks.

35. Check and, if necessary, adjust the curb idle speed.

36. Install the air cleaner assembly including the air intake duct and heat tube.

### V8 Engines

1. Drain the cooling system.
2. Remove the intake manifold and the carburetor as an assembly.
3. Disconnect the spark plug wires, marking them as to placement. Position them out of the way of the cylinder head. Remove the spark plugs.
4. Disconnect the exhaust pipes at the manifolds.
5. Remove the rocker arm covers.
6. On cars with air conditioning, remove the mounting bolts and the drive belt, and position the compressor out of the way of the left cylinder head. Remove the compressor upper mounting bracket from the cylinder head.

NOTE: *If the compressor refrigerant lines do not have enough slack to permit repositioning of the compressor without first disconnecting the refrigerant lines, the air conditioning system will have to be evacuated by a trained air conditioning serviceman. Under no circumstances should an untrained person attempt to disconnect the air conditioning refrigerant lines.*

7. In order to remove the left cylinder head, on cars equipped with power steering, it may be necessary to remove the steering pump and bracket, remove the drive belt, and wire or tie the pump out of the way, but in such a way as to prevent the loss of its fluid.
8. In order to remove the right head it may be necessary to remove the alternator mounting bracket bolt and spacer, the ignition coil, and the air cleaner inlet duct from the right cylinder head.
9. In order to remove the left cylinder head on a car equipped with a Thermactor air pump system, disconnect the hose from the air manifold on the left cylinder head.
10. If the right cylinder head is to be removed on a car equipped with a Thermactor system, remove the Thermactor air pump and its mounting bracket. Disconnect the hose from the air manifold on the right cylinder head.
11. Loosen the rocker arm stud nuts enough to rotate the rocker arms to the side, in order to facilitate the removal of the pushrods. Remove the pushrods in sequence, so that they may be installed in their original positions.

Remove the exhaust valve stem caps, if equipped

12. Remove the cylinder head attaching bolts, noting their positions. Lift the cylinder head off the block. Remove and discard the old cylinder head gasket. Clean all mounting surfaces.

Installation is as follows:

1. Position the new cylinder head gasket over the dowels on the block. Position new gaskets on the muffler inlet pipes at the exhaust manifold flange.
2. Position the cylinder head to the block, and install the head bolts, each in its original position. On engines on which the exhaust manifold has been removed from the head to facilitate removal, it is necessary to properly guide the exhaust manifold studs into the muffler inlet pipe flange when installing the head.
3. Step-torque the cylinder head retaining bolts first to 50 ft. lbs. then to 60 ft. lbs., and finally to the torque specification listed in the "Torque Specifications" chart. Tighten the exhaust manifold to cylinder head attaching bolts to specifications.
4. Tighten the nuts on the exhaust manifold studs at the muffler inlet flanges to 18 ft. lbs.
5. Clean and inspect the pushrods one at a time. Clean the oil passage within each pushrod with solvent and blow the passage out with compressed air. Check the ends of the pushrods for nicks, grooves, roughness, or excessive wear. Visually inspect the pushrods for straightness, and replace any bent ones. Do not attempt to straighten pushrods.
6. Install the pushrods in their original positions. Apply Lubriplate® or a similar product to the valve stem tips and to the pushrod guides in the cylinder head. Install the exhaust valve stem caps.
7. Apply Lubriplate® or a similar product to the fulcrum seats and sockets. Turn the rocker arms to their proper position and tighten the stud nuts enough to hold the rocker arms in position. Make sure that the lower ends of the pushrods have remained properly seated in the valve lifters. Tighten the stud nuts 17–23 ft. lbs. in the order given under Valve Adjustment.
8. Install the valve covers.
9. Install the intake manifold and carburetor, following the procedure under "Intake Manifold Installation."
10. Reinstall all other items removed.

### Cylinder Head Overhaul

1. Remove the cylinder head(s) from the car engine (see Cylinder Head Removal and In-

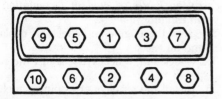

**V8 cylinder head torque sequence**

**De-carbon the cylinder head and valves:**

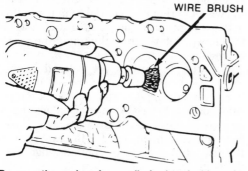

WIRE BRUSH

Remove the carbon from cylinder head with a wire brush and electric drill

stallation). Place the head(s) on a workbench and remove any manifolds that are still connected. Remove all rocker arm retaining parts and the rocker arms, if still installed. On four cylinder engines, remove the camshaft (see Camshaft Removal).

2. Turn the cylinder head over so that the mounting surface is facing up and support evenly on wooden blocks.

CAUTION: *V6 engines use aluminum cylinder heads, exercise care when cleaning.*

3. Use a scraper and remove all of the gasket material stuck to the head mounting surface. Mount a wire carbon removal brush in an electric drill and clean away the carbon on the valves and head combustion chambers.

CAUTION: *When scraping or decarbonizing the cylinder head take care not to damage or nick the gasket mounting surface.*

4. Number the valve heads with a permanent felt-tip marker for cylinder location.

### RESURFACING

If the cylinder head is warped resurfacing by a machine shop is required. Place a straight-edge across the gasket surface of the head. Using feeler gauges, determine the clearance at the center and along the length between the head and straight-edge. Measure clearance at the center and along the lengths of both diag-

**Check the cylinder head for warpage:**

1 & 3 CHECK DIAGONALLY
2 CHECK ACROSS CENTER

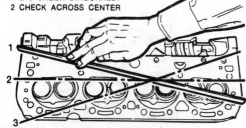

Check the cylinder head for warpage

onals. If warpage exceeds .003 inches in a six inch span, or .006 inches over the total length the cylinder head must be resurfaced.

## Valves and Springs
### REMOVAL AND INSTALLATION

1. Block the head on its side, or install a pair of head-holding brackets made especially for valve removal.

2. Use a socket slightly larger than the valve stem and keepers, place the socket over the valve stem and gently hit the socket with a plastic hammer to break loose any varnish buildup.

3. Remove the valve keepers, retainer, spring shield and valve spring using a valve spring compressor (the locking C-clamp type is the easiest kind to use).

4. Put the parts in a separate container numbered for the cylinder being worked on; do not mix them with other parts removed.

5. Remove and discard the valve stem oil seal, a new seal will be used at assembly time.

6. Remove the valve from the cylinder head and place, in order, through numbered holes punched in a stiff piece of cardboard or wooden valve holding stick.

NOTE: *The exhaust valve stems, on some engines, are equipped with small metal caps. Take care not to lose the caps. Make sure to reinstall them at assembly time. Replace any caps that are worn.*

7. Use an electric drill and rotary wire brush to clean the intake and exhaust valve ports, combustion chamber and valve seats. In some cases, the carbon will need to be chipped away. Use a blunt pointed drift for carbon chipping, be careful around the valve seat areas.

8. Use a wire valve guide cleaning brush and safe solvent to clean the valve guides.

9. Clean the valves with a revolving wire brush. Heavy carbon deposits may be removed with the blunt drift.

NOTE: *When using a wire brush to clean carbon on the valve ports, valves etc., be sure that the deposits are actually removed, rather than burnished.*

10. Wash and clean all valve springs, keepers, retaining caps etc., in safe solvent.

11. Clean the head with a brush and some safe solvent and wipe dry.

12. Check the head for cracks. Cracks in the cylinder head usually start around an exhaust valve seat because it is the hottest part of the combustion chamber. If a crack is suspected but cannot be detected visually have the area checked with dye penetrant or other method by the machine shop.

13. After all cylinder head parts are reasonably clean check the valve stem-to-guide clearance. If a dial indicator is not on hand, a visual inspection can give you a fairly good idea if the guide, valve stem or both are worn.

14. Insert the valve into the guide until slightly away from the valve seat. Wiggle the valve sideways. A small amount of wobble is normal, excessive wobble means a worn guide or valve stem. If a dial indicator is on hand, mount the indicator so that the stem of the valve is at 90° to the valve stem, as close to the valve guide as possible. Move the valve off the seat, and measure the valve guide-to-stem clearance by rocking the stem back and forth to actuate the dial indicator. Measure the valve stem using a micrometer and compare to specifications to determine whether stem or guide wear is causing excessive clearance.

15. The valve guide, if worn, must be repaired before the valve seats can be resurfaced. Ford supplies valves with oversize stems to fit valve guides that are reamed to oversize for repair. The machine shop will be able to handle the guide reaming for you. In some cases, if the guide is not too badly worn, knurling may be all that is required.

16. Reface, or have the valves and valve seats refaced. The valve seats should be a true 45° angle. Remove only enough material to clean up any pits or grooves. Be sure the valve seat is not too wide or narrow. Use a 60° grinding wheel to remove material from the bottom of the seat for raising and a 30° grinding wheel to remove material from the top of the seat to narrow.

17. After the valves are refaced by machine, hand lap them to the valve seat. Clean the grinding compound off and check the position of face-to-seat contact. Contact should be close to the center of the valve face. If contact is close to the top edge of the valve narrow the seat; if to close to the bottom edge, raise the seat.

18. Valves should be refaced to a true angle of 44°. Remove only enough metal to clean up the valve face or to correct runout. If the edge of a valve head, after machining, is 1/32 inch or less replace the valve. The tip of the valve stem should also be dressed on the valve grinding machine, however, do not remove more than .010 inch.

19. After all valve and valve seats have been machined, check the remaining valve train parts (springs, retainers, keepers, etc.) for wear. Check the valve springs for straightness and tension.

20. Reassemble the head in the reverse order of disassembly using new valve guide seals and lubricating the valve stems. Check the valve spring installed height, shim or replace as necessary.

### CHECKING VALVE SPRINGS

Place the valve spring on a flat surface next to a carpenters square. Measure the height of the spring, and rotate the spring against the edge of the square to measure distortion. If the spring height varies (by comparsion) by more than 1/16 inch or if the distortion exceeds 1/16 inch, replace the spring.

Have the valve springs tested for spring pressure at the installed and compressed (installed height minus valve lift) height using a

**Resurface the valve seats using reamers or grinder:**

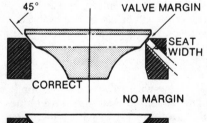

CORRECT

INCORRECT

**Valve seat width and centering**

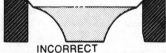

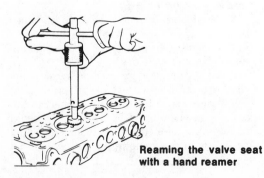

**Reaming the valve seat with a hand reamer**

**Check the valve springs:**

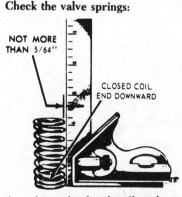

**Check the valve spring free length and squareness**

valve spring tester. Springs should be within one pound, plus or minus each other. Replace springs as necessary.

## VALVE SPRING INSTALLED HEIGHT

After installing the valve spring, measure the distance between the spring mounting pad and the lower edge of the spring retainer. Compare the measurement to specifications. If the installed height is incorrect, add shim washers between the spring mounting pad and the spring. Use only washers designed for valve springs; available at most parts houses.

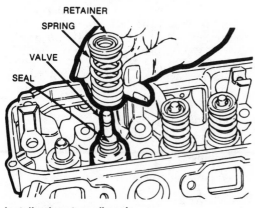

Install valve stem oil seals

## VALVE STEM OIL SEALS

Umbrella type oil seals fitting on the valve stem over the top of the valve guide are used on the in-line six and eight cylinder engines. The four cylinder and V6 engine uses a positive valve stem seal using a Teflon insert. Teflon seals are available for other engines but usually require valve guide machining, consult your automotive machine shop for advice on having positive valve stem oil seals installed.

When installing valve stem oil seals, ensure that a small amount of oil is able to pass the seal to lubricate the valve stems and guide walls; otherwise, excessive wear will occur.

## VALVE SEATS

If a valve seat is damaged or burnt and cannot be serviced by refacing, it may be possible to have the seat machined and an insert installed. Consult the automotive machine shop for their advice.

NOTE: *The aluminum heads on V6 engines are equipped with inserts.*

## VALVE GUIDES

Worn valve guides can, in most cases, be reamed to accept a valve with an oversized stem. Valve guides that are not excessively worn or distorted may, in some cases, be knurled rather than reamed. However, if the valve stem is worn reaming for an oversized valve stem is the answer since a new valve would be required.

Knurling is a process in which metal is displaced and raised, thereby reducing clearance. Knurling also produces excellent oil control. The possibility of knurling instead of reaming the valve guides should be discussed with a machinist.

## HYDRAULIC VALVE CLEARANCE

Hydraulic valve lifters operate with zero clearance in the valve train, and because of this the rocker arms are nonadjustable. The only means by which valve system clearances can be altered is by installing over or undersize pushrods; but, because of the hydraulic lifter's natural ability to compensate for slack in the valve train, all components of all the valve system should be checked for wear if there is excessive play in the system.

When a valve in the engine is in the closed position, the valve lifter is resting on the base circle of the camshaft lobe and the pushrod is in its lowest position. To remove this additional clearance from the valve train, the valve lifter expands to maintain zero clearance in the valve system. When a rocker arm is loosened or removed from the engine, the lifter expands to its fullest travel. When the rocker arm is reinstalled on the engine, the proper valve setting is obtained by tightening the rocker arm to a specified limit. But with the lifter fully expanded, if the camshaft lobe is on a high point it will require excessive torque to compress the lifter and obtain the proper setting. Because of this, when any component of the valve system has been removed, a preliminary valve adjustment procedure must be followed to ensure that when the rocker arm is reinstalled on the engine and tightened, the camshaft lobe for that cylinder is in the low position.

To determine whether a shorter or longer push rod is necessary, make the following check:

### SIX CYLINDER ENGINES

1. Connect an auxiliary starter switch in the starting circuit. Crank the engine with the ignition switch OFF until the No. 1 piston is on TDC after the compression stroke.

2. With the crankshaft in the position designated in Steps 3 and 4, position the hydraulic lifter compressor tool on the rocker arm. Slowly apply pressure to bleed down the hydraulic lifter until the plunger is completely bottomed. Take care to avoid excessive pressure that might bend the push rod. Hold the

Checking the valve clearance on 6 cylinder engines

lifter in this position and check the available clearance between the rocker arm and the valve stem tip with a feeler gauge.

If the clearance is less than specified, install an under-size push rod. If the clearance is greater than specified, install an oversize push rod.

3. With the No. 1 piston on TDC after compression stroke, use the procedure in Step 2, check the following valves:

**In-Line Engines**

- No. 1 Intake
- No. 1 Exhaust
- No. 2 Intake
- No. 3 Exhaust
- No. 4 Intake
- No. 5 Exhaust

**V6 Engines**

- No. 1 Intake
- No. 1 Exhaust
- No. 3 Intake
- No. 3 Exhaust
- No. 6 Intake
- No. 4 Exhaust

4. Now rotate the crankshaft 360° (1 revolution of the crankshaft). By using the procedure in step 2, check the following valves:

**In-Line Engines**

- No. 2 Exhaust
- No. 3 Intake
- No. 4 Exhaust
- No. 5 Intake
- No. 6 Intake
- No. 6 Exhaust

**V6 Engines**

- No. 2 Intake
- No. 3 Exhaust

- No.4 Intake
- No. 5 Exhaust
- No. 5 Intake
- No. 6 Exhaust

5. When compressing the valve spring to remove the push rods, be sure the piston in the individual cylinder is below TDC to avoid contact between the valve and the piston. To replace a push rod, it will be necessary to remove the valve rocker arm shaft assembly. Upon replacement of a valve push rod, valve rocker arm shaft assembly or hydraulic valve lifter, the engine should not be cranked or rotated until the hydraulic lifters have had an opportunity to leak down to their normal operating position. The leak down rate can be accelerated by using the tool shown on the valve rocker arm and applying pressure in a direction to collapse the lifter.

Note: Collapsed tappet gap:

**In-Line Engines**

- Allowable—.085–.209
- Desired—.110–.184

**V6 Engines**

- Allowable—.088–.189

### V8 ENGINES

1. Connect an auxiliary starter switch in the starting circuit. Crank the engine with the ignition switch OFF until the No. 1 piston is on TDC after the compression stroke.

2. With the crankshaft in the positions designated in Steps 3, 4 and 5 position the hydraulic lifter compressor tool on the rocker

Checking the valve clearance on V8 engines

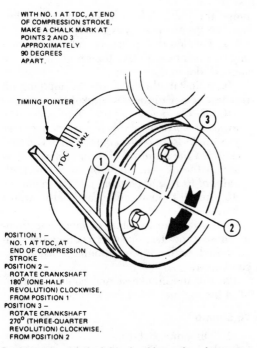

WITH NO. 1 AT TDC, AT END
OF COMPRESSION STROKE,
MAKE A CHALK MARK AT
POINTS 2 AND 3
APPROXIMATELY
90 DEGREES
APART.

TIMING POINTER

POSITION 1 –
NO. 1 AT TDC, AT
END OF COMPRESSION
STROKE
POSITION 2 –
ROTATE CRANKSHAFT
180° (ONE-HALF
REVOLUTION) CLOCKWISE,
FROM POSITION 1
POSITION 3 –
ROTATE CRANKSHAFT
270° (THREE-QUARTER
REVOLUTION) CLOCKWISE,
FROM POSITION 2

**Position of crankshaft for checking valve clearance**

arm. Slowly apply pressure to bleed down the tappet until the plunger is completely bottomed. Hold the tappet in this position and check the available clearance between the rocker arm and the valve stem tip with a feeler gauge. The feeler gauge width must not exceed ⅜ inch, in order to fit between the rails on the rocker arm. If the clearance is less than specifications, install a shorter push rod. If the clearance is greater than specifications, install a longer push rod.

3. With the No. 1 piston on TDC at the end of the compression stroke (Position No. 1 in illustration) check the following valves:
• No. 1 Intake No. 1 Exhaust
• No. 7 Intake No. 5 Exhaust
• No. 8 Intake No. 4 Exhaust

4. Rotate the crankshaft to Position No. 2 in the illustration and check the following valves:
• No. 5 Intake No. 2 Exhaust
• No. 4 Intake No. 6 Exhaust

5. Rotate the crankshaft to Position No. 3 in the illustration and check the following valves:
• No. 2 Intake No. 7 Exhaust
• No. 3 Intake No. 3 Exhaust
• No. 6 Intake No. 8 Exhaust
Note: Collapse tappet gap:
• (255 cu in.)
Allowable—.098–.198
Desired—.123–.173
• (302 cu in. and 351)
Allowable—.–.193
Desired—.096–.163

## VALVE CLEARANCE—HYDRAULIC VALVE LASH ADJUSTERS
### Four Cylinder 140 Cu In. Engine

Hydraulic valve lash adjusters are used in the valve train. These units are placed at the fulcrum point of the cam followers (or rocker arms). Their action is similar to the hydraulic tappets used in push rod engines.

1. Position the camshaft so that the base circle of the lobe is facing the cam follower of the valve to be checked.

2. Using the tool shown in the illustration, slowly apply pressure to the cam follower until the lash adjuster is completely collapsed. Hold the follower in this position and insert 0.045 in. feeler gauge between the base circle of the cam and the follower.

NOTE: *The minimum gap is 0.035 in. and the maximum is 0.055 in. The desire gap is between 0.040 in. and 0.050 in.*

3. If the clearance is excessive, remove the cam follower and inspect it for damage.

4. If the cam follower seems OK measure the valve spring assembled height to be sure the valve is not sticking. See the Valve Specifications chart in this chapter.

5. If the valve spring assembled height is OK check the dimensions of the camshaft.

6. If the camshaft dimensions are OK the lash adjuster should be cleaned and tested.

7. Replace any worn parts as necessary.

NOTE: *For any repair that includes removal of the camshaft follower (rocker arm), each affected hydraulic lash adjuster must be collapsed after reinstallation of the camshaft follower, and then released. This step must be taken prior to any rotation of the camshaft.*

## HYDRAULIC VALVE LIFTER INSPECTION

Remove the lifters from their bores and remove any gum and varnish with safe solvent. Check the lifters for concave wear. If the bottom of the lifter is worn concave or flat, replace the lifter. Lifters are built with a convex bottom, flatness indicates wear. If a worn lifter is detected, carefully check the camshaft for wear.

To test lifter leak down, submerge the lifter in a container of kerosene. Chuck a used pushrod or its equivalent into a drill press. Position the container of kerosene so the pushrod acts on the lifter plunger. Pump the lifter with the drill press until resistance increases. Pump several more times to bleed any air from the lifter. Apply very firm, constant pressure to the lifter and observe the rate which fluid bleeds out of the lifter. If the lifter bleeds down very quickly (less than 15 seconds), the lifter should be replaced. If the time exceeds 60 seconds, the lifter is sticking and should be cleaned or replaced. If the lifter is operating properly (leak down time 15–60 seconds) and not worn, lubricate and reinstall in engine.

## Timing Cover and Chain
### REMOVAL AND INSTALLATION
#### In-Line Six Cylinder Engines

1. Drain the cooling system and crankcase.

2. Disconnect the upper radiator hose from the intake manifold and the lower hose from the water pump. On cars with automatic transmission, disconnect the cooler lines from the radiator.

3. Remove the radiator, fan and pulley, and engine drive belts. On models with air conditioning, remove the condenser retaining bolts and position the condenser forward. *Do not disconnect the refrigerant lines.*

4. Remove the cylinder front cover retaining bolts and front oil pan bolts and gently pry the cover away from the block.

NOTE: *On 6-250 engine the oil pan must be removed prior to the front cover.*

5. Remove the crankshaft pulley bolt and use a puller to remove the vibration damper.

6. With a socket wrench of the proper size on the crankshaft pulley bolt, gently rotate the crankshaft in a colckwise direction until all slack is removed from the lift side of the timing chain. Scribe a mark on the engine block parallel to the present position on the left side of the chain. Next, turn the crankshaft in a counterclockwise direction to remove all the slack from the right side of the chain. Force the left side of the chain outward with the fingers and measure the distance between the reference point and the present position of the chain. If the distance exceeds ½ inch, replace the chain and sprockets.

7. Crank the engine until the timing marks are aligned as shown in the illustration. Re-

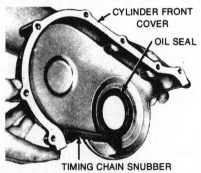

CYLINDER FRONT COVER

OIL SEAL

TIMING CHAIN SNUBBER

**Timing gear cover on 6-200, 250 engines**

move the bolt, slide sprocket and chain forward and remove as an assembly.

8. Position the sprockets and chain on the engine, making sure that the timing marks are aligned, dot to dot.

9. Reinstall the front cover, applying oil resistant sealer to the new gasket.

NOTE: *On 6-200 engines. Trim away the exposed portion of the old oil pan gasket flush with front of the engine block. Cut and position the required portion of a new gasket to the oil pan, applying sealer to both sides of it. Install oil pan on 6-250 engines.*

10. Install the fan, pulley and belts. Adjust belt tension.

11. Install the radiator, connect the radiator hoses and transmission cooling lines. If equipped with air conditioning, install the condenser.

12. Fill the crankcase and cooling system. Start the engine and check for leaks.

#### V6 Engine

1. Disconnect the negative battery cable from the battery. Drain the cooling system.

2. Remove the air cleaner and air duct assemblies.

3. Remove the radiator fan shroud and position back over the water pump. Remove the fan clutch assembly and shroud.

4. Remove all drive belts. If equipped with power steering, remove the pump with hoses attached and position out of the way. Be sure to keep the pump upright to prevent fluid leakage.

5. If your car is equipped with air conditioning, remove the front compressor mounting bracket. It is not necessary to remove the compressor.

6. Disconnect the coolant by-pass hose and the heater hose at the water pump.

7. Disconnect the upper radiator hose at the thermostat housing. Remove the distributor.

8. If your car is equipped with a tripminder, remove the flow meter support bracket and allow the meter to be supported by the hoses.

9. Raise the front of the car and support on jackstands.

10. Remove the crankshaft pulley using a suitable puller. Remove the fuel pump shield.

11. Disconnect the fuel line from the carburetor at the fuel pump. Remove the mounting bolts and the fuel pump. Position pump out of the way with tank line still attached.

12. Drain the engine oil and remove the oil filter.

13. Disconnect the lower radiator hose at the water pump.

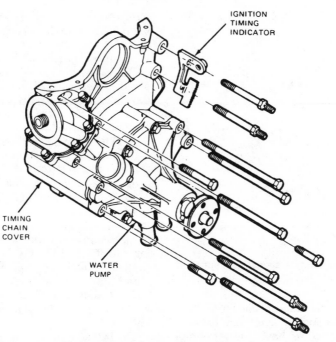

**Timing gear and water pump—V6 engine**

14. Remove the oil pan mounting bolts and lower the oil pan.

NOTE: *The front cover cannot be removed unless the oil pan is lowered.*

15. Lower the car from the jackstands.

16. Remove the front cover mounting bolts.

NOTE: *Water pump removal is not necessary.*

CAUTION: *A front cover mounting bolt is located behind the oil filter adapter. If the bolt is not removed and the cover is pried upon breakage will occur.*

17. Remove the timing indicator. Remove the front cover and water pump assembly.

18. Remove the camshaft thrust button and spring from the end of the camshaft. Remove the camshaft sprocket attaching bolts.

19. Remove the camshaft sprocket, crankshaft sprocket and timing chain by pulling forward evenly on both sprockets. If the crankshaft sprocket is difficult to remove, position two small prybars, one on each side, behind the sprocket and pry forward.

20. Clean all gasket surfaces on the front cover, cylinder black, fuel pump and oil pan.

21. Install a new front cover oil seal. If a new front cover is to be installed: Install the oil pump, oil filter adapter and intermediate shaft from the old cover. Remove the water pump from the old cover, clean the mounting surface, install a new mounting gasket and the pump on the new front cover. Pump attaching bolt torque is 13–22 ft. lbs.

22. Rotate the crankshaft, if necessary, to bring No. 1 piston to TDC with the crankshaft keyway at the 12 o'clock position.

23. Lubricate the timing chain with motor oil. Install the chain over the two gears making sure the marks on both gears are positioned across from each other. Install the gears and chain on the cam and crankshaft. Install the camshaft mounting bolts. Tighten the bolts to 15–22 ft. lbs.

24. Install the camshaft thrust button and spring. Lubricate the thrust button with Polyethylene grease before installation.

NOTE: *The thrust button and spring must be bottomed in the camshaft seat and must not be allowed to fall out during front cover installation.*

25. Position a new cover gasket on the front of the engine and install the cover and water pump assemblies. Install the timing indicator. Torque the front cover bolts to 15–22 ft. lbs.

26. The remaining steps of installation are in the reverse order of removal.

CAUTION: *When installing the fuel pump, turn the crankshaft 180 degrees to position the fuel pump drive eccentric away from the fuel pump arm. Failure to turn the drive eccentric away from the pump arm can cause stress on the pump mounting threads and strip them out when installing the pump.*

### V8 Engines

1. Drain cooling system, remove air cleaner and disconnect the battery.

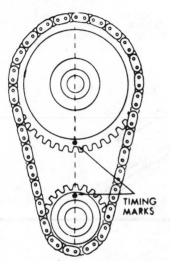

**Timing gear marks must be aligned (except 4-140 engine)**

2. Disconnect the transmission cooler lines and radiator hoses and remove the radiator.

3. Disconnect heater hose at water pump. Slide water pump by-pass hose clamp toward the pump.

4. Loosen alternator mounting bolts at the alternator. Remove the alternator support bolt at the water pump. Remove Thermactor pump on all engines so equipped. If equipped with power steering or air conditioning, unbolt the component, remove the belt, and lay the pump aside with the lines attached.

5. Remove the fan, spacer, pulley, and drive belt.

6. Drain the crankcase.

7. Remove pulley from crankshaft pulley adapter. Remove cap screw and washer from front end of crankshaft. Remove crankshaft pulley adapter with a puller.

8. Disconnect fuel pump outlet line at the pump. Remove fuel pump retaining bolts and lay the pump to the side. Remove the engine oil dipstick.

9. Remove the front cover attaching bolts.

10. Remove the crankshaft oil slinger if so equipped.

11. Check timing chain deflection, using the procedure outlined in Step 6 of the 200 cu in. six cylinder cover and chain removal.

12. Rotate the engine until sprocket timing marks are aligned as shown in valve timing illustration.

13. Remove crankshaft sprocket cap screw, washers, and fuel pump eccentric. Slide both sprockets and chain forward and off as an assembly.

14. Position sprockets and chain on the camshaft and crankshaft with both timing marks dot to dot on a centerline. Install fuel pump eccentric, washers and sprocket attaching bolt. Torque the sprocket attaching bolt to 40–45 ft. lbs.

15. Install crankshaft front oil slinger.

16. Clean front cover and mating surfaces of old gasket material. Install a new oil seal in the cover. Use a seal driver tool, if available.

17. Coat a new cover gasket with sealer and position it on the block.

NOTE: *Trim away the exposed portion of the oil pan gasket flush with the cylinder block. Cut and position the required portion of a new gasket to the oil pan, applying sealer to both sides of it.*

18. Install front cover, using a crank-shaft-to-cover alignment tool. Coat the threads of the attaching bolts with sealer. Torque attaching bolts to 12–15 ft. lbs.

19. Install fuel pump, connect fuel pump outlet tube.

20. Install crankshaft pulley adapter and torque attaching bolt. Install crankshaft pulley.

21. Install water pump pulley, drive belt, spacer and fan.

22. Install alternator support bolt at the water pump. Tighten alternator mounting bolts. Adjust drive belt tension. Install Thermactor pump if so equipped.

23. Install radiator and connect all coolant and heater hoses. Connect battery cables.

24. Refill cooling system and the crankcase. Install the dipstick.

25. Start engine and operate at fast idle.

26. Check for leaks, install air cleaner. Adjust ignition timing and make all final adjustments.

## Front Cover Oil Seal

### REMOVAL AND INSTALLATION

#### All-Except 4-140

It is recommended to replace the cover seal any time the front cover is removed.

NOTE: *On V6 engines, the seal may be removed, after the crank pulley is off without removing the cover.*

1. With the cover removed from the car, drive the old seal from the rear of cover with a pinpunch. Clean out the recess in the cover.

2. Coat the new seal with grease and drive it into the cover until it is fully seated. Check the seal after installation to be sure the spring is properly positioned in the seal.

## Camshaft Drive Belt and Cover

### Four Cylinder 140 cu in. Engine

The correct installation and adjustment of the camshaft drive belt is mandatory if the engine

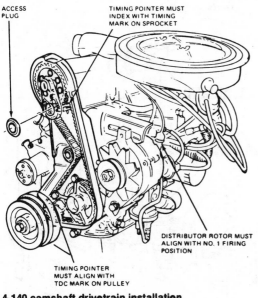

ACCESS PLUG

TIMING POINTER MUST INDEX WITH TIMING MARK ON SPROCKET

DISTRIBUTOR ROTOR MUST ALIGN WITH NO. 1 FIRING POSITION

TIMING POINTER MUST ALIGN WITH TDC MARK ON PULLEY

**4-140 camshaft drivetrain installation**

is to run properly. The camshaft controls the opening of the camshaft and the crankshaft. When any given piston is on the intake stroke the corresponding intake valve must be open to admit air/fuel mixture into the cylinder. When the same piston is on the compression and power strokes, both valves in that cylinder must be closed. When the piston is on the exhaust stroke, the exhaust valve for that cylinder must be open. If the opening and closing of the valves is not coordinated with the movements of the pistons, the engine will run very poorly, if at all.

The camshaft drive belt also turns the engine auxiliary shaft. The distributor is driven by the engine auxiliary shaft. Since the distributor controls ignition timing, the auxiliary shaft must be coordinated with the camshaft and the crankshaft, since both valves in any given cylinder must be closed and the piston in that cylinder near the top of the compression stroke when the spark plug fires.

Due to this complex interrelationship between the camshaft, the crankshaft and the auxiliary shaft, the cogged pulleys on each component must be aligned when the camshaft drive belt is installed.

## TROUBLESHOOTING

Should the camshaft drive belt jump timing by a tooth or two, the engine could still run; but very poorly. To visually check for correct timing of the crankshaft, auxiliary shaft, and the camshaft follow this procedure:

NOTE: *There is an access plug provided in the cam drive belt cover so that the cam-*

shaft timing can be checked without moving the drive belt cover.

1. Remove the access plug.
2. Turn the crankshaft until the timing marks on the crankshaft indicate TDC.
3. Make sure that the timing mark on the camshaft drive sprocket is aligned with the pointer on the inner belt cover. Also, the rotor of the distributor must align with the No. 1 cylinder firing position.

NOTE: *Never turn the crankshaft of any of the overhead cam engines in the opposite direction of normal rotation. Backward rotation of the crankshaft may cause the timing belt to slip and alter the timing.*

## REMOVAL AND INSTALLATION

1. Set the engine to TDC as described in the troubleshooting section. The crankshaft and camshaft timing marks should align with their respective pointers and the distributor rotor should point to the No. 1 plug tower.
2. Loosen the adjustment bolts on the alternator and acessories and remove the drive belts. To provide clearance for removing the camshaft belt, remove the fan and pulley.
3. Remove the belt outer cover.
4. Remove the distributor cap from the distributor and position it out of the way.
5. Loosen the belt tensioner adjustment and pivot bolts. Lever the tensioner away from the belt and retighten the adjustment bolt to hold it away.
6. Remove the crankshaft bolt and pulley. Remove the belt guide behind the pulley.
7. Remove the camshaft drive belt.
8. Install the new belt over the crankshaft pulley first, then counter-clockwise over the auxiliary shaft sprocket and the camshaft sprocket. Adjust the belt fore and aft so that it is centered on the sprockets.
9. Loosen the tensioner adjustment bolt, allowing it to spring back against the belt.
10. Rotate the crankshaft two complete turns in the normal rotation direction to remove any belt slack. Turn the crankshaft until the timing check marks are lined up. If the timing has slipped, remove the belt and repeat the procedure.
11. Tighten the tensioner adjustment bolt to 14–21 ft. lbs., and the pivot bolt to 28–40 ft. lbs.
12. Replace the belt guide and crankshaft pulley, distributor cap, belt outer cover, fan and pulley, drive belts and accessories. Adjust the accessory drive belt tension. Start the engine and check the ignition timing.

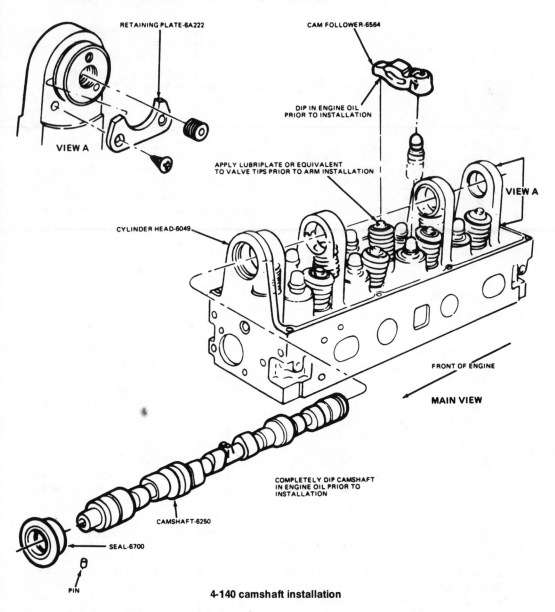

RETAINING PLATE-6A222

CAM FOLLOWER-6564

DIP IN ENGINE OIL
PRIOR TO INSTALLATION

VIEW A

APPLY LUBRIPLATE OR EQUIVALENT
TO VALVE TIPS PRIOR TO ARM INSTALLATION

CYLINDER HEAD-6049

VIEW A

FRONT OF ENGINE

MAIN VIEW

COMPLETELY DIP CAMSHAFT
IN ENGINE OIL PRIOR TO
INSTALLATION

CAMSHAFT-6250

SEAL-6700

PIN

**4-140 camshaft installation**

## Camshaft

### REMOVAL AND INSTALLATION

#### Four Cylinder 140 cu in. Engine

NOTE: *The following procedure covers camshaft removal and installation with the cylinder head on or off the engine. If the cylinder head has been removed start at Step 9.*

1. Drain the cooling system. Remove the air cleaner assembly and disconnect the negative battery cable.

2. Remove the spark plug wires from the plugs, disconnect the retainer from the valve cover and position the wires out of the way. Disconnect rubber vacuum lines as necessary.

3. Remove all drive belts. Remove the al-ternator mounting bracket-to-cylinder head mounting bolts, position bracket and alternator out of the way.

4. Disconnect and remove the upper radiator hose. Disconnect the radiator shroud.

5. Remove the fan blades and water pump pulley and fan shroud. Remove cam belt and valve covers.

6. Align engine timing marks at TDC. Remove cam drive belt.

7. Jack up the front of the car and support on jackstands. Remove the front motor mount bolts. Disconnect the lower radiator hose from the radiator. Disconnect and plug the automatic transmission cooler lines.

8. Postion a piece of wood on a floor jack and raise the engine carefully as far as it will

go. Place blocks of wood between the engine mounts and crossmember pedestals.

9. Remove the rocker arms as described earlier in this chapter.

10. Remove the camshaft drive gear and belt guide using a suitable puller. Remove the front oil seal with a sheet metal screw and slide hammer.

11. Remove the camshaft retainer located on the rear mounting stand by unbolting the two bolts.

12. Remove the camshaft by carefully withdrawing toward the front of the engine. Caution should be used to prevent damage to cam bearings, lobes and journals.

13. Check the camshaft journals and lobes for wear. Inspect the cam bearings, if worn (unless the proper bearing installing tool is on hand), the cylinder head must be removed for new bearings to be installed by a machine shop.

14. Cam installation is in the reverse order of removal. See following notes.

NOTE: *Coat the camshaft with heavy SF oil before sliding it into the cylinder head. Install a new front seal. Apply a coat of sealer or teflon tape to the cam drive gear bolt before installation.*

NOTE: *After any procedure requiring removal of the rocker arms, each lash adjuster must be fully collapsed after assembly, then released. This must be done before the camshaft is turned. See Valve Clearance-Hydraulic Valve Lash Adjusters.*

### In-Line Six Cylinder Engines

1. Remove the cylinder head.

2. Remove the cylinder front cover, timing chain and sprockets as outlined in the preceding section.

3. Disconnect and remove the radiator, condenser and grille. Remove the gravel deflector.

4. Using a magnet, remove the valve lifters and keep them in order so that they can be installed in their original positions.

5. Remove the camshaft thrust plate and remove the camshaft by pulling it from the front of the engine. Use care not to damage the camshaft lobes or journals while removing the cam from the engine.

6. Before installing the camshaft, coat the lobes with engine assembly lubricant and the journals and all valve parts with heavy oil. Clean the oil passage at the rear of the cylinder block with compressed air.

### V6 and V8 Engines

1. Remove or reposition the radiator, A/C condenser and grille components as necessary to provide clearance to remove the camshaft.

2. Remove the cylinder front cover and timing chain as previously described in this chapter.

3. Remove the intake manifold and related parts described earlier in this chapter.

4. Remove the crankcase ventilation valve and tubes from the valve rocker covers. Remove the EGR cooler, if so equipped.

5. Remove the rocker arm covers and loosen the valve rocker arm fulcrum bolts and rotate the rocker arms to the side.

6. Remove the valve push rods and identify them so that they can be installed in their original positions.

7. Remove the valve lifters and place them in a rack so that they can be installed in their original bores.

8. Remove the camshaft thrust plate or button and spring and carefully remove the camshaft by pulling toward the front of the engine. Be careful not to damage the camshaft bearings.

9. Before installing, oil the camshaft journals with heavy engine oil SF and apply Lubriplate® or equivalent to the lobes. Carefully slide the camshaft through the bearings.

10. Install the camshaft thrust plate with the groove towards the cylinder block.

11. Lubricate the lifters with heavy SE engine oil and install in their original bores.

12. Apply Lubriplate® or equivalent to the valve stem tips and each end of the push rods. Install the push rods in their original position.

13. Lubricate the rocker arms and fulcrum seats with heavy SF engine oil and position the rocker arms over the push rods.

14. Install all other parts previously removed.

15. Fill the crankcase and cooling system and adjust the timing.

## CHECKING CAMSHAFT

Degrease the camshaft using safe solvent, clean all oil grooves. Visually inspect the cam lobes and bearing journals for excessive wear. If a lobe is questionable, check all lobes and journals with a micrometer.

Measure the lobes from nose to base and again at 90°. The lift is determined by subtracting the second measurement from the first. If all exhaust lobes and all intake lobes are not identical, the camshaft must be reground or replaced. Measure the bearing journals and compare to specifications. If a journal is worn there is a good chance that the cam bearings are worn too, requiring replacement.

If the lobes and journals appear intact, place the front and rear cam journals in V-blocks and rest a dial indicator on the center journal. Rotate the camshaft to check for straightness, if deviation exceeds .001 inch, replace the camshaft.

## Auxiliary Shaft
### REMOVAL AND INSTALLATION
#### Four Cylinder 140 cu in. Engine

1. Remove the camshaft drive belt cover.
2. Remove the drive belt. Remove the auxiliary shaft sprocket. A puller may be necessary to remove the sprocket.

3. Remove the distributor and fuel pump.
4. Remove the auxiliary shaft cover and thrust plate.
5. Withdraw the auxiliary shaft from the block.

NOTE: *The distributor drive gear and the fuel pump eccentric on the auxiliary shaft must not be allowed to touch the auxiliary shaft bearings during removal and installation. Completely coat the shaft with oil before sliding it into place.*

6. Slide the auxiliary shaft into the hous-

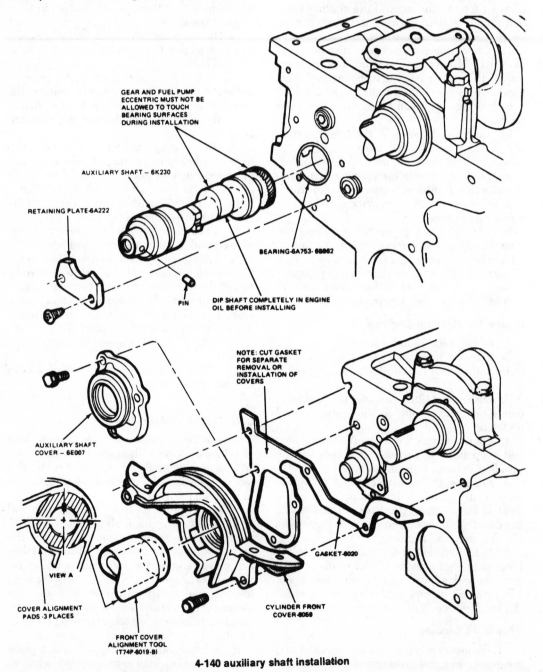

GEAR AND FUEL PUMP ECCENTRIC MUST NOT BE ALLOWED TO TOUCH BEARING SURFACES DURING INSTALLATION

AUXILIARY SHAFT – 6K230

RETAINING PLATE-6A222

BEARING-6A753- 6B862

PIN

DIP SHAFT COMPLETELY IN ENGINE OIL BEFORE INSTALLING

NOTE: CUT GASKET FOR SEPARATE REMOVAL OR INSTALLATION OF COVERS

AUXILIARY SHAFT COVER – 6E007

GASKET-6020

VIEW A

COVER ALIGNMENT PADS -3 PLACES

FRONT COVER ALIGNMENT TOOL (T74P-6019-B)

CYLINDER FRONT COVER-6050

**4-140 auxiliary shaft installation**

ing and insert the thrust plate to hold the shaft.

7. Install a new gasket and auxiliary shaft cover.

NOTE: *The auxiliary shaft cover and cylinder front cover share a gasket. Cut off the old gasket around the cylinder cover and use half of the new gasket on the auxiliary shaft cover.*

8. Fit a new gasket into the fuel pump and install the pump.

9. Insert the distributor and install the auxiliary shaft sprocket.

10. Align the timing marks and install the drive belt.

11. Install the drive belt cover.

12. Check the ignition timing.

## Pistons and Connection Rods
### REMOVAL AND INSTALLATION

NOTE: *Although, in most cases, the pistons and connecting rods can be removed from the engine (after the cylinder head and oil pan are removed) while the engine is still in the car; it is far easier to remove the engine from the car. If removing pistons with the engine still installed, disconnect the radiator hoses, automatic transmission cooler lines and radiator shroud. Unbolt front mounts before jacking up the engine. Block the engine in position with wooden blocks between the mounts.*

1. Remove the engine from the car. Remove cylinder head(s), oil pan and front cover (if necessary).

2. Because the top piston ring does not travel to the very top of the cylinder bore, a ridge is built up between the end of the travel and the top of the cylinder. Pushing the piston and connecting rod assembly past the ridge is difficult and may cause damage to the piston. If new rings are installed and the ridge has not been removed, ring breakage and piston damage can occur when the ridge is encountered at engine speed.

3. Turn the crankshaft to position the piston at the bottom of the cylinder bore. Cover the top of the piston with a rag. Install a ridge reamer in the bore and follow the manufacturer's instructions to remove the ridge. Use caution; avoid cutting too deeply or into the ring travel area. Remove the rag and cuttings from the top of the piston. Remove the ridge from all cylinders.

4. Check the edges of the connecting rod and bearing cap for numbers or matchmarks, if none are present mark the rod and cap numerically and in sequence from front to back of engine. The numbers or marks not only tell from which cylinder the piston came from but also ensures that the rod caps are installed in the correct matching position.

5. Turn the crankshaft until the connecting rod is at the bottom of travel. Remove the two attaching nuts and the bearing cap. Take two pieces of rubber tubing and cover the rod bolts to prevent crank or cylinder scoring. Use a wooden hammer handle to help push the piston and rod up and out of the cylinder. Reinstall the rod cap in proper position. Remove all pistons and connecting rods. Inspect cylinder walls and deglaze or hone as necessary.

6. Installation is in the reverse order of removal. Lubricate each piston, rod bearing and cylinder wall. Install a ring compressor over the piston, position piston with mark toward front of engine and carefully install. Position connecting rod with bearing insert installed over the crank journal. Install the rod cap with bearing in proper position. Secure with rod nuts and torque to proper specifications. Install all rod and piston assemblies.

### CLEANING AND INSPECTION

1. Use a piston ring expander and remove the rings from the piston.

2. Clean the ring grooves using an appropriate cleaning tool, exercise care to avoid cutting too deeply.

3. Clean all varnish and carbon from the piston with a safe solvent. Do not use a wire brush or caustic solution on the pistons.

4. Inspect the pistons for scuffing, scoring, cracks, pitting or excessive ring groove wear. If wear is evident, the piston must be replaced.

5. Have the piston and connecting rod assembly checked by a machine shop for correct alignment, piston pin wear and piston diameter. If the piston has "collapsed" it will have to be replaced or knurled to restore original diameter. Connecting rod bushing replacement, piston pin fitting and piston changing can be handled by the machine ship.

### CYLINDER BORE

1. Check the cylinder bore for wear using a telescope gauge and a micrometer, measure the cylinder bore diameter perpendicular to the piston pin at a point 2½ inches below the top of the engine block. Measure the piston skirt perpendicular to the piston pin. The difference between the two measurements is the piston clearance. If the clearance is within specifications, finish honing or glaze breaking is all that is required. If clearance is excessive a slightly oversize piston may be required. If greatly oversize, the engine will have to be

## PISTON RING SPACING

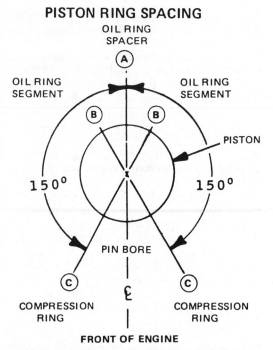

Recommended piston ring spacing. Refer to the ring manufacturer's instruction sheet before installing new piston rings

bored and .010 inch or larger oversized pistons installed.

### FITTING AND POSITIONING PISTON RINGS

1. Take the new piston rings and compress them, one at a time into the cylinder that they will be used in. Press the ring about one inch below the top of the cylinder block using an inverted piston.

2. Use a feeler gauge and measure the distance between the ends of the ring; this is called measuring the ring end-gap. Compare the reading to the one called for in the specifications table. File the ends of the ring with a fine file to obtain necessary clearance.

NOTE: *If inadequate ring end-gap is utilized, ring breakage will result.*

RING COMPRESSOR

**Install the piston using a ring compressor**

3. Inspect the ring grooves on the piston for excessive wear or taper. If necessary have the grooves recut for use with a standard ring and spacer. The machine shop can handle the job for you.

4. Check the ring grooves by rolling the new piston ring around the groove to check for burrs or carbon deposits. If any are found, remove with a fine file. Hold the ring in the groove and measure side clearance with a feeler gauge. If clearance is excessive, spacer(s) will have to be added.

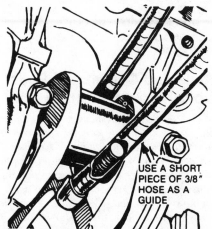

USE A SHORT PIECE OF 3/8" HOSE AS A GUIDE

**Use lengths of vacuum hose or rubber tubing to protect the crankshaft journals and cylinder walls during installation**

NOTE: *Always add spacers above the piston ring.*

5. Install the rings on the piston, lower oil ring first. Use a ring installing tool on the compression rings. Consult the instruction sheet that comes with the rings to be sure they are installed with the correct side up. A mark on the ring usually faces upward.

6. When installing oil rings; first, install the expanding ring in the groove. Hold the ends of the ring butted together (they must not overlap) and install the bottom rail (scraper) with the end about one inch away from the butted end of the control ring. Install the top rail about an inch away from the butted end of the control but on the opposite side from the lower rail.

7. Install the two compression rings.

8. Consult the illustration for ring positioning, arrange the rings as shown, install a ring compressor and insert the piston and rod assembly into the engine.

## Crankshaft and Bearings

1. Rod bearings can be installed when the pistons have been removed for servicing (rings

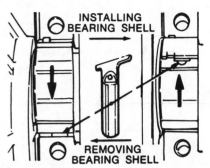

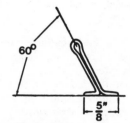

Remove or install the upper main bearing insert using a roll-out pin

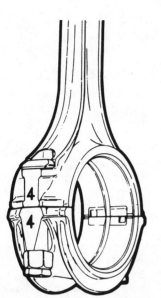

Match the connecting rod and cap to themselves and the cylinder using stamped numbers

Home made roll-out pin

etc.) or, in most cases, while the engine is still in the car. Bearing replacement, however, is far easier with the engine out of the car and disassembled.

2. For in car service, remove the oil pan, spark plugs and front cover if necessary. Turn the engine until the connecting rod to be serviced is at the bottom of travel. Remove the bearing cap, place two pieces of rubber hose over the rod cap bolts and push the piston and rod assembly up the cylinder bore until enough room is gained for bearing insert removal. Take care not to push the rod assembly up too far or the top ring will engage the cylinder ridge or come out of the cylinder and require head removal for reinstallation.

3. Clean the rod journal, the connecting rod end and the bearing cap after removing the old bearing inserts. Install the new inserts in the rod and bearing cap, lubricate them with oil. Position the rod over the crankshaft journal and install the rod cap. Make sure the cap and rod numbers match, torque the rod nuts to specifications.

4. Main bearings may be replaced while the engine is still in the car by "rolling" them out and in.

5. Special roll out pins are available from automotive parts houses or can be fabricated from a cotter pin. The roll out pin fits in the oil hole of the main bearing journal. When the crankshaft is rotated opposite the direction of the bearing lock tab, the pin engages the end of the bearing and "rolls" out the insert.

6. Remove main bearing cap and roll out upper bearing insert. Remove insert from main bearing cap. Clean the inside of the bearing cap and crankshaft journal.

7. Lubricate and roll upper insert into position, make sure the lock tab is anchored and the insert is not "cocked". Install the lower bearing insert into the cap, lubricate and install on the engine. Make sure the main bearing cap is installed facing in the correct direction and torque to specifications.

8. With the engine out of the car. Remove

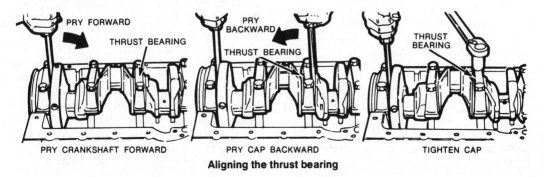

Aligning the thrust bearing

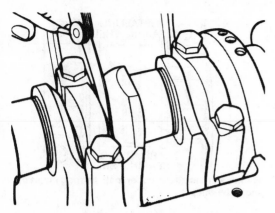

**Check the crankshaft end-play with a feeler gauge**

the intake manifold, cylinder heads, front cover, timing gears and/or chain, oil pan, o pump and flywheel.

9. Remove the piston and rod assemblies. Remove the main bearing caps after marking them for position and direction.

10. Remove the crankshaft, bearing inserts and rear main oil seal. Clean the engine block and cap bearing saddles. Clean the crankshaft and inspect for wear. Check the bearing journals with a micrometer for out-of-round condition and to determine what size rod and main bearing inserts to install.

11. Install the main bearing upper inserts and rear main oil seal half into the engine block.

12. Lubricate the bearing inserts and the crankshaft journals. Slowly and carefully lower the crankshaft into position.

13. Install the bearing inserts and rear main seal into the bearing caps, install the caps working from the middle out. Torque cap bolts to specifications in stages, rotate the crankshaft after each torque state. Note the illustration for thrust bearing alignment.

14. Remove bearing caps, one at a time and check the oil clearance with Plastigage®. Reinstall if clearance is within specifications. Check the crankshaft end-play, if within specifications install connecting rod and piston assem-

blies with new rod bearing inserts. Check connecting rod bearing oil clearance and side play, if correct assemble the rest of the engine.

### BEARING OIL CLEARANCE

Remove cap from the bearing to be checked. Using a clean, dry rag, thoroughly clean all oil from crankshaft journal and bearing insert.

NOTE: *Plastigage® is soluble in oil; therefore, oil on the journal or bearing could result in erroneous readings.*

Place a piece of Plastigage® along the full width of the bearing insert, reinstall cap, and torque to specifications.

NOTE: *Specifications are given in the engine specifications earlier in this chapter.*

Remove bearing cap, and determine bearing clearance by comparing width of Plastigage® to the scale on Plastigage® envelope. Journal taper is determined by comparing width of the bearing insert, reinstall cap, and torque to specifications.

journal eccentricity.

NOTE: *Do not rotate crankshaft with Plastigage® installed. If bearing insert and journal appear intact, and are within tolerances, no further main bearing service is required. If bearing or journal appear defective, cause of failure should be determined before replacement.*

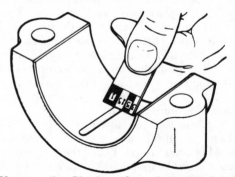

**Measure the Plastigage® to determine bearing clearance**

### CRANKSHAFT END-PLAY/CONNECTING ROD SIDE PLAY

Place a pry bar between a main bearing cap and crankshaft casting taking care not to damage any journals. Pry backward and forward, measure the distance between the thrust bearing and crankshaft with a feeler gauge. Compare reading with specifications. If too great a clearance is determined, a main bearing with a larger thrust surface or crank machining may be required. Check with an automotive machine shop for their advice.

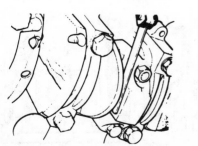

**Check the connecting rod side clearance with a feeler gauge**

Connecting rod clearance between the rod and crankthrow casting can be checked with a feeler gauge. Pry the rod carefully to one side as far as possible and measure the distance on the other side of the rod.

### CRANKSHAFT REPAIRS

If a journal is damaged on the crankshaft, repair is possible by having the crankshaft machined to a standard undersize.

In most cases, however, since the engine must be removed from the car and disassembled, some thought should be given to replacing the damaged crankshaft with a reground shaft kit. A reground crankshaft kit contains the necessary main and rod bearings for installation. The shaft has been ground and polished to undersize specifications and will usually hold up well if installed correctly.

## Completing the Rebuilding Process

Complete the rebuilding process as follows:

Fill the oil pump with oil, to prevent cavitating (sucking air) on initial engine start up. Install the oil pump and the pickup tube on the engine. Coat the oil pan gasket as necessary, and install the gasket and the oil pan. Mount the flywheel and the crankshaft vibration damper or pulley on the crankshaft.

NOTE: *Always use new bolts when installing the flywheel. Inspect the clutch shaft pilot bushing in the crankshaft. If the bushing is excessively worn, remove it with an expanding puller and a slide hammer, and tap a new bushing into place.*

Position the engine, cylinder head side up. Lubricate the lifters, and install them into their bores. Install the cylinder head, and torque it as specified. Insert the pushrods (where applicable), and install the rocker shaft(s) (if so equipped) or position the rocker.

Install the intake and exhaust manifolds, the carburetor(s), the distributor and spark plugs. Mount all accessories and install the engine in the car. Fill the radiator with coolant, and the crankcase with high quality engine oil.

## Break-in Procedure

Start the engine, and allow it to run at low speed for a few minutes, while checking for leaks. Stop the engine, check the oil level, and fill as necessary. Restart the engine, and fill the cooling system to capacity. Check and adjust the ignition timing. Run the engine at low to medium speed (800–2500 rpm) for approximately ½ hour, and retorque the cylinder

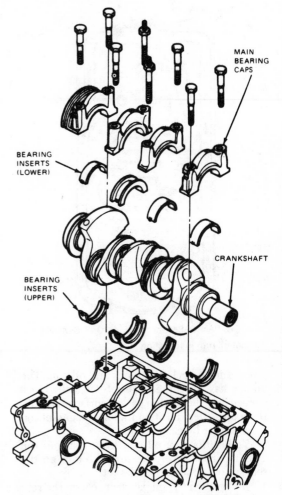

**Typical crankshaft and main bearing assembly—V6 shown**

head bolts. Road test the car, and check again for leaks.

## Oil Pan

### REMOVAL AND INSTALLATION

#### 4-140, 6-200, 250

1. Drain the crankcase.
2. Remove the oil level dipstick and the flywheel housing inspection cover.
3. Remove the oil pan retaining nuts, and drop the pan and gasket. It may be necessary to crank the engine to obtain clearance to remove the pan. On some models with rack and pinion steering it may be necessary to unmount the steering assembly for clearance.
4. Remove the oil pump screen and inlet tube assembly.
5. Clean and install the oil pump inlet tube and screen assembly.
6. Clean the gasket surfaces of the block and oil pan. Be sure to clean the seal retainer

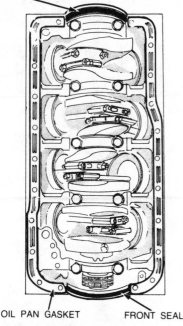

REAR SEAL

OIL PAN GASKET          FRONT SEAL

**Typical oil pan installation**

grooves in the cylinder block and oil pan. The oil pan has a two-piece gasket. Coat the block surface and the oil pan gasket surface with oil-resistant sealer. Position the oil pan gaskets on the cylinder block.

7. Position the oil pan front seal mn the cylinder front cover. Be sure the tabs on the seal are over the oil pan gasket.

8. Position the oil pan rear seal on the rear main bearing cap. Be sure the tabs on the seal are over the oil pan gasket.

9. Hold the oil pan in place against the block and install a bolt, finger-tight, on each side of the oil pan. Install the remaining bolts. Torque the bolts from the center outward in each direction to specifications.

10. Install the dipstick. Fill the crankcase with the proper grade and quantity of oil, and check for leaks.

NOTE: *Some engines have been built using RTV silicone gasket material in place of gaskets. To assemble a part using the gasket material, run a ⅛ inch bead of gasket material around the pan sealing surface, enclosing all bolt holes. This material starts to cure in 10–15 minutes, so don't take too long to position and attach the pan.*

**All V6 and V8 Engines**

1. Remove the oil level dipstick. Remove the bolts attaching the fan shroud to the radiator. Position the shroud over the fan.

2. Raise the vehicle and install safety stands.

3. Drain the crankcase.

4. Remove the stabilizer bar from the chassis. On some models with rack and pinion steering it may be necessary to unmount the steering assembly for clearance.

5. Remove the engine front support thru-bolts.

6. Raise the engine and place wood blocks between the engine front supports and chassis brackets.

7. If equipped with an automatic transmission, disconnect the oil cooler lines at the radiator.

8. Remove the oil pan retaining bolts and lower the oil pan onto the crossmember.

9. Remove oil pump pick-up tube and screen from the oil pump. Rotate the crankshaft for clearance and remove the oil pan.

10. Clean the gasket surfaces of the block and oil pan. The oil pan has a two-piece gasket.

11. Clean the oil pump pick-up tube and screen.

12. Coat the block surface and the oil pan gasket with sealer. Position the oil pan gaskets on the cylinder block.

13. Position the oil pan front seal on the cylinder front cover. Be sure the tabs on the seal are over the oil pan gasket.

14. Position the oil pan rear seal on the rear main bearing cap. Be sure the tabs nn the seal are over the oil pan gasket.

15. Position the oil pan on the crossmember. Install a new gasket on the oil pump and install the oil pump pick-up tube.

16. Position the oil pan against the block and install a bolt, finger-tight, on each side of the block. Install the remaining bolts. Tighten the bolts from the center outward in each direction to specifications.

17. If equipped with an automatic transmission, connect the oil cooler lines at the radiator.

18. Raise the engine and remove the wood blocks from between the engine supports and the chassis brackets. Lower the engine and install the engine support thru-bolts. Tighten the bolts to specifications.

19. Install the stabilizer bar to the chassis.

20. Lower the vehicle.

21. Install the fan shroud.

22. Install the oil level dipstick. Fill the crankcase with the proper grade and quantity of engine oil. Start the engine and check for oil leaks.

## Rear Main Oil Seal

### *REMOVAL AND INSTALLATION*

**All Engines**

NOTE: *The rear oil seal installed in these engines is a rubber type seal.*

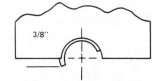

INSTALL SEAL WITH LIP
TOWARDS FRONT OF ENGINE

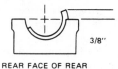

3/8''

SEAL HALVES TO PROTRUDE BEYOND
PARTING FACES THIS DISTANCE TO
ALLOW FOR CAP TO BLOCK ALIGNMENT

3/8''

REAR FACE OF REAR
MAIN BEARING CAP
AND CYLINDER BLOCK

FRONT OF
ENGINE

VIEW LOOKING AT PARTING
FACE OF SPLIT, LIP-TYPE
CRANKSHAFT SEAL

**Rear main bearing oil seal installation**

1. Remove the oil pan, and, if required, the oil pump.

2. Loosen all main bearing caps allowing the crankshaft to lower slightly.

NOTE: *The crankshaft should not be allowed to drop more than* $1/32$ *in.*

3. Remove the rear main bearing cap and remove the seal from the cap and block. Be very careful not to scratch the sealing surface. Remove the old seal retaining pin from the cap, if equipped. It is not used with the replacement seal.

4. Carefully clean the seal grooves in the cap and block with solvent.

5. Soak the new seal halves in clean engine oil. Remove locating tabs if equipped.

6. Install the upper half of the seal in the block with the undercut side of the seal toward the front of the engine. Slide the seal around the crankshaft journal until ⅜ in. protrudes beyond the base of the block.

7. Tighten all the main bearing caps (except the rear main bearing) to specifications.

8. Install the lower seal into the rear cap, with the undercut side facing the front of the engine. Allow ⅜ in. of the seal to protrude above the surface, at the opposite end from the block seal.

9. Squeeze a $1/16$ in. bead of silicone sealant onto the areas at the corners of the bearing cap and block.

10. Install the rear cap and torque to specifications.

11. Install the oil pump and pan. Fill the crankcase with oil, start the engine, and check for leaks.

## Oil Pump

### REMOVAL AND INSTALLATION

#### All Engines Except V6

1. Remove the oil pan as outlined previously in this chapter.

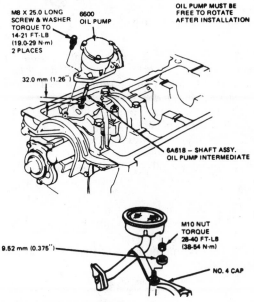

M8 X 25.0 LONG
SCREW & WASHER
TORQUE TO
14-21 FT-LB
(19.0-29 N·m)
2 PLACES

6600
OIL PUMP

OIL PUMP MUST BE
FREE TO ROTATE
AFTER INSTALLATION

32.0 mm (1.26'')

6A618 — SHAFT ASSY.
OIL PUMP INTERMEDIATE

M10 NUT
TORQUE
28-40 FT-LB
(38-54 N·m)

9.52 mm (0.375'')

NO. 4 CAP

**4-140 oil pump installation**

2. Remove and clean the oil pump inlet tube and screen assembly.

3. Remove the oil pump attaching bolts. Lower the oil pump, gasket and intermediate driveshaft from the crankcase.

4. Install the oil pump assembly:

a. Prime the pump by filling it with engine oil and rotating the pump shaft to distribute the oil within the pump body.

b. Position the intermediate driveshaft into the distributor socket. With the shaft firmly seated in the socket, the stop on the shaft should contact the roof of the crankcase. Remove the shaft and position the stop as necessary.

c. Insert the intermediate driveshaft into the oil pump. Using a new gasket, install the pump and shaft as an assembly.

NOTE: *Do not attempt to force the pump*

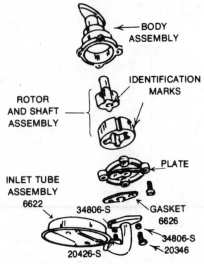

BODY ASSEMBLY

IDENTIFICATION MARKS

ROTOR AND SHAFT ASSEMBLY

PLATE

INLET TUBE ASSEMBLY
6622

34806-S

GASKET 6626

34806-S
20346

20426-S

**In-line 6 and V8 oil pump**

*into position if it will not seat readily. If necessary, rotate the intermediate driveshaft hex into a new position so that it will mesh with the distributor shaft.*

5. Torque the oil pump attaching bolts to the following specifications:
  • 6-cyl. engines—12–15 ft. lbs.;
  • V8 engines—22–32 ft. lbs.;
6. Install the oil pan as outlined previously.

**V6**

1. If necessary remove the oil filter.
2. Remove the oil pump cover attaching bolts and remove the cover.
3. Lift the pump gears of the pocket in the front cover.
4. Remove the cover gasket. Discard the gasket.

5. If necessary, remove the pump gears from the cover.
6. Pack the gear pocket with petroleum jelly. DO NOT USE CHASSIS LUBRICANTS.
7. Install the gears in the cover pocket making sure the petroleum jelly fills all voids between the gears and the pocket.
CAUTION: *Failure to properly pack the oil pump gears with petroleum jelly may result in failure of the pump to prime when the engine is started.*
8. Position the cover gasket and install the pump cover.
9. Tighten the pump cover attaching bolts to 18–22 ft. lbs.

## Radiator

### REMOVAL AND INSTALLATION

1. Drain the cooling system.
2. Disconnect the upper and lower hoses at the radiator.
3. On cars with automatic transmissions, disconnect the oil cooler lines at the radiator.
4. On vehicles with a fan shroud, remove the shroud retaining screws and position the shroud out of the way.
5. Remove the radiator attaching bolts and lift out the radiator.
6. If a new radiator is to be installed, transfer the petcock from the old radiator to the new one. On cars with automatic transmissions, transfer the oil cooler line fittings from the old radiator to the new one.
7. Position the radiator and install, but do not tighten, the radiator support bolts. On cars with automatic transmissions, connect the oil

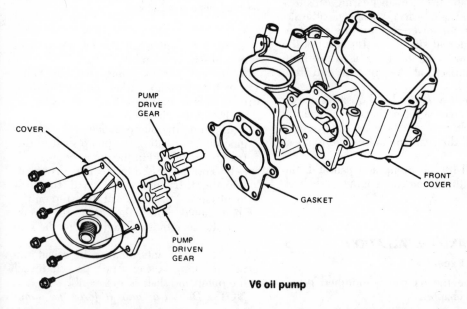

COVER

PUMP DRIVE GEAR

FRONT COVER

GASKET

PUMP DRIVEN GEAR

**V6 oil pump**

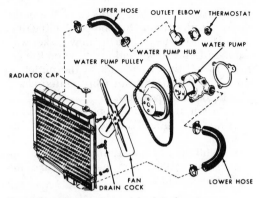

UPPER HOSE   OUTLET ELBOW   THERMOSTAT

WATER PUMP HUB   WATER PUMP

WATER PUMP PULLEY

RADIATOR CAP

FAN   LOWER HOSE
DRAIN COCK

**Typical cooling system and related parts**

cooler lines. Then tighten the radiator support bolts.

8. On vehicles with a fan shroud, reinstall the shroud.

9. Connect the radiator hoses. Close the radiator petcock. Then fill the cooling system.

10. Start the engine and bring to operating temperature. Check for leaks.

11. On cars with automatic transmissions, check the cooler lines for leaks and interference. Check the transmission fluid level.

## Water Pump

### REMOVAL AND INSTALLATION

#### Four Cylinder 140 cu in. Engine

1. Drain the cooling system.

2. Disconnect the lower radiator hose and heater hose from the water pump.

3. Loosen the alternator retaining and adjusting bolt, and remove the drive belt.

4. Remove the fan shroud, fan and water pump pulley. On 2300 cc engines, remove the camshaft drive belt cover first. It is not necessary to remove the cam belt or inner cover.

5. Remove the water pump retaining bolts and remove the pump from the engine.

6. Clean all mating surfaces and install the pump with a new gasket coated with sealer. If a new pump is being installed, transfer the heater hose fitting from the old pump.

7. Reverse the removal steps to install the pump. Refill the cooling system.

#### All except 4-140

1. Drain the cooling system.

2. Disconnect the negative battery cable.

3. If equipped with a fan shroud, remove the shroud attaching bolts and position the shroud over the fan.

4. Remove the fan and spacer from the water pump shaft. Remove the shroud, if so equipped.

5. Remove the air conditioning drive belt

and idler pulley, if so equipped. Remove the alternator, power steering and Thermactor drive belts, if so equipped. Remove the power steering pump attaching bolts, if so equipped, and position it to one side (leaving it connected).

6. Remove all accessory brackets which attach to the water pump. Remove the water pump pulley.

7. Disconnect the lower radiator hose, heater hose, and the water pump by-pass hose at the water pump.

8. Remove the bolts attaching the water pump to the front cover. Remove the pump and gasket. Discard the old gasket.

9. Clean all gasket surfaces.

NOTE: *The 250 six-cylinder engine originally had a one-piece gasket for the cylinder front cover and the water pump. Trim away the old gasket at the edge of the cylinder cover and replace with a service gasket.*

10. Coat both sides of a new gasket with water-resistant sealer and place it on the front cover. Install the water pump and tighten the attaching bolts diagonally, in rotation, to 15 ft. lbs.

11. Connect the lower radiator hose, heater hose, and water pump by-pass hose at the water pump.

12. Install all accessory brackets attaching to the water pump. Install the pump pulley on the pump shaft.

13. Install the power steering pump and drive belt, if so equipped. Install the alternator, air conditioning, and Thermactor drive belts, if so equipped. Install the air conditioner idler pulley bracket, if so equipped. Adjust the drive belt tension of all accessory drive belts.

14. Position the fan shroud, if so equipped, over the water pump pulley. Install the spacer and fan. Install the shroud attaching bolts, if so equipped.

15. Fill the cooling system. Operate the engine until normal running temperature is reached. Check for leaks.

## Thermostat

### REMOVAL AND INSTALLATION

1. Open the drain cock and drain the radiator so that the coolant level is below the coolant outlet elbow which houses the thermostat.

2. Remove the outlet elbow retaining bolts and position the elbow clear of the intake manifold or cylinder head sufficiently to provide access to the thermostat.

3. Remove the thermostat and old gasket. The thermostat must be rotated counterclockwise for removal.

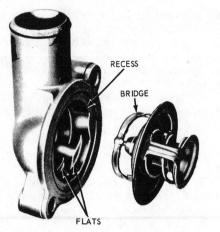

RECESS

BRIDGE

FLATS

**Typical thermostat installation**

4. Clean the mating surfaces of the outlet elbow and the engine to remove all old gasket material and sealer. Coat the new gasket with water-resistant sealer and install in on the engine. Install the thermostat in the outlet elbow. The thermostat must be rotated clockwise to lock it in position.

5. Install the outlet elbow and retaining bolts on the engine. Torque the bolts to 12–15 ft. lbs.

6. Refill the radiator. Run the engine at operating temperature and check for leaks. Recheck the coolant level.

# Emission Controls and Fuel System

**4**

## EMISSION CONTROLS

There are three basic sources of automotive pollution in the modern internal combustion engine. They are the crankcase with its accompanying blow-by vapors, the fuel system with its evaporation of unburned gasoline and the combustion chambers with their resulting exhaust emissions. Pollution arising from the incomplete combustion of fuel generally falls into three categories: hydrocarbons (HC), carbon monoxide (CO) and oxides of nitrogen ($NO_x$).

## Positive Crankcase Ventilation System

All Granadas and Monarchs are equipped with a positive crankcase ventilation (PCV) system to control crankcase blow-by vapors. The system consists of a PCV valve and oil separator mounted on top of the valve cover, a nonventilated oil filter cap and a pair of hoses supplying filtered intake air to the valve cover and delivering the crankcase vapors from the valve cover to the intake manifold (six cylinder) or carburetor (V8).

The system functions as follows: When the engine is running, a small portion of the gases which are formed in the combustion chamber leaks by the piston rings and enters the crankcase. Since these gases are under pressure, they tend to escape from the crankcase and enter the atmosphere. If these gases are allowed to remain in the crankcase for any period of time, they contaminate the engine oil and cause sludge to build up in the crankcase. If the gases are allowed to escape into the atmosphere, they pollute the air with unburned hydrocarbons. The job of the crankcase emission control equipment is to recycle these gases

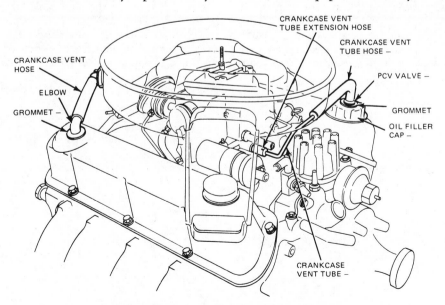

**Positive crankcase ventilation system—V8**

back into the engine combustion chamber where they are reburned.

These crankcase (blow-by) vapors are recycled in the following way: as the engine is running, clean filtered air is drawn through the air filter and into the crankcase. As the air passes through the crankcase, it picks up the combustion gases and carries them out of the crankcase through the oil separator, through the PCV valve and into the induction system. As the gases enter the intake manifold, they are drawn into the combustion chamber where they are reburned.

The most critical component in the system is the PCV valve. This valve controls the amount of gases which is recycled into the combustion chamber. At low engine speeds, the valve is partially closed, limiting the flow of gases into the intake manifold. As engine speed increases, the valve opens to admit greater quantities of the gases into the intake manifold. If the valve should become blocked or plugged, the gases will be prevented from escaping from the crankcase by the normal route. Since these gases are under pressure, they will find their own way out of the crankcase. This alternate route is usually a weak oil seal or gasket in the engine. As the gas escapes by the gasket, it also creates an oil leak. Besides causing oil leaks, a clogged PCV valve also allows these gases to remain in the crankcase for an extended period of time, promoting the formation of sludge in the engine.

## Fuel Evaporative Control System

All Monarchs and Granadas are equipped with a fuel evaporative control system to prevent the evaporation of unburned gasoline. This system consists of a special vacuum/pressure relief filler cap, an expansion area at the top of the fuel tank, a foam-filled vapor separator

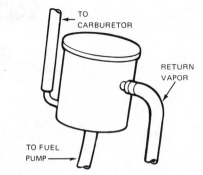

**Vapor separator**

mounted on top of the fuel tank, a carbon canister which stores fuel vapors and hoses which connect this equippment. The carburetor fuel bowl vapors are retained within the fuel bowl until the engine is started, at which point they are internally vented into the engine for burning.

The rest of the system functions as follows: Change in atmospheric temperature causes the gasoline in fuel tanks to expand or contract. If this expansion and consequent vaporization take place in a conventional fuel tank, the fuel vapors escape through the filler cap or vent hose, and pollute the atmosphere. The fuel evaporative emission control system prevents this by routing the gasoline vapors to the engine, where they are burned.

As the gasoline in the fuel tank of a parked car begins to expand due to heat, the vapor that forms rises to the top of the fuel tank. The fuel tanks on all Granadas and Monarchs are enlarged so that there exists an area representing 10–20% of the total fuel tank volume above the level of the fuel tank filler tube where these gases may collect. The vapors then travel upward into the vapor separator which prevents liquid gasoline from escaping from the fuel tank. The fuel vapor is then drawn through

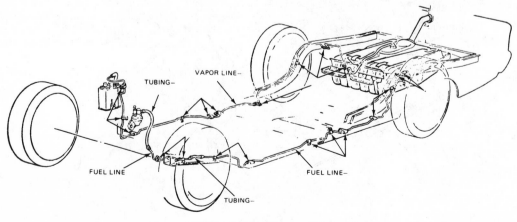

**Fuel and vapor line routing**

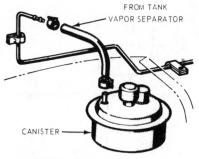

**Carbon canister**

the vapor separator outlet hose, then to the charcoal canister in the engine compartment. The vapor enters the canister, passes through a charcoal filter, then exits through the canister's grated bottom. As the vapor passes through the charcoal, it is cleansed of hydrocarbons, so that the air that passes out of the bottom of the canister is free of pollutants.

When the engine is started, vacuum from the carburetor draws fresh air into the canister. As the entering air passes through the charcoal in the canister, it picks up the hydrocarbons that were deposited there by the fuel vapors. This mixture of hydrocarbons and fresh air is then carried through a hose to the air cleaner. In the carburetor, it combines with the incoming fuel-air mixture and enters the combustion chambers of the engine, where it is burned.

To solve the problem of allowing air into the tank to replace the gasoline displaced during normal use and the problem of relieving excess pressure from the fuel tank should it reach a dangerous level, a special filler cap was devised. Under normal circumstances, this filler cap functions as a check valve, allowing air to enter the tank to replace the fuel consumed. At the same time, it prevents vapors from escaping from the cap. In case of severe pressure within the tank, the filler cap valve opens, venting the pollutants to the atmosphere.

## Heated Air Intake System

The heated air intake portion of the air cleaner consists of a bimetal switch and vacuum motor

and a spring-loaded temperature control door in the snorkel of the air cleaner. The temperature control door is located between the end of the air cleaner snorkel, which draws in air from the engine compartment, and the duct that carries heated air up from the exhaust manifold. When the temperature under the hood is below 90°F, the control door prevents underhood air from entering the air cleaner, allowing only heated air from the exhaust manifold to be drawn into the air cleaner. When underhood temperatures rise above 130°F, the control door blocks off heated air from the exhaust manifold and allows only underhood air to be drawn into the air cleaner.

By controlling the temperature of the engine intake air this way, exhaust emissions are lowered and fuel economy is improved. In addition, throttle plate icing is reduced and cold weather driveability is improved.

## Dual Diaphragm Distributors

Some models are equipped with dual diaphragm distributors. The dual diaphragm is a two-chambered housing which is mounted on the side of the distributor. The outer side is a conventional vacuum advance mechanism, connected to the carburetor by a vacuum hose. The purpose of the vacuum advance unit is to advance ignition timing in response to the conditions under which the engine is operating. Vacuum advance units have been in use for many years, and their chief advantage is economical engine operation. The inner or second side of the diaphragm is the side that has been added to help control exhaust emissions at idle and during deceleration.

This inner side of the dual diaphragm is connected by a vacuum hose to the intake manifold. When the engine is idling or decelerating, intake manifold vacuum is high and carburetor vacuum is low. Under these conditions, intake manifold vacuum, applied to the inner side of the dual diaphragm, retards ignition timing to promote more complete combustion of the fuel-air mixture in the engine combustion chambers.

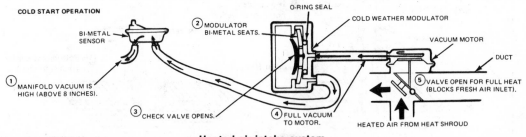

**Heated air intake system**

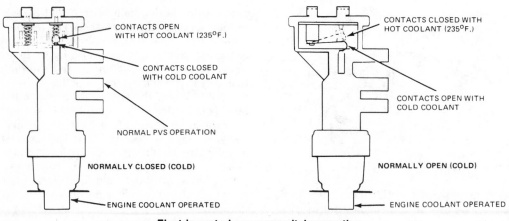

CONTACTS OPEN
WITH HOT COOLANT (235°F.)

CONTACTS CLOSED
WITH COLD COOLANT

NORMAL PVS OPERATION

NORMALLY CLOSED (COLD)

ENGINE COOLANT OPERATED

CONTACTS CLOSED WITH
HOT COOLANT (235°F.)

CONTACTS OPEN WITH
COLD COOLANT

NORMALLY OPEN (COLD)

ENGINE COOLANT OPERATED

**Electric ported vacuum switch operation**

## 2-PORT PVS OPERATION

- Simple on-off "switch" for vacuum.
- **EGR-PVS valve** – cuts off EGR vacuum when engine is cold.

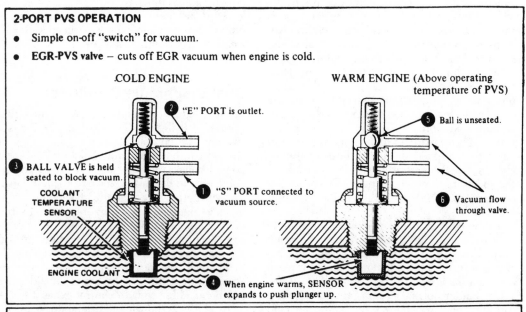

COLD ENGINE

WARM ENGINE (Above operating
temperature of PVS)

**2** "E" PORT is outlet.

**3** BALL VALVE is held
seated to block vacuum.

COOLANT
TEMPERATURE
SENSOR

**1** "S" PORT connected to
vacuum source.

ENGINE COOLANT

**4** When engine warms, SENSOR
expands to push plunger up.

**5** Ball is unseated.

**6** Vacuum flow
through valve.

## 3-PORT PVS OPERATION

- **EGR/CSC** – switches EGR vacuum from EGR system to distributor advance with cold engine.
- **Cold Start Spark Advance (CSSA)** – supplies manifold vacuum to distributor below 125° F. coolant temperature.
- **Coolant Spark Control (CSC)** – cuts off distributor advance below hot engine temperature.
- **Cooling PVS** – switches advance vacuum from spark port to manifold vacuum if engine overheats.

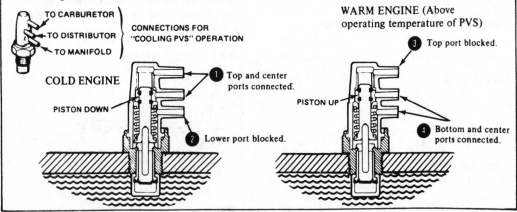

TO CARBURETOR

TO DISTRIBUTOR

TO MANIFOLD

CONNECTIONS FOR
"COOLING PVS" OPERATION

COLD ENGINE

PISTON DOWN

**1** Top and center
ports connected.

**2** Lower port blocked.

WARM ENGINE (Above
operating temperature of PVS)

**3** Top port blocked.

PISTON UP

**4** Bottom and center
ports connected.

**Ported vacuum switch operation**

## Ported Vacuum Switch (Distributor Vacuum Control Valve)

Ported vacuum switches are used to switch vacuum signals with varying engine coolant temperatures. They may have two, three or four vacuum ports and, on models equipped with catalytic converters and Thermactor systems, a set of electrical contacts. There may be as many as three or four separate ported vacuum switches, each with its own special function. PVS switches may be used to cut off exhaust gas recirculation until a predetermined engine temperature is reached, to switch vacuum signals on an ignition spark control system in order to improve cold start driveability, or to provide extra ignition advance and subsequent higher idle speed should the engine begin to overheat. They may also be used to vent Thermactor air pump air to the atmosphere under certain engine conditions, or to regulate a vacuum operated heat control in the exhaust manifold.

Ported vacuum switch

## Spark Delay Valve

The spark delay valve is a plastic, spring-loaded, color-coaded valve which is installed in the vacuum line to the distributor advance diaphragm. Under heavy throttle application, the valve will close, blocking normal carbu-

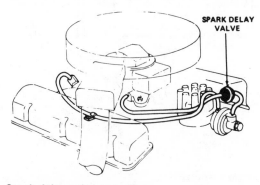

SPARK DELAY VALVE

Spark delay valve operation

retor vacuum to the distributor. After the designated period of closing time, the valve opens, restoring the carburetor vacuum to the distributor.

## Exhaust Gas Recirculation System

All Granadas and Monarchs are equipped with exhaust gas recirculation (EGR) systems to control oxides of nitrogen.

On V6 and V8 engines, exhaust gases travel through the exhaust gas crossover passage in the intake manifold. A portion of these gases are diverted into a spacer which is mounted under the carburetor. The EGR control valve, which is attached to the rear of the spacer, consists of a vacuum diaphragm with an attached plunger which normally block off exhaust gases from entering the intake manifold. On most in-line six cylinder engines, an external tube carries exhaust manifold gases to the carburetor spacer. On all models, the EGR valve is controlled by a vacuum line from the carburetor which passes through a ported vacuum switch. The EGR ported vacuum switch provides a vacuum to the EGR valve at coolant temperature above 125°F. The vacuum diaphragm then opens the EGR valve permitting exhaust gases to flow through the carburetor spacer and enter the intake manifold where they combine with the fuel mixture and enter the combustion chambers. The exhaust gases are relatively oxygen-free, and tend to dilute the combustion charge. This lowers peak combustion temperature thereby reducing oxides of nitrogen.

## EGR System Venturi Vacuum Amplifier

The EGR systems most Monarchs and Granadas include a venturi vacuum amplifier (VVA). The amplifier is used to boost a relatively weak venturi vacuum signal in the throat of the carburetor into a strong intake manifold vacuum signal to operate the EGR valve. By matching venturi air flow to EGR flow more closely, driveability is improved.

The amplifier features a vacuum reservoir and check valve to maintain an adequate vacuum supply regardless of variations in engine mainfold vacuum. Also used in conjunction with the amplifier is a relief valve, which will cancel the output EGR vacuum signal whenever the venturi vacuum signal is equal to, or greater than, the intake manifold vacuum. Thus, the EGR valve may close at or near wide-open throttle acceleration, when maximum power is needed.

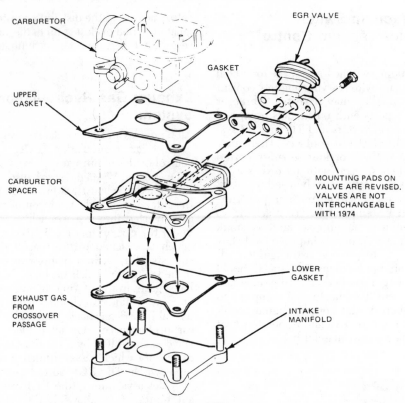

**Spacer entry EGR system**

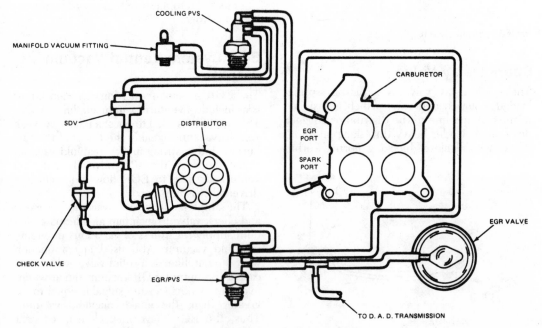

**Typical EGR/CSC system schematic**

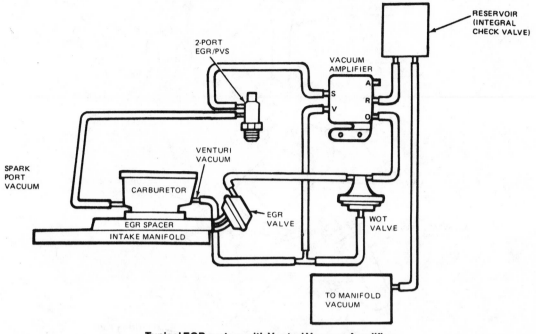

**Typical EGR system with Venturi Vacuum Amplifier**

## EGR/Coolant Spark Control (CSC) System

The EGR/CSC system regulates both distributor spark advance and the EGR valve operation according to coolant temperature by sequentially switching vacuum signals.

The major EGR/CSC system components are:

- 95°F EGR-PVS valve
- Spark Delay Valve (SDV)
- Vacuum check valve

When the engine coolant temperature is below 82°F, the EGR-PVS valve admits carburetor EGR port vacuum (occurring at about 2,500 rpm) directly to the distributor advance diaphragm, through the one-way check valve.

At the same time, the EGR-PVS valve shuts off carburetor EGR vacuum to the EGR valve and transmission diaphragm.

When engine coolant temperature is 95°F and above, the EGR-PVS valve is actuated and directs carburetor EGR vacuum to the EGR valve and transmission instead of the distributor. At temperatures between 82°–95°F, the EGR-PVS valve may be open, closed, or in midposition.

The SDV valve delays carburetor spark vacuum to the distributor advance diaphragm by restricting the vacuum signal through the SDV valve for a predetermined time. During normal acceleration, little or no vacuum is admitted to the distributor advance diaphragm until acceleration is completed, because of (1) the

time delay of the SDV valve and (2) the rerouting of EGR port vacuum if the engine coolant temperature is 95°F or higher.

The check valve blocks off vacuum signal from the SDV to the EGR-PVS so that carburetor spark vacuum will not be dissipated when the EGR-PVS is actuated above 95°F.

## Thermactor System

The Thermactor emission control system makes use of a belt-driven air pump to inject fresh air into the hot exhaust stream through the engine exhaust ports. The result is the extended burning of those fumes which were not completely ignited in the combustion chamber, and the subsequent reduction of some of the hydrocarbon and carbon monoxide content of the exhaust emissions into harmless carbon dioxide and water.

The Thermactor system is composed of the following components:

1. Air supply pump (belt-driven)
2. Air bypass valve
3. Check valves
4. Air manifolds (internal or external)
5. Air supply tubes (on external manifolds only)

Air for the Thermactor system is cleaned by means of a centrifugal filter fan mounted on the air pump driveshaft. The air filter does not require a replaceable element.

To prevent excessive pressure, the air pump is equipped with a pressure relief valve which

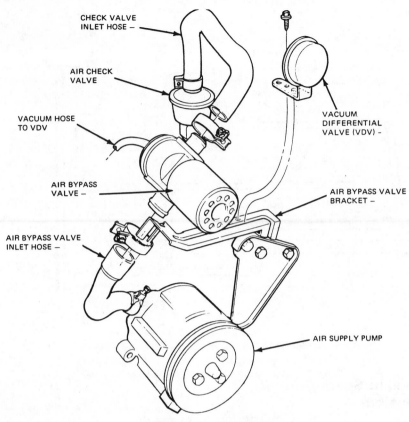

CHECK VALVE
INLET HOSE —

AIR CHECK
VALVE

VACUUM HOSE
TO VDV

AIR BYPASS
VALVE —

AIR BYPASS VALVE
INLET HOSE —

VACUUM
DIFFERENTIAL
VALVE (VDV) -

AIR BYPASS VALVE
BRACKET —

AIR SUPPLY PUMP

**Thermactor system**

uses a replaceable plastic plug to control the pressure setting.

The Thermactor air pump has sealed bearings, which are lubricated for the life of the unit, and preset rotor vane and bearing clearances, which do not require any periodic adjustments.

The air supply from the pump is controlled by the air bypass valve, sometimes called a dump valve. During deceleration, the air bypass valve opens, momentarily diverting the air supply through a silencer and into the atmosphere, thus preventing backfires within the exhaust system.

A check valve is incorporated in the air inlet side of the air manifolds. Its purpose is to prevent exhaust gases from backing up into the Thermactor system. This valve is especially important in the event of drive belt failure and during deceleration, when the air bypass valve is dumping the air supply.

The air manifolds and air supply tubes channel the air from the Thermactor air pump into the exhaust ports of each cylinder, thus completing the cycle of the Thermactor system.

The Thermactor system used on cars with catalytic converters incorporates several com-

ponents to prevent excessive converter temperatures from developing. Since the catalyst requires large quantities of oxygen to function, an air bypass valve and a vacuum differential (VDV) valve are used to control temperatures by dumping air from the Thermactor pump to

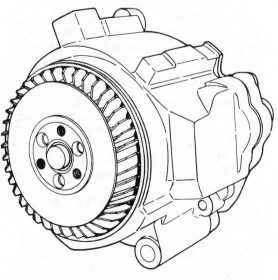

**Air pump**

the atmosphere instead of delivering it to the catalyst.

The purpose of these valves is to "dump" air during periods of vacuum failure, the rich exhaust gas condition during deceleration, prevent backfire when the exhaust gases are overly rich and provide pressure relief (due to excessive air pump volume or restriction downstream).

The air bypass valve used with catalytic converters differs from the valve used on cars without converters and can be identified by the *vacuum port on top of the valve*. The valve functions as follows: During normal operation, engine intake manifold vacuum applied through the VDV holds the valve upward, allowing Thermactor air to flow to the cylinder head(s) and blocking the vent port. When engine intake manifold vacuum rises or drops sharply (such as during acceleration or deceleration, or system blockage or failure), the VDV operates and momentarily cuts off the vacuum to the bypass valve. The spring pulls the stem down, seating the valve to cut off pump air to the exhaust manifold, and opening the dump valve at the lower end of the bypass valve to momentarily divert the pump air to the atmosphere. In the case of excess pump volume or a downstream restriction, the excess pressure will unseat the valve in the lower portion of the bypass valve and allow a partial flow of pump air to the atmosphere. At the same time, the valve in the upper part of the bypass is still unseated, allowing partial flow of pump air to the exhaust manifold to meet system requirements.

The vacuum differential valve (VDV) controls the operation of the new bypass valve used with catalytic converter equipped systems.

The VDV is inserted in the vacuum control line to the bypass valve and serves to cut off the vacuum and deenergize the bypass valve. The differential valve consists of a diaphragm connected to a dump valve that controls the vacuum to the bypass valve. During normal operation, vacuum is equalized on both sides of the diaphragm and the spring holds the dump valve closed. When sudden higher than normal vacuum is encountered, such as under deceleration conditions, vacuum is higher on the dump valve side of the diaphragm and the diaphragm operates the dump valve. As the dump valve operates, the vacuum signal to the bypass valve is diverted through the built-in filter system to atmosphere. When the vacuum bleeding through the bypass timing orifice in the VDV has equalized on both sides of the diaphragm, the diaphragm return spring once again closes the dump valve and applies

vacuum to the bypass valve, which again applies pump air to the exhaust ports.

## PULSED AIR TYPE

Some 4 and 6 cylinder engines are equipped with an air injection system called pulse air or Thermactor II. The system does not use an air pump; instead, it uses the natural pulses present in the exhaust system to pull air into the exhaust manifold through pulsed air valves. The pulse air valve is connected to the exhaust manifold with a long tube and to the air cleaner with a hose.

### Troubleshooting

1. Check that air can flow freely through the air cleaner to the check valve.
2. Blow through the check valve, toward the manifold, then attempt to suck back through the valve. The valve should flow freely in the direction of the exhaust manifold only. If it doesn't, replace the valve.

## Vacuum-Operated Heat Control Valve (VOHV)

To further aid cold start driveability during engine warmup, 1975–76 V8 engines use a VOHV located between the exhaust manifold and the exhaust inlet (header) pipe.

When the engine is first started, the valve is closed, blocking exhaust gases from exiting from one bank of cylinders. These gases are then diverted back through the intake manifold crossover passage under the carburetor. The result is quick heat to the carburetor and choke.

The VOHV is controlled by a ported vacuum switch which uses manifold vacuum to keep the vacuum motor on the valve closed until the coolant reaches a predetermined "warm-up" valve. When the engine is warmed up, the PVS shuts off vacuum to the VOHV, and a strong return spring opens the VOHV butterfly.

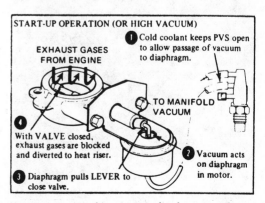

Vacuum operated heat control valve operation

## Catalytic Converter System

Catalytic Converters are used to clean up engine exhaust emissions. Your car may be equipped with one or two converters. Models having only one converter, in the exhaust system, have the "Conventional Oxidation Catalyst" (COC) converter. The COC acts on two of the major pollutants-unburned hydrocarbons (HC) and carbon monoxide (CO). If the exhaust system has two converters, the first (and usually smaller converter, called a "Three-Way Catalyst" (TWC), is designed to control oxides of nitrogen ($NO_x$).

The TWC converter operates on the exhaust gases as they arrive from the engine. As the gases flow from the TWC to the COC converter, they mix with air from the air pump

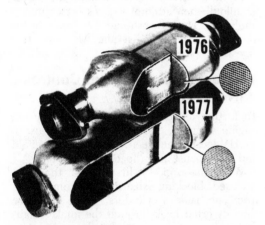

**Typical catalytic converters**

**This is the hot idle compensator, found in the PCV valve line on certain models. It requires no service**

injected into a mixing chamber. This air is required for proper oxidation in the COC converter.

CAUTION: *The temperatures of the exhaust system is very high. Never work on any part of the system until it has cooled down. Use special care when working around a converter, they reach a very high temperature in a very short time.*

*The continued use of leaded gas in a converter equipped car will clog the system and render the converter useless.*

## Feedback Carburetor Electronic Engine Control

This system actually consists of three subsystems: a two part catalytic converter, a Thermactor (air pump) system, and an electronically controlled feedback carburetor.

The converter consists of two catalytic converters in one shell. The front section is designed to control all three engine emissions ($NO_x$, HC, and CO). The rear section acts only on HC and CO. There is a space between the two sections which serves as a mixing chamber. Air is pumped into this area by the Thermactor system to assist in the oxidation of HC and CO.

The Thermactor system is the same as that found on conventional Ford models, with the addition of a second air control valve and a second exhaust check valve.

An electronically controlled feedback carburetor (Motorcraft model 6500 or 7200/2700) is used to precisely calibrate fuel metering. The air/fuel ratio is externally controlled and variable. It is adjusted according to conditions by the Electronic Control Unit (ECU), 1978–79, or the Microprocessor Control Unit (MCU), 1980 and later. There are two modes of operation: closed loop control and open loop control. Under closed loop operation, each component in the chain is sensitive to the signals sent by the other components. This means that the carburetor mixture is being controlled by the vacuum regulator/solenoid, which is adjusted by the control unit, which is receiving signals from the oxygen sensor in the exhaust manifold, which is measuring a mixture determined by the carburetor, and so on. In this case, the feedback loop is complete. Under open loop operation, the carburetor air/fuel mixture is controlled directly by the control unit according to a predetermined setting. Open loop operation takes place when the coolant temperature is below 125°F, or when the throttle is closed, during idle or deceleration.

The control unit receives signals from the exhaust gas oxygen sensor, the throttle angle vacuum switch, and the cold temperature vacuum switch, analyzes them, and sends out commands to the vacuum solenoid/regulator, which in turn adjusts, by means of vacuum, the height of the carburetor fuel metering rod. In this way, the fuel mixture is adjusted according to conditions. The control unit also varies the trensition time from rich to lean (and vice versa) according to engine rpm. The rpm signal is taken from the coil connector TACH terminal.

There are two differences between the ECU, used in 1978 and 1979, and the MCU, used in 1980 and later models. The MCU is programmable, enabling it to be used with many different engine calibrations. Additionally, the MCU controls the Thermactor solenoid valves, thus directing the air flow to the exhaust manifold, the catalytic converter mixing chamber, or the atmosphere when air flow is not needed or wanted.

Because of the complicated nature of the Ford system, special diagnostic tools are necessary for troubleshooting and repair. No attempt at testing or repair should be made unless both the Feedback Control Tester (Ford part no T78L-50-FBC-1) and a digital volt/ohmmeter (Ford part no. T78L-50-DVOM) are available. A tachometer, vacuum gauge, hand vacuum pump and gauge, and a special throttle rpm tool are also required for diagnosis. No troubleshooting procedures will be given here, since they are supplied with the testing equipment.

## Component Service

### POSITIVE CRANKCASE VENTILATION SYSTEM

1. Remove the PCV system components, filler cap, PCV valve, hoses, tubes, fittings, etc. from the engine.

2. Soak the rubber ventilation hose(s) in a low volatility petroleum base solvent.

3. Clean the rubber ventilation hose(s) by passing a suitable cleaning brush through them.

4. Thoroughly wash the rubber hoses in a low volatility petroleum base solvent and dry with compressed air.

5. Thoroughly wash the crankcase breather cap, if so equipped, in a low volatility petroleum base solvent and shake dry. Do not dry with compressed air; damage to the filtering media may result.

6. Thoroughly clean tubes, fittings, connections to assure unobstructed flow of emission gases.

7. Install new PCV valve and reinstall previously removed hoses, tubes, fittings, etc. to their proper location.

8. Replace any system component that shows signs of damage, wear or deterioration as required.

9. Replace any hose or tube that cannot be cleaned satisfactorily.

### FUEL EVAPORATIVE CONTROL SYSTEM

The only service performed on this system is the replacement of the charcoal canister at the intervals listed in the maintenance schedule in Chapter 1.

### EXHAUST GAS RECIRCULATION SYSTEM

NOTE: *Models using unleaded fuel do not require regular EGR system cleaning.*

#### EGR Valve Cleaning

Remove the EGR valve for cleaning. Do not strike or pry on the valve diaphragm housing or supports, as this may damage the valve operating mechanism and/or change the valve

The EGR valve is in the back of the carburetor

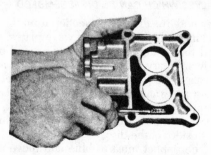

Clean the passages in the carburetor spacer with a wire brush

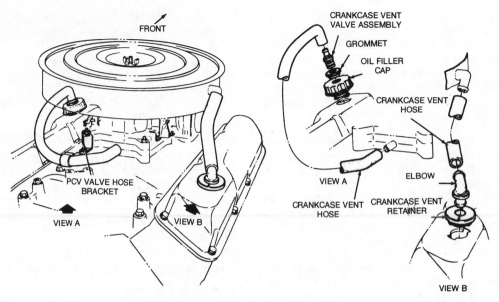

**V8 engine PCV system components**

**Cleaning the EGR valve orifice**

calibration. Check orifice hole in the EGR valve body for deposits. A small hand drill of no more than 0.060-inch diameter may be used to clean the hole if plugged. Extreme care must be taken to avoid enlarging the hole or damaging the surface of the orifice plate.

*VALVES WHICH CANNOT BE DISASSEMBLED*

Valves which are riveted or otherwise permanently assembled should be replaced if highly contaminated; they cannot be cleaned.

*VALVES WHICH CAN BE DISASSEMBLED*

Separate the diaphragm section from the main mounting body. Clean the valve plates, stem, and the mounting plate, using a small power driven rotary wire brush. Take care not to damage the parts. Remove deposits between stem and valve disc by using a steel blade or shim, approximately 0.028 inch thick, in a sawing motion around the stem shoulder at both sides of the disc.

The poppet must wobble and move axially before reassembly.

Clean the cavity and passages in the main body of the valve with a power driven rotary wire brush. If the orifice plate has a hole less than 0.450 inch, it must be removed for cleaning. Remove all loosened debris, using shop compressed air. Reassemble the diaphragm section on the main body using a new gasket between them. Torque the attaching screws to specification. Clean the orifice plate and the counterbore in the valve body. Reinstall the orifice plate, using a small amount of contact cement to retain the plate in place during assembly of the valve to the carburetor spacer. Apply cement only to outer edges of the orifice plate to avoid restriction of the orifice.

## EGR Supply Passages and Carburetor Spacer Cleaning

Remove the carburetor and carburetor spacer on engines so equipped. Clean the supply tube with a small power driven rotary wire brush or blast cleaning equipment. Clean the ex-

**External exhaust gas supply tube—six cylinder**

haust gas passages in the spacer, using a suitable wire brush and/or scraper. The machined holes in the spacer can be cleaned by using a suitable round wire brush. Hard encrusted material should be probed loose first, then brushed out. On six-cylinder engines, the external tube from the exhaust manifold must be removed and cleaned with a brush.

### EGR Exhaust Gas Channel Cleaning

Clean the exhaust gas channel, where applicable, in the intake manifold, using a suitable carbon scraper. Clean the exhaust gas entry port in the intake manifold by hand, passing a suitable drill bit through the holes to auger out the deposits. Do not use a wire brush. The manifold riser bore(s) should be suitably plugged during the above action to prevent any of the residue from entering the induction system

### *THERMACTOR AIR PUMP DRIVE BELT REPLACEMENT AND/OR ADJUSTMENT*

1. Loosen the air pump adjusting bolt. Loosen the air pump-to-mounting bracket bolt and push the air pump toward the cylinder block. Remove the belt.

2. Install a new drive belt. With a suitable bar, pry against the rear cover of the air pump to obtain the specified belt tension.

3. Retighten the pump mounting bolts.

NOTE: *It is highly advisable to use a belt tension gauge (T63L-8620-A) to check belt tension. When using this tool, follow the manufacturer's instructions and specifications. Any belt which has been operated for 10 minutes or more is considered to be a "used" belt and should be adjusted accordingly.*

In the event that a belt tension gauge is not available, the thumb deflection method of belt tension adjustment must be employed. This method is discussed in Chapter 1.

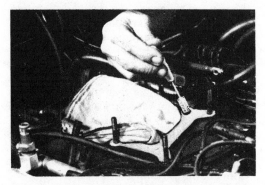

**Cleaning EGR entry port in the intake manifold**

## Component Testing

### *POSITIVE CRANKCASE VENTILATION SYSTEM*

#### PCV Valve Test

1. See if any deposits are present in the carburetor passages, the oil filler cap or the hoses. Clean these as required.

2. Connect a tachometer, as instructed by its manufacturer, to the engine.

3. With engine idling, do one of the following:

   a. Remove the PCV valve hose from the crankcase or the oil filter connection.

   b. On cars with the PCV valve located in a grommet on the valve cover, remove both the valve and the grommet.

NOTE: *If the valve and the hoses are not clogged up, a hissing sound should be present.*

4. Check the tachometer reading. Place a finger over the valve or hose opening (a suction should be felt).

5. Check the tachometer again. The engine speed should have dropped at least 50 rpm. It should return to normal when the finger is removed from the opening.

6. If the engine does not change speed or if the change is less than 50 rpm, the hose is clogged or the valve is defective. Check the hose first. If the hose is not clogged, replace, do not attempt to repair, the PCV valve.

7. Test the new valve in the above manner, to make sure that it is operating properly.

### *HEATED AIR INTAKE SYSTEM*

#### Duct and Valve Assembly Test

1. Either start with a cold engine or remove the air cleaner from the engine for at least half an hour. While cooling the air cleaner, leave the engine compartment hood open.

2. Tape a thermometer, of known accuracy, to the inside of the air cleaner so that it is near the temperature sensor unit. Install the air cleaner on the engine but do not fasten its securing nut.

3. Start the engine. With the engine cold and the outside temperature less than 90°F, the door should be in the "heat on" position (closed to outside air).

4. Operate the throttle lever rapidly to one-half the three-quarters of its opening and release it. The air door should open to allow outside air to enter and then close again.

5. Allow the engine to warm up to normal temperature. Watch the door. When it opens to the outside air, remove the cover from the air cleaner, the temperature should be over

90°F and no more than 130°F; 105°F is about normal. If the door does not work within these temperature ranges, or fails to work at all, check for linkage or door binding.

If binding is not present and the air door is not working, proceed with the vacuum tests given below. If these indicate no faults in the vacuum motor and the door is not working, the temperature sensor is defective and must be replaced.

### Vacuum Motor Test

Be sure that the vacuum hose that runs between the temperature switch and the vacuum motor is not pinched by the retaining clip under the air cleaner. This could prevent the air door from closing.

1. Check all the vacuum lines and fittings for leaks. Correct any leaks. If none are found, proceed with the test.
2. Remove the hose which runs from the sensor to the vacuum motor. Run a hose directly from the manifold vacuum source to the vacuum motor.
3. If the motor closes the air door, it is functioning properly and the temperature sensor is defective.
4. If the motor does *not* close the door and no binding is present in its operation, the vacuum motor is defective and must be replaced.

   NOTE: *If an alternate vacuum source is applied to the motor, insert a vacuum gauge in the line by using a T-fitting. Apply at least 9 in. Hg of vacuum in order to operate the motor.*

### DUAL DIAPHRAGM DISTRIBUTOR ADVANCE AND RETARD MECHANISMS TEST

1. Connect a timing light to the engine. Check the ignition timing.

   NOTE: *Before proceeding with the tests, disconnect any spark control devices, distributor vacuum valves, etc. If these are left connected, inaccurate results may be obtained.*
2. Remove the retard hose from the distributor and plug it. Increase the engine speed. The timing should advance. If it fails to do so, then the vacuum unit is faulty and must be replaced.
3. Check the timing with the engine at normal idle speed. Unplug and retard hose and connect it to the vacuum unit. The timing should instantly be retarded from 4°–10°. If this does not occur, the retard diaphragm has a leak and the vacuum unit must be replaced.

### PORTED VACUUM SWITCH (DISTRIBUTOR VACUUM CONTROL VALVE) TEST

1. Check the routing and connection of all vacuum hoses.
2. Attach a tachometer to the engine.
3. Bring the engine up to the normal operating temperature. The engine must not be overheated.
4. Note the engine rpm, with the transmission in neutral, and the throttle in the curb idle position.
5. Disconnect the vacuum hose from the intake manifold at the termperature-sensing valve. Plug or clamp the hose.
6. Note the idle rpm with the hose disconnected. If there is no change in rpm, the valve is good. If there is a drop of 100 or more rpm, the valve should be replaced. Replace the vacuum line.
7. Check to make sure that the all-season cooling mixture meets specifications, and that the correct radiator cap is in place and functioning.
8. Block the radiator air flow to induce a higher-than-normal temperature condition.
9. Continue to operate until the engine temperature or heat indicator shows above normal.

   If engine speed by this time has increased 100 or more rpm, the temperature-sensing valve is satisfactory. If not, it should be replaced.

### SPARK DELAY VALVE TEST

NOTE: *If the distributor vacuum line contains a cut-off solenoid, it must be open during this test.*
1. Detach the vacuum line from the distributor at the spark delay valve end. Connect a vacuum gauge to the valve, in its place.
2. Connect a tachometer to the engine. Start the engine and rapidly increase its speed to 2,000 rpm with the transmission in neutral.
3. As soon as the engine speed is increased, the vacuum gauge reading should drop to zero.
4. Hold the engine speed at a steady 2,000 rpm. It should take longer than two seconds for the gauge to register 6 in. Hg. If it takes less than two seconds, the valve is defective and must be replaced.
5. If it takes longer than the number of seconds specified in the application chart for the gauge to reach 6 in. Hg, disconnect the vacuum gauge from the spark delay valve. Disconnect the hose which runs from the spark delay valve to the carburetor at the valve end. Connect the vacuum gauge to this hose.

6. Start the engine and increase its speed to 2,000 rpm. The gauge should indicate 10–16 in. Hg. If it does not, there is a blockage in the carburetor vacuum port or else the hose itself is plugged or broken. If the gauge reading is within specification, the valve is defective.

7. Reconnect all vacuum lines and remove the tachometer, once testing is completed.

## EXHAUST GAS RECIRCULATION SYSTEM

### System Test

1. Allow the engine to warm up, so that the coolant temperature has reached at least 125°F.

2. Disconnect the vacuum hose which runs from the temperature cut-in valve to the EGR valve at the EGR valve end. Connect a vacuum gauge to this hose with a T-fitting.

3. Increase engine speed. Do not exceed half throttle or 3,000 rpm. The gauge should indicate a vacuum. If no vacuum is present, check the following:

a. The carburetor—look for a clogged vacuum port.

b. The vacuum hoses—including the vacuum hoses to the transmission modulator.

c. The temperature cut-in valve—if no vacuum is present at its outlet with the engine temperature above 125°F and vacuum available from the carburetor, the valve is defective.

4. If all the above tests are positive, check the EGR valve itself.

5. Connect an outside vacuum source and a vacuum gauge to the valve.

6. Apply vacuum to the EGR valve. The valve should open at 3–10 in. Hg, the engine idle speed should slow down and the idle quality should become more rough.

7. If this does not happen, i.e., the EGR valve remains closed, the EGR valve is defective and must be replaced.

8. If the valve stem moves but the idle remains the same, the valve orifice is clogged and must be cleaned.

NOTE: *If an outside vacuum source is not available, disconnect the hose which runs between the EGR valve and the temperature cut-in valve and plug the hose connections on the cut-in valve. Connect the EGR valve hose to a source of intake manifold vacuum and watch the idle. The results should be the same as in steps 6–7, above.*

### Temperature Cut-In Valve EGR Ported Vacuum Switch

#### VALVE BENCH TEST

1. Remove the valve from the engine.

2. Connect an outside source of vacuum to the top port on the valve. Leave the bottom port vented to the atmosphere.

3. Use ice or an aerosol spray to cool the valve below 60°F.

4. Apply 20 in. Hg vacuum to the valve. The valve should hold a minimum of 19 in. Hg vacuum for 5 minutes without leaking down.

5. Leave the vacuum source connected to the valve and place it, along with a high temperature thermometer, into a nonmetallic, heat-resistant container full of water.

6. Heat the water. The vacuum in the valve should drop to zero once the temperature of the water reaches about 125°F.

7. Replace the valve if it fails either of the tests.

#### VACUUM MODULATOR TEST

NOTE: *The vacuum modulator is used only with an automatic transmission.*

1. Remove the vacuum modulator from the car.

2. Connect the modulator to an outside vacuum source: a distributor tester, for example.

NOTE: *The vacuum source should be adjusted to supply 18 in. Hg, with the end of the vacuum line blocked off.*

3. Connect the vacuum line from the vacuum source to the EGR port on the vacuum modulator.

4. The vacuum modulator should hold the 18 in. Hg reading. If it does not, then the diaphragm is leaking and must be replaced.

## EGR VENTURI VACUUM AMPLIFIER SYSTEM

### System Test

The amplifiers have built-in calibrations and no external adjustments are required. If the amplifier tests reveal it is malfunctioning, replace the amplifier. All connections are located on one side of the amplifier. A vacuum connector and hose assembly is used to assure that proper connections are made at the amplifier. The amplifier is retained with a sheet-metal screw.

1. Operate the engine until normal operating temperatures are reached.

2. Before the vacuum amplifier is checked, inspect all other basic components of the EGR System (EGR valve, EGR/PVS valve, hoses, routing, etc.).

3. Check vacuum amplifier connections for proper routing and installation. If necessary, refer to the typical vacuum amplifier schematic.

4. Remove hose at EGR valve.

5. Connect vacuum gauge to EGR hose. Gauge must read in increments of at least 1 in. Hg graduation.

6. Remove hose at carburetor venturi (leave off).

7. With engine at curb idle speed, vacuum gauge reading should be with ±0.3 in. Hg of specified bias valve as shown in amplifier specifications for other than zero bias. Zero bias may read from 0 to 0.5 in. Hg. If out of specification, replace amplifier.

8. Depress accelerator and release after engine has reached 1500 to 2000 rpm. After engine has returned to idle, the vacuum must return to bias noted in step 7. If bias has changed, replace amplifier. Also, if vacuum shows a marked increase (greater than 1 in. Hg) during acceleration period, the amplifier should be replaced.

9. Hook up venturi hose at carburetor with engine at curb idle rpm. If a sizeable increase in output vacuum is observed, (more than 0.5 in. Hg above step 7), check idle speed. High idle speed could increase output vacuum due to venturi vacuum increase. See engine decal for correct idle specifications.

10. Check amplifier reservoir and connections as follows: Disconnect external reservoir hose at amplifier and AP or plug. Depress accelerator rapidly to 1500 to 2000 rpm. The vacuum should increase to 4 in. Hg or more. If out of specifications, replace amplifier.

## THERMACTOR SYSTEM

Before performing an extensive diagnosis of the emission control systems, verify that all specifications on the Certification Label are met, because the following systems or components may cause symptoms that appear to be emission related.

   a. Improper vacuum connections
   b. Vacuum leaks
   c. Ignition timing
   d. Plugs, wires, cap and rotor
   e. Carburetor float level
   f. Carburetor main metering jets
   g. Choke operation

### Fabricating a Test Gauge Adapter

In order to test the three major components of a Thermactor system (air pump, check valve and bypass valve), a pressure gauge and adapter are required. The adapter can be fabricated as follows:

  1. Obtain these items:

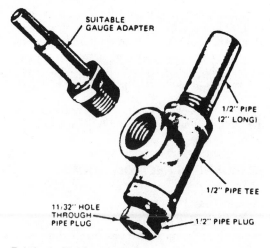

**Fabricated test gauge adapter**

   a. ½-inch pipe tee
   b. ½-inch pipe, 2 inches long and threaded at one end
   c. ½-inch pipe plug
   d. ½-inch reducer bushing or other suitable gauge adapter

2. Apply sealer to threaded ends of pipe, plug and bushing. Assemble as shown in the illustration.

3. Drill ¹¹/₃₂ inch (0.3437) diameter hold through center of pipe plug. Clean out chips after drilling.

4. Attach pressure gauge with ¼-psi increments to bushing or adapter.

### Air Pump Tests

CAUTION: *Do not hammer on, pry, or bend the pump housing while tightening the drive belt or testing the pump.*

#### BELT TENSION AND AIR LEAKS

1. Before proceeding with the tests, check the pump drive belt tension to see if it is within specifications.

2. Turn the pump by hand. If it has seized, the belt will slip, producing noise. Disregard any chirping, squealing, or rolling sounds from inside the pump; these are normal when it is turned by hand.

3. Check the hoses and connections for leaks. Hissing or a blast of air is indicative of a leak. Soapy water, applied lightly around the area in question, is a good method for detecting leaks.

#### AIR OUTPUT TESTS

1. Disconnect the air supply hose at the antibackfire valve.

2. Connect a vacuum gauge, using a suitable adaptor, to the air supply hose.

NOTE: *If there are two hoses plug the second one.*

3. With the engine at normal operating temperature, increase the idle speed and watch the vacuum gauge.

4. The air flow from the pump should be steady and fall between 2–6 psi. If it is unsteady or falls below this, the pump is defective and must be replaced.

### PUMP NOISE DIAGNOSIS

The air pump is normally noisy; as engine speed increases, the noise of the pump will rise in pitch. The rolling sound the pump bearings make is normal; however, if this sound becomes objectionable at certain speeds, the pump is defective and will have to be replaced.

A continual hissing sound from the air pump pressure relief valve at idle, indicates a defective valve. Replace the relief valve.

If the pump rear bearing fails, a continual knocking sound will be heard. Since the rear bearing is not separately replaceable, the pump will have to be replaced as an assembly.

### Check Valve Test

1. Before starting the test, check all of the hoses and connections for leaks.

2. Detach the air supply hose(s) from the check valve(s).

3. Insert a suitable probe into the check valve and depress the plate. Release it; the plate should return to its original position against the valve seat. If binding is evident, replace the valve.

4. Repeat step 3 if two valves are used.

5. With the engine running at normal operating temperature, gradually increase its speed to 1,500 rpm. Check for exhaust gas leakage. If any is present, replace the valve assembly.

NOTE: *Vibration and flutter of the check valve at idle speed is a normal condition and does not mean that the valve should be replaced.*

### Air Bypass Valve Test

1. Detach the hose, which runs from the bypass valve to the check valve, at the bypass valve hose connection.

2. Connect a tachometer to the engine. With the engine running at normal idle speed, check to see that air is flowing from the bypass valve hose connection.

3. Speed the engine up, so that it is running at 1,500–2,000 rpm. Allow the throttle to snap shut. The flow of air from the bypass valve at the check valve hose connection should stop momentarily and air should then flow from the

exhaust port on the valve body or the silencer assembly.

4. Repeat step 3 several times. If the flow of air is not diverted into the atmosphere from the valve exhaust port or if it fails to stop flowing from the hose connection, check the vacuum lines and connections. If these are tight, the valve is defective and requires replacement.

5. A leaking diaphragm will cause the air to flow out both the hose connection and the exhaust port at the same time. If this happens, replace the valve.

## Component Replacement

### PCV VALVE

Disconnect the ventilation hose at the oil filler cap on V8 applications and pull out the PCV valve from its grommet. On six-cylinder engines, disconnect the ventilation hose from its connection at the front of the valve cover and pull out the PCV valve from its grommet. Clean out all of the passageways in the hoses and fittings with a kerosene soaked rag. Install a new PCV valve in its grommet and connect the ventilation hose.

### EVAPORATIVE CONTROL CHARCOAL CANISTER

Loosen and remove the canister mounting bolts from the mounting bracket. Disconnect the purge hose from the air cleaner and the feed hose from the fuel tank. Discard the old canister and install a new unit. Make sure that the hoses are connected properly.

### PORTED VACUUM SWITCH (DISTRIBUTOR VACUUM CONTROL VALVE)

1. Drain about one gallon of coolant out of the radiator.

2. Tag the vacuum hoses that attach to the control valve and disconnect them.

3. Unscrew and remove the control valve.

4. Install the new control valve.

5. Connect the vacuum hoses.

6. Fill the cooling system.

### VACUUM-OPERATED DUCT AND VALVE ASSEMBLY

1. Disconnect the vacuum hose at the vacuum motor.

2. Remove the hex-head cap screws that secure the air intake duct and valve assembly to the air cleaner.

3. Remove the duct and valve assembly from the engine.

4. Position the duct and valve assembly to

the air cleaner and heat stove tube. Install the attaching cap screws.

5. Connect the vacuum line at the vacuum motor.

### SPARK DELAY VALVE

1. Locate the spark delay valve in the distributor vacuum line and disconnect it from the line.

2. Install a new spark delay valve in the line, making sure that the black end of the valve is connected to the line from the carburetor and the color coded end is connected to the line from the spark delay valve to the distributor.

### THERMACTOR AIR PUMP

1. Disconnect the air outlet hose at the air pump.

2. Loosen the pump belt tension adjuster.

3. Disengage the drive belt.

4. Remove the mounting bolt and air pump.

5. To install, position the air pump on the mounting bracket and install the mounting bolt.

6. Place drive belt in pulleys and attach the adjusting arm to the air pump.

7. Adjust the drive belt tension to specifications and tighten the adjusting arm and mounting bolts.

8. Connect the air outlet hose to the air pump.

### THERMACTOR AIR PUMP FILTER FAN

1. Loosen the air pump adjusting arm bolt and mounting bracket bolt to relieve drive belt tension.

2. Remove drive pulley attaching bolts and pull drive pulley off the air pump shaft.

3. Pry the outer disc loose; then, pull off the centrifugal filter fan with slip-joint pliers.

CAUTION: *Do not attempt to remove the metal drive hub.*

4. Install a new filter fan by drawing it into position, using the pulley and bolts as an installer. Draw the fan evenly by alternately tightening the bolts, making certain that the outer edge of the fan slips into the housing.

NOTE: *A slight interference with the housing bore is normal. After a new fan is installed, it may squeal upon initial operation, until its outer diameter sealing lip has worn in, which may require 20 to 30 miles of operation.*

### THERMACTOR CHECK VALVE

1. Disconnect the air supply hose at the valve. (Use a 1¼-inch crowfoot wrench; the valve has standard, righthand pipe thread.)

2. Clean the threads on the air manifold adaptor (air supply tube on V8 engine) with a

wire brush. Do not blow compressed air through the check valve in either direction.

3. Install the check valve and tighten.

4. Connect the air supply hose.

### THERMACTOR AIR BYPASS VALVE

1. Disconnect the air and vacuum hoses at the air bypass valve body.

2. Position the air bypass valve and connect the respective hoses.

## Fuel Pump

### REMOVAL AND INSTALLATION

1. Disconnect the plug and inlet and outlet lines from the fuel pump.

2. Remove the fuel pump retaining bolts and carefully pull the pump and old gasket away from the block.

3. Discard the old gasket. Clean the mating surfaces on the block and position a new gasket on the block, using oil-resistant sealer.

CAUTION: *On V6 engines turn the crankshaft to position the drive eccentric away from the fuel pump arm. Failure to turn the eccentric away can cause stress on mounting threads and strip them out when installing the pump.*

4. Mount the fuel pump and gasket to the engine block, being careful to insert the pump lever (rocker arm) in the engine block, aligning it correctly above the camshaft lobe.

NOTE: *If resistance is felt while positioning the fuel pump on the block, the camshaft lobe is probably on the high position. To ease installation, connect a remote engine starter switch to the engine and "tap" the switch until resistance fades.*

5. While holding the pump securely against the block, install the retaining bolts. Torque the mounting bolts; 4 cyl; 14–21 ft lbs: 6 cyl; 11–19 ft. lbs: V6, 14–21 ft. lbs. and V8, 19–27 ft. lbs.

6. Unplug and reconnect the fuel lines at the pump.

7. Start the engine and check for fuel leaks. Also check for oil leaks where the fuel pump attaches to the block.

### TESTING AND ADJUSTMENT

No adjustments may be made to the fuel pump. Before removing and replacing the old fuel pump, the following test may be made while the pump is still installed on the engine.

1. If a fuel pressure gauge is available, connect the gauge to the engine and operate the engine until the pressure stops rising. Stop the engine and take the reading. If the reading is within the specifications given in the "Tune-Up Specifications" chart in Chapter 2, the

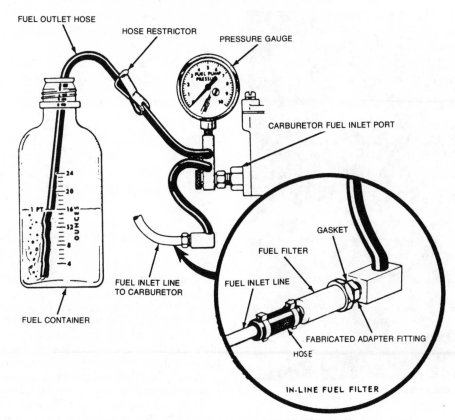

**Fuel pump pressure and capacity test equipment**

malfunction is not in the fuel pump. Also check the pressure drop after the engine is stopped. A large pressure drop below the minimum specification indicates leaky valves. If the pump proves to be satisfactory, check the tank and inlet line.

2. If a fuel pressure gauge is not available, disconnect the fuel line at the pump outlet, place a vessel beneath the pump outlet, and crank the engine. A good pump will force the fuel out of the outlet in steady spurts. A worn diaphragm spring may not provide proper pumping action.

3. As a further test, disconnect and plug the fuel line from the tank at the pump, and hold your thumb over the pump inlet. If the pump is functioning properly, a suction should be felt on your thumb. No suction indicates that the pump diaphragm is leaking or that the diaphragm linkage is worn.

4. Check the crankcase for gasoline. A ruptured diaphragm may leak fuel into the engine.

## Electric Choke

Most Monarchs and Granadas use an electri-

cally assisted choke to reduce exhaust emissions of carbon monoxide during warmup. The system consists of a choke cap, a thermostatic spring, a bimetal sensing disc (switch) and a ceramic position temperature coefficient (PTC) heater.

The choke is powered from the center tap of the alternator, so that current is constantly applied to the temperature sensing disc. The system is grounded through the carburetor body. At temperatures below approximately 60°F, the switch is open and no current is supplied to the ceramic heater, thereby resulting in normal unassisted thermostatic spring choking action. When the temperature rises above about 60°F, the temperature sensing disc closes and current is supplied to the heater, which in turn, acts on the thermostatic spring. Once the heater starts, it causes the thermostatic spring to pull the choke plate(s) open within 1½ minutes, which is sooner than it would open if not assisted.

### ELECTRIC CHOKE OPERATIONAL TEST

1. Detach the electrical lead from the choke cap.

**Electric choke hookup**

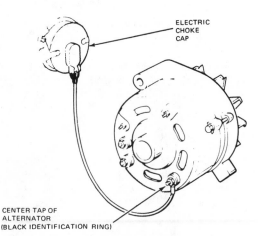

Typical electric assist choke wiring

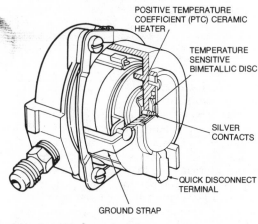

POSITIVE TEMPERATURE
COEFFICIENT (PTC) CERAMIC
HEATER

TEMPERATURE
SENSITIVE
BIMETALLIC DISC

SILVER
CONTACTS

QUICK DISCONNECT
TERMINAL

GROUND STRAP

**Electric choke components**

the lead, since it is not passing current to the choke assist.

CAUTION: *Do not ground the terminal on the alternator while performing step 6.*

7. If the light still does not glow, the fault lies somewhere in the electrical system. Check the system out. If the electrically assisted choke receives power but still does not appear to be functioning properly, reconnect the choke lead and proceed with the rest of the test.

8. Tape the bulb end of the thermometer to the metallic portion of the choke housing.

9. If the electrically assisted choke operates below 55°F, it is defective and must be replaced.

10. Allow the engine to warm up to between 80° and 110°F; at these temperatures the choke should operate for about 1½ minutes.

11. If it does not operate for this length of time, check the bimetallic spring to see if it is connected to the tang on the choke lever.

12. If the spring is connected and the choke is not operating properly, replace the cap assembly.

2. Use a jumper lead to connect the terminal on the choke cap and the wire terminal, so that the electrical circuit is still completed.

3. Start the engine.

4. Hook up a test light between the connector on the choke lead and ground.

5. The test light should glow. If it does not, current is not being supplied to the electrically assisted choke.

6. Connect the test light between the terminal on the alternator and the terminal on the choke cap. If the light now glows, replace

## Carburetors

### THROTTLE SOLENOID (ANTI-DIESELING SOLENOID) TEST

1. Turn the ignition key on and open the throttle. The solenoid plunger should extend (solenoid energize).

2. Turn the ignition off. The plunger should retract, allowing the throttle to close.

NOTE: *With the anti-dieseling solenoid de-energized, the carburetor idle speed adjusting screw must make contact with the throttle shaft to prevent the throttle plates from jamming in the throttle bore when the engine is turned off.*

3. If the solenoid is functioning properly and the engine is still dieseling, check for one of the following:
   a. High idle or engine shut off speed
   b. Engine timing not set to specification
   c. Binding throttle linkage
   d. Too low an octane fuel being used.

Correct any of these problems as necessary.

4. If the solenoid fails to function as outlined in steps 1–2, disconnect the solenoid leads; the solenoid should deenergize. If it does not, it is jammed and must be replaced.

5. Connect the solenoid to a 12 V power source and to ground. Open the throttle so that the plunger can extend. If it does not, the solenoid is defective.

6. If the solenoid is functioning correctly and no other source of trouble can be found, the fault probably lies in the wiring between the solenoid and the ignition switch or in the ignition switch itself. Remember to reconnect the solenoid when finished testing.

## Carburetor Usage

| Engine | Model |
|--------|-------|
| 4 Cylinder | 5200/6500 |
| 6 Cylinder | YFA/1946 |
| V6 | 2150/7200 |
| V8 | 2150/2700/7200 |

### REMOVAL AND INSTALLATION

1. Remove the air cleaner.

2. Disconnect the throttle cable or rod at the throttle lever. Disconnect the distributor vacuum line, EGR line, inline fuel filter, choke heat tube and the positive crankcase ventilation hose at the carburetor.

3. Disconnect the throttle solenoid (if so equipped) and electric choke assist at their connectors.

4. Remove the carburetor retaining nuts. Lift the carburetor off carefully, taking care not to spill any fuel. Remove and discard the carburetor mounting gasket. Remove the carburetor spacer, if so equipped, from the intake manifold.

5. Before reinstalling the carburetor, clean the gasket mounting surfaces of the intake manifold, spacer and carburetor. When using a spacer, use two new gaskets, sandwiching the spacer between the gaskets. If a spacer is not used, only one new carburetor mounting gasket is required.

6. Place the new gasket and spacer (if so equipped) on the carburetor mounting studs. Position the carburetor on the gasket and tighten the retaining nuts by hand. Then tighten the nuts in a crisscross pattern to 10–15 ft. lbs.

7. Connect the throttle linkage, the distributor vacuum line, EGR line, inline fuel filter, choke heat tube, positive crankcase ventilation hose, throttle solenoid and electric choke assist.

8. Adjust the curb idle speed, the idle fuel mixture and the accelerator pump stroke (2150 only). Install the air cleaner.

### OVERHAUL

Efficient carburetion depends greatly on careful cleaning and inspection during overhaul, since dirt, gum, water, or varnish in or on the carburetor parts are often responsible for poor performance.

Overhaul your carburetor in a clean, dust-free area. Carefully disassemble the carburetor, referring often to the exploded views. Keep all similar and lookalike parts segregated during the disassembly and cleaning to avoid accidental interchange during assembly. Make a note of all jet sizes.

When the carburetor is disassembled, wash all parts (except diaphragms, electric choke units, pump plunger, and any other plastic, leather, fiber, or rubber parts) in clean carburetor solvent. Do not leave parts in the solvent any longer than necessary to sufficiently loosen the deposits. Excessive cleaning may remove the special finish from the float bowl and choke valve bodies, leaving those parts unfit for service. Rinse all parts in clean solvent and blow them dry with compressed air or allow them to air dry. Wipe clean all cork, plastic, leather and fiber parts with a clean, lint-free cloth.

Blow out all passages and jets with compressed air and be sure that there are no restrictions or blockages. Never use wire or similar tools to clean jets, fuel passages, or air bleeds. Clean all jets and valves separately to avoid accidental interchange.

Check all parts for wear or damage. If wear or damage is found, replace the defective parts. Especially check the following:

1. Check the float needle and seat for wear. If wear is found, replace the complete assembly.

2. Check the float hinge pin for wear and the float(s) for dents or distortion. Replace the float if fuel has leaked into it.

3. Check the throttle and choke shaft bores for wear on an out-of-round condition. Damage or wear to the throttle arm, shaft, or shaft bore will often require replacement of the throttle body. These parts require a close tolerance of fit; wear may allow air leakage, which could affect starting and idling.

NOTE: *Throttle shafts and bushings are not included in overhaul kits. They can be purchased separately.*

4. Inspect the idle mixture adjusting needles for burrs or grooves. Any such condition requires replacement of the needle, or you will not be able to obtain a satisfactory idle.

5. Test the accelerator pump check valves. They should pass air one way but not the other. Test for proper seating by blowing and sucking on the valve. Replace the valve if necessary. If the valve is satisfactory, wash the valve again to remove breath moisture.

6. Check the bowl cover for warped surfaces with a straightedge.

7. Closely inspect the valves and seats for wear and damage, replacing as necessary.

8. After the carburetor is assembled, check the choke valve for freedom of operation.

Carburetor overhaul kits are recommended for each overhaul. These kits contain all gaskets and new parts to replace those which deteriorate most rapidly. Failure to replace all parts supplied with the kit (especially gaskets) can result in poor performance.

Some carburetor manufacturers supply overhaul kits of three basic types: minor repair: major repair; and gasket kits. Basically, they contain the following;

Minor Repair Kits:
- All gaskets
- Float needle valve
- Volume control screw
- All diaphragms
- Spring for the pump diaphragm

Major Repair Kits:
- All jets and gaskets
- All diaphragms
- Float needle valve
- Volume control screw

- Pump ball valve
- Float
- Complete intermediate rod
- Intermediate pump lever
- Some cover hold-down screws and washers

Gasket Kits:
- All gaskets

After cleaning and checking all components, reassemble the carburetor, using new parts and referring to the exploded view. When reassembling, make sure that all screw and jets are tight in their seats, but do not overtighten as the tips will be distorted. Tighten all screws gradually, in rotation. Do not tighten idle mixture needle valves into their seats; uneven idling will result. Always use new gaskets. Always adjust the float for correct drop and level.

## 5200 Carburetor Adjustment
### *FLOAT LEVEL ADJUSTMENT*

1. Remove the air cleaner.

2. Disconnect the fuel and deceleration valve (if equipped) hoses from the carburetor.

3. Remove the small clip that attaches the choke rod to the choke plate shaft and disconnect the rod from the shaft.

4. Remove the screws that attach the upper body of the carburetor to the main body of the carburetor and carefully lift the upper body off the main body. Be careful not to tear the upper body gasket.

5. Turn the carburetor upper body upside down and measure the clearance between the bottom of each float and the bottom of the carburetor upper body.

6. If the clearance is incorrect, bend the float level adjusting tang to correct.

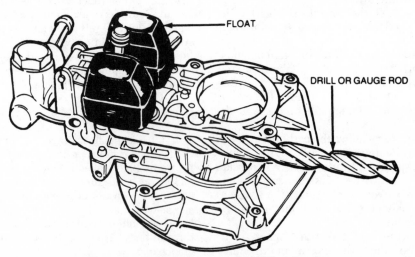

**Measuring the float clearance on 5200 carburetor**

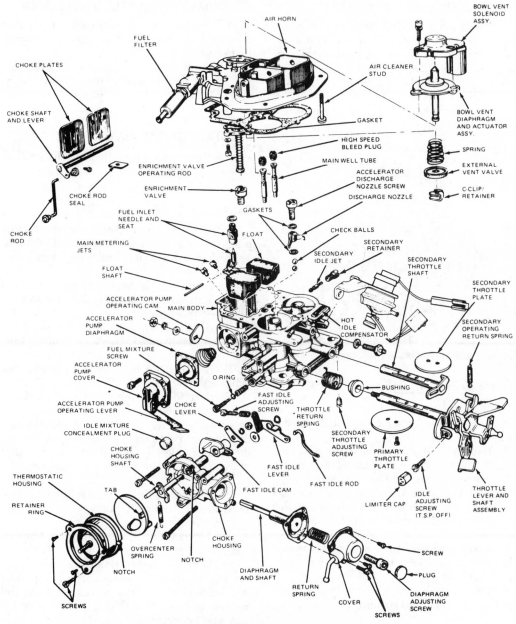

**Motorcraft 5200 carburetor**

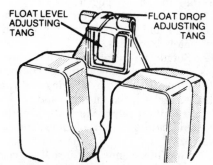

FLOAT LEVEL ADJUSTING TANG

FLOAT DROP ADJUSTING TANG

**Motorcraft 5200 float adjustment**

NOTE: *Both floats must be adjusted to the same clearance.*

7.  Position the upper body and gasket of the main body of the carburetor and connect the choke rod to the choke plate lever. Install the choke rod attaching clip in the hole in the rod.

8.  Install the upper body attaching screws.

9.  Connect the fuel and deceleration valve hoses to the carburetor.

10.  Install the air cleaner.

### FAST IDLE CAM ADJUSTMENT

1. Insert a $5/32$ in. drill between the lower edge of the choke plate and the air horn wall.
2. With the fast idle screw held on the second step of the fast idle cam, measure the clearance between the tang of the choke lever and the arm on the fast idle cam.
3. Bend the choke lever tang to adjust it if it is not up to specification.

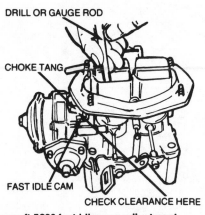

Motorcraft 5200 fast idle cam adjustment

### CHOKE PLATE PULLDOWN ADJUSTMENT

1. Remove the choke thermostatic spring cover.
2. Pull the water cover and the thermostatic spring cover assembly out of the way.
3. Set the fast idle cam on the second step.
4. Push the diaphragm stem against its stop and insert the specified gauge between the lower edge of the choke valve and the air horn wall.
5. Apply sufficient pressure to the upper edge of the choke valve to take up any slack in the choke linkage.
6. Turn the adjusting screw in or out to adjust the choke plate-to-air horn clearance.

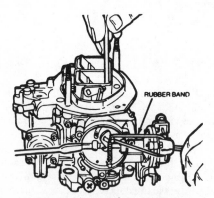

Motorcraft 5200 choke pulldown adjustment

### SECONDARY THROTTLE STOP SCREW

1. Turn the secondary throttle stop screw counterclockwise until the secondary throttle plate seats in its bore.
2. Turn the screw clockwise until it touches the tab on the secondary throttle lever, then add ¼ turn.

### ELECTRIC CHOKE ADJUSTMENT

For electric choke procedures refer to the 2150 carburetor section.

### FAST IDLE SPEED ADJUSTMENT

1. Remove the air cleaner assembly and plug the vacuum line at the source of vacuum.
2. Set the parking brake and block the wheels.
3. Connect a tachometer to the engine.
4. Start the engine and warm up to normal operating temperature.
5. Reinstall any distributor vacuum lines that were removed and check the ignition timing.
6. Remove the EGR vacuum line at the valve and plug the line.
7. If applicable, remove the spark delay valve and route the primary distributor advance vacuum signal directly to the primary distributor diaphragm (advance side). If the distributor has a secondary (retard) diaphragm, leave the vacuum connection intact.
8. Disconnect and plug the fuel deceleration valve hose (if so equipped) at the carburetor connection.
9. Air conditioner, if so equipped, must be "off."
10. With the engine running at normal operating temperature and choke plate fully opened (automatic transmission in Park and manual in Neutral) set the throttle so that the fast idle adjustment screw contacts the kickdown step of the choke cam and adjust the fast idle adjusting screw to obtain the specified rmp according to vehicle specifications.
11. Set the throttle to the high step of the choke cam and allow the engine to run approximately 5 seconds.
12. Rotate the choke cam until the fast idle adjustment screw contacts the kickdown step of the choke cam. After allowing the rpm to stabilize, recheck fast idle rmp and readjust if necessary by repeating Steps 10–12 until the specified fast idle speed is obtained and can be repeated.
13. Stop the engine and install air cleaner and vacuum lines.

## Overhaul-Model 5200

### DISASSEMBLY

During disassembly operations, refer to the exploded view of the components which accompanies this section. Keep the parts from the different sections of the carburetor separated. Clean and inspect all components. Wash components (except the accelerating pump diaphragm and any other rubber goods) in a suitable commercial solvent. Rince all solvent-cleaned parts in kerosene to remove traces of the cleaning solvent, then dry with compressed air.

1. Remove the float bowl cover screws and washers. Disconnect the choke rod by removing the plastic retaining bushings and remove the float bowl cover.

2. Turn the bowl cover over and remove the choke rod seal, the float hinge pin, the float, fuel inlet needle and seat with gasket.

3. Remove the three enrichment (power) valve vacuum diaphragm screws, washers and diaphragm.

4. Remove the three vent cover/solenoid attaching screws and remove the cover.

5. Pry the vent arm pivot pin toward the fuel inlet seat and remove the pin and vent arm.

6. Remove the E-clip from the vent diaphragm stem, remove diaphragm assembly, vent spring, retainer and valve.

7. Remove the choke cover housing retaining screws; remove the ring, housing and electric heater assembly.

8. Remove the choke housing assembly mounting screws-note from where the different length screws come. Slip the housing away from the carb body disengage the fast idle rod. Remove the O-ring gasket from the vacuum passage.

9. Remove the choke shaft nut and washer, choke lever, fast idle cam, fast idle lever screw and fast idle lever spring.

10. Remove the choke diaphragm cover screws, the cover, return spring, diaphragm and rod assembly.

11. Remove the four accelerator pump-to-body screws and pump cover assembly. Remove the pump diaphragm and return spring.

12. From the center of the main body of the carburetor remove the accelerator pump discharge screw assembly, pump discharge nozzle and two gaskets. Cover the main body with your hand, invert it and catch the two pump discharge balls as they free the discharge passage.

13. Remove the primary high speed bleeds and main well tube and the secondary high speed bleeds and main well tube. Be sure to note the sizes of the air bleed plugs and main well tubes so they may be reinstalled in the proper position.

14. Remove the primary and secondary

## Model 5200

| Year | (9510)* Carburetor Identification | Dry Float Level (in.) | Pump Hole Setting | Choke Plate Pulldown (in.) | Fast Idle Cam Linkage (in.) | Fast Idle (rpm) | Dechoke (in.) | Choke Setting |
|------|------|------|------|------|------|------|------|------|
| 1981 | EIZE-YA | .41 –.51 | 2 | 0.200 | .080 | ① | 0.200 | ① |
| | EOEE-RB | .41 –.51 | 2 | 0.200 | .080 | ① | 0.200 | ① |
| | EIZE-VA | .41 –.51 | 2 | 0.200 | .080 | ① | 0.200 | ① |
| | D9EE-ANA | .41 –.51 | 2 | 0.240 | 0.720 | ① | 0.200 | ① |
| | D9EE-APA | .41 –.51 | 2 | 0.240 | 0.120 | ① | 0.200 | ① |
| 1982 | E1ZE-ADB | .41 –.51 | 3 | 0.275 | 0.240 | 1600 | 0.393 | ① |
| | E1ZE-ACA | .41 –.51 | 2 | 0.200 | .080 | 1800 | 0.196 | ① |
| | E1BE-RA | .41 –.51 | 2 | 0.200 | .080 | 1800 | 0.196 | ① |
| | E1ZE-YA | .41 –.51 | 2 | 0.200 | .080 | 2000 | 0.196 | ① |
| | E1ZE-VA | .41 –.51 | 2 | 0.200 | .080 | 2000 | 0.196 | ① |
| | E2ZE-AFA | .41 –.51 | 2 | 0.236 | 0.118 | 1800 | 0.236 | ① |
| | E2ZE-AHA | .41 –.51 | 2 | 0.236 | 0.118 | 2000 | 0.236 | ① |
| | E2ZE-ABA | .41 –.51 | 2 | 0.236 | 0.118 | 2000 | 0.236 | ① |
| | E2ZE-AGA | .41 –.51 | 2 | 0.236 | 0.118 | 2000 | 0.236 | ① |
| | E2ZE-AAA | .41 –.51 | 2 | 0.236 | 0.118 | 2000 | 0.236 | ① |

*Basic carburetor number    ① See underhood specifications sticker

main metering jets. Note the different size jets and their proper locations.

15. Remove the power valve and gasket. Remove the secondary idle jet retainer and jets located on the side of the carburetor body.

16. Turn the idler limiter cap in (clockwise) to the stop. Remove the limiter cap. Count the turns required to lightly seat the idle adjustment needle. Count to the nearest $1/16$ turn. Remove the needle and spring.

17. Remove the secondary throttle operating lever return spring. Remove the primary throttle shaft nut, lock washer, flat washer and accelerator pump cam. Remove the idle speed screws and spring from the throttle shaft lever.

### ASSEMBLY

1. Install the idle speed screw and spring. Install the accelerator pump cam, flat washer, lock washer and nut on the primary throttle shaft.

2. Install the idle mixture adjusting screw. Turn the screw in until it gently bottoms. Back out the needle screw the exact number of turns recorded when you disassembled it. Install a new limiter cap with its step resting on the lean side of the stop on the carb body.

3. Install the idle jet and retainer assembly on the secondary side. Install the power valve gasket and power valve. Install the primary and secondary main jets, primary and secondary main well tubes and high speed bleeds.

NOTE: *Be sure they are reinstalled in the correct place.*

4. Install the two accelerator pump discharge check balls. Install the pump discharge nozzle and the two gaskets. Install the accelerator pump discharge screw.

5. Install the accelerator pump return spring, pump diaphragm and cover. Start the four pump cover screws and, holding the pump operating lever slightly opened to align the diaphragm gasket, tighten the four screws evenly.

6. Install the automatic choke diaphragm adjusting screw. Adjust the screw so that the threads are flush with the inside of the cover. Install the choke diaphragm and rod assembly, the return spring and cover. Install the cover screws and lockwashers.

7. Install the fast idle adjusting screw and spring on the fast idle arm. Install the flat spacer, fast idle arm and attaching screw. Install the choke shaft into the housing and position the fast idle cam on the housing post. Install the choke lever, lockwasher and nut.

8. Place a new O-ring washer on the vacuum passage. Install the fast idle rod with the end with one tab in the fast idle adjusting lever and the other end in the long leg of the housing. Install the retaining screws.

9. Adjust the choke plate pull down. Refer to the adjustment section of this chapter.

10. Install the electric choke heater, housing, retaining ring and attaching screws. Index the housing and tighten the screws.

NOTE: *Be sure that the choke plate is in the full closed position before installing the electric choke heater element.*

11. With fuel bowl cover inverted, install bowl vent diaphragm, vent valve, spring, retainer and E-clip. Position vent arm and install vent arm pivot pin. Install vent valve cover/solenoid with the three retaining screws and tighten them.

12. Install the needle seat and gasket. Install the power valve vacuum diaphragm. Depress the spring and install the screws and washers to finger tightness. Hold the stem so the diaphragm is horizontal and tighten the screw equally.

13. Install the float needle clip on the float tab, position the float and needle, install the needle into the seat and secure the float with the float pivot shaft.

14. Adjust the dry float setting and the float drop. Refer to the adjustment section in this chapter.

15. Install the choke rod seal. Install the choke rod and fasten it to the choke lever. Install the retaining clip.

16. Place the bowl cover gasket in position, install the choke link into position on the choke lever and install the retaining clip.

17. Place the float bowl cover in position and install the retaining bolts. Tighten them evenly.

18. Install the throttle positioner.

## Holley 6500 Feedback Carburetor

California models using the 4 cylinder, 2.3 liter, 140 cubic inch engine may be equipped with a Feedback Engine Control system. This system requires more precise fuel metering and is equipped with the Holley/Weber 6500 Feedback carburetor.

The Holley/Weber 6500 Feedback carburetor is basically a Model 5200 carburetor that has an externally-variable auxiliary fuel metering system in place of the usual enrichment valve.

### ADJUSTMENTS

Refer to the Model 5200 section.

NOTE: *If the feedback valve piston and diaphragm assembly is removed for any rea-*

*son it is essential that the following proce-
dure is followed during reassembly.*

1. Apply one drop of Loctite® 271 or equivalent to the threads of the retaining screw
holes.

2. Position the feedback fuel diaphragm and
piston assembly over the spring, so that the
attaching holes are aligned with the tapped
holes in the air horn. Make sure the diaphragm spring is properly installed with one
end of the spring over the end of the adjustment screw and the other centered within the
cupped washer of the diaphragm and piston
assembly.

3. Install the three retaining screws and
tighten to 4–5 in. lbs.

## Carter YFA Adjustment

### AUTOMATIC CHOKE HOUSING ADJUSTMENT

By rotating the spring housing of the automatic choke, the reaction of the choke to engine temperature can be controlled. To adjust, remove the air cleaner assembly, loosen
the thermostatic spring housing retaining
screws and set the spring housing to the specified index mark. After adjusting the setting,
tighten the retaining screws and replace the
air cleaner assembly to the carburetor.

### CHOKE PLATE PULL-DOWN CLEARANCE

1. Remove the carburetor air cleaner and
remove the choke thermostatic spring housing.

2. Bend a section of 0.026-inch-diameter

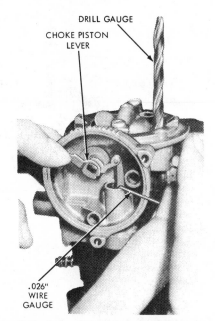

**Carter YFA choke plate pull-down clearance**

wire at a 90° angle, approximately ⅛ inch from
one end.

3. Insert the bent end of the wire gauge between the choke piston slot and the righthand
slot in the choke housing. Rotate the choke
piston lever counterclockwise until the gauge
is snug in the piston slot.

4. Exert light pressure upon the choke piston lever to hold the gauge in position. Check
the specified clearance with a drill of the correct diameter between the lower edge of the
choke plate and the carburetor bore.

5. Choke plate pull-down clearance may be

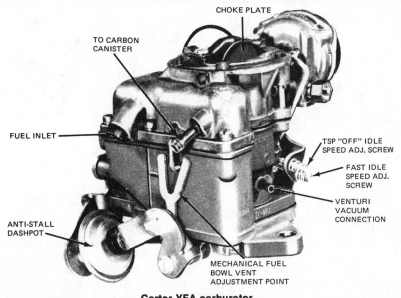

**Carter YFA carburetor**

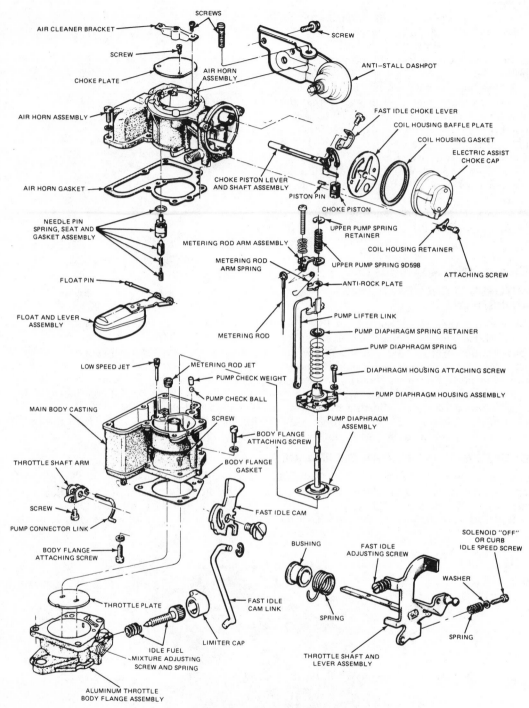

**Typical Carter YFA carburetor**

adjusted by bending the choke piston lever as required to obtain the desired clearance. It is recommended the choke piston lever be removed prior to bending, in order to prevent distorting the piston link.

6. Install the choke thermostatic spring housing and gasket, and set the housing to the proper specification.

## FLOAT LEVEL ADJUSTMENT

The float level is adjusted dry in the following manner: Remove the carburetor air horn and gasket from the carburetor. Using a gauge made to the proper dimension, invert the air horn assembly and check the clearance between the top of the float and the bottom of

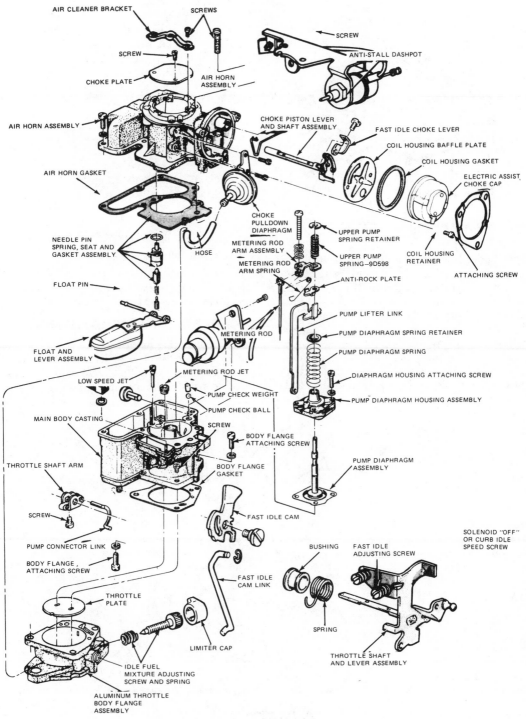

AIR CLEANER BRACKET

SCREWS

SCREW

ANTI-STALL DASHPOT

SCREW

CHOKE PLATE

AIR HORN ASSEMBLY

CHOKE PISTON LEVER AND SHAFT ASSEMBLY

FAST IDLE CHOKE LEVER

COIL HOUSING BAFFLE PLATE

AIR HORN ASSEMBLY

COIL HOUSING GASKET

ELECTRIC ASSIST CHOKE CAP

AIR HORN GASKET

CHOKE PULLDOWN DIAPHRAGM

UPPER PUMP SPRING RETAINER

NEEDLE PIN SPRING, SEAT AND GASKET ASSEMBLY

METERING ROD ARM ASSEMBLY

HOSE

UPPER PUMP SPRING—9D598

COIL HOUSING RETAINER

METERING ROD ARM SPRING

ANTI-ROCK PLATE

ATTACHING SCREW

FLOAT PIN

PUMP LIFTER LINK

PUMP DIAPHRAGM SPRING RETAINER

METERING ROD

PUMP DIAPHRAGM SPRING

FLOAT AND LEVER ASSEMBLY

METERING ROD JET

DIAPHRAGM HOUSING ATTACHING SCREW

LOW SPEED JET

PUMP CHECK WEIGHT

PUMP DIAPHRAGM HOUSING ASSEMBLY

MAIN BODY CASTING

PUMP CHECK BALL

SCREW

BODY FLANGE ATTACHING SCREW

PUMP DIAPHRAGM ASSEMBLY

THROTTLE SHAFT ARM

BODY FLANGE GASKET

SCREW

PUMP CONNECTOR LINK

FAST IDLE CAM

BODY FLANGE ATTACHING SCREW

SOLENOID "OFF" OR CURB IDLE SPEED SCREW

THROTTLE PLATE

BUSHING

FAST IDLE ADJUSTING SCREW

FAST IDLE CAM LINK

SPRING

LIMITER CAP

THROTTLE SHAFT AND LEVER ASSEMBLY

IDLE FUEL MIXTURE ADJUSTING SCREW AND SPRING

ALUMINUM THROTTLE BODY FLANGE ASSEMBLY

**Typical Carter YFA carburetor**

the air horn. Float level is ⅜ inch. When checking the float level, the air horn should be held at eye level and the float lever arm should be resting on the pin of the needle valve. Bend the float lever arm to adjust the float clearance. However, do not bend the tab at the end of the float arm, as this will prevent the float from bottoming in the fuel bowl when the bowl is empty. Using a new gasket, install the carburetor air horn.

## METERING ROD ADJUSTMENT

With the carburetor air horn and gasket removed from the carburetor, unscrew the idle

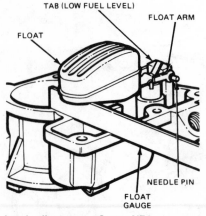

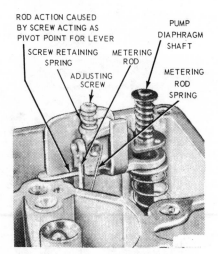

**Float level adjustment—Carter YFA**

**Carter YFA metering rod adjustment**

speed adjusting screw until the throttle plate is tightly closed in the throttle bore. Press downward on the end of the diaphragm shaft until the metering rod arm contacts the lifter link at the diaphragm stem. With the metering rod in the preceding position, turn the rod adjustment screw (see accompanying illustration) until the metering rod just bottoms in the body casting. Turn the metering rod adjusting screw one additional turn in the clock-

wise direction. Install the carburetor air horn along with a new gasket.

### DECHOKE CLEARANCE ADJUSTMENT

1. Remove the air cleaner.
2. Hold the throttle plate to the full open position while closing the choke plate as far as possible without forcing it. Use a drill of the

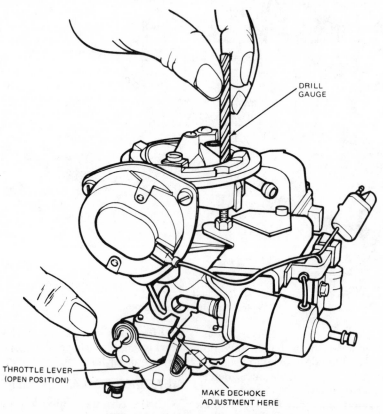

**YFA dechoke clearance adjustment**

proper diameter (see Specifications) to check the clearance between the choke plate and air horn.

3. To adjust, bend the arm on the choke trip lever of the throttle lever. To decrease the clearance, bend the arm downward; to increase the clearance bend the arm upward. Recheck the clearance after making the adjustment.

### FAST IDLE CAM INDEX SETTING

1. Position the fast idle screw on the kickdown step of the fast idle cam against the shoulder of the high step.

2. Adjust by bending the choke plate connecting rod to obtain the specified clearance between the lower edge of the choke plate and the carburetor bore.

## Overhaul—Carter YFA

### DISASSEMBLY

During the disassembly operations, refer to the exploded view of components which accompanies this section. Separate the throttle connector rod retainer from the choke connector rod and remove the rod from the fast idle link. Remove the automatic choke components, including housing retaining screws, housing assembly, housing gasket and baffle plate, trip lever and pin assembly and fast idle link. Remove the air horn retaining screws, the dashpot and bracket, and the air horn and air horn gasket from the carburetor main body. With the air horn assembly inverted, remove the float pin and the float and lever assembly. With the air horn assembly turned upright, catch the needle pin, spring, needle and seat. Remove the float needle seat and gasket. Remove the air cleaner bracket and the choke

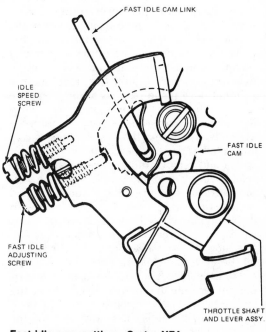

Fast idle cam setting—Carter YFA

plate retaining screws. If necessary, the ends of the screws may be filed and new screws used during assembly. Remove the choke plate. With the fast idle cam spring disengaged from the cam spring lever on the choke piston lever and shaft assembly, rotate the choke shaft and piston assembly in the counterclockwise direction until the choke piston is withdrawn from the choke piston cylinder. Remove the choke assembly from the air horn and remove the piston pin, piston, fast idle cam and spring from the piston lever and shaft assembly. With the main body casting inverted, catch the accelerating pump check needle as it falls out.

## Carter YFA

| Year | Float Level (in.) | Fast Idle Setting (in.) | Choke Plate Pulldown Clearance (in.) | Dechoke Clearance (minimum in.) | Choke Housing Adjustment |
|------|------|------|------|------|------|
| 1975 | 3/8 ① | .140 | 0.290 | .250 | 200 eng—index<br>250 eng—2 rich |
| 1976–'77 | 25/32 | .140 | 200 eng—0.260<br>250 eng—0.290 ② | .250 | 200 eng 49 states—1 rich<br>250 eng 49 states—index<br>250 eng Cal—2 rich |
| 1978 | 25/32 | .140 | .230 ② | .250 | 2 rich |
| 1979–80 | 25/32 | .140 | .260 ④ | .250 | 1 rich |

① Float level is ¾ inch on D5DE-NB and D5DE-RB carburetors
② Pull-down clearance is 0.230 inch on D6DE-BB carburetor
③ .200 for carburetor D8DE-EA
④ D9BE-RA—.180
   D9DE-AA, D9DE-BA and D9DE-EA—.230

With the throttle shaft arm spring disconnected, loosen the throttle shaft arm screw and remove the arm and pump connector link. Remove the retaining screws of the accelerating pump diaphragm housing and withdraw the diaphragm assembly, lifter link, metering rod and fuel bowl baffle plate as a unit. Separate the metering rod arm spring from the metering rod and remove the metering rod from the assembly. Compress the upper pump spring and remove the retainer. Lift off the upper spring and remove the metering rod arm assembly and pump lifter link from the diaphragm shaft. Compress the lower spring and remove the spring retainer, spring and pump diaphragm assembly from the housing. Use a special tool or a screwdriver of appropriate size to remove the low speed jet and metering rod jet. Remove the retaining screws which attach the throttle body flange to the main body casting and separate the components. Remove the gasket between the throttle body and main body. Filing the ends if necessary, remove the screws which retain the throttle plate (use new screws during assembly) and slide the throttle shaft and lever assembly out of the throttle body flange.

NOTE: *Do not remove the idle mixture limiter caps or the mixture screws from the throttle body.*

## ASSEMBLY

Prior to assembly, clean and inspect all components. Wash all components (except the accelerating pump diaphragm and the antistall dashpot assembly) in a suitable commercial solvent. Rinse all solvent-cleaned parts in kerosene to remove traces of the cleaning solvent, then dry with compressed air. Do not use wire or drills to clean openings in the carburetor—use of such devices will enlarge the hole or passage being cleaned, thus changing the operating characteristics of the carburetor.

Install the throttle shaft and lever assembly to the throttle body flange, then position the throttle plate on its shaft so that the notch in the plate is lined up with the slotted idle port in the throttle body flange. Install the throttle plate retaining screws so that they are snug, but not tight. Move and rotate the shaft to ensure that the throttle plate does not bind in its bore and reposition the plate if necessary. Tighten the throttle plate retaining screws and stake or peen into place.

Using a new gasket, join the main body casting with the throttle body flange and evenly tighten the retaining screws. Using the proper size screwdriver or special jet tool, install the metering rod jet and low speed jet. Install the pump diaphragm to the accelerating pump

diaphragm housing and position the lower spring on the diaphragm shaft and housing. Install the spring retainer, pump lifter link, metering rod arm and spring assembly, and the upper spring on the diaphragm shaft. Depress the spring and install the upper retainer. Install the metering rod to the meter rod arm as shown in the illustration accompanying the preceding section. Line up the pump diaphragm with its housing and install the retaining screws. Position the fuel bowl baffle plate on the pump assembly and line up the pump housing, pump lifter link, metering rod and baffle plate with the main body casting.

NOTE: *Be sure that the vacuum passage in the diaphragm housing is lined up with that of the main body.*

Install the assembly to the main body casting, being sure that the pump lifter link is engaged with the main body, that the baffle plate has its grooves in the main body, and that the metering rod is inserted into the metering rod jet. Install the pump housing screws so that they are snug, but not tight. Pushing down on the diaphragm shaft to compress the diaphragm, tighten the retaining screws evenly. Adjust the metering rod. Install the throttle shaft arm and pump connector link to the throttle shaft and pump lifter link. Tighten the locking screw and connect the throttle shaft arm return spring. Install the fast idle cam and spring to the choke lever and shaft assembly. Install the choke piston and pin to the choke piston lever and shaft, then disengage the cam spring from the lever and install the choke shaft assembly to the air horn. Align the piston with the cylinder, rotate the shaft assembly in the clockwise direction until the piston pin is inside the cylinder. Position the cam spring on the cam spring lever of the choke lever assembly.

NOTE: *When the cam spring is properly positioned, the tangs on the cam and the choke lever will be lined up with one on front of the other.*

With the choke plate in position on the shaft, install the retaining screws without tightening fully. As with the throttle plate, move and rotate the shaft to ensure that the plate moves freely, then tighten the screws and peen or stake to secure.

Install the needle valve seat and gasket in the air horn. Invert the air horn and install the needle, pin spring, needle pin, float and lever, the float pin. Adjust the float lever, and float pin. Adjust the float lever. Install the pump check needle to the main body casting and position the air horn (with new gasket) and the antistall dashpot and bracket on the main body. Secure the dashpot bracket and evenly tighten the screws attaching the air horn to the main body. Install the choke trip lever and fast idle link to the choke housing. Be sure that the lever and link properly engage each other and the choke piston lever and shaft. Install the coil housing, gasket and baffle plate (with identification mark facing outward). The gasket should be between the baffle and the coil housing, and the thermostatic spring should engage the tang of the choke lever. Install the retainers and screws, set the housing to the proper setting, and tighten the screws. Install the air cleaner bracket and attach the throttle connector rod retainer to the fast idle link. Install the choke connector rod to the throttle lever and fast idle link. Secure the air horn to the main body and connect the connector rod retainer to the choke connector rod.

## Holley Model 1946 Carburetor Adjustments

### FAST IDLE CAM ADJUSTMENT

Fast idle cam position adjustment is necessary to make sure the fast idle screw contacts the various steps of the fast idle cam at the proper time during engine warm-up. This adjustment can be made with the carburetor on the engine (with the engine off) or with the carburetor removed from the engine.

1. With the fast idle speed adjusting screw contacting the second highest step of the fast idle cam (kickdown step), move the choke plate toward the closed position with light pressure on the choke lever or choke plate.

2. Check the fast idle cam setting using the specified size gauge or drill bit between the upper edge of the choke plate and the wall of the air horn.

3. Bend the fast idle cam link to achieve the specified setting.

NOTE: *To fabricate a convenient bending*

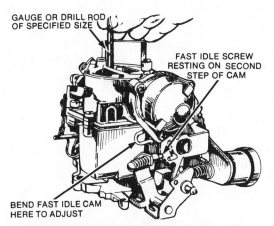

GAUGE OR DRILL ROD OF SPECIFIED SIZE

FAST IDLE SCREW RESTING ON SECOND STEP OF CAM

BEND FAST IDLE CAM HERE TO ADJUST

**Holley 1946 fast idle cam position adjustment**

*tool, file a slot in the blade of a flat screwdriver just wide enough to slip over the 1/8 inch fast idle cam link. The tool can also be used in other applications where bending a similar rod for adjustment is required.*

### ACCELERATOR PUMP STROKE ADJUSTMENT

The accelerator pump stroke is pre-set at the factory and should not be adjusted to improve driveability.

### DECHOKE CLEARANCE ADJUSTMENT

The dechoke feature provides a means of partially opening the choke plate during cold engine starts, even though the choke bimetal spring is holding it closed. By depressing the accelerator pedal fully, engines that may have become 'flooded' or that have stalled due to excessive choke action can be cleared. To adjust the dechoke clearance, proceed as follows:

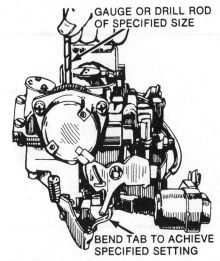

GAUGE OR DRILL ROD OF SPECIFIED SIZE

BEND TAB TO ACHIEVE SPECIFIED SETTING

**Holley 1946 dechoke adjustment**

1. With the engine off, hold the throttle in the wide open position.

2. Insert the specified size gauge or drill bit between the upper edge of the choke plate and the inner wall of the air horn.

3. With light pressure against the choke shaft lever, a slight drag should be felt as the gauge or drill bit is withdrawn.

4. To adjust, bend the tang on the throttle lever until the correct opening is obtained. The tab can be bent with a pair of pliers or other suitable bending tool. Bending the tab upward will increase the dechoke clearance.

### CHOKE PULLDOWN ADJUSTMENT

Adjust choke pulldown by bending the choke pulldown diaphragm connecting link. Use a

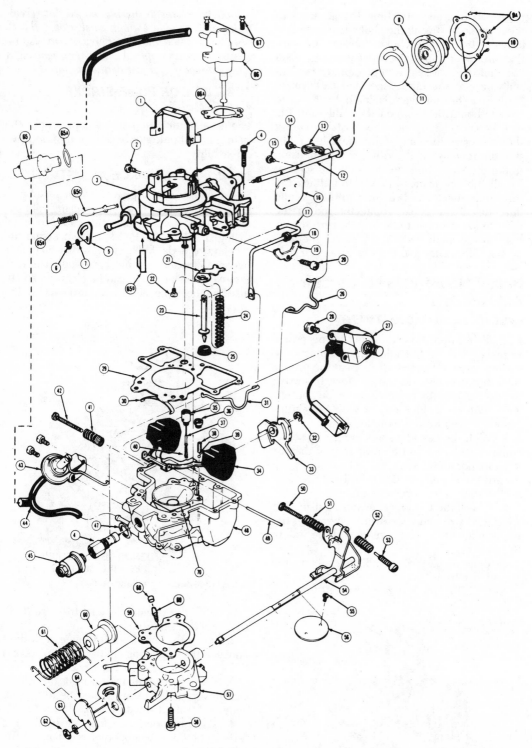

Holley 1946 carburetor

gauge or drill bit of the specified diameter to check the clearance between the top of the choke plate and the air horn.

## DASHPOT ADJUSTMENT

Adjust the dashpot by loosening the locknut and turning the dashpot in the bracket. The dashpot plunger must be fully collapsed. Use a feeler gauge to check the clearance between the plunger and the throttle pad.

## EXTERNAL FUEL BOWL VENT ADJUSTMENT

Adjust the external fuel bowl vent with the carburetor installed on the engine and the ignition OFF, after having first adjusted the curb idle speed.

1. Remove the air cleaner assembly.
2. Disconnect the canister vent hose from the bowl vent tube on the air horn.
3. Attach a hand operated vacuum pump (Rotunda 21-0014 or equivalent) to the bowl vent tube, using a ⅜ inch adaptor.
4. Remove the three bowl vent cover screws located on the top of the air horn.

5. Remove the bowl vent cover gasket and spring.
6. Turn the vent adjusting screw (located on the nylon vent arm) clockwise until no more than ⅛ inch of the adjustment screw threads is visible above the vent arm.
7. While operating the hand vacuum pump, gradually turn the adjusting screw counterclockwise ⅛ turn at a time until vacuum is indicated on the gauge, showing that the valve is closed. Release the vacuum and turn the adjusting screw ½ turn clockwise. Disconnect the hand vacuum pump and adaptor from the vent hose.
8. Reconnect the canister vent hose and install the air cleaner assembly.

## FLOAT ADJUSTMENT

1. Remove the carburetor upper body (air horn assembly.
2. With the upper body assembly removed, place a finger over the float hinge pin retainer and invert the main body. Catch the accelerator pump check ball and weight as they drop from the pump channel.

1. Air cleaner bracket (1)
2. Air cleaner bracket screw (2)
3. Air horn
4. Screw and washer (8)
5. Choke pulldown lever
6. Choke shaft nut
7. Lockwasher (1)
8. Choke bimetal assembly
9. Screw (2)
9A. Rivet (2)
10. Choke cover retainer
11. Choke thermostatic housing locating disc
12. Choke shaft and lever assembly
13. Choke control lever
14. Screw (1)
15. Screw (1)
16. Choke plate
17. Accelerator pump operating rod
18. Accelerator pump rod grommet
19. Rod retaining clamp
20. Screw (1)
21. Accelerator pump spring retaining plate
22. Screw (1)
23. Accelerator pump piston stem
24. Accelerator pump spring
25. Accelerator pump piston cup
26. Fast idle cam link
27. Anti-diesel solenoid
28. Screw (2)
29. Air horn gasket
30. Float-hinge retainer
31. Accelerator pump operating link
32. Retaining clip (fast idle cam)
33. Fast idle cam
34. Float assembly
35. Power valve body
36. Main metering jet
37. Power valve pin
38. Accelerator pump weight

39. Accelerator pump check ball
40. Power valve spring
41. Spring
42. Low idle (solenoid off) adjusting screw
43. Choke pulldown diaphragm assembly
44. Choke diaphragm vacuum hose
45. Fuel filter
46. Fuel inlet needle & seat assembly
47. Gasket
48. Main body assembly
49. Float hinge pin
50. Curb idle adjusting screw
51. Spring
52. Spring
53. Fast idle adjusting screw
54. Throttle shaft & lever assembly
55. Screw (2)
56. Throttle plate
57. Throttle body assembly
58. Throttle body screw (3)
59. Throttle body gasket
60. Throttle return spring bushing
61. Throttle return spring
62. Nut
63. Lock washer
64. Throttle return spring bracket
65. Bowl vent solenoid
65A. Washer
65B. Spring
65C. Pintle
65D. Seal
66. Power valve piston assembly
66A. Gasket
67. Screw (2)
68. Idle mixture
69. Concealment plug
    idle mixture needle
70. Fuel bowl filler

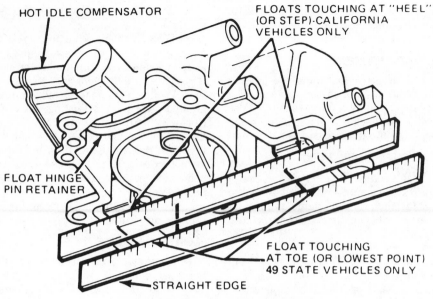

HOT IDLE COMPENSATOR

FLOATS TOUCHING AT "HEEL"
(OR STEP)-CALIFORNIA
VEHICLES ONLY

FLOAT HINGE
PIN RETAINER

FLOAT TOUCHING
AT TOE (OR LOWEST POINT)
49 STATE VEHICLES ONLY

STRAIGHT EDGE

**Holley 1946 float clearance adjustment**

3. Using a straight edge, check the position of the floats as shown in the illustration.
• For all exc. California carburetors:
The straight edge should just touch the lowest point on the float (toe when held as pictured.
• For California carburetors:
The straight edge should just contact the step (or heel of the float.
4. Once the adjustment is correct, turn the main body right side up and check the float alignment. The float should move freely throughout its range without contacting the fuel bowl walls. If the float pontoons are misaligned, straighten by bending the float arms. Recheck the float level adjustment.

## Overhaul-Holley 1946

### DISASSEMBLY

To help prevent damage to the throttle plates, use the EGR spacer, a carburetor stand, or some bolts, held in place by nuts, as a holding device while you are working on the carburetor.

1. Remove the choke cover attaching screws, the retainer, bimetal cover and gasket.

CAUTION: *Do not put cover assembly in carb cleaner. Clean by wiping and blowing out with air.*

2. Remove the choke pulldown bracket screws (2), disconnect the vacuum hose from

## Holley Model 1946

| Year | Part Number | Float Level (in.) | Choke Pulldown (in.) | Dechoke (in.) | Fast Idle Cam (in.) | Accelerator Pump Stroke Slot |
|------|-------------|-------------------|----------------------|---------------|---------------------|------------------------------|
| 1981 | EIBE-AFA | .69 | .113 | .150 | .082 | #2 |
|      | EIBE-AKA | .69 | .113 | .150 | .082 | #2 |
|      | EOBE-CA | .69 | .100 | .150 | .070 | #2 |
|      | EOBE-AA | .69 | .100 | .150 | .070 | #2 |
| 1982 | EIBE-AGA | .69 | .120 | .150 | .086 | #2 |
|      | E2BE-CA | .69 | .110 | .150 | .078 | #2 |
|      | E2BE-BA | .69 | .110 | .150 | .078 | #2 |
|      | E2BE-JA | .69 | .110 | .150 | .078 | #2 |
|      | E2BE-HA | .69 | .110 | .150 | .078 | #2 |
|      | E2BE-TA | .69 | .110 | .150 | .078 | #2 |
|      | E2BE-SA | .69 | .110 | .150 | .078 | #2 |

the carb body and remove the pulldown and linkage.

3. Remove the fuel bowl vent cover (3 screws). Remove the cover, spring and gasket from the air horn. Note the position of the spring when you remove it. Remove the bowl vent attaching screw and lift the bowl vent assembly from its seat.

CAUTION: *Do not put the bowl vent assembly in carb cleaner.*

4. Remove the fast idle cam, the choke lever retaining screw and the throttle return spring bracket. Remove the accelerator pump link, remember which slot it is located in for proper reassembly.

5. Remove the remaining air horn screws (7) and remove the air horn. Place the air horn upside down and remove the gasket. Make sure all of the gasket material is cleaned from the gasket surface.

CAUTION: *Do not scrape with a metal scraper; use a nylon or plastic scraper.*

6. A screw and a clamp attach the accelerator pump operating rod; remove them. Remove the pump spring retaining plate, rotate the pump rod and disconnect the pump drive spring and accelerator pump assembly. *Do not put the pump plunger in carb cleaner.*

7. Rotate the pump operating rod and remove the rod and grommet from the bowl cover.

8. The main well tube is not removable. Blow it out with air.

9. Remove the choke housing (3 screws).

10. Place your hand over the top of the main body and turn it upside down. The accelerator pump discharge weight and ball will be dislodged and fall in your hand. Retain them for reinstallation. Remove the fuel inlet valve and fitting, the float retainer, float shaft and float.

11. Remove the main metering jet with a jet wrench. If you do not own or cannot borrow a suitable jet wrench, a ⅜-inch deep slot screwdriver may be used.

CAUTION: *When using a screwdriver take care not to burr the edges of the main jet.*

12. Remove the enrichment valve. A tool can be made for this purpose by taking a ⅜-inch wide screwdriver and grinding a $1/16$ inch wide by ⅜-inch deep slot in the blade. The slot will provide the necessary clearance for the enrichment valve stem.

13. Remove the hot idle compensator cover, the hot idle compensator valve, and the mounting gaskets from the main carb body.

14. Remove the three screws that attach the throttle body to the main body; separate the two parts.

Remove the low idle speed screw and the solenoid.

15. Turn the idle mixture cap on the leanest position (clockwise). The limiter cap stop should be against the throttle body. Remove the limiter cap.

16. Note the position of the idle mixture screw slot. Slowly turn the screw in until it lightly seats, record the number of turns required. Remove the idle mixture screw.

## ASSEMBLY

1. Install the idle mixture screw into the throttle body. Lightly seat it and back off the number of turns recorded when you remove it. Position the slot in the screw head at the same point as recorded when you removed the limiter cap. Install a new limiter cap, lean stop against the throttle body.

2. Install the low speed screw and solenoid. Position a new throttle body gasket on the main body and attach the throttle body. Before tightening the mounting screws, work the throttle several times to make sure it is not binding. Secure the mounting screws.

3. Install a new hot idle compensator valve gasket and the valve in the carb main body. Place the cover and gasket over the valve and secure the attaching screws.

4. Snap the small diameter end of the enrichment valve spring over the shoulder on the large end of the pin. Insert the pin into the valve body from the threaded end. Install the enrichment valve. Install the main metering jet.

5. Replace the hinge pin into the float arm and place the float into position. Install the hinge retainer and the fuel inlet valve with gasket.

6. Make dry float adjustment. Refer to the adjustment section in this chapter.

7. Install the accelerator ball and weight.

8. Install the accelerator pump operating rod and grommet on the air horn. Push the accelerator pump cup over the retaining tab on the end of the pump piston rod. Assemble the pump spring and retainer plate to the piston rod. The larger end of the spring should contact the retainer plate and seat over the shoulder.

9. While holding the accelerator pump assembly together, connect the pump operating rod through the slotted hole in the piston rod and rotate the rod so the plate can be positioned and the attaching screw installed. Tighten the attaching screw. Install the pump operating clamp and attaching screw.

10. Put a new air horn gasket in position over the alignment pin. Guide the accelerator pump cup into the pump well and the main well tube into the main well in the carb body. Align the air horn and lower it into place. Make

sure the enrichment valve stem squarely contacts the enrichment valve pin.

11. Attach the air horn with seven screws. Hook the accelerator pump link to the pump operating rod and the correct slot in the throttle return spring bracket. Slide the throttle return spring mounting bracket assembly over the throttle shaft and align with the shoulders on the end of the shaft. Install the attaching nut and washer, engage the throttle return spring over the throttle stop.

12. Engage the fast idle cam link in the fast idle cam slot. Install the cam, retainer, choke control lever and screw.

13. Install the bowl vent assembly and hinge pin, secure with hinge pin screw. Place the small diameter of the bowl vent spring over the shoulder of the vent arm. Install the vent cover and gasket.

14. Connect the choke pulloff linkage, install the bracket and reconnect the vacuum line.

15. Install the bimetal choke, make sure the spring tab is engaged in the slotted choke shaft lever. Index the cover and tighten the mounting screws.

NOTE: *Be sure to use a new choke cap gasket.*

## 2150 2V Carburetor Adjustments
### *FLOAT LEVEL ADJUSTMENT—WET*

1. Run the engine to normal operating temperature and stop the engine.

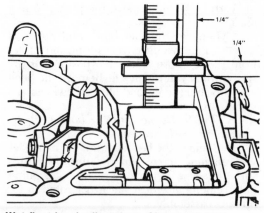

**Wet float level adjustment—Motorcraft 2150**

2. Remove the air cleaner.

3. Remove the air horn attaching screws and the carburetor identification tag. Leave the air horn and gasket in position on the carburetor main body and start the engine. Let the engine idle a few minutes, then remove the air cleaner stud and the air horn and gasket to provide access to the float assembly.

4. While the engine is idling use a standard depth scale to measure the vertical distance from the top machined surface of the carburetor main body to the level of the fuel in the fuel bowl. The measurement must be made at least a ¼ inch away from any vertical surface to assure an accurate reading. The fuel level should be measured at the point of contact of the float with the fuel. To raise the fuel level

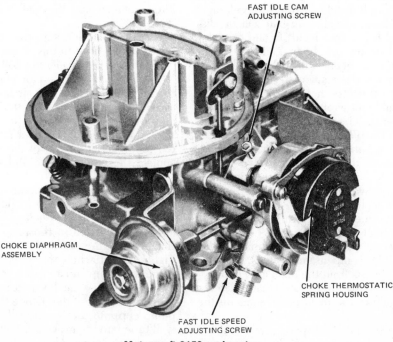

**Motorcraft 2150 carburetor**

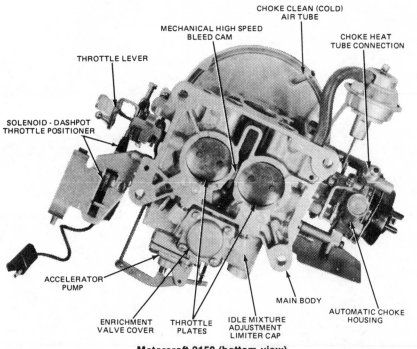

**Motorcraft 2150 (bottom view)**

bend the flat tab contacting the fuel inlet valve upward and downward to lower it.

5. Install a new air horn gasket and install the air horn assembly.

6. Install the air cleaner anchor stud and install the air cleaner.

### FLOAT LEVEL ADJUSTMENT—DRY

The dry float adjustment is a preliminary fuel level adjustment only. The wet float adjustment must be made after the carburetor is mounted on the engine.

1. With the air horn removed, the air float raised and the inlet needle seated, check the distance between the top surface of the main body (gasket removed) and the surface of the float.

    a. Depress the float tab to seat the fuel inlet needle.

    b. Measure near the center of the float around ⅛ inch from the free end.

    c. Bend the tab on the float to adjust.

### ELECTRIC CHOKE

#### Linkage Check

1. With the engine off, remove the air cleaner and make sure that the holddown wingnut has not been over torqued and caused

**Dry float level adjustment—Motorcraft 2150**

**Choke housing index marks**

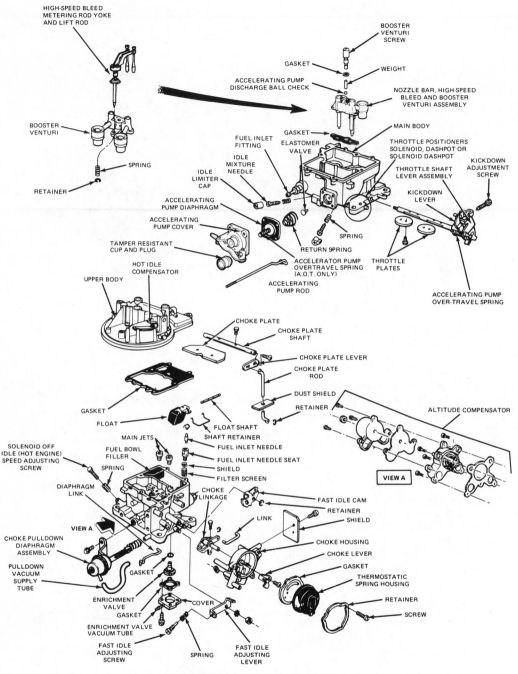

**Typical Motorcraft 2150 carburetor**

the A/C housing to interfere with the choke plate operation.

2. Make sure that the vacuum hoses, solenoid, and electrical choke wires are properly connected.

3. Check throttle system, choke plate, linkage and fast idle cam for freedom of operation.

### Electrical Test

1. Disconnect the choke lead wire from the choke cap and connect a jumper wire between the choke cap terminal and the wire terminal. Start the engine.

2. Connect a test light between the connector of the choke lead wire and ground. If the light glows, current is available to the choke cap. The choke cap should be replaced. If the light does not glow, connect the test light between the alternator stator and the choke lead wire. If the light glows, replace the lead wire. If the light does not glow, the problem lies in the engine electrical circuit.

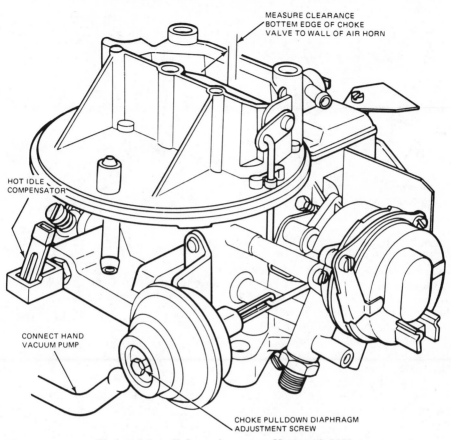

MEASURE CLEARANCE
BOTTOM EDGE OF CHOKE
VALVE TO WALL OF AIR HORN

HOT IDLE
COMPENSATOR

CONNECT HAND
VACUUM PUMP

CHOKE PULLDOWN DIAPHRAGM
ADJUSTMENT SCREW

**Choke plate pull-down clearance—Motorcraft 2150**

### Automatic Choke Adjustment

The automatic choke has an adjustment to control its reaction to engine temperature.

1. Remove the air cleaner.

2. Remove the heater hose from the bracket (if so equipped).

3. Loosen the thermostatic spring housing clamp retaining screws.

4. Set the spring housing to the specified index mark and tighten the clamp attaching screws.

5. Replace the heater hose and air cleaner assembly.

### CHOKE PLATE PULLDOWN AND FAST/IDLE CAM

The Model 2150 2V carburetor is equipped with a choke pulldown diaphragm assembly. Vacuum is metered to the diaphragm through internal passages in the carburetor, through a connecting external tube. As the vacuum bleeds through the orifices in the carburetor, the choke diaphragm pulls the choke plate to the pulldown position.

### Choke Pulldown Check

1. Set the throttle on the fast idle cam top step.

2. Note the index position of the choke bimetallic cap. Loosen the retaining screws and rotate the cap 90 degrees in the rich (closing) direction.

3. Manually force the pulldown control diaphragm link in the direction of the applied vacuum or apply vacuum to the external vacuum tube to activate the pulldown motor.

4. Measure the vertical hard gauge clearance between the choke plate and the center of the carburetor air horn wall nearest the fuel bowl. Adjust the choke plate pulldown to specification by adjusting the diaphragm stop on the end of the choke pulldown diaphragm.

5. Set the choke bimetallic cap to specification.

### Fast Idle Speed Adjustment

1. Remove the EGR vacuum line and air cleaner and plug both vacuum lines.

2. Check the ignition timing.

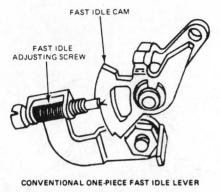

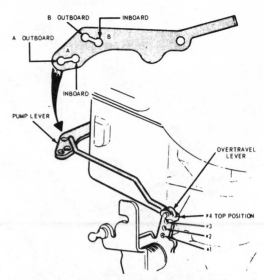

Fast idle cam setting—Motorcraft 2150

3. Place the transmission in Neutral and engage the parking brake.

4. Start the engine and bring to normal operation temperature.

5. Remove the spark delay valve (if so equipped) and route part throttle vacuum signal directly to advance side of distributor. If the distributor is a dual diaphragm model, leave the manifold vacuum line connected to the retard side of the distributor.

6. Set the throttle to the kickdown step on the choke cam and make sure the adjusting screw is against the shoulder of the kickdown step.

7. Adjust the rpm to specifications.

### Accelerator Pump Stroke Adjustment

The accelerator pump stroke has been preset at the factory for each particular engine and should not be readjusted. However if the rod has been changed from the specified hole it should be reset.

1. Lift up on the retaining clip and release the rod.

2. Position the slip over the hole specified in the carburetor specifications chart and in-

Accelerator pump stroke adjustment through 1979—Motorcraft 2150

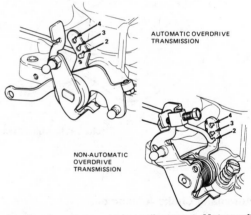

Accelerator pump stroke adjustment Motorcraft 2150 from 1980

sert the operating rod through the clip and the overtravel lever. Snap the end of the clip over the rod to secure.

## Model 2150

| Year | (9510)* Carburetor Identification | Dry Float Level (in.) | Wet Float Level (in.) | Pump Setting Hole # ① | Choke Plate Pulldown (in.) | Fast Idle Cam Linkage Clearance (in.) | Fast Idle (rpm) | Dechoke (in.) | Choke Setting |
|---|---|---|---|---|---|---|---|---|---|
| 1975–76 | All | 7/16 | 13/16 | 2 | 0.140 | ② | ③ | — | 3 Rich |
| 1977 | All | 7/16 | 13/16 | 2 | 0.147 | ② | ③ | — | 1 Rich |
| 1978 | D84E-EA | 7/16 | 13/16 | 2 | 0.110 | ② | ③ | — | 3 Rich |
| | D8AE-JA | 3/8 | 3/4 | 3 | 0.167 | ② | ③ | — | 3 Rich |
| | D8BE-ACA | 7/16 | 3/4 | 4 | 0.155 | ② | ③ | — | 2 Rich |
| | D8BE-ADA | 7/16 | 13/16 | 2 | 0.110 | ② | ③ | — | 3 Rich |

## Model 2150 (continued)

| Year | (9510)* Carburetor Identification | Dry Float Level (in.) | Wet Float Level (in.) | Pump Setting Hole # ① | Choke Plate Pulldown (in.) | Fast Idle Cam Linkage Clearance (in.) | Fast Idle (rpm) | Dechoke (in.) | Choke Setting |
|------|-----------------------------------|-----------------------|-----------------------|------------------------|------------------------------|----------------------------------------|-----------------|----------------|----------------|
| 1978 | D8BE-AEA | 7/16 | 13/16 | 2 | 0.110 | ② | ③ | — | 4 Rich |
| | D8BE-AFA | 7/16 | 13/16 | 2 | 0.110 | ② | ③ | — | 4 Rich |
| | D8BE-MB | 3/8 | 13/16 | 3 | 0.122 | ② | ③ | — | Index |
| | D8DE-HA | 19/32 | 13/16 | 3 | 0.157 | ② | ③ | — | Index |
| | D8KE-EA | 19/32 | 13/16 | 2 | 0.135 | ② | ③ | — | 3 Rich |
| | D8OE-BA | 3/8 | 3/4 | 3 | 0.167 | ② | ③ | — | 3 Rich |
| | D8OE-EA | 19/32 | 13/16 | 2 | 0.136 | ② | ③ | — | Index |
| | D8OE-HA | 7/16 | 13/16 | 3 | 0.180 | ② | ③ | — | 2 Rich |
| | D8SE-CA | 19/32 | 13/16 | 3 | 0.150 | ② | ③ | — | 2 Rich |
| | D8ZE-TA | 3/8 | 3/4 | 4 | 0.135 | ② | ③ | — | Index |
| | D8ZE-UA | 3/8 | 3/4 | 4 | 0.135 | ② | ③ | — | Index |
| | D8WE-DA | 7/16 | 13/16 | 4 | 0.143 | ② | ③ | — | 1 Rich |
| | D8YE-AB | 3/8 | 13/16 | 3 | 0.122 | ② | ③ | — | Index |
| | D8SE-DA, EA | 7/16 | 13/16 | 3 | 0.147 | ② | ③ | — | 3 Rich |
| | D8SE-FA, GA | 3/8 | 13/16 | 3 | 0.147 | ② | ③ | — | 3 Rich |
| 1979 | D9AE-AHA | 7/16 | 13/16 | 3 | 0.147 | ② | ③ | 1/4 | 3 Rich |
| | D9AE-AJA | 7/16 | 13/16 | 3 | 0.147 | ② | ③ | 1/4 | 3 Rich |
| | D9AE-ANB | 7/16 | 13/16 | 3 | 0.129 | ② | ③ | — | 1 Rich |
| | D9AE-APB | 7/16 | 13/16 | 3 | 0.129 | ② | ③ | — | 1 Rich |
| | D9AE-AVB | 7/16 | 13/16 | 3 | 0.129 | ② | ③ | — | 1 Rich |
| | D9AE-AYA | 7/16 | 13/16 | 3 | 0.129 | ② | ③ | — | 1 Rich |
| | D9AE-AYB | 7/16 | 13/16 | 3 | 0.129 | ② | ③ | — | 1 Rich |
| | D9AE-TB | 7/16 | 13/16 | 3 | 0.129 | ② | ③ | — | 2 Rich |
| | D9AE-UB | 7/16 | 13/16 | 3 | 0.129 | ② | ③ | — | 2 Rich |
| | D9BE-VB | 7/16 | 13/16 | 3 | 0.153 | ② | ③ | 1/4 | 2 Rich |
| | D9BE-YB | 7/16 | 13/16 | 3 | 0.153 | ② | ③ | — | 2 Rich |
| | D9DE-NB | 7/16 | 13/16 | 3 | 0.153 | ② | ③ | 1/4 | 2 Rich |
| | D9DE-RA | 7/16 | 13/16 | 2 | 0.125 | ② | ③ | 0.115 | 3 Rich |
| | D9DE-RB | 7/16 | 13/16 | 2 | 0.125 | ② | ③ | 0.115 | 3 Rich |
| | D9DE-RD | 7/16 | 13/16 | 2 | 0.125 | ② | ③ | — | 3 Rich |
| | D9DE-SA | 7/16 | 13/16 | 2 | 0.125 | ② | ③ | 1/4 | 3 Rich |
| | D9DE-SC | 7/16 | 13/16 | 2 | 0.125 | ② | ③ | — | 3 Rich |
| | D9ME-BA | 7/16 | 13/16 | 2 | 0.136 | ② | ③ | 0.115 | Index |
| | D9ME-CA | 7/16 | 13/16 | 2 | 0.136 | ② | ③ | 0.115 | Index |
| | D9OE-CB | 7/16 | 13/16 | 3 | 0.132 | ② | ③ | 0.115 | 3 Rich |
| | D9OE-DB | 7/16 | 13/16 | 3 | 0.132 | ② | ③ | — | 3 Rich |
| | D9OE-EA | 7/16 | 13/16 | 3 | 0.132 | ② | ③ | 0.115 | 2 Rich |
| | D9OE-FA | 7/16 | 13/16 | 3 | 0.132 | ② | ③ | 0.115 | 2 Rich |
| | D9SE-GA | 7/16 | 13/16 | 3 | 0.150 | ② | ③ | 1/4 | 2 Rich |

## Model 2150 (continued)

| Year | (9510)* Carburetor Identification | Dry Float Level (in.) | Wet Float Level (in.) | Pump Setting Hole # ① | Choke Plate Pulldown (in.) | Fast Idle Cam Linkage Clearance (in.) | Fast Idle (rpm) | Dechoke (in.) | Choke Setting |
|---|---|---|---|---|---|---|---|---|---|
| 1979 | D9VE-LC | ⅜ | ¾ | 3 | 0.145 | ② | ③ | ¼ | 3 Rich |
| | D9VE-SA | ⁷⁄₁₆ | ¹³⁄₁₆ | 3 | 0.147 | ② | ③ | — | 3 Rich |
| | D9VE-UB | ⁷⁄₁₆ | ¹³⁄₁₆ | 3 | 0.155 | ② | ③ | ¼ | 3 Rich |
| | D9VE-VA | ⅜ | ¾ | 3 | 0.145 | ② | ③ | — | 3 Rich |
| | D9VE-YB | ⅜ | ¾ | 2 | 0.145 | ② | ③ | ¼ | 3 Rich |
| | D9WE-CB | ⁷⁄₁₆ | ¹³⁄₁₆ | 3 | 0.132 | ② | ③ | — | 3 Rich |
| | D9WE-DB | ⁷⁄₁₆ | ¹³⁄₁₆ | 3 | 0.132 | ② | ③ | — | 3 Rich |
| | D9WE-EB | ⁷⁄₁₆ | ¹³⁄₁₆ | 3 | 0.132 | ② | ③ | — | 2 Rich |
| | D9WE-FB | ⁷⁄₁₆ | ¹³⁄₁₆ | 3 | 0.132 | ② | ③ | — | 2 Rich |
| | D9WE-JA | ⁷⁄₁₆ | ¹³⁄₁₆ | 3 | 0.150 | ② | ③ | ¼ | 2 Rich |
| | D9WE-MB | ⁷⁄₁₆ | ¹³⁄₁₆ | 3 | 0.132 | ② | ③ | — | 1 Rich |
| | D9WE-NB | ⁷⁄₁₆ | ¹³⁄₁₆ | 3 | 0.132 | ② | ③ | — | 1 Rich |
| | D9YE-EA | ⁷⁄₁₆ | ¹³⁄₁₆ | 3 | 0.118 | ② | ③ | 0.115 | 1 Rich |
| | D9YE-FA | ⁷⁄₁₆ | ¹³⁄₁₆ | 3 | 0.118 | ② | ③ | 0.115 | 1 Rich |
| | D9YE-AB | ⁷⁄₁₆ | ¹³⁄₁₆ | 3 | 0.118 | ② | ③ | 0.115 | Index |
| | D9YE-BB | ⁷⁄₁₆ | ¹³⁄₁₆ | 3 | 0.118 | ② | ③ | 0.115 | Index |
| | D9YE-CA | ⁷⁄₁₆ | ¹³⁄₁₆ | 2 | 0.118 | ② | ③ | 0.115 | Index |
| | D9YE-DA | ⁷⁄₁₆ | ¹³⁄₁₆ | 2 | 0.118 | ② | ③ | 0.115 | Index |
| | D9ZE-AYA | ⁷⁄₁₆ | ¹³⁄₁₆ | 3 | 0.138 | ② | ③ | 0.115 | Index |
| | D9ZE-BFB | ⁷⁄₁₆ | ¹³⁄₁₆ | 2 | 0.125 | ② | ③ | — | 3 Rich |
| | D9ZE-BGB | ⁷⁄₁₆ | ¹³⁄₁₆ | 2 | 0.125 | ② | ③ | — | 3 Rich |
| | D9ZE-BHB | ⁷⁄₁₆ | ¹³⁄₁₆ | 2 | 0.125 | ② | ③ | ¼ | 3 Rich |
| | D9ZE-BJB | ⁷⁄₁₆ | ¹³⁄₁₆ | 2 | 0.125 | ② | ③ | — | 3 Rich |
| 1980 | EO4E-PA, RA | — | ¹³⁄₁₆ | 2 | 0.104 | ② | ③ | ¼ | ③ |
| | EOBE-AUA | — | ¹³⁄₁₆ | 3 | 0.116 | ② | ③ | ¼ | ③ |
| | EODE-SA, TA | — | ¹³⁄₁₆ | 2 | 0.104 | ② | ③ | ¼ | ③ |
| | EOKE-CA, DA | — | ¹³⁄₁₆ | 3 | 0.116 | ② | ③ | ¼ | ③ |
| | EOKE-GA, HA | — | ¹³⁄₁₆ | 3 | 0.116 | ② | ③ | ¼ | ③ |
| | EOKE-JA, KA | — | ¹³⁄₁₆ | 3 | 0.116 | ② | ③ | ¼ | ③ |
| | D84E-TA, UA | — | ¹³⁄₁₆ | 2 | 0.125 | ② | ③ | ¼ | ③ |
| | EO4E-ADA, AEA | — | ¹³⁄₁₆ | 2 | 0.104 | ② | ③ | ¼ | ③ |
| | EO4E-CA | — | ¹³⁄₁₆ | 2 | 0.104 | ② | ③ | ¼ | ③ |
| | EO4E-EA, FA | — | ¹³⁄₁₆ | 2 | 0.104 | ② | ③ | ¼ | ③ |
| | EO4E-JA, KA | — | ¹³⁄₁₆ | 2 | 0.137 | ② | ③ | ¼ | ③ |
| | EO4E-SA, TA | — | ¹³⁄₁₆ | 2 | 0.104 | ② | ③ | ¼ | ③ |
| | EO4E-VA, YA | — | ¹³⁄₁₆ | 2 | 0.104 | ② | ③ | ¼ | ③ |
| | EODE-TA, VA | — | ¹³⁄₁₆ | 2 | 0.104 | ② | ③ | ¼ | ③ |
| | EOSE-GA, HA | — | ¹³⁄₁₆ | 2 | 0.104 | ② | ③ | ¼ | ③ |
| | EOSE-LA, MA | — | ¹³⁄₁₆ | 2 | 0.104 | ② | ③ | ¼ | ③ |

55 WAYS TO IMPROVE FUEL ECONOMY

# CHILTON'S
# FUEL ECONOMY
# & TUNE-UP TIPS

**Tune-up • Spark Plug Diagnosis • Emission Controls**

**Fuel System • Cooling System • Tires and Wheels**

**General Maintenance**

# CHILTON'S FUEL ECONOMY & TUNE-UP TIPS

Fuel economy is important to everyone, no matter what kind of vehicle you drive. The maintenance-minded motorist can save both money and fuel using these tips and the periodic maintenance and tune-up procedures in this Repair and Tune-Up Guide.

There are more than 130,000,000 cars and trucks registered for private use in the United States. Each travels an average of 10-12,000 miles per year, and, and in total they consume close to 70 billion gallons of fuel each year. This represents nearly ⅔ of the oil imported by the United States each year. The Federal government's goal is to reduce consumption 10% by 1985. A variety of methods are either already in use or under serious consideration, and they all affect you driving and the cars you will drive. In addition to "down-sizing", the auto industry is using or investigating the use of electronic fuel delivery, electronic engine controls and alternative engines for use in smaller and lighter vehicles, among other alternatives to meet the federally mandated Corporate Average Fuel Economy (CAFE) of 27.5 mpg by 1985. The government, for its part, is considering rationing, mandatory driving curtailments and tax increases on motor vehicle fuel in an effort to reduce consumption. The government's goal of a 10% reduction could be realized — and further government regulation avoided — if every private vehicle could use just 1 less gallon of fuel per week.

## How Much Can You Save?

Tests have proven that almost anyone can make at least a 10% reduction in fuel consumption through regular maintenance and tune-ups. When a major manufacturer of spark plugs sur-

## TUNE-UP

1. Check the cylinder compression to be sure the engine will really benefit from a tune-up and that it is capable of producing good fuel economy. A tune-up will be wasted on an engine in poor mechanical condition.

2. Replace spark plugs regularly. New spark plugs alone can increase fuel economy 3%.

3. Be sure the spark plugs are the correct type (heat range) for your vehicle. See the Tune-Up Specifications.

Heat range refers to the spark plug's ability to conduct heat away from the firing end. It must conduct the heat away in an even pattern to avoid becoming a source of pre-ignition, yet it must also operate hot enough to burn off conductive deposits that could cause misfiring.

The heat range is usually indicated by a number on the spark plug, part of the manufacturer's designation for each individual spark plug. The numbers in bold-face indicate the heat range in each manufacturer's identification system.

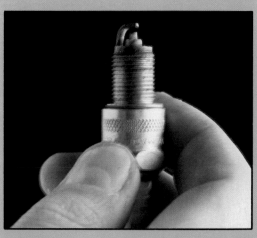

Periodically, check the spark plugs to be sure they are firing efficiently. They are excellent indicators of the internal condition of your engine.

| Manufacturer | Typical Designation |
|---|---|
| AC | R **45** TS |
| Bosch (old) | WA **145** T30 |
| Bosch (new) | HR **8** Y |
| Champion | RBL **15** Y |
| Fram/Autolite | **415** |
| Mopar | P-**62** PR |
| Motorcraft | BRF-**42** |
| NGK | BP **5** ES-15 |
| Nippondenso | W **16** EP |
| Prestolite | 14GR **5** 2A |

On AC, Bosch (new), Champion, Fram/Autolite, Mopar, Motorcraft and Prestolite, a higher number indicates a hotter plug. On Bosch (old), NGK and Nippondenso, a higher number indicates a colder plug.

4. Make sure the spark plugs are properly gapped. See the Tune-Up Specifications in this book.

5. Be sure the spark plugs are firing efficiently. The illustrations on the next 2 pages show you how to "read" the firing end of the spark plug.

6. Check the ignition timing and set it to specifications. Tests show that almost all cars have incorrect ignition timing by more than 2°.

veyed over 6,000 cars nationwide, they found that a tune-up, on cars that needed one, increased fuel economy over 11%. Replacing worn plugs alone, accounted for a 3% increase. The same test also revealed that 8 out of every 10 vehicles will have some maintenance deficiency that will directly affect fuel economy, emissions or performance. Most of this mileage-robbing neglect could be prevented with regular maintenance.

Modern engines require that all of the functioning systems operate properly for maximum efficiency. A malfunction anywhere wastes fuel. You can keep your vehicle running as efficiently and economically as possible, by being aware of your vehicle's operating and performance characteristics. If your vehicle suddenly develops performance or fuel economy problems it could be due to one or more of the following:

| PROBLEM | POSSIBLE CAUSE |
|---|---|
| Engine Idles Rough | Ignition timing, idle mixture, vacuum leak or something amiss in the emission control system. |
| Hesitates on Acceleration | Dirty carburetor or fuel filter, improper accelerator pump setting, ignition timing or fouled spark plugs. |
| Starts Hard or Fails to Start | Worn spark plugs, improperly set automatic choke, ice (or water) in fuel system. |
| Stalls Frequently | Automatic choke improperly adjusted and possible dirty air filter or fuel filter. |
| Performs Sluggishly | Worn spark plugs, dirty fuel or air filter, ignition timing or automatic choke out of adjustment. |

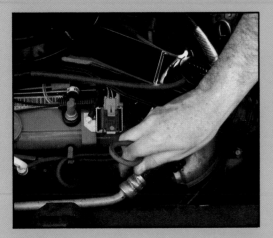

*Check spark plug wires on conventional point type ignition for cracks by bending them in a loop around your finger.*

*Be sure that spark plug wires leading to adjacent cylinders do not run too close together. (Photo courtesy Champion Spark Plug Co.)*

7. If your vehicle does not have electronic ignition, check the points, rotor and cap as specified.

8. Check the spark plug wires (used with conventional point-type ignitions) for cracks and burned or broken insulation by bending them in a loop around your finger. Cracked wires decrease fuel efficiency by failing to deliver full voltage to the spark plugs. One misfiring spark plug can cost you as much as 2 mpg.

9. Check the routing of the plug wires. Misfiring can be the result of spark plug leads to adjacent cylinders running parallel to each other and too close together. One wire tends to pick up voltage from the other causing it to fire "out of time".

10. Check all electrical and ignition circuits for voltage drop and resistance.

11. Check the distributor mechanical and/or vacuum advance mechanisms for proper functioning. The vacuum advance can be checked by twisting the distributor plate in the opposite direction of rotation. It should spring back when released.

12. Check and adjust the valve clearance on engines with mechanical lifters. The clearance should be slightly loose rather than too tight.

# SPARK PLUG DIAGNOSIS

## Normal

APPEARANCE: This plug is typical of one operating normally. The insulator nose varies from a light tan to grayish color with slight electrode wear. The presence of slight deposits is normal on used plugs and will have no adverse effect on engine performance. The spark plug heat range is correct for the engine and the engine is running normally.

CAUSE: Properly running engine.

RECOMMENDATION: Before reinstalling this plug, the electrodes should be cleaned and filed square. Set the gap to specifications. If the plug has been in service for more than 10-12,000 miles, the entire set should probably be replaced with a fresh set of the same heat range.

## Oil Deposits

APPEARANCE: The firing end of the plug is covered with a wet, oily coating.

CAUSE: The problem is poor oil control. On high mileage engines, oil is leaking past the rings or valve guides into the combustion chamber. A common cause is also a plugged PCV valve, and a ruptured fuel pump diaphragm can also cause this condition. Oil fouled plugs such as these are often found in new or recently overhauled engines, before normal oil control is achieved, and can be cleaned and reinstalled.

RECOMMENDATION: A hotter spark plug may temporarily relieve the problem, but the engine is probably in need of work.

## Incorrect Heat Range

APPEARANCE: The effects of high temperature on a spark plug are indicated by clean white, often blistered insulator. This can also be accompanied by excessive wear of the electrode, and the absence of deposits.

CAUSE: Check for the correct spark plug heat range. A plug which is too hot for the engine can result in overheating. A car operated mostly at high speeds can require a colder plug. Also check ignition timing, cooling system level, fuel mixture and leaking intake manifold.

RECOMMENDATION: If all ignition and engine adjustments are known to be correct, and no other malfunction exists, install spark plugs one heat range colder.

Photos Courtesy Fram Corporation

## Carbon Deposits

APPEARANCE: Carbon fouling is easily identified by the presence of dry, soft, black, sooty deposits.

CAUSE: Changing the heat range can often lead to carbon fouling, as can prolonged slow, stop-and-start driving. If the heat range is correct, carbon fouling can be attributed to a rich fuel mixture, sticking choke, clogged air cleaner, worn breaker points, retarded timing or low compression. If only one or two plugs are carbon fouled, check for corroded or cracked wires on the affected plugs. Also look for cracks in the distributor cap between the towers of affected cylinders.

RECOMMENDATION: After the problem is corrected, these plugs can be cleaned and reinstalled if not worn severely.

## MMT Fouled

APPEARANCE: Spark plugs fouled by MMT (Methycyclopentadienyl Maganese Tricarbonyl) have reddish, rusty appearance on the insulator and side electrode.

CAUSE: MMT is an anti-knock additive in gasoline used to replace lead. During the combustion process, the MMT leaves a reddish deposit on the insulator and side electrode.

RECOMMENDATION: No engine malfunction is indicated and the deposits will not affect plug performance any more than lead deposits (see Ash Deposits). MMT fouled plugs can be cleaned, regapped and reinstalled.

## High Speed Glazing

APPEARANCE: Glazing appears as shiny coating on the plug, either yellow or tan in color.

CAUSE: During hard, fast acceleration, plug temperatures rise suddenly. Deposits from normal combustion have no chance to fluff-off; instead, they melt on the insulator forming an electrically conductive coating which causes misfiring.

RECOMMENDATION: Glazed plugs are not easily cleaned. They should be replaced with a fresh set of plugs of the correct heat range. If the condition recurs, using plugs with a heat range one step colder may cure the problem.

## Ash (Lead) Deposits

APPEARANCE: Ash deposits are characterized by light brown or white colored deposits crusted on the side or center electrodes. In some cases it may give the plug a rusty appearance.

CAUSE: Ash deposits are normally derived from oil or fuel additives burned during normal combustion. Normally they are harmless, though excessive amounts can cause misfiring. If deposits are excessive in short mileage, the valve guides may be worn.

RECOMMENDATION: Ash-fouled plugs can be cleaned, gapped and reinstalled.

## Detonation

APPEARANCE: Detonation is usually characterized by a broken plug insulator.

CAUSE: A portion of the fuel charge will begin to burn spontaneously, from the increased heat following ignition. The explosion that results applies extreme pressure to engine components, frequently damaging spark plugs and pistons.

Detonation can result by over-advanced ignition timing, inferior gasoline (low octane) lean air/fuel mixture, poor carburetion, engine lugging or an increase in compression ratio due to combustion chamber deposits or engine modification.

RECOMMENDATION: Replace the plugs after correcting the problem.

Photos Courtesy Champion Spark Plug Co.

# EMISSION CONTROLS

13. Be aware of the general condition of the emission control system. It contributes to reduced pollution and should be serviced regularly to maintain efficient engine operation.

14. Check all vacuum lines for dried, cracked or brittle conditions. Something as simple as a leaking vacuum hose can cause poor performance and loss of economy.

15. Avoid tampering with the emission control system. Attempting to improve fuel econ-

# FUEL SYSTEM

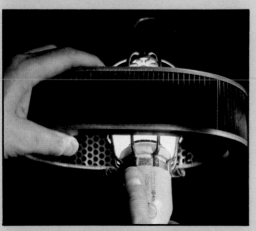

*Check the air filter with a light behind it. If you can see light through the filter it can be reused.*

*Extremely clogged filters should be discarded and replaced with a new one.*

18. Replace the air filter regularly. A dirty air filter richens the air/fuel mixture and can increase fuel consumption as much as 10%. Tests show that ⅓ of all vehicles have air filters in need of replacement.

19. Replace the fuel filter at least as often as recommended.

20. Set the idle speed and carburetor mixture to specifications.

21. Check the automatic choke. A sticking or malfunctioning choke wastes gas.

22. During the summer months, adjust the automatic choke for a leaner mixture which will produce faster engine warm-ups.

# COOLING SYSTEM

29. Be sure all accessory drive belts are in good condition. Check for cracks or wear.

30. Adjust all accessory drive belts to proper tension.

31. Check all hoses for swollen areas, worn spots, or loose clamps.

32. Check coolant level in the radiator or expansion tank.

33. Be sure the thermostat is operating properly. A stuck thermostat delays engine warm-up and a cold engine uses nearly twice as much fuel as a warm engine.

34. Drain and replace the engine coolant at least as often as recommended. Rust and scale

# TIRES & WHEELS

38. Check the tire pressure often with a pencil type gauge. Tests by a major tire manufacturer show that 90% of all vehicles have at least 1 tire improperly inflated. Better mileage can be achieved by over-inflating tires, but never exceed the maximum inflation pressure on the side of the tire.

39. If possible, install radial tires. Radial tires deliver as much as ½ mpg more than bias belted tires.

40. Avoid installing super-wide tires. They only create extra rolling resistance and decrease fuel mileage. Stick to the manufacturer's recommendations.

41. Have the wheels properly balanced.

omy by tampering with emission controls is more likely to worsen fuel economy than improve it. Emission control changes on modern engines are not readily reversible.

16. Clean (or replace) the EGR valve and lines as recommended.

17. Be sure that all vacuum lines and hoses are reconnected properly after working under the hood. An unconnected or misrouted vacuum line can wreak havoc with engine performance.

---

23. Check for fuel leaks at the carburetor, fuel pump, fuel lines and fuel tank. Be sure all lines and connections are tight.

24. Periodically check the tightness of the carburetor and intake manifold attaching nuts and bolts. These are a common place for vacuum leaks to occur.

25. Clean the carburetor periodically and lubricate the linkage.

26. The condition of the tailpipe can be an excellent indicator of proper engine combustion. After a long drive at highway speeds, the inside of the tailpipe should be a light grey in color. Black or soot on the insides indicates an overly rich mixture.

27. Check the fuel pump pressure. The fuel pump may be supplying more fuel than the engine needs.

28. Use the proper grade of gasoline for your engine. Don't try to compensate for knocking or "pinging" by advancing the ignition timing. This practice will only increase plug temperature and the chances of detonation or pre-ignition with relatively little performance gain.

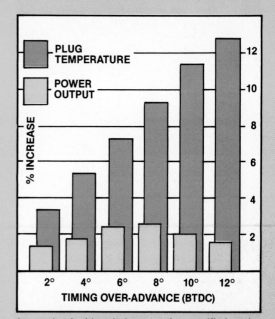

*Increasing ignition timing past the specified setting results in a drastic increase in spark plug temperature with increased chance of detonation or preignition. Performance increase is considerably less. (Photo courtesy Champion Spark Plug Co.)*

---

that form in the engine should be flushed out to allow the engine to operate at peak efficiency.

35. Clean the radiator of debris that can decrease cooling efficiency.

36. Install a flex-type or electric cooling fan, if you don't have a clutch type fan. Flex fans use curved plastic blades to push more air at low speeds when more cooling is needed; at high speeds the blades flatten out for less resistance. Electric fans only run when the engine temperature reaches a predetermined level.

37. Check the radiator cap for a worn or cracked gasket. If the cap does not seal properly, the cooling system will not function properly.

---

42. Be sure the front end is correctly aligned. A misaligned front end actually has wheels going in differed directions. The increased drag can reduce fuel economy by .3 mpg.

43. Correctly adjust the wheel bearings. Wheel bearings that are adjusted too tight increase rolling resistance.

*Check tire pressures regularly with a reliable pocket type gauge. Be sure to check the pressure on a cold tire.*

# GENERAL MAINTENANCE

*Check the fluid levels (particularly engine oil) on a regular basis. Be sure to check the oil for grit, water or other contamination.*

*A vacuum gauge is another excellent indicator of internal engine condition and can also be installed in the dash as a mileage indicator.*

44. Periodically check the fluid levels in the engine, power steering pump, master cylinder, automatic transmission and drive axle.

45. Change the oil at the recommended interval and change the filter at every oil change. Dirty oil is thick and causes extra friction between moving parts, cutting efficiency and increasing wear. A worn engine requires more frequent tune-ups and gets progressively worse fuel economy. In general, use the lightest viscosity oil for the driving conditions you will encounter.

46. Use the recommended viscosity fluids in the transmission and axle.

47. Be sure the battery is fully charged for fast starts. A slow starting engine wastes fuel.

48. Be sure battery terminals are clean and tight.

49. Check the battery electrolyte level and add distilled water if necessary.

50. Check the exhaust system for crushed pipes, blockages and leaks.

51. Adjust the brakes. Dragging brakes or brakes that are not releasing create increased drag on the engine.

52. Install a vacuum gauge or miles-per-gallon gauge. These gauges visually indicate engine vacuum in the intake manifold. High vacuum = good mileage and low vacuum = poorer mileage. The gauge can also be an excellent indicator of internal engine conditions.

53. Be sure the clutch is properly adjusted. A slipping clutch wastes fuel.

54. Check and periodically lubricate the heat control valve in the exhaust manifold. A sticking or inoperative valve prevents engine warm-up and wastes gas.

55. Keep accurate records to check fuel economy over a period of time. A sudden drop in fuel economy may signal a need for tune-up or other maintenance.

## Model 2150 (continued)

| Year | (9510) *<br>Carburetor<br>Identification | Dry<br>Float<br>Level<br>(in.) | Wet<br>Float<br>Level<br>(in.) | Pump<br>Setting<br>Hole # ① | Choke<br>Plate<br>Pulldown<br>(in.) | Fast<br>Idle Cam<br>Linkage<br>Clearance<br>(in.) | Fast<br>Idle<br>(rpm) | Dechoke<br>(in.) | Choke<br>Setting |
|---|---|---|---|---|---|---|---|---|---|
| 1980 | EOSE-NA | — | 13/16 | 2 | 0.104 | ② | ③ | ¼ | ③ |
| | EOSE-PA | — | 13/16 | 2 | 0.137 | ② | ③ | ¼ | ③ |
| | EOVE-FA | — | 13/16 | 2 | 0.104 | ② | ③ | ¼ | ③ |
| | EOWE-BA, CA | — | 13/16 | 2 | 0.137 | ② | ③ | ¼ | ③ |
| | D9AE-ANA, APA | — | 13/16 | 3 | 0.129 | ② | ③ | ¼ | ③ |
| | D9AE-AVA, AYA | — | 13/16 | 3 | 0.129 | ② | ③ | ¼ | ③ |
| | EOAE-AGA | — | 13/16 | 3 | 0.159 | ② | ③ | ¼ | ③ |
| 1981 | EIKE-CA | 7/16 | 0.810 | 3 | 0.124 | ② | ③ | 0.250 | ③ |
| | EIKE-EA | 7/16 | 0.810 | 3 | 0.124 | ② | ③ | 0.250 | ③ |
| | EIKE-DA | 7/16 | 0.810 | 3 | 0.124 | ② | ③ | 0.250 | ③ |
| | EIKE-FA | 7/16 | 0.810 | 3 | 0.124 | ② | ③ | 0.250 | ③ |
| | EIWE-FA | 7/16 | 0.810 | 2 | 0.120 | ② | ③ | 0.250 | ③ |
| | EIWE-EA | 7/16 | 0.810 | 2 | 0.120 | ② | ③ | 0.250 | ③ |
| | EIWE-CA | 7/16 | 0.810 | 2 | 0.120 | ② | ③ | 0.250 | ③ |
| | EIWE-DA | 7/16 | 0.810 | 2 | 0.120 | ② | ③ | 0.250 | ③ |
| | EIAE-YA | 7/16 | 0.810 | 3 | 0.124 | ② | ③ | 0.250 | ③ |
| | EIAE-ZA | 7/16 | 0.810 | 3 | 0.124 | ② | ③ | 0.250 | ③ |
| | EIAE-ADA | 7/16 | 0.810 | 3 | 0.124 | ② | ③ | 0.250 | ③ |
| | EIAE-AEA | 7/16 | 0.810 | 3 | 0.124 | ② | ③ | 0.250 | ③ |
| | EIAE-TA | — | 0.810 | 2 | 0.104 | ② | ③ | 0.250 | ③ |
| | EIAE-UA | — | 0.810 | 2 | 0.104 | ② | ③ | 0.250 | ③ |
| 1982 | E2BE-UA | 7/16 | 0.810 | 2 | 0.110 | ② | 2200 | 0.250 | ⑤ |
| | E2BE-AAA | 7/16 | 0.810 | 2 | 0.110 | ② | 2200 | 0.250 | ⑤ |
| | E2BE-VA | 7/16 | 0.810 | 2 | 0.113 | ② | 2200 | 0.250 | ⑤ |
| | E2BE-ABA | 7/16 | 0.810 | 2 | 0.113 | ② | 2200 | 0.250 | ⑤ |
| | E2BE-AGA | 7/16 | 0.810 | 2 | 0.113④ | ② | 2200 | 0.250 | ⑤ |
| | E2BE-AHA | 7/16 | 0.810 | 2 | 0.113 | ② | 2200 | 0.250 | ⑤ |
| | E2VE-CA | 7/16 | 0.810 | 2 | 0.113 | ② | 2200 | 0.250 | ⑤ |
| | E24E-CA | 7/16 | 0.810 | 2 | 0.110 | ② | 1200 | 0.250 | ⑤ |
| | E24E-DA | 7/16 | 0.810 | 2 | 0.110 | ② | 1200 | 0.250 | ⑤ |
| | E24E-AA | 7/16 | 0.810 | 2 | 0.110 | ② | 2100 | 0.250 | ⑤ |
| | E24E-BA | 7/16 | 0.810 | 2 | 0.110 | ② | 2100 | 0.250 | ⑤ |
| | E24E-EA | 7/16 | 0.810 | 2 | 0.110 | ② | ③ | 0.250 | ⑤ |
| | E24E-FA | 7/16 | 0.810 | 2 | 0.110 | ② | ③ | 0.250 | ⑤ |
| | E2KE-AA | 7/16 | 0.810 | 2 | 0.140 | ② | 1500 | 0.250 | ⑤ |
| | E2KE-BA | 7/16 | 0.810 | 2 | 0.140 | ② | 1500 | 0.250 | ⑤ |
| | E2WE-EA | 7/16 | 0.810 | 2 | 0.137 | ② | 1500 | 0.250 | ⑤ |
| | E2WE-FA | 7/16 | 0.810 | 2 | 0.137 | ② | 1500 | 0.250 | ⑤ |
| | E2DE-JA | 7/16 | 0.810 | 2 | 0.137 | ② | 1600 | 0.250 | ⑤ |

## Model 2150 (continued)

| Year | (9510)* Carburetor Identification | Dry Float Level (in.) | Wet Float Level (in.) | Pump Setting Hole # ① | Choke Plate Pulldown (in.) | Fast Idle Cam Linkage Clearance (in.) | Fast Idle (rpm) | Dechoke (in.) | Choke Setting |
|---|---|---|---|---|---|---|---|---|---|
| 1982 | E2DE-KA | 7/16 | 0.810 | 2 | 0.137 | ② | 1600 | 0.250 | ⑤ |
| | E2DE-LA | 7/16 | 0.810 | 2 | 0.137 | ② | 1700 | 0.250 | ⑤ |
| | E2DE-MA | 7/16 | 0.810 | 2 | 0.137 | ② | 1700 | 0.250 | ⑤ |
| | E25E-DA | 7/16 | 0.810 | 2 | 0.144 | ② | 1500 | 0.250 | ⑤ |
| | E2AE-SA | 7/16 | 0.810 | 2 | 0.172 | ② | 1550 | 0.250 | ⑤ |
| | E25E-CA | 7/16 | 0.810 | 2 | 0.137 | ② | 1700 | 0.250 | ⑤ |
| | E2ZE-BAA | 13/32 | 0.780 | 2 | 0.172 ④ | ② | 1400 | 0.250 | ⑤ |
| | E2ZE-BBA | 13/32 | 0.780 | 2 | 0.172 ④ | ② | 1400 | 0.250 | ⑤ |

\* Basic carburetor number for Ford products
① With link in inboard hole of pump lever
② Opposite "V" notch; see text
③ See underhood decal
④ ± .010"
⑤ V-notch

## Overhaul—Model 2150

### DISASSEMBLY

To facilitate workong on the carburetor, and to prevent damage to the throttle plates, install carburetor legs on the base. If legs are unavailable, install four bolts (about 2¼ inches long of the correct diameter) and eight nuts on the carburetor base.

Use a separate container for the component parts of the various assemblies to facilitate cleaning, inspection and assembly.

The following is a step-by-step sequence of operations for completely overhauling the carburetor. However certain components of the carburetor can be serviced without a complete disassembly of the entire unit. For complete carburetor overhaul, follow all of the steps. To partially overhaul a carburetor or to install a new gasket kit, follow only the applicable steps.

### Air Horn

1. Remove the air cleaner anchor screw.
2. Remove the automatic choke control rod retainer.
3. Remove the air horn attaching screws, lockwashers and the carburetor identification tag. Remove the air horn and air horn gasket.
4. Remove the choke control rod by loosening the screws which secure the choke shaft lever to the choke shaft. Remove the rod from the air horn. Slide the plastic dust seal out of the air horn.
5. If it is necessary to remove the choke plate, remove the staking marks on the choke plate attaching screws and remove the screws. Remove the choke plate by sliding it out of the shaft from the top of the air horn. Remove any burrs around screw holes prior to removing the choke shaft out of the air horn.

### Choke Pulldown Diaphragm Assembly

1. Disconnect the choke pulldown link by removing the rod retainer and pulling the rod out of the diaphragm link slot.
2. Remove the two screws from the attaching bracket. Disconnect the vacuum supply tube and remove the pulldown diaphragm.
3. To install, position the choke pulldown diaphragm mounting bracket against the main body casting and install the two attaching screws.
4. Connect the vacuum supply tube to the correct vacuum base tube connection.
5. Insert the choke pulldown control rod through the slot in the diaphragm link. Install the retainer clip over the end of the rod in the slot.
6. Perform an automatic choke pulldown clearance and fast idle cam index setting adjustment as described previously in this chapter.

### Automatic Choke

1. Remove the fast idle cam retainer.
2. Remove the thermostatic choke spring housing retaining screws and remove the clamp, housing and gasket.
3. Remove the choke housing assembly retaining screws. If the air horn was not previously removed, remove the choke control rod retainer. Remove the choke control rod retainer. Remove the choke housing assembly, gasket and the fast idle cam rod from the fast idle cam lever.
4. Remove the choke lever retaining screw

and washer. Disconnect the choke control rod from the choke lever. Remove the choke lever and fast idle cam lever from the choke housing.

## Main Body

1. With the use of a screwdriver, pry the float retainer from the fuel inlet seat. Remove the float, float shaft retainer and fuel inlet needle assembly. Remove the retainer and float shaft from the float lever.

2. Remove the fuel inlet needle, seat, filter screen and main jets with a jet wrench.

3. Remove the booster venturi screw (accelerator pump discharge), air distribution plate, booster venturi and metering rod assembly and gasket. Invert the main body. Let the accelerating pump discharge weight and ball and the mechanical high speed bleed lift rod and spring fall into your hand.

4. Remove the accelerator pump operating rod from the overtravel lever to the retainer. To release the operating rod from the overtravel lever retainer, press upward on the part of the retainer which snaps over the rod. Disengage the rod from the retainer and from the overtravel lever. Remove the rod and retainer.

5. Remove the accelerating pump cover attaching screws. Remove the accelerating pump cover, diaphragm assembly and spring.

6. If it is necessary to remove the Elastomer (power) valve, grasp it firmly and pull it out. If the Elastomer valve tip broke off during the removal, be sure to remove the tip from the fuel bowl. An Elastomer valve must be replaced whenever it has been removed from the carburetor, as it will dry out and crack.

7. Invert the main body and remove the enrichment valve with a box wrench or socket wrench. Remove the enrichment valve gasket. Discard the gasket.

8. Remove the idle fuel mixture adjusting screws (needles) and the springs. Remove the limiters from the adjusting screws.

9. If necessary, remove the nut and washer securing the fast idle adjusting lever assembly to the throttle shaft and remove the lever assembly. If necessary, remove the idle screw and the retainer from the fast idle adjusting lever.

10. Remove the anti-stall dashpot, solenoid or solenoid-dashpot (if so equipped).

11. If it is necessary to remove the throttle plates, lightly scribe the throttle plates along the throttle shaft, and mark each plate and its corresponding bore with a number or letter for proper installation.

12. Slide the throttle shaft out of the main body, making sure that you catch the mechan-

ical high speed bleed actuator located on the throttle shaft between the throttle plates.

Clean and inspect the carburetor components.

## ASSEMBLY

Make sure that all holes in new gaskets have been properly punched and that no foreign material has adhered to the gaskets. Make sure that the accelerating pump diaphragm is not torn or cut.

## Main Body

1. Slide the throttle shaft assembly into the main body until it begins to enter the high speed bleed cam slot in the body.

2. Holding the cam by the edge of the point, hold it in the slot and rotate the throttle shaft until it will pass through the cam. Rotate the shaft clockwise until the throttle lever clears the boss for the TSP "off" idle speed screw. Continue inserting the shaft into the proper position, rotating as necessary to properly position the cam.

3. Refer to the lines scribed on the throttle plates and install the throttle plates in their proper location with the screws snug, but not tight. Always use new screws when installing throttle plates.

4. Close the throttle plates. Invert the main body, and hold it up to the light. Little or no light should show between the throttle plates and the throttle bores. Tap the plates lightly with a screwdriver handle to seat them. Hold the throttle plates closed and tighten and stake the attaching screws. Stake hardened screws by crimping the exposed threads with diagonal cutters.

5. If necessary, install the fast idle screw on the fast idle adjusting lever.

6. Install the anti-stall dashpot, solenoid or solenoid-dashpot (if so equipped).

7. Place the fast idle adjusting lever assembly on the throttle shaft and install the retaining washer and nut.

8. If the Elastomer power valve was removed, lubricate the tip of the new Elastomer valve and insert the tip into the accelerator pump cavity center hole. Using a pair of needle-nose pliers, reach into the fuel bowl and grasp the valve tip. Pull the valve in until it seats in the pump cavity wall and cut off the tip forward of the retaining shoulder. Remove the tip from the bow.

9. Install the accelerating pump diaphragm return spring on the boss in the chamber. Insert the diaphragm assembly into position on the main body. Install the cover screws.

10. Insert the accelerating pump operating rod retainer over the specified hole in the ov-

ertravel lever. Insert the operating rod through the retainer and the hole in the overtravel lever and snap the retainer down over the rod.

11. Invert the main body. Install the enrichment valve and new gasket with a wrench. Tighten the valve securely.

12. Install the idle mixture adjusting screws (needles) and springs. Turn the needles in gently with your fingers until they just touch the seat, then back them off 1½ turns for a preliminary idle fuel mixture adjustment. Do not install the idle mixture limiters at this time. Install the enrichment valve cover and new gasket. The cover must be installed with the limiter stops on the cover in position to provide a positive stop for the tabs on the idle mixture adjusting screw limiters.

13. Install the main jets and the fuel inlet seat, filter screen, baffle and new gasket. Be sure that the correct jets are installed.

14. Install the fuel inlet needle assembly in the fuel inlet seat.

15. Slide the float shaft into the float lever. Position the float shaft retainer on the float shaft.

16. Insert the float assembly into the fuel bowl and hook the float lever tab under the fuel inlet needle assembly. Insert the float shaft into its guides at the sides of the fuel bowl.

17. With a screwdriver, position the float shaft retainer in the groove on the fuel needle inlet seat. Check the float setting.

18. Drop the accelerating pump discharge ball and weight into the passage in the main body.

19. Position the new booster assembly gasket and the booster venturi assembly in the main body. Install the air distribution plate and the accelerator pump discharge screw. Tighten the screw.

### Automatic Choke

1. Position the fast idle cam lever on the thermostatic choke shaft and lever assembly. The bottom of the fast idle cam lever adjusting screw must rest against the tang on the choke lever. Insert the choke lever into the rear of the choke housing. Position the choke lever so that the hole in the lever is to the left side of the choke housing.

2. Install the fast idle cam rod on the fast idle cam lever. Place the fast idle cam on the fast idle cam rod and install the retainer. Place the choke housing vacuum pickup port to main body gasket on the choke housing flange.

3. Position the choke housing on the main body and at the same time, install the fast idle cam on the hub on the main body. Position the gasket and install the choke housing at-

taching screws. Install the fast idle cam retainer. Install the thermostatic spring housing.

### Air Horn

1. If the choke plate shaft was removed, position the shaft in the air horn, then install the choke plate rod on the end of the choke shaft.

2. If the choke plate was removed, insert the choke plate into the choke plate shaft. Install the choke plate screws snug, but not tight. Check for proper plate fit, binding in the air horn and free rotation of the shaft by moving the plate from the closed position to the open position. If necessary, remove the choke plate and grind or file the plate edge where it is binding or scraping on the air horn wall. If the choke plate and shaft move freely, tighten the choke plate screws while holding the choke in the fully closed position.

3. Position the main body gasket and the choke rod plastic seal on the main body. Position the air horn on the main body and gasket so that the choke plate rod fits through the seal and the opening in the main body. Insert the end of the choke plate rod into the automatic choke lever. Install the air horn attaching screws and the carburetor identification tag. Tighten the attaching screws. Install the choke plate rod retainer. Install the air cleaner anchor screw. Tighten the air cleaner anchor screw to the specified torque.

Perform all automatic choke adjustments and other carburetor functions to specifications.

## Motorcraft 2700 VW and 7200 VV
### DESIGN

Since the design of the 2700 VV (variable venturi) carburetor differs considerably from the other carburetors in the Ford lineup, an explanation in the theory and operation is presented here.

In exterior appearance, the variable venturi carburetor is similar to conventional carburetors and, like a conventional carburetor, it uses a normal float and fuel bowl system. However, the similarity ends there. In place of a normal choke plate and fixed area venturis, the 2700 VV carburetor has a pair of small oblong castings in the top of the upper carburetor body where you would normally expect to see the choke plate. These castings slide back and forth across the top of the carburetor in response to fuel-air demands. Their movement is controlled by a spring-loaded diaphragm valve regulated by a vacuum signal taken below the venturis in the throttle bores. As the throttle is opened, the strength of the

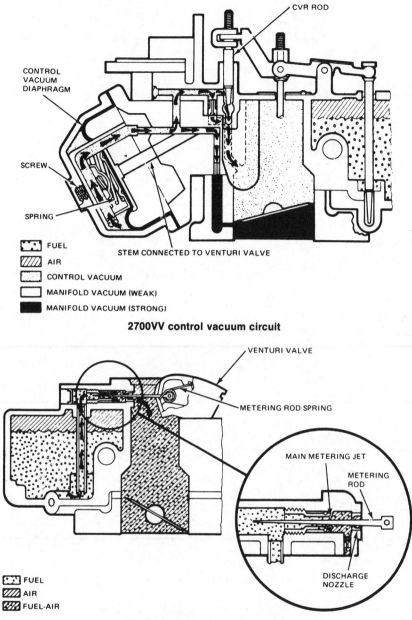

CVR ROD

CONTROL
VACUUM
DIAPHRAGM

SCREW

SPRING

[FUEL symbol] FUEL
[AIR symbol] AIR
[CONTROL VACUUM symbol] CONTROL VACUUM
[MANIFOLD VACUUM (WEAK) symbol] MANIFOLD VACUUM (WEAK)
[MANIFOLD VACUUM (STRONG) symbol] MANIFOLD VACUUM (STRONG)

STEM CONNECTED TO VENTURI VALVE

**2700VV control vacuum circuit**

VENTURI VALVE

METERING ROD SPRING

MAIN METERING JET

METERING
ROD

[FUEL symbol] FUEL
[AIR symbol] AIR
[FUEL-AIR symbol] FUEL-AIR

DISCHARGE
NOZZLE

**2700VV main metering system**

vacuum signal increases, opening the venturis and allowing more air to enter the carburetor.

Fuel is admitted into the venturi area by means of tapered metering rods that fit into the main jets. These rods are attached to the venturis, and, as the venturis open or close in response to air demand, the fuel needed to maintain the proper mixture increases or decreases as the metering rods slide in the jets. In comparison to a conventional carburetor with fixed venturis and a variable air supply, this system provides much more precise control of the fuel-air supply during all modes of operation. Because of the variable venturi principle, there are fewer fuel metering systems and fuel passages. The only auxiliary fuel metering systems required are an idle trim, accelerator pump (similar to a conventional carburetor), starting enrichment, and cold running enrichment.

NOTE: *Adjustment, assembly and disassembly of this carburetor require special tools for some of the operations. These tools are available (see the Tools and Equipment Section). Do not attempt any operations on this carburetor without first checking to see if you*

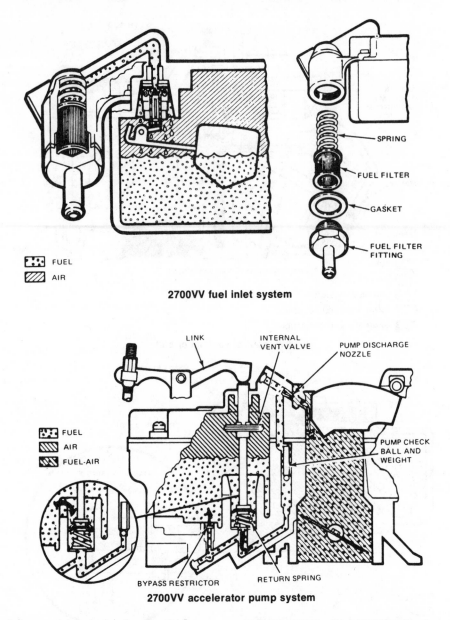

FUEL
AIR

SPRING

FUEL FILTER

GASKET

FUEL FILTER
FITTING

**2700VV fuel inlet system**

LINK

INTERNAL
VENT VALVE

PUMP DISCHARGE
NOZZLE

FUEL
AIR
FUEL-AIR

PUMP CHECK
BALL AND
WEIGHT

BYPASS RESTRICTOR

RETURN SPRING

**2700VV accelerator pump system**

*need the special tools for that particular operation. The adjustment and repair procedures given here mention when and if you will need the special tools.*

The Motorcraft model 7200 variable venturi (VV) carburetor shares most of its design features with the model 2700 VV. The major difference between the two is that the 7200 is designed to work with Ford's EEC (electronic engine control) feedback system. The feedback system precisely controls the air/fuel ratio by varying signals to the feedback control monitor located on the carburetor, which opens or closes the metering valve in response. This expands or reduces the amount of control vacuum above the fuel bowl, leaning or richening the mixture accordingly.

## FLOAT LEVEL ADJUSTMENT

1. Remove and invert the upper part of the carburetor, with the gasket in place.
2. Measure the vertical distance between the carburetor body, outside the gasket, and the bottom of the float.
3. To adjust, bend the float operating lever that contacts the needle valve. Make sure that the float remains parallel to the gasket surface.

## FLOAT DROP ADJUSTMENT

1. Remove and hold upright the upper part of the carburetor.
2. Measure the vertical distance between the carburetor body, outside the gasket, and the bottom of the float.

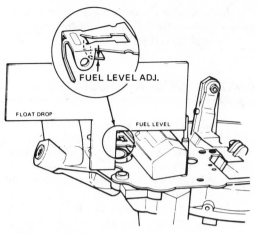

**Fuel level adjustment**

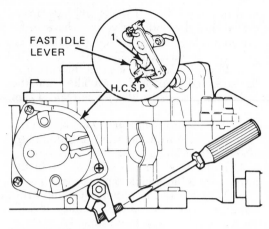

**Fast idle speed adjustment**

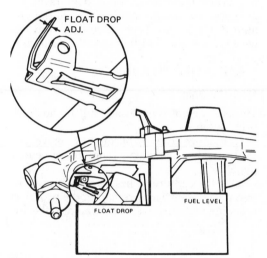

**Float drop adjustment**

3. Adjust by bending the stop tab on the float lever that contacts the hinge pin.

## FAST IDLE SPEED ADJUSTMENT

1. With the engine warmed up and idling, place the fast idle lever on the step of the fast idle cam specified on the engine compartment sticker or in the specifications chart. Disconnect and plug the EGR vacuum line.

2. Make sure the high speed cam positioner lever is disengaged.

3. Turn the fast idle speed screw to adjust to the specified speed.

## FAST IDLE CAM ADJUSTMENT

You will need a special tool for this job; Ford calls it a stator cap (#T77L-9848-A). It fits over the choke thermostatic lever when the choke cap is removed.

1. Remove the choke coil cap. On 1980 and later California models, the choke cap is riv-

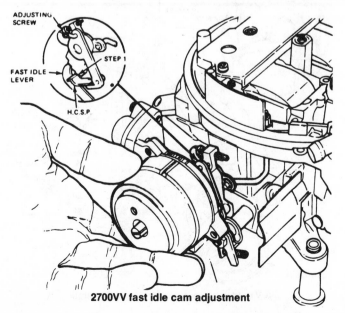

**2700VV fast idle cam adjustment**

eted in place. The top rivets will have to be drilled out; the bottom rivet will have to be driven out from the rear. New rivets must be used upon installation.

2. Place the fast idle lever in the corner of the specified step of the fast idle cam (the highest step is first) with the high speed cam positioner retracted.

3. If the adjustment is being made with the carburetor removed, hold the throttle lightly closed with a rubber band.

4. Turn the stator cap clockwise until the lever contacts the fast idle cam adjusting screw.

5. Turn the fast idle cam adjusting screw until the index mark on the cap lines up with the specified mark on the casting.

6. Remove the stator cap. Install the choke coil cap and set to the specified housing mark.

### COLD ENRICHMENT METERING ROD ADJUSTMENT

**1977–79**

A dial indicator and the stator cap are required for this adjustment.

1. Remove the choke coil cap. See Step 1 of the "Fast Idle Cam Adjustment."

2. Attach a weight to the choke coil mechanism to seat the cold enrichment rod.

3. Install and zero a dial indicator with the tip on top of the enrichment rod. Raise and release the weight to verify zero on the dial indicator.

4. With the stator cap at the index position,

the dial indicator should read the specified dimension. Turn the adjusting nut to correct.

5. Install the choke cap at the correct setting.

### CONTROL VACUUM ADJUSTMENT

**1977 Only**

1. Make sure the idle speed is correct.

2. Using a $5/32$ in. Allen wrench, turn the venturi valve diaphragm adjusting screw clockwise until the valve is firmly closed.

3. Connect a vacuum gauge to the vacuum tap on the venturi valve cover.

4. Idle the engine and use a ⅛ in. Allen wrench to turn the venturi by-pass adjusting screw to the specified vacuum setting. You may have to correct the idle speed.

5. Turn the venturi valve diaphragm adjusting screw counter-clockwise until the vacuum drops to the specified setting. You will have to work the throttle to get the vacuum to drop.

6. Reset the idle speed.

**1980–82 Only**

This adjustment is necessary only on nonfeedback systems.

1. Remove the carburetor. Remove the venturi valve diaphragm plug with a centerpunch.

2. If the carburetor has a venturi valve bypass plug, remove it by removing the two cover retaining screws; invert and remove the by-

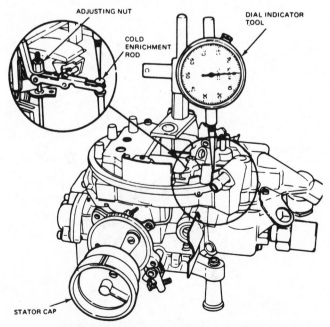

**2700VV cold enrichment metering rod adjustment**

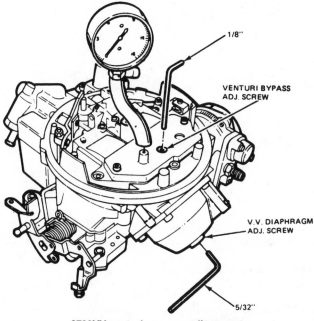

1/8"

VENTURI BYPASS
ADJ. SCREW

V.V. DIAPHRAGM
ADJ. SCREW

5/32"

**2700VV control vacuum adjustment**

pass screw plug from the cover with a drift. Install the cover.

3. Install the carburetor. Start the engine and allow it to reach normal operating temperature. Connect a vacuum gauge to the venturi valve cover. Set the idle speed to 500 rpm with the transmission in Drive.

4. Push and hold the venturi valve closed. Adjust the bypass screw to obtain a reading of 8 in. $H_2O$ on the vacuum gauge. Make sure the idle speed remains constant. Open and close the throttle and check the idle speed.

5. With the engine idling, adjust the venturi valve diaphragm screw to obtain a reading of 6 in. $H_2O$. Set the curb idle to specification. Install new venturi valve bypass and diaphragm plugs.

### INTERNAL VENT ADJUSTMENT

#### Through 1978 Only

This adjustment is required whenever the idle speed adjustment is changed.

1. Make sure the idle speed is correct.
2. Place a 0.010 in. feeler gauge between the accelerator pump stem and the operating link.
3. Turn the nylon adjusting nut until there is a slight drag on the gauge.

### VENTURI VALVE LIMITER ADJUSTMENT

1. Remove the carburetor. Take off the venturi valve cover and the two rollers.
2. Use a center punch to loosen the expan-

sion plug at the rear of the carburetor main body on the throttle side. Remove it.

3. Use an Allen wrench to remove the venturi valve wide open stop screw.
4. Hold the throttle wide open.
5. Apply a light closing pressure on the venturi valve and check the gap between the valve and the air horn wall. To adjust, move the venturi valve to the wide open position and insert an Allen wrench into the stop screw hole. Turn clockwise to increase the gap. Remove the wrench and check the gap again.
6. Replace the wide open stop screw and turn it clockwise until it contacts the valve.
7. Push the venturi valve wide open and check the gap. Turn the stop screw to bring the gap to specifications.
8. Reassemble the carburetor with a new expansion plug.

### CONTROL VACUUM REGULATOR ADJUSTMENT

There are two systems used. The earlier system's C.V.R. rod threads directly through the arm. The revised system, introduced in late 1977, has a ⅜ in. nylon hex adjusting nut on the C.V.R. rod and a flange on the rod.

#### Early System

1. Make sure that the cold enrichment metering rod adjustment is correct.
2. Rotate the choke coil cap half a turn clockwise from the index mark. Work the throttle to set the fast idle cam.
3. Press down lightly on the regulator rod.

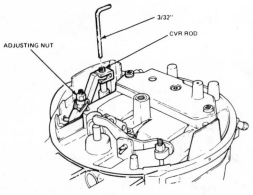

**Control vacuum regulator adjustment**

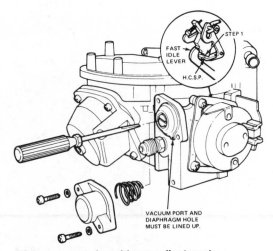

**High cam speed positioner adjustment**

If there is no down travel, turn the adjusting screw counter-clockwise until some travel is felt.

4. Turn the regulator rod clockwise with an Allen wrench until the adjusting nut just begins to rise.

5. Press lightly on the regulator rod. If there is any down travel, turn the adjusting screw clockwise in ¼ turn increments until it is eliminated.

6. Return the choke coil cap to the specified setting.

### Revised System

The cold enrichment metering rod adjustment must be checked and set before making this adjustment.

1. After adjusting the cold enrichment metering rod, leave the dial indicator in place but remove the stator cap. Do not re-zero the dial indicator.

2. Press down on the C.V.R. rod until it bottoms on its seat. Measure this amount of travel with the dial indicator.

3. If the adjustment is incorrect, hold the ⅜ in. C.V.R. adjusting nut with a box wrench to prevent it from turning. Use a ³/₃₂ in. Allen wrench to turn the C.V.R. rod; turning counter-clockwise will increase the travel, and vice versa.

## HIGH SPEED CAM POSITIONER ADJUSTMENT

### Through 1979 Only

1. Place the high speed cam positioner in the corner of the specified cam step, counting the highest step as the first.

2. Place the fast idle lever in the corner of the positioner.

3. Hold the throttle firmly closed.

4. Remove the diaphragm cover. Adjust the diaphragm assembly clockwise until it lightly bottoms. Turn it counter-clockwise ½ to 1½

turns until the vacuum port and diaphragm hole line up.

5. Replace the cover.

## IDLE MIXTURE ADJUSTMENT

### Through 1977 Only

The results of this adjustment should be checked with an emissions tester, to make sure that emission limits are not exceeded. Idle mixture (idle trim) is not adjustable 1978 and later models.

1. Remove the air cleaner cover only.

2. Use a ³/₃₂ in. Allen wrench to adjust the mixture for each barrel by turning the air adjusting screw. Turn clockwise to richen.

## DISASSEMBLY

NOTE: *Special tools are required. If you have any doubts about your ability to successfully complete this procedure, leave it to a professional service person.*

### Upper Body

1. Remove the fuel inlet fitting, fuel filter, gasket and spring.

2. Remove the screws retaining the upper body assembly and remove the upper body.

3. Remove the float hinge pin and float assembly.

4. Remove the fuel inlet valve, seat and gasket.

5. Remove the accelerator pump rod and the choke control rod.

6. Remove the accelerator pump link retaining pin and the link.

7. Remove the accelerator pump swivel and the retaining nut.

8. Remove the E-ring on the choke hinge pin and slide the pin out of the casting.

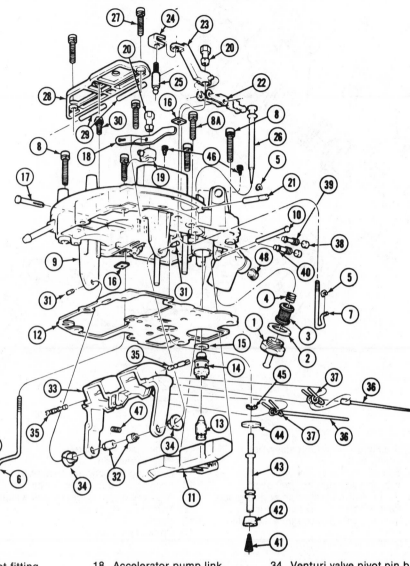

1. Fuel inlet fitting
2. Fuel inlet fitting gasket
3. Fuel filter
4. Fuel filter spring
5. Retaining E-ring
6. Accelerator pump rod
7. Choke control rod
8. Screw
8A. Screw
9. Upper body
10. Float hinge pin
11. Float assembly
12. Float bowl gasket
13. Fuel inlet valve
14. Fuel inlet seat
15. Fuel inlet seat gasket
16. Dust seal
17. Pin

18. Accelerator pump link
19. Accelerator pump swivel
20. Nut
21. Choke hinge pin
22. Cold enrichment rod lever
23. Cold enrichment rod swivel
24. Control vacuum regulator
    adjusting nut
25. Control vacuum regulator
26. Cold enrichment rod
27. Screw
28. Venturi valve cover plate
29. Roller bearing
30. Venturi air bypass screw
31. Venturi valve pivot plug
32. Venturi valve pivot pin
33. Venturi valve

34. Venturi valve pivot pin bushing
35. Metering rod pivot pin
36. Metering rod
37. Metering rod spring
38. Cup plug
39. Main metering jet assembly
40. O-ring
41. Accelerator pump return spring
42. Accelerator pump cup
43. Accelerator pump plunger
44. Internal vent valve
45. Retaining E-ring
46. Idle trim screw
47. Venturi valve limiter adjusting
    screw
48. Pipe plug

**1977 2700VV upper body assembly view. Each year some very slight changes in design were made. Always refer to the assembly drawing supplied with the rebuilding kit**

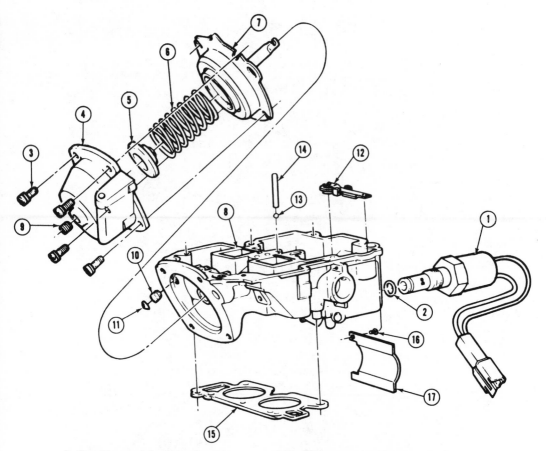

1. Cranking enrichment solenoid
2. O-ring seal
3. Screw
4. Venturi valve diaphragm cover
5. Venturi valve diaphragm spring guide
6. Venturi valve diaphragm spring
7. Venturi valve diaphragm assembly
8. Main body
9. Venturi valve adjusting screw
10. Wide open stop screw
11. Plug expansion
12. Cranking fuel control assembly
13. Accelerator pump check ball
14. Accelerator pump check ball weight
15. Throttle body gasket
16. Screw
17. Choke heat shield

**2700VV main body**

9. Remove the cold enrichment rod adjusting nut, lever and swivel; remove the control vacuum nut and regulator as an assembly.

10. Remove the cold enrichment rod.

11. Remove the venturi valve cover plate and roller bearings. Remove the venturi air bypass screw.

12. Using special tool T77P-9928-A, press the tapered plugs out of the venturi valve pivot pins.

13. Remove the venturi valve pivot pins, bushings and the venturi valve.

14. Remove the metering rod pivot pins, springs and metering rods. Be sure to mark the rods so that you know on which side they belong. Also, keep the venturi valve blocked open when working on the jets.

15. Using tool T77L-9533-B, remove the cup plugs.

16. Using tool T77L-9533-A, turn each main metering jet clockwise, counting the number of turns, until they bottom in the casting. You will need to know the number of turns when you reassemble the carburetor. Remove the jets and mark them so that you know on which side they belong. Don't lose the O-rings.

17. Remove the accelerator pump plunger assembly.

18. Remove the idle trim screws. Remove the venturi valve limiter adjusting screw.

19. To assemble the upper body, reverse the order.

### Main Body

1. Remove the cranking enrichment solenoid and the O-ring seal.

2. Remove the venturi valve cover, spring guide, and spring. Remove the venturi valve.

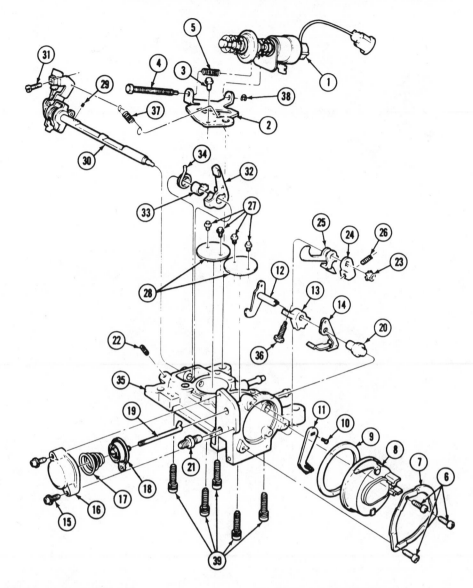

1. Throttle return control device
2. Throttle return control device bracket
3. Mounting screw
4. Adjusting screw
5. Adjusting screw spring
6. Screw
7. Choke thermostatic housing retainer
8. Choke thermostatic housing
9. Choke thermostatic housing gasket
10. Screw
11. Choke thermostatic lever
12. Choke lever and shaft assembly
13. Fast idle cam
14. High cam speed positioner assembly
15. Screw
16. High cam speed positioner diaphragm cover
17. High cam speed positioner diaphragm spring
18. High cam speed positioner diaphragm assembly
19. High cam speed positioner rod
20. Choke housing bushing
21. Choke heat tube fitting
22. Curb idle adjusting screw
23. Retaining nut
24. Fast idle adjusting lever
25. Fast idle lever
26. Fast idle adjusting screw
27. Throttle plate screws
28. Throttle plates
29. Venturi valve limiter stop pin
30. Throttle shaft assembly
31. Transmission kickdown adjusting screw
32. Venturi valve limiter lever
33. Venturi valve limiter bushing
34. Venturi valve limiter spring
35. Throttle body
36. Fast idle cam adjusting screw
37. Transmission kickdown lever return spring
38. Retaining E-ring
39. Screw

**1977 2700VV throttle body**

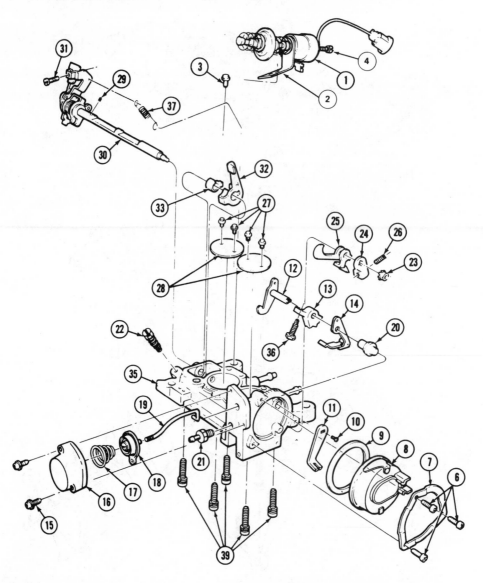

1. Throttle return control device
2. Throttle return control device bracket
3. Mounting screw
4. Adjusting screw (tsp on)
5. (Not applicable 1978)
6. Screw (3)
7. Choke thermostatic housing retainer
8. Choke thermostatic housing
9. Choke thermostatic housing gasket
10. Screw
11. Choke thermostatic lever
12. Choke lever and shaft assembly
13. Fast idle cam
14. High cam speed positioner assembly
15. Screw (2)
16. High cam speed positioner diaphragm cover
17. High cam speed positioner diaphragm spring
18. High cam speed positioner diaphragm assembly
19. High cam speed positioner rod
20. Choke housing bushing
21. Choke heat tube fitting
22. Curb idle adjusting screw (TSP off)
23. Retaining nut
24. Fast idle adjusting lever
25. Fast idle lever
26. Fast idle adjusting screw
27. Throttle plate screws (4)
28. Throttle plates
29. Venturi valve limiter stop pin
30. Throttle shaft assembly
31. Transmission kickdown adjusting screw
32. Venturi valve limiter lever
33. Venturi valve limiter bushing
34. (Not applicable 1978)
35. Throttle body
36. Fast idle cam adjusting screw
37. Transmission kickdown lever return spring
38. (Not applicable 1978)
39. Screw (5)

**2700VV throttle body from 1980**

## Model 2700 VV

| Year | Model | Float Level (in.) | Float Drop (in.) | Fast Idle Cam Setting (notches) | Cold Enrichment Metering Rod (in.) | Control Vacuum (in. H₂O) | Venturi Valve Limiter (in.) | Choke Cap Setting (notches) | Control Vacuum Regulator Setting (in.) |
|---|---|---|---|---|---|---|---|---|---|
| 1977–78 | All | 1³/₆₄ | 1¹⁵/₃₂ | 1 Rich/3rd step | .125 | 5.0 | ⁶¹/₆₄ | Index | — |
| 1979 | D9ZE-LB | 1³/₆₄ | 1¹⁵/₃₂ | 1 Rich/2nd step | .125 | ① | ② | Index | .230 |
| | D84E-KA | 1³/₆₄ | 1¹⁵/₃₂ | 1 Rich/3rd step | .125 | 5.5 | ⁶¹/₆₄ | Index | — |
| 1980 | All | 1³/₆₄ | 1¹⁵/₃₂ | 1 Rich/4th step | .125 | ③ | ④ | ⑤ | .075 |
| 1981 | EIAE-AAA | 1.015–1.065 | 1.435–1.485 | — | — | ③ | ④ | ⑤ | — |

① Venturi Air Bypass 6.8–7.3
  Venturi Valve Diaphragm 4.6–5.1
② Limiter Setting .38–.42
  Limiter Stop Setting .73–.77
③ See text
④ Opening gap: 0.99–1.01
  Closing gap: 0.94–0.98
⑤ See underhood decal

3. Remove the throttle body.
4. Remove the choke heat shield.
5. Assembly is in reverse order.

## Motorcraft 7200VV Feedback Carburetor

Some California models are equipped with a Motorcraft 7200VV Feedback carburetor.

The Model 7200VV Feedback carburetor shares the same basic systems with the 2700VV (variable venturi) carburetor. However, the 7200VV carburetor's feedback system is controlled by an electronic engine control system (EEC III). This system provides precise control of the air/fuel ratio, thereby, improving exhaust emissions, drive-ability and fuel economy.

Methods of testing the 7200VV carburetor and the EEC III system are possibly beyond the resources of the do-it-yourselfer. It therefore, is suggested that you consult your Ford dealer or a qualified repair shop for any service or repair.

## Fuel Tank

### REMOVAL

1. Raise the vehicle up on a hoist.
2. Drain the fuel from the tank.
3. Disconnect the fuel lines and hoses from the tank assembly.
4. Loosen the retaining straps at the adjusting bolts and remove the tank.

### INSTALLATION

1. Position the fuel tank and install the retaining straps.
2. Connect all fuel lines, replacing any cracked, split, or dried out hoses.
3. Replace the fuel separator if found to be damaged or inoperative.
4. Tighten the retaining straps securely.

# Chassis Electrical

**5**

## HEATER: VEHICLES WITHOUT AIR CONDITIONING

### Heater Assembly
#### REMOVAL AND INSTALLATION
**1975–80**

1. Drain the cooling system.
2. Disconnect the heater hoses from the core tubes.
3. Remove the glove box.
4. Remove the right register air duct.
5. Remove the floor discharge duct and the floor nozzle.
6. Disconnect the two air door control cables from the heater case and doors.
7. Remove the right vent cable from the instrument panel.
8. Disconnect the resistor.
9. Remove the vent duct-to-upper cowl bolt.
10. Remove the three heater case-to-firewall mounting stud nuts and remove the heater case.
11. Installation is the reverse of removal.

### Heater Core
#### REMOVAL AND INSTALLATION
**1975–80**

The heater core is located inside the heater case. With the heater assembly removed, remove the heater core cover and pad and remove the core. Reverse the procedure to install. If a new core is being installed, transfer the rubber pads from the old one.

**1981–82**

It is not necessary to remove the heater case for access to the heater core.
1. Drain enough coolant from the radiator to drain the heater core.
2. Loosen the heater hose clamps on the engine side of the firewall and disconnect the heater hoses. Cap the heater core tubes.
3. Remove the glove box liner.
4. Remove the instrument panel-to-cowl brace retaining screws and remove the brace.
5. Move the temperature lever to warm.
6. Remove the heater core cover screws. Remove the cover through the glove box.
7. Loosen the heater case mounting nuts on the engine side of the firewall.
8. Push the heater core tubes and seal toward the interior of the car to loosen the core.
9. Remove the heater core through the glove box opening.

### Blower Motor
#### REMOVAL AND INSTALLATION
**1975–80**

The blower motor is located inside the heater assembly. With the assembly removed, unbolt and remove the blower motor. The motor and cage are removed as an assembly. Reverse the procedure to install.

**1981–82**

The right side ventilator assembly must be removed for access to the blower motor and wheel.
1. Remove the retaining screw for the right register duct mounting bracket.
2. Remove the screws holding the control cable lever assembly to the instrument panel.
3. Remove the glove box liner.
4. Remove the plastic rivets securing the grille to the floor outlet, and remove the grille.
5. Remove the right register duct and register assembly:
   a. Remove the register duct bracket retaining screw on the lower edge of the instrument panel, and disengage the duct from the opening and remove through the glove box opening.

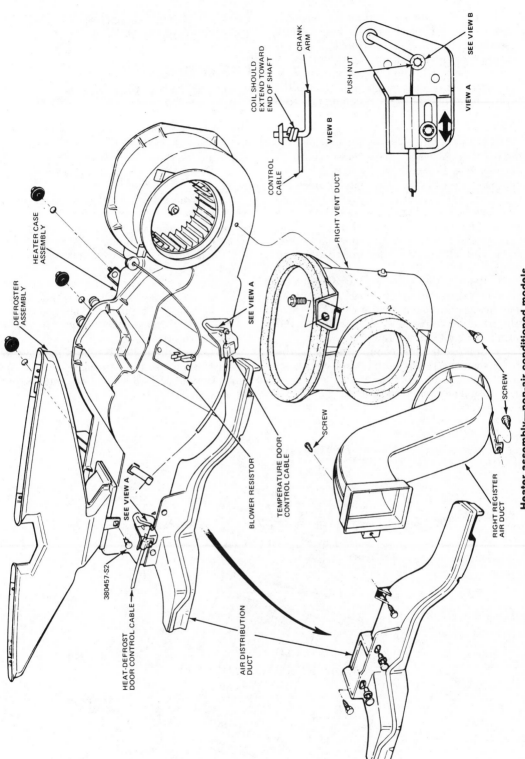

COIL SHOULD
EXTEND TOWARD
END OF SHAFT

CRANK
ARM

VIEW B

CONTROL
CABLE

SEE VIEW B

PUSH NUT

VIEW A

HEATER CASE
ASSEMBLY

DEFROSTER
ASSEMBLY

RIGHT VENT DUCT

SEE VIEW A

380457-S2

SEE VIEW A

BLOWER RESISTOR

TEMPERATURE DOOR
CONTROL CABLE

SCREW

SCREW

SCREW

HEAT-DEFROST
DOOR CONTROL CABLE

AIR DISTRIBUTION
DUCT

RIGHT REGISTER
AIR DUCT

**Heater assembly—non-air conditioned models**

b.  Insert a thin blade under the retaining tab and pry the tab toward the louvers until retaining tab pivot clears the hole in the register opening. Pull the register assembly end out from the housing only enough to prevent the pivot from going back into the pivot hole. Pry the other retaining tab loose and remove the register assembly from the opening.

6.  Remove the retaining screws securing the ventilator assembly to the blower housing. The upper right screw can be reached with a long extension through the register opening; the upper left screw can be reached through the glove box opening. The other two screws are on the bottom of the assembly.

7.  Slide the assembly to the right, then down and out from under the instrument panel.

8.  Remove the motor lead wire connector from the register and push it back through the hole in the case. Remove the right side cowl trim panel for access, and remove the ground terminal lug retaining screw.

9.  Remove the hub clamp spring from the motor shaft and remove the blower wheel.

10.  Remove the blower motor bolts from the housing and remove the motor.

# HEATER: VEHICLES WITH AIR CONDITIONING

## Heater Core
### *REMOVAL AND INSTALLATION*
**1975–80**

The refrigerant system components and charge do not have to be disturbed when removing and installing the heater core.

1.  Drain the coolant and disconnect the negative battery cable.

2.  Disconnect the heater hoses at the dash panel in the engine compartment. Plug the tubes to prevent coolant leakage.

3.  On models through 1978, remove the heat distribution duct from the instrument panel.

4.  Remove the seat belt interlock module and bracket. Remove the glove box liner.

5.  Loosen the right door sill scuff plate, right A-pillar trim cover and remove the right cowl side trim panel.

6.  Loosen the bolt that retains the cowl to the instrument panel and remove the instrument panel brace bolt at the lower rail, below the glove box.

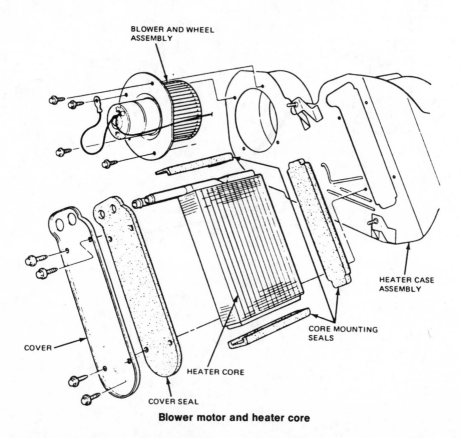

BLOWER AND WHEEL ASSEMBLY

HEATER CASE ASSEMBLY

CORE MOUNTING SEALS

COVER

HEATER CORE

COVER SEAL

**Blower motor and heater core**

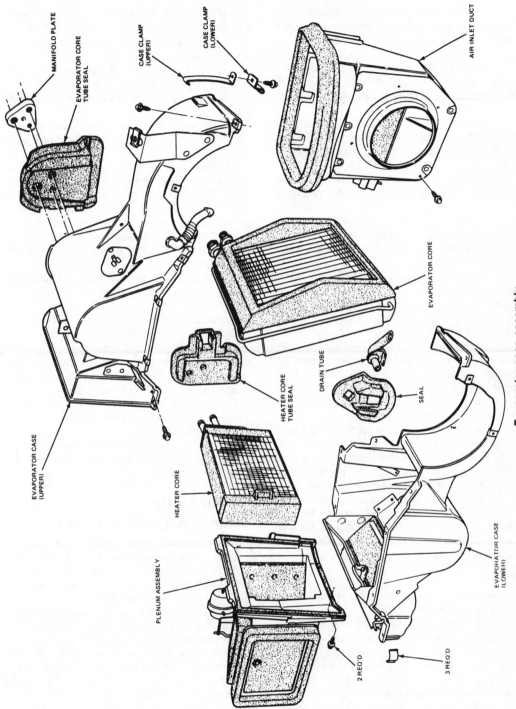

MANIFOLD PLATE

EVAPORATOR CORE TUBE SEAL

CASE CLAMP (UPPER)

CASE CLAMP (LOWER)

AIR INLET DUCT

EVAPORATOR CORE

EVAPORATOR CASE (UPPER)

HEATER CORE TUBE SEAL

DRAIN TUBE

SEAL

HEATER CORE

PLENUM ASSEMBLY

2 REQ'D

3 REQ'D

EVAPORATOR CASE (LOWER)

**Evaporator case assembly**

7. On 1975–76 models, remove the instrument panel crash pad. Remove the radio speaker or panel cowl brace if the car does not have a radio.

8. Remove the four screws which retain the defroster nozzle to the cowl bracket. Lift the defroster nozzle upward through the crash pad opening.

9. Disconnect the vacuum hoses from the door motors. Remove the screw from the clip holding the vacuum harness to the plenum assembly.

10. Remove the heater-defroster door mounting nuts and swing the motor rearward on the door crankarm.

11. Remove the two screws attaching the plenum to the left mounting bracket. Then remove the screws and clips securing the plenum to the evaporator case.

12. Swing the bottom of the plenum away from the evaporator case to disengage the S-clip on the forward flange of the plenum. Raise the plenum to clear the tabs on top of the evaporator case.

13. Since there is very little clearance between the plenum and the wiper motor assembly, move the plenum as far to the left as possible while pulling rearward on the instrument panel to gain clearance. Be careful not to crack the instrument panel.

14. Pull the heater core to the left, using the tab molded into the rear heater core seal. As the rear surface of the heater core clears the evaporator case, pull the core rearward and downward to clear the instrument panel.

15. Reverse the above procedure to install. NOTE: *Before installing the core, make sure that the heater core tube to dash panel seal is in place between the evaporator case and the dash panel.*

**1981–82**

The instrument panel must be removed for access to the heater core.

1. Disconnect the battery ground cable.

2. Remove the instrument panel pad:

a. Remove the screws attaching the instrument cluster trim panel to the pad.

b. Remove the screw attaching the pad to the panel at each defroster opening.

c. Remove the screws attaching the edge of the pad to the panel.

3. Remove the steering column opening cover.

4. Remove the nuts and bracket retaining the steering column to the instrument panel and lay the column against the seat.

5. Remove the instrument panel to brake pedal support screw at the column opening.

6. Remove the screws attaching the lower brace to the panel below the radio, and below the glove box.

7. Disconnect the temperature cable from the door and case bracket.

8. Unplug the 7-port vacuum hose connectors at the evaporator case.

9. Disconnect the resistor wire connector and the blower feed wire.

10. Remove the screws attaching the top of the panel to the cowl. Support the panel while doing this.

11. Remove the one screw at each end attaching the panel to the cowl side panels.

12. Move the panel rearward and disconnect the speedometer cable and any wires preventing the panel from lying flat on the seat.

13. Drain the coolant and disconnect the heater hoses from the heater core. Plug the core tubes.

14. Remove the nuts retaining the evaporator case to the firewall in the engine compartment.

15. Remove the case support bracket screws and air inlet duct support bracket.

16. Remove the nut retaining the bracket to the dash panel at the left side of the evaporator case, and the nut retaining the bracket below the case to the dash panel.

17. Pull the case assembly away from the panel to get to the screws retaining the heater core cover to the case.

18. Remove the cover screws and the cover.

19. Lift the heater core and seals from the evaporator case.

## Blower Motor
### REMOVAL AND INSTALLATION

1. Disconnect the negative battery cable.

2. Remove the right cowl side trim panel.

3. Remove the bolt retaining the lower side of the instrument panel to the cowl. Remove the right cowl side brace bolt.

4. Disconnect the wiring harness connectors at the blower motor. If so equipped, remove the cooling tube from the blower motor.

5. Remove the four screws retaining the blower motor and remove the blower assembly. Pull rearward on the lower edge of the instrument panel to provide clearance.

6. Installation is in reverse order. If necessary, cement the cooling tube to the blower motor.

**1981–82**

The air inlet duct and blower housing assembly must be removed for access to the blower motor.

1. Remove the glove box liner and disconnect the hose from the vacuum motor.

2. Remove the instrument panel lower right side to cowl attaching bolt.

3. Remove the screw attaching the brace to the top of the air inlet duct.

4. Disconnect the motor wire.

5. Remove the housing lower support bracket to case nut.

6. Remove the side cowl trim panel and remove the ground wire screw.

7. Remove the attaching screw at the top of the air inlet duct.

8. Remove the air inlet duct and housing assembly down and away from the evaporator case.

9. Remove the four blower motor mounting plate screws and remove the blower motor and wheel as an assembly from the housing. Do not remove the mounting plate from the motor.

## RADIO

### REMOVAL AND INSTALLATION

#### 1975–80

1. Disconnect the negative battery cable.

2. Remove the headlight control knob and shaft by depressing the release button on the rear of the switch.

3. Remove the bezel nut that attaches the switch to the instrument panel and remove the switch.

4. Remove the heater, air conditioner, windshield wiper knobs, and radio knobs and discs.

5. Remove the screws retaining the applique to the instrument panel and remove the applique. Disconnect the antenna cable.

6. Remove the four screws retaining the radio bezel and slide the radio and bezel out of the lower rear support bracket. Disconnect the electrical connections and remove the radio.

7. To install, replace the rear support bracket on the radio. Install the bezel and the washers and nuts on the radio shafts.

8. Insert the radio through the instrument panel opening far enough to connect the electrical leads and the antenna cable. Install the radio upper rear support bracket into the lower rear support bracket.

9. Center the radio in the opening and install the four bezel attaching screws.

10. Install the instrument panel applique. Install all the knobs removed earlier. Install the headlight switch.

11. Connect the battery cable.

#### 1981–82

1. Disconnect the negative battery cable.

2. Disconnect the electrical, speaker, and antenna leads from the radio.

3. Remove the knobs, discs, and control shaft nuts and washers from the radio shafts.

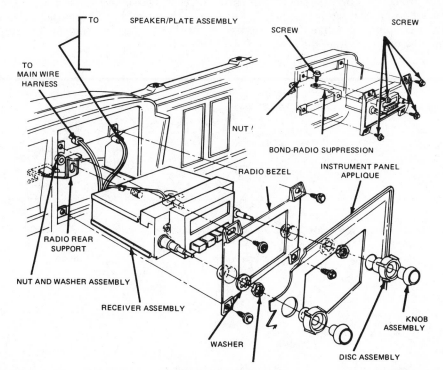

**Radio installation**

4. Remove the ash tray receptacle and bracket.

5. Remove the rear support nut from the radio.

6. Remove the instrument panel lower reinforcement and the heater or air conditioning floor ducts.

7. Remove the radio from the rear support, and drop the radio down and out from behind the instrument panel.

8. To install, reverse the removal procedure.

# WINDSHIELD WIPERS

## Blade and Arm

### REPLACEMENT

Raise the blade end of the wiper off the windshield and move the slide latch away from the pivot shaft. The wiper arm can now be pulled off the shaft. No tools are necessary. To install a new arm, simply push the arm head down over the pivot shaft while holding the slide latch out of the way. Lower the blade onto the windshield. If the blade does not touch the windshield, then the slide latch is not completely in place.

Blades used are of two types: the bayonet type and the sidesaddle type. To remove the bayonet type, press inward on the tab and pull the blade from the arm. To remove the pin type, insert a small flat screwdriver blade between the arm and the tab and press down, while pulling the blade from the arm.

For more information on wiper blade replacement, refer to Chapter 1.

## Wiper Motor

### REMOVAL AND INSTALLATION

The wiper motor contains glass-like elements which can easily be damaged by mishandling. Never tap or strike the motor with a solid object.

### Through 1977

1. Disconnect the negative battery cable.
2. Remove the evaporator case center distribution duct.
3. Remove the wiper motor pivot clip and work it over the top of the brake support assembly.
4. Disconnect the linkage from the arm. Some models are equipped with an additional instrument panel brace which must be detached from the floor pan and swung to one side for clearance.
5. Remove the wiper motor mounting bolts and remove the motor.
6. Reverse the above to install.

### 1978–80

1. Disconnect the negative battery cable.
2. Remove the eight instrument panel pad screws.
3. Remove the radio speaker mounting bracket. Disconnect and remove the speaker.
4. Remove the defroster nozzle and the air distribution duct by removing the four attaching screws.

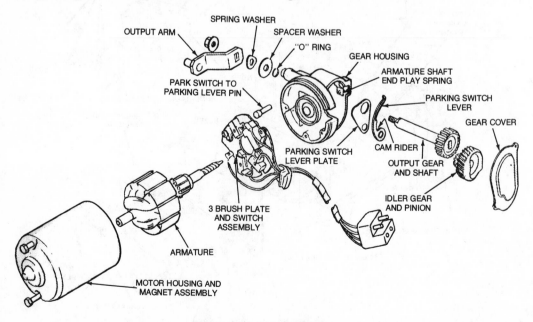

**Wiper motor—exploded view**

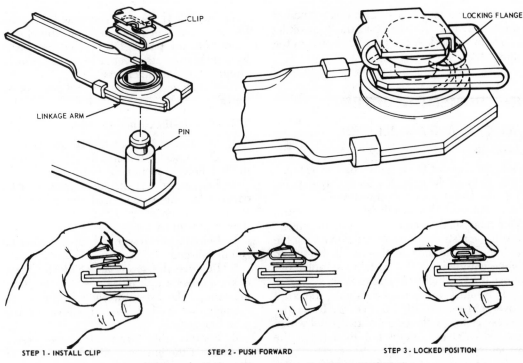

STEP 1 - INSTALL CLIP     STEP 2 - PUSH FORWARD     STEP 3 - LOCKED POSITION

**Installation of wiper arm connector clips, if so equipped**

5. Remove the wiper motor mounting bolts and remove the motor and the drive arm clip.

6. Transfer the drive arm and the motor bracket to the new motor. Reverse the removal procedure to install.

### 1981–82

1. Disconnect the ground cable.

2. Remove the right hand wiper arm from the pivot shaft and lay it on the top grille.

3. Remove the cowl top grille screws.

4. Reach under the left front corner of the grille to disconnect the linkage drive arm from the motor crank by removing the retaining clip.

5. Disconnect the electrical connector. Remove the motor mounting bolts and remove the motor.

6. Install in reverse order.

## Pivot Shaft and Linkage
### REMOVAL AND INSTALLATION

#### 1975–80
#### Left Side

1. Remove the instrument cluster.

2. Remove the wiper arm and blade assembly from the pivot shaft.

3. Working through the cluster opening, disconnect both pivot shaft links from the motor drive arm by removing the connecting clip.

4. Remove the three bolts that retain the left pivot shaft assembly to the cowl and take the left pivot shaft assembly out through the cluster opening.

5. Before installing, cement a new gasket on the pivot shaft mounting flange. Tighten the retaining bolts to 3–7 ft. lb. After installing the pivot shaft and link assembly to the cowl, connect the right pivot shaft link to the motor drive arm first, then connect the left link. Be sure that the connecting clip is locked, as shown in the illustration.

#### Right Side

1. Disconnect the negative battery cable.

2. Remove the wiper arm and blade assembly from the pivot shaft.

3. If the car is air conditioned, remove the right duct assembly. Unclip the duct from the right connector, slide the left end out of the plenum chamber and lower the duct assembly out from under the instrument panel.

4. From under the instrument panel, disconnect first the left and then the right pivot shaft link from the motor drive arm by removing the remaining clip.

5. Remove the three bolts that retain the right pivot shaft and link assembly to the cowl. Lower the assembly out from under the instrument panel.

6. Before installing, cement a new gasket to the pivot shaft mounting flange. After installing the pivot shaft and link assembly to the cowl, be sure the right pivot shaft link is con-

nected to the motor drive arm before the left pivot shaft link. Be sure that the connecting clip is in the locked position, as shown in the illustration.

## INSTRUMENT CLUSTER

### REMOVAL AND INSTALLATION

#### 1975-80

1. Disconnect the negative battery cable.
2. Remove the lower cluster applique cover. Remove the steering column shroud.
3. Remove the headlight switch control knob and shaft assembly by reaching underneath the instrument panel and depressing the bottom on the side of the headlight switch while withdrawing the switch assembly. Remove the headlight switch bezel.
4. Remove the screws retaining the front cover and remove the front cover. It may be necessary to pry the edges of the panel with a screwdriver. Be careful not to damage the panel.
5. If the vehicle is equipped with an automatic transmission, remove the screw retaining the PRND2L control cable bracket to the steering column. Detach the cable loop from the pin on the steering column.
6. Disconnect the speedometer cable by pressing the flat surface of the plastic connector and pulling the cable away from the head.

7. Remove the screws retaining the cluster to the instrument panel and pull the cluster away from the panel. Disconnect the cluster feed plug from its receptacle in the printed circuit. Remove the cluster.
8. Installation is in the reverse order of removal.

#### 1981-82 Non-Electronic Cluster

1. Disconnect the negative battery cable.
2. Disconnect the speedometer cable (refer to the following section for instructions).
3. Remove the instrument cluster trim cover attaching screws and the lower two steering column cover attaching screws. Remove the trim covers.
4. Remove the lower half of the steering column shroud.
5. Remove the screw attaching the transmission selector indicator bracket to the steering column. Unfasten the cable loop from the retainer on the shift lever. Remove the column bracket.
6. Remove the cluster attaching screws. Disconnect the cluster feed plug and remove the cluster.
7. Reverse the procedure for installation. Be sure to lubricate the speedometer drive head. Adjust the selector indicator if necessary.

#### 1981-82 Electronic Cluster

1. Disconnect the negative battery cable.
2. Remove the steering column trim cover

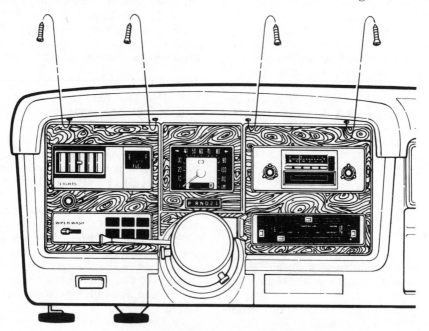

Pull cover slightly away at top; then carefully pull rearward
at bottom to unsnap four cover to panel retainers.

**Instrument panel attaching screws**

and lower instrument panel trim cover. Remove the keyboard trim panel and the trim panel on the left of the column.

3. Remove the instrument cluster trim cover screws and remove the trim panel.

4. Remove the instrument cluster mounting screws and pull the cluster forward. Disconnect the feed plugs and the ground wire from the back of the cluster. Disconnect the speedometer cable (see following section for details).

5. Remove the screw attaching the transmission indicator cable bracket to the steering column. Unfasten the cable loop from the retainer. Remove the bracket.

6. Unfasten the plastic clamp from around the steering column. Remove the cluster.

7. To install the cluster: Apply a small amount of silicone lubricant into the drive hole of the speedometer head.

8. Connect the feed plugs and the ground wire to the cluster. Install the speedometer cable. Attach the instrument cluster to the instrument panel.

9. Install the plastic indicator cable clamp around the steering column and engage the clamp locator pin in the column tube.

10. Place the transmission selector in the "Drive" position. Install the mounting screw into the retainer but do not tighten.

11. Rotate the plastic cable clamp until the indicator flag covers *both* location dots. Tighten the retainer screw.

12. Move the selector through all positions. Readjust if necessary.

13. The rest of the installation is in the reverse order of removal.

## Speedometer Cable
### REMOVAL AND REPLACEMENT

1. Raise the car in the air and support it with jackstands.

2. The speedometer cable is attached to the transmission. Locate the cable and remove the bolt retaining the speedometer gear in the transmission. Remove the retaining clip and pull the speedometer gear out of the transmission.

3. Remove the clips retaining the cable to the underside of the car. Remove the retaining clips (if any) near the steering column.

4. Reach under the instrument panel and remove the speedometer cable from the back of the instrument cluster by pressing the flat surface of the plastic connector and pulling the cable away from the head.

NOTE: *It may be necessary to remove the instrument cluster to gain access to the speedometer cable.*

**The speedometer cable attaches to the left side of the transmission extension housing**

5. Remove the speedometer cover plate on the floor panel.

6. Remove the speedometer cable assembly.

7. Installation is in the reverse order. Do not bend the cable any more than necessary. The minimum bend radius for the entire length of the cable is 6 inches.

## Ignition Lock Cylinder
### REPLACEMENT

1. Disconnect the negative battery cable.

2. On cars with a fixed steering column, remove the steering wheel trim pad and the steering wheel. Insert a stiff wire into the hole located in the lock cylinder housing. On cars with a tilt steering wheel, this hole is located on the outside of the column near the 4-way flasher button. It is not necessary to remove the wheel. On 1981–82 models, remove the four column shroud screws. The hole in the casting is angled down toward the seat. Insert a ⅛ in. diameter wire.

3. Place the gear shift lever in Reverse on standard shift cars and in Park on cars with automatic transmissions and turn the ignition key to the "on" position.

4. Depress the wire and remove the lock cylinder and wire.

5. Insert a new cylinder into the housing and turn to the "off" position. This will lock the cylinder into position.

6. Reinstall the steering wheel and pad.

7. Connect the negative battery cable.

## Ignition Switch
### REPLACEMENT

1. Disconnect the negative battery cable.

2. Remove shrouding from the steering

column. Detach and lower the steering column from the brake support bracket on all except 1981–82 models.

3. Disconnect the switch wiring at the multiple plug.

4. Remove the two nuts that retain the switch to steering column. On the models specified in Step 2, the break-off head bolts that attach the switch to the lock cylinder housing must be drilled out with a ⅛ in. drill. Remove the bolts with an Easy-Out extractor. Disengage the ignition switch from the pin.

5. On models with a steering column-mounted gearshift lever, disconnect the ignition switch plunger from the ignition switch actuator rod and remove the ignition switch. On models with a floor mounted gearshift lever, remove the pin that connects the switch plunger to the switch actuator and remove the switch.

6. To re-install the switch, place both locking mechanism at top of column and switch itself in lock position for correct adjustment. To hold column in lock position, place automatic shift lever in PARK or manual shift lever in reverse, and turn to LOCK and remove the key. New switches are held in lock by plastic shipping pins. To pin existing switches, pull the switch plunger out as far as it will go and push back in to first detent. Insert ³/₃₂ in. diameter wire into locking hole in the top of the switch.

7. Connect the switch plunger to the switch actuator rod.

8. Position the switch on the column and install the attaching nuts. Be sure the proper break-off head bolts are used on the models mentioned in Step 2. Do not tighten them.

9. Move the switch up and down to locate the mid-position of rod lash, and then tighten the nuts. On the models specified in Step 2, tighten the bolts until the heads break off.

10. Remove the locking pin or wire. Connect the electrical connector. Reconnect the battery cable and check for proper switch operation.

11. Attach the steering column to the brake support bracket and install the shrouding.

## HEADLIGHTS

### *REMOVAL AND INSTALLATION*

1. Remove the headlight door mounting screws and the headlight door.

2. Remove the screws that hold the bulb retainer to the adjusting ring and remove the retainer.

3. Pull the headlight forward and disconnect the wiring assembly plug. Remove the headlight.

4. Attach the new headlight to the wiring plug.

5. Install the new light in the housing and replace the retainer ring and attaching screws.

6. Reinstall the headlight door.

## SEATBELT/STARTER INTERLOCK SYSTEM

On some early 1975 models, a starter interlock system is employed, consisting of a warning light, buzzer, seat sensors, switches in the outboard belt retractors and an electronic logic module. Basically, the starter will not engage

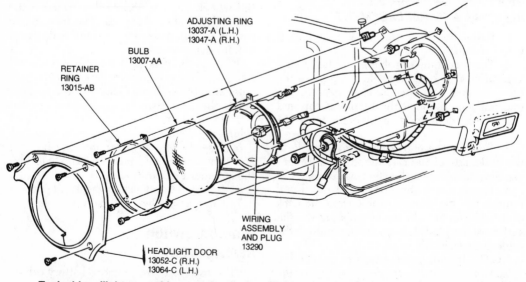

**Typical headlight assembly—rectangular headlights are assembled in the same manner**

## 1981–82 Fuse Identification

| Circuit Protected | Position | Size |
|---|---|---|
| Stop Lamps, Hazard Warning Lamps | 1 | 15 Amp. |
| Windshield Wiper, Windshield Washer Pump, Interval Wiper, Washer Fluid Level Indicator | 2 | 6 Amp. C.B. |
| (Not Used) | 3 | Spare |
| Taillamps, Parking Lamps, Side Marker Lamps, Instrument Cluster Illumination Lamps, License Lamps | 4 | 15 Amp. |
| Optional Lamp Outage System and same system as above | 4 | 10 Amp. |
| Turn Signal Lamps, Back-up Lamps | 5 | 15 Amp. |
| A/C Clutch, Heated Backlite Relay Timer, Trunk Lid Release, Speed Control Module, Electronic Digital Clock Display, Graphic Warning Display Module, Illuminated Entry | 6 | 20 Amp. |
| (Not Used) | 7 | Spare |
| Courtesy Lamps, Key Warning Buzzer, Illuminated Entry Module, Analog Clock, Tension Reliever | 8 | 15 Amp. |
| Heater Blower Motor | 9 | 15 Amp. |
| A/C Blower Motor | 9 | 30 Amp. |
| Flash-to-Pass | 10 | 20 Amp. |
| Radio, Tape Player, Premium Sound | 11 | 15 Amp. |
| (Not Used) | 12 | Spare |
| Instrument Cluster Illumination Lamps, Radio, Climate Control, Ashtray Lamps | 13 | 5 Amp. |
| Power Windows (2 Door) | 14 | 20 Amp. C.B. |
| Power Window Relay (4 Door) | 14 | 15 Amp. |
| (Not Used) | 15 | Spare |
| Horn, Front Cigar Lighter, Electronic Console Clock | 16 | 20 Amp. |
| (Not Used) | 17 | Spare |
| Warning Indicator Lamps, Throttle Solenoid Positioner, Low Fuel Module, Dual Timer Buzzer, Tachometer, Engine Idle Track Relay | 18 | 10 Amp. |

## 1981–82 Circuit Protection

| Circuit Protected | Location | Size |
|---|---|---|
| Windshield Wiper/Washer | Fuse Panel | 6 Amp. C.B. |
| Headlights, High Beam Indicator | Headlight Switch | 22 Amp. C.B. |
| Power Windows (4 Door), | Starter Motor | 20 Amp. C.B. |
| Power Door Locks and Power Seats | Relay | |

| Fuse Link | Location | GA |
|---|---|---|
| Lamp Feed | Near Voltage Regulator | 16 |
| Ignition Feed | Near Voltage Regulator | 16 |
| Charging Circuit | Near Starter Motor Relay | 14 |
| Heated Backlite and Power Door Locks | Near Starter Motor Relay | 16 |
| Engine Compartment Lamp | Near Starter Motor Relay | 20 |
| Electric Choke Feed | Near Master Cylinder | 20 |
| MCU Feed | Near Master Cylinder | 20 |

unless the driver and other front seat occupants pull out their seat belts. Unless the driver and passengers have remained seated and buckled, the sequence must be repeated every time the engine is started. A starter interlock bypass switch is located in the engine compartment on the left wheel well. Since the legal requirement for these interlock systems has been dropped, the system can be legally disconnected.

### DISABLING THE INTERLOCK SYSTEM

1. Locate the interlock override relay under the hood. It is almost always on the left wheel well.

2. Remove the connector.

3. Cut the white wire(s) with the pink dots (#33 circuit) and the red wire(s) with the light blue stripe (#32 circuit).

4. Splice the two (or four) wires together and tape the splice.

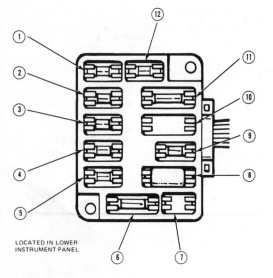

LOCATED IN LOWER
INSTRUMENT PANEL

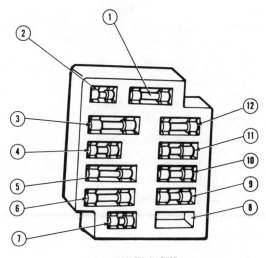

LOCATED IN LOWER
INSTRUMENT PANEL

1. (15 amp. fuse) Heater
    (30 amp. fuse) Air conditioning
2. (15 amp. fuse) Turn signal lamps, backup lamps
3. (15 amp. fuse) Courtesy lamps, stop lamps
4. (20 amp. fuse) Horns, cigar lighter
5. (15 amp. fuse) Hazard flasher
6. (14 amp. fuse) Instrument panel warning lamps
7. Blank
8. (6 amp. C.B.) Windshield wiper
9. (15 amp. fuse) Windshield washer, accessories
10. Blank
11. (7.5 amp. fuse) Radio (or tape player)
12. (4 amp. fuse) Instrument panel and cluster lights, (PRND21) light

**1975–77 fuse box layout**

NOTE: *Do not cut and splice any of the other connector wires. If the red/yellow hash wire is spliced to any of the other wires, the car will start in gear.*

5. Install the connector back on the override switch.

6. Buckle the seat belt and turn the key to the "on" position. If the starter cranks in "on" or in any gear selected, then the wrong wires have been spliced. Repeat steps three and four.

7. Unbuckle the belt and try to start the car. If the car won't start, repeat steps 3 and 4. If the car starts, everything is fine.

8. To stop the warning buzzer from operating, remove it from its connector and throw it away. Tape the connector to the wiring harness so that it can't rattle.

## CIRCUIT PROTECTION

### Fusible Links

In addition to fuses and circuit breakers some wiring harnesses incorporate fusible links to protect the wiring.

① 14 amp. fuse—warning lights, ignition system
② 15 amp. fuse—heated backlite indicator lamp, heated mirror
③ 35 amp. fuse—A/C blower motor & controls
④ 20 amp. fuse—turn signal flasher, back-up lights
⑤ 6 amp. fuse—windshield wiper & washer
⑥ 15 amp. fuse—radio & power antenna
⑦ 4 amp. fuse—illumination lamps (instr. panel)
⑧ Blank
⑨ 20 amp. fuse—heated backlite switch and relay control feed, horn warning actuator, speed control amplifier, cornering lamps, window reg. safety relay control feed, illum. entry lamps feed
⑩ 15 amp. fuse—stop lamps, courtesy lamps —luggage compt. glove box, doors, instr. panel, dome, vanity mirror, garage door opener
⑪ 30 amp. fuse—cigar lighter, horns
⑫ 20 amp. fuse—emergency warning flasher

**1978 fuse box layout**

NOTE: *Refer to the Circuit Protection Chart to find out what circuits use fusible links.*

The fusible link is a short length of special, Hypalon (high temperature) insulated wire, integral with the engine compartment wiring harness and should not be confused with standard wire. It is several wire gauges smaller than the circuit which it protects. Under no circumstances should a fuse link replacement repair be made using a length of standard wire cut from bulk stock or from another wiring harness.

To repair any blown fuse use the following procedure:

1. Determine which circuit is damaged, its location and the cause of the open fuse link. If the damaged fuse link is one of three fed by a common No. 10 or 12 gauge feed wire, determine the specific affected circuit.

2. Disconnect the negative battery cable.

3. Cut the damaged fuse link from the wiring harness and discard it. If the fuse link is one of three circuits fed by a single feed wire,

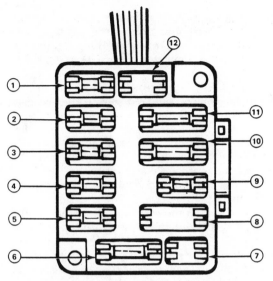

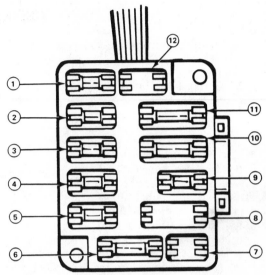

1. 30 amp. fuse—power window (2-door only)
2. 20 amp. fuse—accessories
3. 15 amp. fuse—courtesy lamps
4. 20 amp. fuse—cigar lighter, horns
5. 20 amp. fuse—stop lamps, emergency warning lamps
6. 14 amp. fuse—warning lights, ignition system
7. Blank
8. 15 amp. fuse—heater blower motor
9. 35 amp. fuse—A/C blower motor
   15 amp. fuse—turn signal flasher, back-up lamps
10. 6 amp. C.B.—windshield wiper and washer
11. 7.5 amp. fuse—radio
12. 4 amp. fuse—instrument panel illumination lamps

**1979 fuse box layout**

1. 20 amp. fuse—electric choke
2. 15 amp. fuse—tail lamps
3. 15 amp. fuse—courtesy lamps
4. 20 amp. fuse—cigar lighter, horns
5. 20 amp. fuse—stop lamps, emergency warning lamps
6. 14 amp. fuse—warning lights, ignition system
7. 15 amp. fuse—radio
8. 15 amp. fuse—heater blower motor (A/C) (35 amp. fuse with A/C)
9. 15 amp. fuse—turn signal flasher, back-up lamps
10. 6 amp. C.B.—windshield wiper and washer
11. 20 amp. fuse—accessories
12. 4 amp. fuse—instrument panel illumination lamps

**1980 fuse box layout**

## Bulb Specifications

| | '75–77 | '78–80 | '81–82 |
|---|---|---|---|
| Headlights | 6014 | 6052 | ④ |
| Front park/turn signal | 1157NA | 1157NA ② | 1157 |
| Rear tail/stop/turn signal | 1157 | 1157 | 1157 |
| Back-up light | 1156 | 1156 | 1156 |
| License plate light | 1178 | 168 | 168 |
| Dome light | 561 | 561 | 906 |
| Front side markers | 97NA ① | 194 ③ | 194 |
| Rear side markers | 1157 | 1157 | 194 |
| High beam indicator | 194 | 194 | 194 |
| Turn signal indicator | 194 | 194 | 194 |
| Warning lights (oil, alternator, etc.) | 194 | 194 | 194 |
| Heater and A/C control lights | 161 | 161 | 161 |
| Ashtray light | 1892 | 1816 | 1892 |
| Trunk light | 631 | 89 | 89 |
| Engine compartment light | 631 | 89 | 89 |
| Glove box light | 1816 | 1816 | 1816 |
| Instrument panel courtesy light | 631 | 89 | 89 |
| Speedometer and odometer | 194 | 194 | — |
| Fuel gauge | 194 | 194 | — |

① 1976: 1157NA
② 1980: 1157
③ 1979–80: 168
④ Hi: H4651
   Lo: H4656

cut it out of the harness at each splice end and discard it.

4. Identify and procure the proper fuse link and butt connectors for attaching the fuse link to the harness.

5. To repair any fuse link in a 3-link group with one feed:

a. After cutting the open link out of the harness, cut each of the remaining undamaged fuse links close to the feed wire weld.

b. Strip approximately ½ inch of insulation from the detached ends of the two good fuse links. Then insert two wire ends into one end of a butt connector and carefully push one stripped end of the replacement fuse link into the same end of the butt connector and crimp all three firmly together.

NOTE: *Care must be taken when fitting the three fuse links into the butt connector as the internal diameter is a snug fit for three wires. Make sure to use a proper crimping tool. Pliers, side cutters, etc. will not apply the proper crimp to retain the wires and withstand a pull test.*

c. After crimping the butt connector to the three fuse links, cut the weld portion from the feed wire and strip approximately ½ inch of insulation from the cut end. Insert the stripped end into the open end of the butt connector and crimp very firmly.

d. To attach the remaining end of the replacement fuse link strip approximately ½ inch of insulation from the wire end of the circuit from which the blown fuse link was removed, and firmly crimp a butt connector or equivalent to the stripped wire. Then, insert the end of the replacement link into the other end of the butt connector and crimp firmly.

e. Using rosin core solder with a consistency of 60 percent tin and 40 percent lead, solder the connectors and the wires at the repairs and insulate with electrical tape.

6. To replace any fuse link on a single circuit in a harness, cut out the damaged portion, strip approximately ½ inch of insulation from the two wire ends and attach the appropriate replacement fuse link to the stripped wire ends with two proper size butt connectors. Solder the connectors and wires and insulate with tape.

7. To repair any fuse link which has an eyelet terminal on one end such as the charging circuit, cut off the open fuse link behind the weld, strip approximately ½ inch of insulation from the cut end and attach the appropriate new eyelet fuse link to the cut stripped wire with an appropriate size butt connector. Solder the connectors and wires at the repair and insulate with tape.

8. Connect the negative battery cable to the battery and test the system for proper operation.

NOTE: *Do not mistake a resistor wire for a fuse link. The resistor wire is generally longer and has print stating "Resistor don't cut or splice."*

NOTE: *When attaching a single No. 16, 17, 18 or 20 gauge fuse link to a heavy gauge wire, always double the stripped wire end of the fuse link before inserting and crimping it into the butt connector for positive wire retention.*

## Circuit Breaker

A circuit breaker is an electrical switch which breaks the circuit in case of an overload. The circuit breaker is located at the top of the fuse panel.

## WIRING DIAGRAMS

Wiring diagrams have been omitted from this book. As cars have become more complex, wiring diagrams have grown in size and complexity as well. It has become impossible to provide a readable reproduction in a reasonable number of pages. Information on ordering wiring diagrams from the vehicle manufacturer can be found in the owner's manual.

# Clutch and Transmission

# 6

## UNDERSTANDING THE MANUAL TRANSMISSION AND CLUTCH

Because of the way the gasoline engine breathes, it can produce torque, or twisting force, only within a narrow speed range. Most modern engines must turn at about 2,500 rpm to produce their peak torque. By 4,500 rpm they are producing so little torque that continued increases in engine speed produce no power increases.

The transmission and clutch are employed to vary the relationship between engine speed and the speed of the wheels so that adequate engine power can be produced under all circumstances. The clutch allows engine torque to be applied to the transmission input shaft gradually, due to mechanical slippage. The car can, consequently, be started smoothly from a full stop.

The transmission changes the ratio between the rotating speeds of the engine and the wheels by the use of gears. Three-speed or four-speed transmissions are most common. The lower gears allow full engine power to be applied to the rear wheels during acceleration at low speeds.

The clutch driven plate is a thin disc, the center of which is splined to the transmission input shaft. Both sides of the disc are covered with a layer of material which is similar to brake lining and which is capable of allowing slippage without roughness or excessive noise.

The clutch cover is bolted to the engine flywheel and incorporates a diaphragm spring which provides the pressure to engage the clutch. The cover also houses the pressure plate. The driven disc is sandwiched between the pressure plate and the smooth surface of the flywheel when the clutch pedal is released, thus forcing it to turn at the same speed as the engine crankshaft.

The transmission contains a mainshaft which passes all the way through the transmission, from the clutch to the driveshaft. This shaft is separated at one point, so that front and rear portions can turn at different speeds.

Power is transmitted by a countershaft in the lower gears and reverse. The gears of the countershaft mesh with gears on the mainshaft, allowing power to be carried from one to the other. All the countershaft gears are integral with that shaft, while several of the mainshaft gears can either rotate independently of the shaft or be locked to it. Shifting from one gear to the next causes one of the gears to be freed from rotating with the shaft, and locks another to it. Gears are locked and unlocked by internal dog clutches which slide between the center of the gear and the shaft. The forward gears usually employ synchronizers: friction members which smoothly bring gear and shaft to the same speed before the toothed dog clutches are engaged.

The clutch is operating properly if:

1. It will stall the engine when released with the vehicle held stationary.

2. The shift lever can be moved freely between first and reverse gears when the vehicle is stationary and the clutch disengaged.

A clutch pedal free-play adjustment is incorporated in the linkage. If there is 1 inch of motion before the pedal begins to release the clutch, it is adjusted properly. Inadequate free-play wears all parts of the clutch releasing mechanisms and may cause slippage. Excessive free-play may cause inadequate release and hard shifting of gears.

## MANUAL TRANSMISSION

Two types of manual transmissions have been offered in the Granada and Monarch. In 1975 and 1976, a three-speed transmission was offered. In 1977, the three speed was replaced by a four-speed overdrive transmission and in 1981 and later a regular four-speed was used.

## REMOVAL AND INSTALLATION

1. Raise the car in the air and support it with jackstands.

2. Mark the driveshaft so that it can be replaced in its original position. Disconnect the driveshaft from the differential, and slide the front of the driveshaft from the transmission extension housing. Seal the extension housing with a plastic bag or something similar to prevent lubricant from leaking from the transmission.

3. Remove the bolt and retainer securing the speedometer cable to the extension housing and withdraw the cable from the housing.

4. If the car is equipped with a three-speed transmission, remove the shift rods from the levers at the transmission. If the car has the four-speed overdrive transmission, remove the shift rods if equipped and the shift control unit from the extension housing.

5. Raise the rear of the engine enough to remove the weight from the crossmember, and remove the crossmember.

6. With the transmission supported, remove the transmission or bell housing mounting bolts. Pull the transmission to the rear until the input shaft clears the flywheel housing or engine.

NOTE: *On 1981 and later models, the bell housing is removed with the transmission.*

7. Lower the transmission from the vehicle. *Do not depress the clutch pedal while the transmission is removed.*

Installation of the transmission is as follows:

1. After making sure the mating surfaces of the transmission case and flywheel housing are clean, install a guide pin in each lower mounting bolt hole.

2. Start the input shaft through the throwout bearing and line up the splines on the input shaft with those in the clutch disc.

3. Slide the transmission forward on the guide pins until the input shaft pilot enters the bushing on the crankshaft. It may be necessary to wiggle the transmission slightly.

4. When the transmission is snug against the flywheel housing, install the upper transmission mounting bolts. Remove the two guide pins and install the two lower bolts. Torque the mounting bolts to 37–42 ft. lb. on three speed models, 42–50 ft. lb. on four speeds.

5. With the rear of the engine raised high enough to provide clearance, install the crossmember.

6. Install the shift rods and the shift control assembly on four-speed models. Install the speedometer cable.

7. Install the driveshaft, making sure it is in its original position.

8. Check the lubricant level and add lubricant if necessary. Adjust the shift linkage if necessary.

9. Lower the car.

## LINKAGE ADJUSTMENT

### Three Speed Column-Mounted Shifter

1. Place the shift lever in neutral.

2. Loosen the two gearshift rod adjustment nuts at the transmission. Make sure the shift levers on the transmission are in the neutral (parallel) position.

3. Use a $^3/_{16}$-inch allen wrench as an alignment tool. Insert the short end through the first and reverse lever, the second and third lever and both holes in the lower casting.

4. Tighten the adjustment nuts.

5. Remove the alignment tool. Start the engine and move the shifter through the gears to make sure it operates properly.

### Three Speed Floor-Mounted Shifter

1. Place the shift lever in neutral.

2. Loosen the two shift linkage adjustment nuts, making sure the shift rods remain in the transmission shift levers.

3. Use an allen wrench as an alignment tool. Insert the alignment tool through the hole in the boot and into the shift control assembly alignment hole.

4. Tighten the adjustment nuts, making sure the slotted ends of the shift rods are over the flats of the studs on the shift control assembly.

5. Remove the alignment pin. Check to make sure the linkage operates smoothly.

### Four Speed

NOTE: *This procedure is for 1977–78 models only. 1979 and later models are equipped with internal shift rails, having no provision for adjustment.*

1. Place shifter lever in neutral position, then raise car on a hoist.

2. Insert a ¼ in. rod into the alignment holes of the shift levers.

3. If the holes are not in exact alignment, check for bent connecting rods or loose lever locknuts at the rod ends. Make replacements or repairs, then adjust as follows.

4. Loosen the three rod-to-lever retaining lock nuts and move the levers until the ¼ in. gauge rod will enter the alignment holes. Be sure that the transmission shift levers are in neutral and the reverse shifter lever is in the neutral detent.

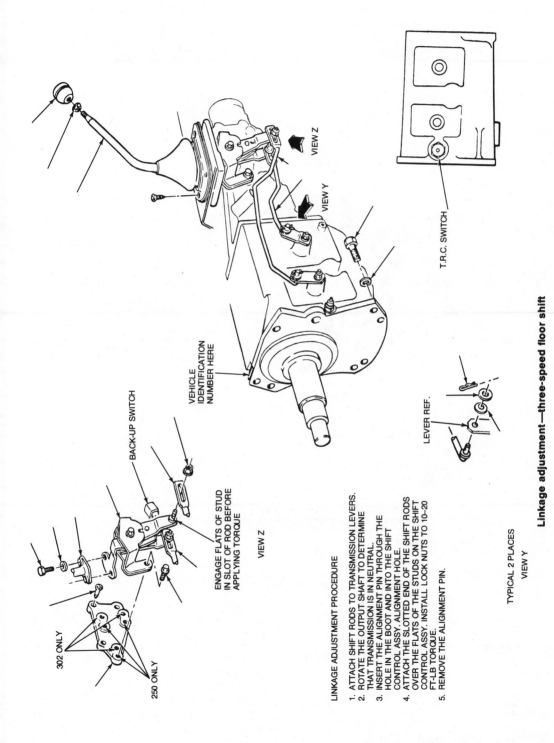

T.R.C. SWITCH

VIEW Z

VIEW Y

VEHICLE
IDENTIFICATION
NUMBER HERE

BACK-UP SWITCH

VIEW Z

ENGAGE FLATS OF STUD
IN SLOT OF ROD BEFORE
APPLYING TORQUE

302 ONLY

250 ONLY

LEVER REF.

LINKAGE ADJUSTMENT PROCEDURE

1. ATTACH SHIFT RODS TO TRANSMISSION LEVERS.
2. ROTATE THE OUTPUT SHAFT TO DETERMINE
   THAT TRANSMISSION IS IN NEUTRAL.
3. INSERT THE ALIGNMENT PIN THROUGH THE
   HOLE IN THE BOOT AND INTO THE SHIFT
   CONTROL ASSY. ALIGNMENT HOLE.
4. ATTACH THE SLOTTED END OF THE SHIFT RODS
   OVER THE FLATS OF THE STUDS ON THE SHIFT
   CONTROL ASSY. INSTALL LOCK NUTS TO 10-20
   FT-LB TORQUE.
5. REMOVE THE ALIGNMENT PIN.

TYPICAL 2 PLACES

VIEW Y

**Linkage adjustment—three-speed floor shift**

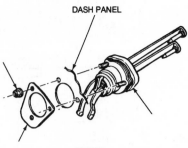

VIEW Z

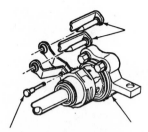

PIN—REMOVE AFTER LINKAGE
ADJUSTMENT

VIEW Y

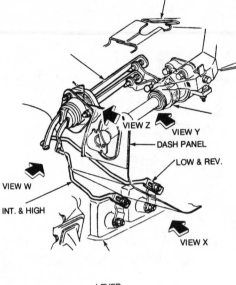

VIEW Z

VIEW Y

DASH PANEL

LOW & REV.

VIEW W

INT. & HIGH

VIEW X

LINKAGE ADJUSTMENT PROCEDURE

1. PLACE GEAR SHIFT LEVER IN
   NEUTRAL POSITION.
2. LOOSEN GEAR SHIFT ROD AD-
   JUSTMENT NUTS
3. BE SURE TRANSMISSION IS IN
   NEUTRAL.
4. INSTALL ADJUSTMENT PIN AS
   SHOWN IN VIEW Y.
5. TIGHTEN AND TORQUE THE GEAR
   SHIFT ROD ADJUSTMENT NUTS.
6. REMOVE THE ALIGNMENT PIN AND
   CHECK THE SHIFT LEVER OPERATION.

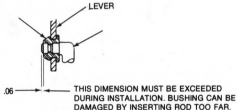

LEVER

.06 — THIS DIMENSION MUST BE EXCEEDED
DURING INSTALLATION. BUSHING CAN BE
DAMAGED BY INSERTING ROD TOO FAR.

BUSHING MUST BE INSTALLED IN LEVERS
IN DIRECTION INDICATED BY ARROW
VIEW W

TYPICAL TWO PLACES

VIEW X

**Shift linkage adjustment—column mounted shifter**

5. Install the shift rods and tighten the locknuts.

6. Remove the ¼ in. gauge rod.

7. Operate the shift levers to assure correct shifting.

# CLUTCH

### *REMOVAL AND INSTALLATION*

1. Raise the car in the air and support it with jackstands.

2. Remove the transmission as outlined earlier.

3. Unhook the throwout bearing lever release spring. Loosen the adjusting rod nuts and remove the adjusting rod from the throwout bearing arm.

4. Remove the starter cable from the starter and then remove the starter from the flywheel housing.

5. Unbolt the flywheel housing from the cylinder block. Remove the engine rear plate from the flywheel housing. Remove the clutch equalizer bar pivot bracket from the flywheel housing.

6. Remove the flywheel housing. Try not to disturb the clutch linkage.

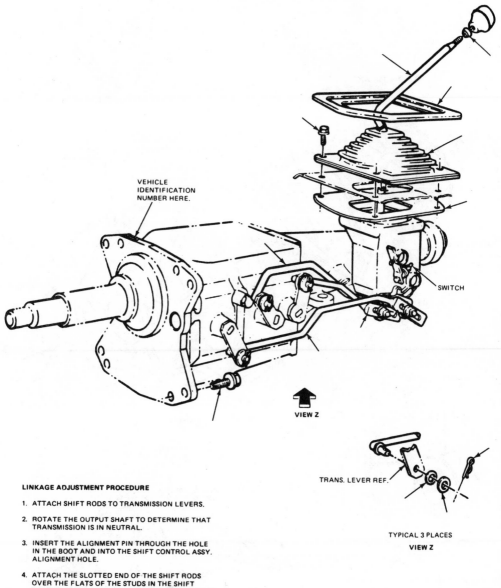

VEHICLE
IDENTIFICATION
NUMBER HERE.

SWITCH

VIEW Z

TRANS. LEVER REF.

TYPICAL 3 PLACES
VIEW Z

**LINKAGE ADJUSTMENT PROCEDURE**

1. ATTACH SHIFT RODS TO TRANSMISSION LEVERS.

2. ROTATE THE OUTPUT SHAFT TO DETERMINE THAT
   TRANSMISSION IS IN NEUTRAL.

3. INSERT THE ALIGNMENT PIN THROUGH THE HOLE
   IN THE BOOT AND INTO THE SHIFT CONTROL ASSY.
   ALIGNMENT HOLE.

4. ATTACH THE SLOTTED END OF THE SHIFT RODS
   OVER THE FLATS OF THE STUDS IN THE SHIFT
   CONTROL ASSY. INSTALL LOCK NUTS TO 10-20 FT-LB
   TORQUE.

5. REMOVE THE ALIGNMENT PIN.

LUBRICATE WITH ESA-M1C75-B GREASE.

**Linkage adjustment—four-speed overdrive transmission**

7. Remove the clutch release lever by pulling it through the window in the housing until the retainer spring becomes disengaged from the pivot.

8. Unbolt the pressure plate from the flywheel. If the plate is to be reinstalled, mark it so that it can be returned to its original position.

9. Remove the pressure plate and clutch disc from the flywheel.

10. Inspect the flywheel, clutch disc, pressure plate, throw-out bearing, and the clutch fork and pivot shaft assembly for wear. Replace the parts as required. If the flywheel shows any signs of overheating or if it is badly grooved or scored, it should be refaced or replaced.

Installation is as follows:

1. Position the clutch disc and pressure plate assembly on the flywheel. Start the bolts to hold the pieces in place, but don't tighten them down yet. Avoid getting the disc oily or greasy, as clutch chatter may result.

2. Align the clutch disc, using an alignment

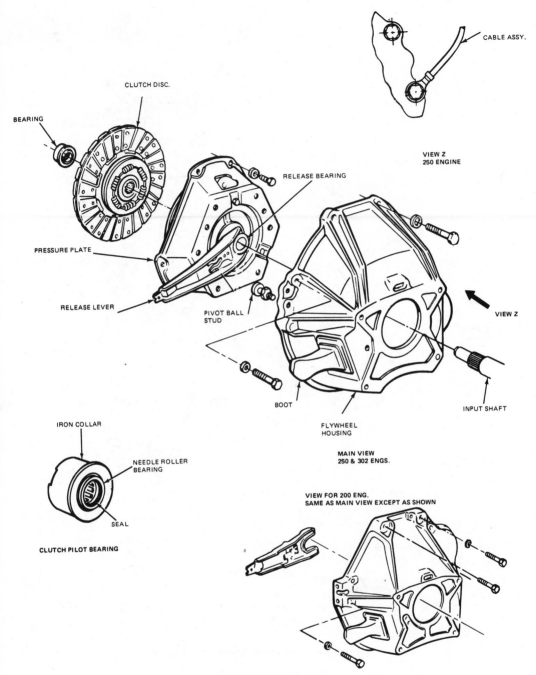

CABLE ASSY.

VIEW Z
250 ENGINE

CLUTCH DISC.

BEARING

RELEASE BEARING

PRESSURE PLATE

VIEW Z

RELEASE LEVER

PIVOT BALL
STUD

BOOT

INPUT SHAFT

FLYWHEEL
HOUSING

MAIN VIEW
250 & 302 ENGS.

IRON COLLAR

NEEDLE ROLLER
BEARING

VIEW FOR 200 ENG.
SAME AS MAIN VIEW EXCEPT AS SHOWN

SEAL

CLUTCH PILOT BEARING

**Clutch components**

tool or a transmission input shaft. Alternately tighten the pressure plate bolts until they are all tight. Then torque them to 12–20 ft. lb. Remove the alignment tool.

3. Lightly grease the throwout bearing where it contacts the pressure plate fingers and fill the grease groove of the throwout bearing. Lithium base grease is specified for all clutch lubrication applications.

4. Install the flywheel housing and the equalizer bar pivot bracket. Torque the housing bolts to 38–55 ft. lb.

5. Install the starter and starter cable. Install the engine rear plate.

6. Install the throwout bearing and the transmission.

7. Install the spring on the throwout bearing arm.

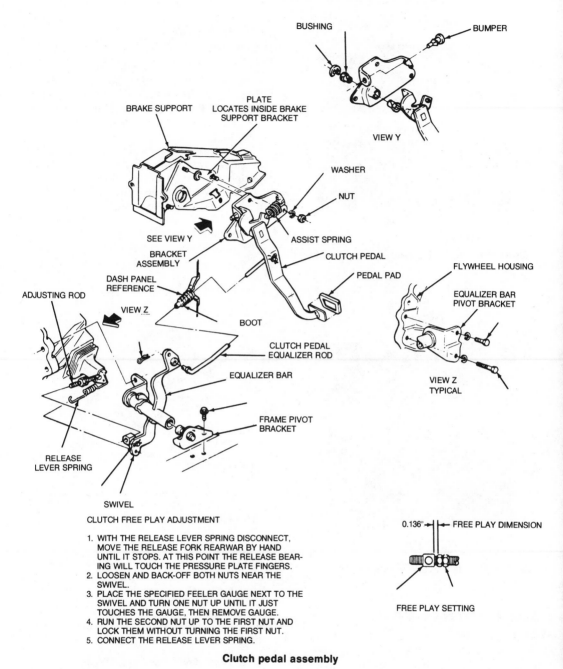

**Clutch pedal assembly**

Labels in figure:

BUSHING

BUMPER

VIEW Y

BRAKE SUPPORT

PLATE
LOCATES INSIDE BRAKE
SUPPORT BRACKET

WASHER

NUT

SEE VIEW Y

ASSIST SPRING

CLUTCH PEDAL

FLYWHEEL HOUSING

BRACKET
ASSEMBLY

DASH PANEL
REFERENCE

PEDAL PAD

EQUALIZER BAR
PIVOT BRACKET

ADJUSTING ROD

VIEW Z

BOOT

CLUTCH PEDAL
EQUALIZER ROD

EQUALIZER BAR

VIEW Z
TYPICAL

RELEASE
LEVER SPRING

FRAME PIVOT
BRACKET

SWIVEL

CLUTCH FREE PLAY ADJUSTMENT

1. WITH THE RELEASE LEVER SPRING DISCONNECT,
MOVE THE RELEASE FORK REARWAR BY HAND
UNTIL IT STOPS. AT THIS POINT THE RELEASE BEAR-
ING WILL TOUCH THE PRESSURE PLATE FINGERS.
2. LOOSEN AND BACK-OFF BOTH NUTS NEAR THE
SWIVEL.
3. PLACE THE SPECIFIED FEELER GAUGE NEXT TO THE
SWIVEL AND TURN ONE NUT UP UNTIL IT JUST
TOUCHES THE GAUGE, THEN REMOVE GAUGE.
4. RUN THE SECOND NUT UP TO THE FIRST NUT AND
LOCK THEM WITHOUT TURNING THE FIRST NUT.
5. CONNECT THE RELEASE LEVER SPRING.

0.136" — FREE PLAY DIMENSION

FREE PLAY SETTING

8. Install the adjusting rod and adjust the clutch.

9. Lower the car.

## CLUTCH ADJUSTMENT

### Thru 1980

1. Raise the car.

2. Loosen the locknut and the adjusting nut on the throwout bearing adjusting rod.

3. Move the throwout bearing arm to the rear until the throwout bearing just contacts with pressure plate fingers. This can be done with the adjusting nut.

4. Tighten the locknut against the adjusting nut.

5. Check the clutch pedal free-play. There should be one inch. If there isn't, readjust the clutch.

6. Lower the car.

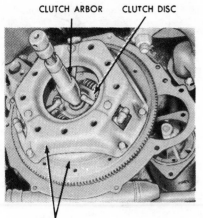

**Installing the clutch disc using the alignment tool**

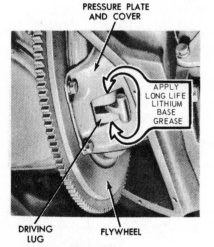

**Pressure plate lubrication points**

### SELF-ADJUSTING CLUTCH

**1981 and Later**

The free play in the clutch is adjusted by a built in mechanism that allows the clutch controls to be self-adjusted during normal operation.

The self-adjusting feature should be checked every 5000 miles. This is accomplished by insuring that the clutch pedal travels to the top of its upward position. Grasp the clutch pedal with your hand or put your foot under the clutch pedal, pull up on the pedal until it stops. Very little effort is required (about 10 lbs.). During the application of upward pressure, a click may be heard which means an adjustment was necessary and has been accomplished.

## Clutch Cable

### REMOVAL AND INSTALLATION

1. Loosen the cable adjustment or, if self adjusting, lift the clutch pedal to its upper position. Disconnect the cable from the clutch pedal or self-adjusting quadrant.

2. Disconnect the cable assembly isolator from the firewall.

3. Pull the cable through the firewall into the engine compartment. Raise the front of the car and support on jackstands.

4. Remove the dust cover from the bell housing and the rubber plug from the clutch release lever. Remove the clip retainer and cable from the bell housing.

5. Remove the clutch cable from the release lever. Remove mounting isolater from cable.

6. Install in the reverse order of removal.

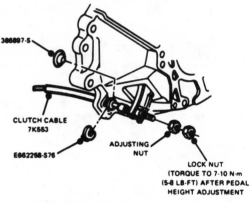

**4-140 clutch pedal adjustment**

## AUTOMATIC TRANSMISSION

### Identification

The transmission may be identified by the code on the Vehicle Certification Label. Refer to the Transmission Code chart.

### REMOVAL AND INSTALLATION

1. Disconnect the negative battery cable. Remove the fan shroud attaching bolts and position the shroud back over the fan.

NOTE: *Shroud removal, radiator base disconnection and thermactor hose removal may be necessary, depending on engine, so damage will not occur when jacking the engine for crossmember or attaching bolt removal.*

2. Remove the upper engine-to-transmission mounting bolts (depending on engine) if they are accessible. Jack up the front and rear of the car and safely support on jackstands.

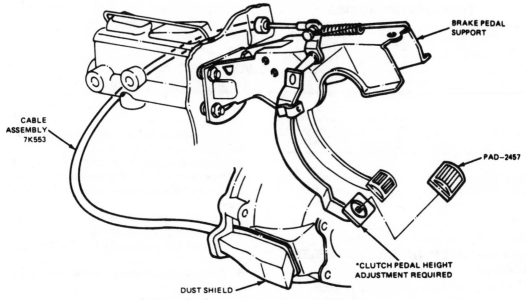

**1981–82 clutch pedal and cable assembly (typical)**

Labels in figure:
- BRAKE PEDAL SUPPORT
- CABLE ASSEMBLY 7K553
- PAD–2457
- *CLUTCH PEDAL HEIGHT ADJUSTMENT REQUIRED
- DUST SHIELD

3. Drain the transmission fluid from the pan and converter.

4. Remove the exhaust pipe(s) and converter(s), if necessary, to gain clearance for transmission removal. Disconnect the sensor wiring or hose.

5. Remove the driveshaft, disconnect the transmission linkage, vacuum line, wiring harness and speedometer cable.

6. Remove the starter motor and lower converter dust shield (inspection plate) and engine brace.

7. Remove the converter-to-flywheel attaching nuts. Turn the engine by placing a wrench or socket on the crankshaft pulley nut to bring the mounting nuts in position for removal. On four cylinder engines, turn the engine in the direction of normal rotation only or the timing belt could be damaged or "jump" time.

8. Disconnect the transmission cooler lines at the transmission and remove the filler tube, if not removed when draining the transmission fluid.

9. Place a transmission jack under the transmission after disconnecting the rear motor mount from the crossmember. Raise the transmission slightly and remove the rear crossmember.

10. Take one last look to make sure everything has been disconnected from the transmission. Remove the remaining engine-to-transmission mounting bolts. On some four cylinder models it will be necessary to disconnect the motor mounts and raise the engine to reach the top engine-to-transmission mount-

ing bolts. Use two jacks, one supporting and transmission and the other to raise the engine; use extreme caution when jacking.

11. Lower the transmission slowly until enough clearance is gained for removal. Be sure enough room is available between the fan blades and radiator and no hoses are stretched. When enough clearance has been gained, support the engine with a jack and slowly move the transmission toward the rear of the car. Be sure the converter remains on the transmission, slightly pry away from the flywheel if necessary.

12. When the transmission and converter are separated from the engine, lower and remove from under the car.

13. Installation is in the reverse order of removal. When installing, take care not to damage the flywheel, be sure the converter

## Torque

**Engine to Transmission Bolts**
- **C3-** 28–38 ft. lbs.
- **C4**
  - 4 and 6 Cyl. 28–38 ft. lbs.
  - V8 Eng.    40–50 ft. lbs.
- **C5-** 40–50 ft. lbs.
- **JATCO** 23–24 ft. lbs.

**Converter to Flywheel**
- **C3-** 27–49 ft. lbs.
- **C4-** 20–30 ft. lbs.
- **C5-** 40–50 ft. lbs.
- **JATCO** 29–36 ft. lbs.

**Converter Drain Plug**
- **C3-** 20–30 ft. lbs.
- **C4-** 17–22 ft. lbs.
- **C5-** 12–17 ft. lbs.

## Transmission Fluids

| | | |
|---|---|---|
| 1975–79 | C3 | Type F |
| | C4 | Type F |
| | JATCO | Dexron II |
| 1980 | C3 | Type F |
| | C4 | Dexron II |
| | JATCO | Dexron II |
| 1981 | C3 | Dexron II |
| | C4 | Dexron II |
| 1982 | C3 | Dexron II |
| | C5 | Type H |

mounting studs are correctly aligned. The converter must rest squarely against the flywheel indicating that the converter pilot is not binding.

## PAN REPLACEMENT, FLUID AND FILTER CHANGE

1. Raise the car on a hoist or jackstands.
2. Some C4 and all C5 models require that the transmission fluid filler tube be disconnected to drain the pan; all others can be drained by loosening the pan bolts and letting the fluid drain out when the pan is lowered.
3. When the fluid has stopped draining to the level of the pan flange, remove the pan bolts starting rear and along both sides of the pan, allowing it to drop and drain gradually. Remove the pan and gasket.
4. Remove the bolts holding the filter in place, remove the filter, clean, and replace it. The filter, may be reused after cleaning it in a nondetergent solution, such as new transmission fluid.

NOTE: *The C4 filter and gasket retain the throttle pressure limit valve within the lower control valve body. The valve and its spring will drop out when the filter is removed. The valve is installed large end first into the valve body; the spring fits over the valve shaft.*

5. After completing any repairs or adjustments, new pan gasket, and the pan on the transmission. Tighten the pan attaching bolts to 12–16 ft.
6. Install three quarts of transmission fluid through the filler tube. If the filler tube was removed to drain the transmission, install the filler tube using a new O-ring.
7. Start and run the engine for a few minutes at low idle speed, and then at the fast idle speed (about 1,200 rpm) until the normal operating temperature is reached. Do not race the engine.
8. Move the selector lever through all gear positions, then place it in the Park position. Check the fluid level and add fluid until the level is between the ADD and FULL marks on the dipstick. Do not overfill.

NOTE: *The level should be at FULL after the engine is completely warmed up. Do not overfill.*

## BAND ADJUSTMENT

### C3 Transmission—Front Band

NOTE: *The torque values and number of turns given in these procedures must be exactly correct to prevent transmission damage.*

1. Wipe clean the area around the adjusting screw on the side of the transmission.
2. Remove the adjusting screw locknut and discard it.
3. Install a new locknut on the adjusting screw but do not tighten it.
4. Tighten the adjusting screw to *exactly 10 ft. lbs.*
5. Back off the adjusting screw *exactly 1½ turns.*
6. Hold the adjusting screw so that it *does not turn* and tighten the adjusting screw locknut to 35–45 ft. lbs.

### C4 and C5 Transmission—Intermediate Band

1. Wipe clean the area around the adjusting screw on the side of the transmission.
2. Remove the adjusting screw locknut and discard it.
3. Install a new locknut on the adjusting screw but do not tighten it yet.
4. Tighten the adjusting screw to *exactly 10 ft. lbs.*
5. Back off the adjusting screw *exactly 1¾ turns* on the C4 and 4¼ turns on the C5.
6. Hold the adjusting screw so that it *does not turn* and tighten the adjusting screw locknut to 35–45 ft. lbs.

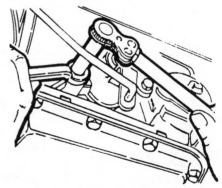

**C4 and C5 intermediate band adjustment**

### JATCO—Intermediate Band

1. Raise and support the vehicle.
2. Remove the servo cover.

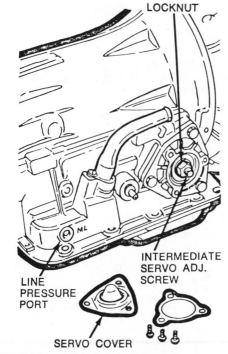

JATCO intermediate band adjustment

3. Loosen the intermediate band adjusting screw locknut and tighten the adjusting screw to *10 ft. lbs.*

4. Back off the adjusting screw *exactly two turns*, hold it stationary and tighten the locknut to 22–29 ft. lbs.

5. Replace the cover using a new gasket.

### LOW-REVERSE BAND ADJUSTMENT

#### C4 and C5 Transmission

1. Wipe clean the area around the adjusting screw on the side of the transmission, near the right-rear corner.

2. Remove the adjusting screw locknut and discard it.

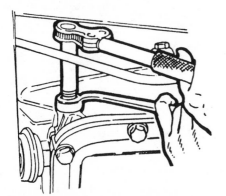

C4 and C5 low-reverse band adjustment

3. Install a new locknut on the adjusting screw but do not tighten it.

4. Tighten the adjusting screw to *exactly 10 ft. lbs.*

5. Back off the adjusting screw *exactly 3 full turns.*

6. Hold the adjusting screw so that it *does not turn* and tighten the adjusting screw to 35–45 ft. lbs.

### NEUTRAL START SWITCH ADJUSTMENT

NOTE: *No adjustment is possible on the C3 transmission.*

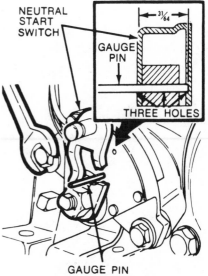

Neutral start switch adjustment (C4 shown)

#### C4 and C5 Transmission

1. Place the transmission selector lever in the Neutral position.

2. Raise the vehicle and support on stands. Loosen the two bolts that attach the neutral switch to the transmission.

3. Rotate the switch until a gauge pin (shank end of a no. 43 drill bit) can be inserted through the gauge pin holes in the switch. The gauge pin must be inserted a full $^{31}/_{64}$ in. into the switch, through all three holes in the switch.

4. Tighten the switch retaining bolts and remove the pin.

### SHIFT LINKAGE ADJUSTMENT

1. Place transmission shift lever in D.

2. Raise vehicle and loosen manual lever shift rod retaining nut. Move transmission lever to D position. D is second from rear.

3. With transmission shift lever and transmission manual lever in position, tighten nut.

4. Check transmission operation for all selector lever detent positions.

## DOWNSHIFT (THROTTLE) LINKAGE ADJUSTMENT

1. With the engine off, disconnect the throttle and downshift return springs, if equipped.

2. Hold the carburetor throttle lever in the wide open position against the stop.

3. Hold the transmission downshift linkage in the full downshift position against the internal stop.

4. Turn the adjustment screw on the carburetor downshift lever to obtain 0.01–0.08 in. clearance between the screw tip and the throttle shaft lever tab.

5. Release the transmission and carburetor to their normal free position.

# Drive Train

## DRIVELINE

The driveshaft is the means by which the power from the engine and transmission (in the front of the car) is transferred to the differential and rear axles and, finally, to the rear wheels.

The driveshaft assembly incorporates two universal joints—one at each end—and a slip yoke at the front end of the assembly, which fits into the back of the transmission.

All driveshafts are balanced when installed in a car. It is therefore imperative that before applying undercoating to the chassis, the driveshaft and universal joint assembly be completely covered to prevent the accidental application of undercoating to their surfaces, and the subsequent loss of balance.

## Driveshaft and U-Joints

### DRIVESHAFT REMOVAL

The procedure for removing the driveshaft assembly—complete with universal joint and slip yoke—is as follows:

1. Mark the relationship of the rear driveshaft yoke and the drive pinion flange of the axle. If the original yellow alignment marks are visible, there is no need for new marks. The purpose of this marking is to facilitate installation of the assembly in its exact original position, thereby maintaining proper balance.

2. Remove the four bolts which hold the rear universal joint to the pinion flange. Wrap tape around the loose bearing caps in order to prevent them from falling off the spider.

3. Pull the driveshaft toward the rear of the vehicle until the slip yoke clears the transmission housing and the seal. Plug the hole at the rear of the transmission housing or place a container under the opening to catch any fluid which might leak.

### UNIVERSAL JOINT OVERHAUL

1. Position the driveshaft assembly in a sturdy vise.

2. Remove the snap-rings which retain the bearings in the slip yoke (front only) and in the driveshaft (front and rear).

3. Using a large punch or an arbor press, drive one of the bearings in toward the center of the universal joint, which will force the opposite bearing out.

4. As each bearing is pressed or punched far enough out of the universal joint assembly that it is accessible, grip it with a pair of pliers, and pull it from the driveshaft yoke. Drive or press the spider in the opposite direction in order to make the opposite bearing accessible, and pull it free with a pair of pliers. Use this procedure to remove all bearings from both universal joints.

5. After removing the bearings, lift the spider from the yoke.

6. Thoroughly clean all dirt and foreign matter from the yoke on both ends of the driveshaft.

NOTE: *When installing new bearings in the yokes, it is advisable to use an arbor press. However, if this tool is not available, the bearings should be driven into position with extreme care, as a heavy jolt on the needle bearings can easily damage or misalign them, greatly shortening their life.*

7. Start a new bearing into the yoke at the rear of the driveshaft.

8. Position a new spider in the rear yoke and press (or drive) the new bearing ¼ inch below the outer surface of the yoke.

9. With the bearing in position, install a new snap-ring.

10. Start a new bearing into the opposite side of the yoke.

11. Press (or drive) the bearing until the opposite bearing—which you have just in-

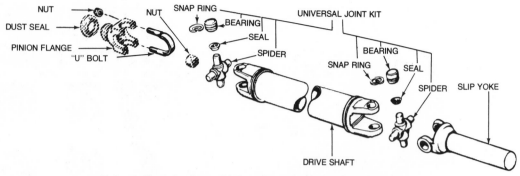

**Driveshaft and universal joints through 1979—exploded view**

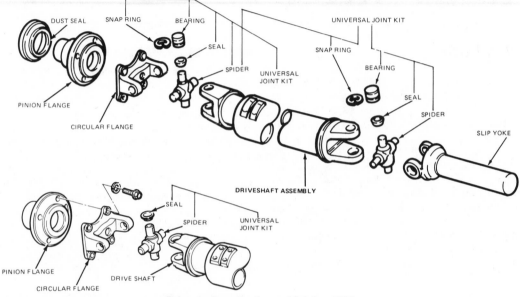

**Driveshaft and universal joints—1980**

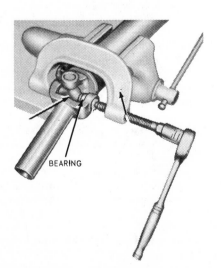

**Removing the universal joint bearing**

stalled—contacts the inner surface of the snap-ring.

12. Install a new snap-ring on the second bearing. It may be necessary to grind the surface of this second snap-ring.

13. Reposition the driveshaft in the vise, so that the front universal joint is accessible.

14. Install the new bearings, new spider, and new snap-rings in the same manner as you did for the rear universal joint.

15. Position the slip yoke on the spider. Install new bearings, nylon thrust bearings, and snap-rings.

16. Check both reassembled joints for freedom of movement. If misalignment of any part is causing a bind, a sharp rap on the side of the yoke with a brass hammer should seat the bearing needles and provide the desired freedom of movement. Care should be exercised to firmly support the shaft end during this operation, as well as to prevent blows to the bearings themselves. *Under no circumstances*

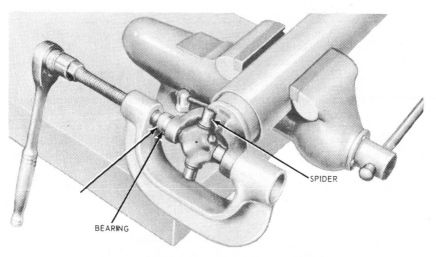

BEARING

SPIDER

**Installing the universal joint bearing**

*should a driveshaft be installed in a car if there is any binding in the universal joints.*

## DRIVESHAFT INSTALLATION

1. Carefully inspect the rubber seal on the output shaft and the seal in end of the transmission extension housing. Replace them if they are damaged.

2. Examine the lugs on the axle pinion flange and replace the flange if the lugs are shaved or distorted.

3. Coat the yoke spline with lithium base chassis grease.

4. Remove the plug from the rear of the transmission housing.

5. Insert the yoke into the transmission housing and onto the transmission output shaft. Make sure that the yoke assembly does not bottom on the output shaft with excessive force.

6. Locate the marks which you made on the rear drive shaft yoke and the pinion flange prior to removal of the driveshaft assembly. Install the driveshaft assembly with the marks properly aligned.

7. Install the U-bolts and nuts that attach the universal joint to the pinion flange. Torque the U-bolt nuts to 8–15 ft. lbs. On 1980, and later, circular flange type shafts, tighten the circular flange bolts to 70–95 ft. lbs.

## REAR AXLE ASSEMBLY

Both integral and removable carrier type axles are used. Traction-Lok (limited slip) axles are available only as removable carrier types.

The axle type and ratio are stamped on a plate attached to a rear housing cover bolt. Axle types also indicate whether the axle shafts are retained by C-locks; on these axles, the bearing is removed with a slide hammer. On other axles, the bearing is housed by a retainer ring which must be split for removal. WER, WGX and WGZ axles have C-locks. All other axles have bearing retainer rings. If the second letter of the axle code is F, it is a Traction-Lok axle (WFA, WFB, etc.). Always use the axle codes and ratio when ordering parts.

## Axle Shaft

### REMOVAL AND INSTALLATION AND/OR BEARING AND SEAL REPLACEMENT

#### Except C-Lock Type

NOTE: *Bearings must be pressed on and off the shaft with an arbor press. Unless you have access to one, it is inadvisable to attempt any repair work on the axle shaft bearing assemblies.*

1. Remove the wheel, tire, and brake drum. With disc brakes, remove the caliper, retainer nuts, and rotor. New anchor plate bolts will be needed for reassembly.

2. Remove the nuts holding the retainer plate to the backing plate, or axle shaft retainer bolts from the housing. Disconnect the brake line with drum brakes.

3. Remove the retainer and install nuts, finger-tight, to prevent the brake backing plate from being dislodged.

4. Pull out the axle shaft and bearing assembly, using a slide hammer.

On models with a tapered roller bearing, the tapered cup will normally remain in the axle housing when the shaft is removed. The cup must be removed from the housing to prevent seal damage when the shaft is reinstalled. The cup can be removed with a slide hammer and an expanding puller.

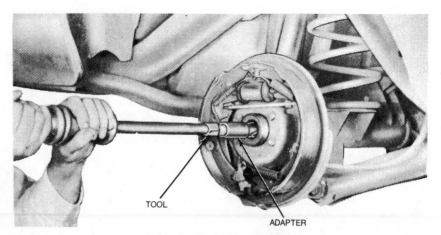

**Typical axle shaft/seal removal**

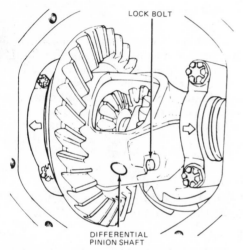

**Location of the pinion shaft and lock on "C" lock axles**

NOTE: *If end-play is found to be excessive, the bearing should be replaced. Shimming the bearing is not recommended as this ignores end-play of the bearing itself and could result in improper seating of the bearing.*

5. Using a chisel, nick the bearing retainer in 3 or 4 places. The retainer does not have to be cut, but merely collapsed sufficiently to allow the bearing retainer to be slid from the shaft.

6. Press off the bearing and install the new one by pressing it into position. With tapered bearings, place the lubricated seal and bearing on the axle shaft (cup rib ring facing the flange). Make sure that the seal is the correct length. Disc brake seal rims are black, drum brake seal rims are grey. Press the bearing and seal onto the shaft.

7. Press on the new retainer.

NOTE: *Do not attempt to press the bearing and the retainer on at the same time.*

8. On ball bearing models, to replace the seal: remove the seal from the housing with an expanding cone type puller and a slide hammer. The seal must be replaced whenever the shaft is removed. Wipe a small amount of sealer onto the outer edge of the new seal before installation; do not put sealer on the sealing lip. Press the seal into the housing with a seal installation tool.

9. Assemble the shaft and bearing in the housing, being sure that the bearing is seated properly in the housing. On ball bearing models, be careful not to damage the seal with the shaft. With tapered bearings, first install the tapered cup on the bearing, and lubricate the outer diameter of the cup and the seal with axle lube. Then install the shaft and bearing assembly into the housing.

10. Install the retainer, drum or rotor and caliper, wheel and tire. Bleed the brakes.

### C-Lock Type

1. Jack up and support the rear of the car.
2. Remove the wheels and tires from the brake drums.

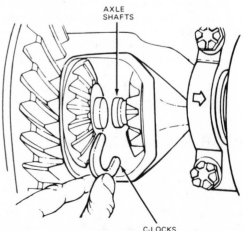

**Removing or installing "C" locks**

3. Place a drain pan under the housing and drain the lubricant by loosening the housing cover.

4. Remove the locks securing the brake drums to the axle shaft flanges and remove the drums.

5. Remove the housing cover and gasket, if used.

6. Position jackstands under the rear frame member and lower the axle housing. This is done to give easy access to the inside of the differential.

7. Working through the opening in the differential case, remove the side gear pinion shaft lockbolt and the side gear pinion shaft.

8. Push the axle shafts inward and remove the C-locks from the inner end of the axle shafts. Temporarily replace the shaft and lockbolt to retain the differential gears in position.

9. Remove the axle shafts with a slide hammer. Be sure the seal is not damaged by the splines on the axle shaft.

10. Remove the bearing and oil seal from the housing. Both the seal and bearing can be removed with a slide hammer. Two types of bearings are used on some axles, one requiring a press fit and the other a loose fit. A loose fitting bearing does not necessarily indicate excessive wear.

11. Inspect the axle shaft housing and axle shafts for burrs or other irregularities. Replace any worn or damaged parts. A light yellow color on the bearing journal of the axle shaft is normal, and does not require replacement of the axle shaft. Slight pitting and wear is also normal.

12. Lightly coat the wheel bearing rollers with axle lubricant. Install the bearings in the axle housing until the bearing seats firmly against the shoulder.

13. Wipe all lubricant from the oil seal bore, before installing the seal.

14. Inspect the original seals for wear. If necessary, these may be replaced with new

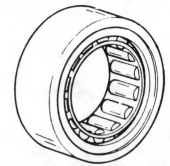

**"C" lock axle shaft wheel bearing**

seals, which are prepacked with lubricant and do not require soaking.

15. Install the oil seal.

16. Remove the lockbolt and pinion shaft. Carefully slide the axle shafts into place. Be careful that you do not damage the seal with the splined end of the axle shaft. Engage the splined end of the shaft with the differential side gears.

17. Install the axle shaft C-locks on the inner end of the axle shafts and seat the C-locks in the counterbore of the differential side gears.

18. Rotate the differential pinion gears until the differential pinion shaft can be installed. Install the differential pinion shaft lockbolt. Tighten to 15–22 ft. lbs.

19. Install the brake drum on the axle shaft flange.

20. Install the wheel and tire on the brake drum and tighten the attaching nuts.

21. Clean the gasket surface of the rear housing and install a new cover gasket and the housing cover. WGY covers do not use a gasket. On these models, apply a bead of silicone sealer on the gasket surface. The bead should run inside of the bolt holes.

22. Raise the rear axle so that it is in the running position. Add the amount of specified lubricant to bring the lubricant level to ½ in. below the filler hole on WER axles, or 1¼ in. below on the WGY.

# Suspension and Steering

**8**

## FRONT SUSPENSION 1975–80

The front wheels rotate on spindles. The upper and lower ends of the spindle are attached to ball joints, which are mounted to an upper and lower arm. The upper control arm pivots on a bushing and shaft assembly which is bolted to the frame. The lower control arm pivots on a bolt in the crossmember. The coil springs are mounted on top of the upper control arms, between the upper arm pivot seats and the top of the spring housings. The shock absorbers are mounted between the pivot seats and the spring housings inside the coil springs.

A stabilizing strut mounts between the two rubber buffer pads at the front crossmember and the lower control arm. A stabilizer bar is used to control front suspension roll.

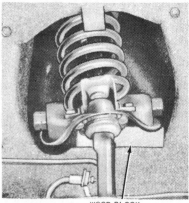

WOOD BLOCK

## Coil Spring

### REMOVAL AND INSTALLATION

Do not attempt to remove or install coil springs without a spring compressor. If a coil spring is removed without the use of a spring compressor, severe injury may result.

1. Remove the shock absorber and mounting bracket.

2. Jack up the car and install a jackstand beneath the inboard end of the lower control arm. Remove the wheel. Place a wooden block next to the control arm, as illustrated.

3. Remove the grease cap, cotter pin, lock nut and outer bearing from the hub.

4. Remove the disc brake caliper and rotor, as outlined in Chapter 9.

5. Install the spring compressor, as shown in the illustration.

6. Remove the two nuts retaining the upper control arm to the spring tower and swing the arms outboard from the tower.

7. Slowly release the spring compressor from the spring and remove the tool from the

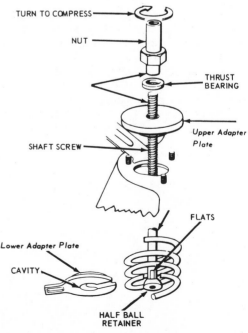

**Spring compressor tool installation**

spring. Then remove the spring from the vehicle.

8. To install, tape the spring upper insulator on the top of the spring. Place the spring in the tower. Install the spring compressor and compress the spring.

9. Swing the upper control arm inboard and insert the retaining bolts through the bolt holes in the spring tower. Install the retaining nuts and torque them to 85–100 ft. lbs. through 1977, 110–130 ft. lbs. for 1978 thru 1980 models.

10. Slowly release the spring compressor, while guiding the lower end of the spring into the upper control arm spring seat. The end of the spring must be no more than ½ inch from the tab on the spring seat.

11. Remove the spring compressor.

12. Reinstall the rotor and the caliper. Install the outer bearing, washer and adjusting nut on the spindle. Adjust the wheel bearing. Install the locknut, cotter pin and grease cap.

13. Install the wheel, remove the jackstand and lower the vehicle. Install the shock absorber and upper mounting bracket.

## Front Shock Absorber
### REMOVAL AND INSTALLATION

1. Raise the hood. Remove the three nuts retaining the shock absorber upper mounting bracket to the spring tower.

2. Jack up the front of the vehicle and install jack stands beneath the lower control arms.

3. Remove the two shock absorber lower retaining nuts, washers and insulators.

4. Lift the shock absorber and upper mounting bracket assembly from the spring tower. Remove the two bolts retaining the upper bracket to the shock absorber and remove the bracket. Remove the insulators from the lower attaching studs.

5. Check the shock absorber by wiping it clean and extending and compressing it several times. Severe leakage or weak damping action requires replacement. All standard equipment shock absorbers are nonrefillable and they cannot be repaired. As a general rule, shock absorbers should be replaced in pairs (front and rear sets).

6. To install, place the upper mounting bracket on the shock absorber and tighten the bolts to 10–16 ft. lbs. through 1978, 14–21 ft. lbs. for 1979, and 22–30 ft. lbs. for 1980. Install the insulators on the lower attaching studs.

7. Position the shock absorber and upper mounting bracket assembly in the spring tower, making sure that the lower studs are located in the pivot plate holes.

8. Install the two nuts on the shock absorber lower studs and tighten them to 8–12 ft. lbs.

9. Install the three nuts retaining the shock absorber upper mounting bracket to the spring tower and torque them to 32–48 ft. lbs.

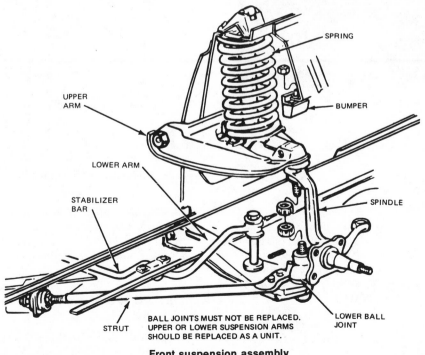

SPRING

UPPER ARM

BUMPER

LOWER ARM

STABILIZER BAR

SPINDLE

STRUT

BALL JOINTS MUST NOT BE REPLACED. UPPER OR LOWER SUSPENSION ARMS SHOULD BE REPLACED AS A UNIT.

LOWER BALL JOINT

**Front suspension assembly**

Remove the three retaining nuts and the shock will come off with its mounting bracket

Upper and lower ball joints (arrows)

The lower shock retaining nuts are hidden in the upper control arm

10. Remove the jackstands and lower the vehicle.

## Upper Ball Joint
### INSPECTION

1. Raise the vehicle on a hoist or floor jack so that the front wheels hang in the full down position. Install jack stands under the crossmember inboard of the lower control arms.
2. Have an assistant grasp the wheel top and bottom and apply alternate in and out pressure to the top and bottom of the wheel.
3. Radial play of ¼ inch is acceptable. It is measured at the inside of the wheel adjacent to the upper arm.

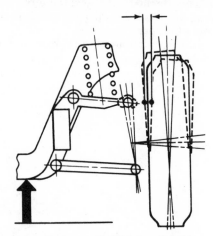

Measuring the upper ball joint radial play

NOTE: *This radial play measurement is multiplied at the other circumference of the tire and should not be measured here. Measure only at the inside of the wheel.*

## Lower Ball Joint
### INSPECTION

The lower ball joint is an integral part of the lower control arm. If the lower ball joint is defective, the entire lower control arm must be replaced.

1. Raise the vehicle on a hoist or floor jack so that the front wheel falls to the full down position. Install jackstands under the cross-member inboard of the lower control arms.

2. Have an assistant grasp the bottom of the tire and move the wheel in and out.

3. As the wheel is being moved, observe the lower control arm where the spindle attaches to it.

4. Any movement between the lower part of the spindle and the lower control arm indicates a bad control arm which must be replaced.

NOTE: *During this check, the upper ball joint will be unloaded and may move; this is normal and not an indication of a bad ball joint. Also, do not mistake a loose wheel bearing for a worn ball joint.*

### REMOVAL AND INSTALLATION

Neither upper nor lower ball joints are replaceable on Granadas and Monarchs. If the ball joint is bad, the entire control arm must be replaced.

## Lower Control Arm
### REMOVAL AND INSTALLATION

1. Position an upper control arm support, a wooden block will do, between the upper arm and the side rail. Refer to Coil Spring Removal and Installation for an illustration of where to place the wood.

2. Raise the vehicle, position jackstands, and remove the wheel and tire.

3. Remove the stabilizer bar-to-link attaching nut and disconnect the bar from the link.

4. Remove the link bolt from the lower arm.

5. Remove the strut bar-to-lower arm attaching nuts and bolts.

6. Remove the lower ball joint cotter pin and back off the nut. Using a suitable tool, loosen the ball joint stud in the spindle.

7. Remove the nut from the arm and lower the arm.

8. Remove the lower arm-to-underbody cam attaching parts and remove the arm.

9. To install, position the lower arm in the underbody and install the ball joint and cam attaching parts loosely.

10. Install the stabilizer and strut. Torque the stabilizer to 6–12 ft. lbs. Torque the strut to 70–80 ft. lbs. through 1978 and 70–80 ft. lbs. for 1979 and later.

11. Torque the lower arm pivot to 85–100 ft. lb. and the ball joint stud to 75–90 ft. lb.

12. Lower the car and remove the upper arm support.

13. Front end alignment must be rechecked.

## Upper Control Arm

When upper control arm bushings become low on lubrication, they become very noisy. This can often be corrected by lubrication and it is not necessary to replace the bushings. On early models that do not contain grease plugs, it is necessary to drill and tap the bushing to accept a grease fitting. On later models with grease plugs it is difficult to remove the plug and grease the bushing with conventional tools. Ford has available an upper A-arm lubrication kit which greatly eases the performance of this operation.

NOTE: *Because suspension damage to one control arm generally affects the other, it is recommended that upper and lower control arms, and their respective ball joints, be replaced as a unit.*

### REMOVAL AND INSTALLATION

1. Install blocks of wood as described in Coil Spring Removal and Installation. Raise the car and support it with jack stands.

2. Remove the wheel.

3. Remove the shock absorber lower attaching nuts.

4. Remove the shock absorber upper mounting bracket attaching nuts and remove the shock and the bracket.

5. Install a spring compressor tool. On models equipped with a V8 engine, it will be necessary to remove the air cleaner to obtain clearance.

6. Position a jack stand under the lower control arm.

7. Remove the cotter pin from the nut on the upper ball joint stud and loosen the nut one or two turns. Do not remove the nut.

8. Place a ball joint remover between the upper and lower ball joint studs. The tool should seat firmly against the ends of the studs, not against the stud nuts.

9. Turn the tool with a wrench until the studs are placed under considerable compression then strike the spindle sharply with a hammer to break the stud loose.

10. Remove the nut from the upper stud and lift the stud out of the spindle.

11. Remove the upper arm attaching nuts from inside the engine compartment and remove the arm.

12. Clean all parts thoroughly but do not clean the ball joint in solvent.

To install:

1. Place the upper arm and spring seat in the spring tower and install the nuts on the two inner shaft attaching bolts. Tighten to 85–100 ft. lbs.

2. Position the upper ball joint stud in the spindle. Install the stud nut. Tighten the nut to 75–90 ft. lbs. Install the cotter pin.

3. Slowly release the coil spring and remove the tool.

4. Install the shock absorber, lower the car to the ground and remove the wood blocks.

5. Check the front end alignment.

## FRONT SUSPENSION 1981–82

1981–82 models use a modified version of the MacPherson strut front suspension. The design utilizes shock struts with coil springs mounted between the lower arm and a spring pocket in the No. 2 crossmember. The lower suspension arm bushings are not separately serviced, and they also must be replaced by replacing the suspension arm assembly.

## Springs

NOTE: *Always use extreme caution when working with coil springs. Make sure the vehicle is supported sufficiently.*

### REMOVAL

1. Raise the front of the vehicle and place safety stands under both sides of the jack pads just back of the lower arms.

2. Remove the wheel and tire assembly.

3. Disconnect the stabilizer bar link from the lower arm.

4. Remove the steering gear bolts, and move the steering gear out of the way.

5. Disconnect the tie rod from the steering spindle.

6. Using a spring compressor, install one plate with the pivot ball seat down into the coils of the spring. Rotate the plate, so that it fully seated into the lower suspension arm spring seat.

7. Install the other plate with the pivot ball seat up into the coils of the spring. Insert the ball nut through the coils of the spring, so it rests in the upper plate.

8. Insert the compression rod into the opening in the lower arm through the lower and upper plate. Install the upper ball nut on the rod, and return the securing pin.

NOTE: *This pin can only be inserted one way into the upper ball nut because of a stepped hole design.*

9. With the upper ball nut secured turn the upper plate, so it walks up the coil until it contacts the upper spring seat.

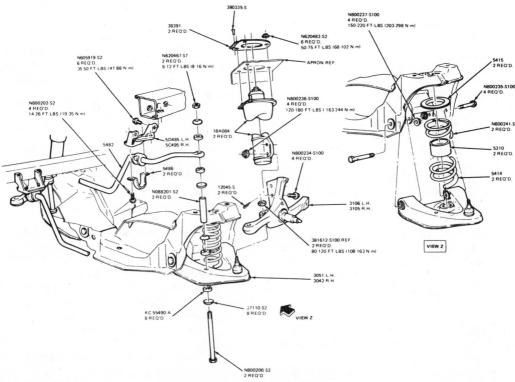

**MacPherson strut front suspension**

10. Install the lower ball nut, thrust bearing and forcing nut on the compression rod.

11. Rotate the nut until the spring is compressed enough so that it is free in its seat.

12. Remove the two lower control arm pivot bolts and nuts, and disengage the lower arm from the frame crossmember and remove the spring assembly.

13. If a new spring is to be installed, mark the position of the upper and lower plates on the spring with chalk. Measure the compressed length of the spring as well as the amount of the spring curvature to assist in the compressing and installation of a new spring.

14. Loosen the nut to relieve spring tension, and remove the tools from the spring.

### INSTALLATION

1. Assemble the spring compressor tool, and locate it in the same position as indicated in Step 13 of the removal procedure.

NOTE: *Before compressing the coil spring, be sure the upper ball nut securing pin is inserted properly.*

2. Compress the coil spring until the spring height reaches the dimension in step 13.

3. Position the coil spring assembly into the lower arm.

NOTE: *Make sure that the lower end of the spring is properly positioned between the two holes in the lower arm spring pocket depression.*

4. To finish installing the coil spring reverse the removal procedure.

## Ball Joints

Ball joints are not replaceable. If the ball joints are found to be defective the lower control arm assembly must be replaced.

### INSPECTION

1. Support the vehicle in normal driving position with both ball joints loaded.

2. Wipe the grease fitting and checking surface, so they are free of dirt and grease. The checking surface is the round boss into which the grease fitting is threaded.

3. The checking surface should project outside the cover. If the checking surface is inside the cover, replace the lower arm assembly.

## Shock Strut

### REMOVAL

1. Place the ignition key in the unlocked position to permit free movement of the front wheels.

2. Working from the engine compartment remove the nut (16 mm) that attaches the strut to the upper mount. A screwdriver in the slot will hold the rod stationary while removing the nut.

NOTE: *The vehicle should not be driven while the nut is removed so make sure the car is in position for hoisting purposes.*

3. Raise the front of the vehicle by the lower control arms, and place safety stands under the frame jacking pads, rearward of the wheels.

4. Remove the tire and wheel assembly.

5. Remove the brake caliper, rotor assembly, and dust shield.

6. Remove the two lower nuts and bolts attaching the strut to the spindle.

7. Lift the strut up from the spindle to compress the rod, then pull down and remove the strut.

### INSTALLATION

1. With the rod half extended, place the rod through the upper mount and hand start the mount as soon as possible.

2. Extend the strut and position into the spindle.

3. Install the two lower mounting bolts and hand start the nuts.

4. Tighten the nut that attaches the strut to the upper body mount to 60–75 ft. lbs. This can be done from inside the engine compartment.

NOTE: *Position a prybar in the slot to hold the rod stationary while the nut is being tightened.*

5. Remove the suspension load from the lower control arms by lowering the hoist and tighten the lower mounting nuts to 150 ft. lbs.

6. Raise the suspension control arms and install the brake caliper, rotor assembly and dust shield.

7. Install the tire and wheel assembly.

8. Remove the safety stands and lower the vehicle.

## Lower Control Arm

### REMOVAL

1. Raise the front of the vehicle and position safety stands under both sides of the jack pads, just to the rear of the lower arms.

2. Remove the wheel and tire assembly.

3. Disconnect the stabilizer bar link from the lower arm.

4. Remove the disc brake caliper, rotor and dust shield.

5. Remove the steering gear bolts and position out of the way.

6. Remove the cotter pin from the ball joint stud nut, and loosen the ball joint nut one or two turns.

7. Tap the spindle sharply to relieve the stud pressure.

8. Remove the tie-rod end from the spindle. Place a floor jack under the lower arm, supporting the arm at both bushings. Remove both lower arm bolts, lower the jack and remove the coil spring as outlined earlier in the chapter.

9. Remove the ball nut and remove the arm assembly.

### INSTALLATION

1. Place the new arm assembly into the spindle and tighten the ball joint nut to 100 ft. lbs. Install the cotter pin.

2. Position the coil spring in the upper spring pocket. Make sure the insulator is on top of the spring and the lower end is properly positioned between the two holes in the depression of the lower arm.

3. Carefully raise the lower arm with the floor jack until the bushings are properly positioned in the crossmember.

4. Install the lower arm bolts and nuts, finger tight only.

5. Install and tighten the steering gear bolts.

6. Connect the tie-rod end and tighten the nut to 35–47 ft. lbs.

7. Connect the stabilizer link bolt and nut and tighten to 10 ft. lbs.

8. Install the brake dust shield, rotor and caliper.

9. Install the wheel and tire assembly.

10. Remove the safety stands and lower the vehicle. After the vehicle has been lowered to the floor and at curb height, tighten the lower arm nuts to 210 ft. lbs.

## FRONT END ALIGNMENT

The procedure for checking and adjusting front wheel alignment requires specialized equipment and professional skills. The following descriptions and adjustment procedures are for general reference only.

NOTE: *Caster and camber on 1981–82 models are set at the factory and cannot be changed. Only toe is adjustable.*

Front wheel alignment is the position of the front wheels relative to each other and to the vehicle. It must be maintained to provide safe, accurate steering with minimum tire wear. Many factors are involved in wheel alignment and adjustments are provided to return those that might change due to normal wear to their original value. The factors which determine wheel alignment are dependent on one another; therefore, when one of the factors is ad-

justed, the others must be adjusted to compensate.

Descriptions of these factors and their effects on the car are provided below.

NOTE: *Do not attempt to check and adjust the front wheel alignment without first making a thorough inspection of the front suspension components.*

## Camber

Camber angle is the number of degrees that the centerline of the wheel is inclined from the vertical. Camber reduces loading of the outer wheel bearing and improves the tire contact patch while cornering.

## Caster

Caster angle is the number of degrees that a line drawn through the steering buckle pivots is inclined from the vertical, toward the front or rear of the car. Caster improves directional stability and decreases susceptibility to crosswinds or road surface deviations.

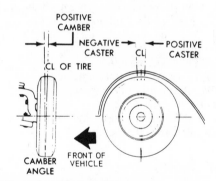

Caster and camber angles

## Steering Axis Inclination

Steering axis inclination is the number of degrees that a line drawn through the steering knuckle pivots is inclined to the vertical, when viewed from the front of the car. This, in combination with caster, is responsible for directional stability and self-centering of the steering. As the steering knuckle swings from lock to lock, the spindle generates an arc, the high point being the straight-ahead position of the wheel. Due to this arc, as the wheel turns, the front of the car is raised. The weight of the car acts against this lift and attempts to return the spindle to the high point of the arc, resulting in self-centering, when the steering wheel is released, and straight-line stability.

## Toe-In

Toe-in is the difference of the distance between the centers of the front and rear of the

# HOW TO READ TIRE WEAR

The way your tires wear is a good indicator of other parts of your car. Abnormal wear patterns are often caused by the need for simple tire maintenance, or for front end alignment.

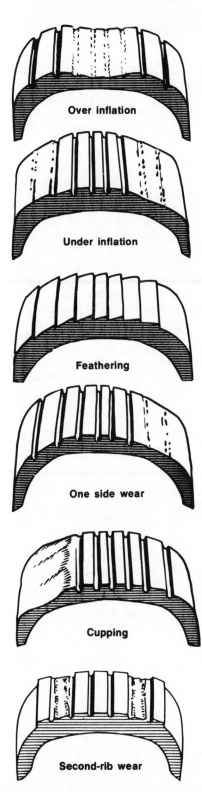

**Over inflation**

**Under inflation**

**Feathering**

**One side wear**

**Cupping**

**Second-rib wear**

Excessive wear at the center of the tread indicates that the air pressure in the tire is consistently too high. The tire is riding on the center of the tread and wearing it prematurely. Occasionally, this wear pattern can result from outrageously wide tires on narrow rims. The cure for this is to replace either the tires or the wheels.

This type of wear usually results from consistent under-inflation. When a tire is under inflated, there is too much contact with the road by the outer treads, which wear prematurely. When this type of wear occurs, and the tire pressure is known to be consistently correct, a bent or worn steering component or the need for wheel alignment could be indicated.

Feathering is a condition when the edge of each tread rib develops a slightly rounded edge on one side and a sharp edge on the other. By running your hand over the tire, you can usually feel the sharper edges before you'll be able to see them. The most common causes of feathering are incorrect toe-in setting or deteriorated bushings in the front suspension.

When an inner or outer rib wears faster than the rest of the tire, the need for wheel alignment is indicated. There is excessive camber in the front suspension, causing the wheel to lean too much putting excessive load on one side of the tire. Misalignment could also be due to sagging springs, worn ball joints, or worn control arm bushings. Be sure the vehicle is loaded the way it's normally driven when you have the wheels aligned.

Cups or scalloped dips appearing around the edge of the tread almost always indicate worn (sometimes bent) suspension parts. Adjustment of wheel alignment alone will seldom cure the problem. Any worn component that connects the wheel to the car can cause this type of wear. Occasionally, wheels that are out of balance will wear like this, but wheel imbalance usually shows up as bald spots between the outside edges and center of the tread.

Second-rib wear is normally found only in radial tires, and appears where the steel belts end in relation to the tread. Normally, it can be kept to a minimum by paying careful attention to tire pressure and frequently rotating the tires. This is frequently considered normal wear but excessive amounts indicate that the tires are too wide for the wheels.

front wheels. It is most commonly measured in inches, but is occasionally referred to as an angle between the wheels. Toe-in is necessary to compensate for the tendency of the wheels to deflect rearward while in motion. Due to this tendency, the wheels of a vehicle, with properly adjusted toe-in, are traveling straight forward when the vehicle itself is traveling straight forward, resulting in directional stability and minimum tire wear.

## ADJUSTMENT PROCEDURES

### Caster 1975–80

Check the caster angle at each front wheel. The caster angle is the fore-aft tilt of the top of the wheel spindle, as shown in the accompanying diagram. Position caster exists when the spindle tilts towards the rear; negative caster is present when the spindle tilts towards the front. The correct caster angle should be between $-1\frac{1}{4}°$ and $+\frac{1}{4}°$. When checking, the maximum caster difference between the two front wheels should not exceed 1°. However, if the caster is to be set, the wheels should be set within $\frac{1}{2}°$ of each other, with both being in the negative $1\frac{1}{2}°$ to positive $\frac{1}{2}°$ range.

NOTE: *Because the front suspension angles are interdependent, the preceding specifications assume that camber is also within permissible limits.*

Caster is adjusted by the position of the front suspension strut, shown in the accompanying illustration. Positive caster is obtained by loosening the strut rear nut and tightening the front nut against the bushing. To obtain negative caster, loosen the strut front nut and tighten the rear nut against the bushing. After the caster has been adjusted, always recheck the camber angles.

### Camber 1975–80

Check the camber angle at each front wheel. Camber is the angle at which the front wheels are tilted at the top (see accompanying diagram). Positive camber exists when the top of the wheel tilts outward; negative camber is present when the top of the wheel tilts inward. Camber angle should be within the range $-\frac{1}{2}°$ to $+1°$, with the maximum camber difference between the front wheels being 1° for checking purposes and $\frac{1}{2}°$ for setting purposes. In other words, when setting the camber angles, the two wheels should be within $\frac{1}{2}°$ of each other, both being in the range of negative $\frac{1}{2}°$ to positive 1°.

The camber adjustment is controlled by the eccentric cam located at the lower arm attachment to the side rail (see accompanying illustration). To adjust the camber, loosen the camber adjustment bolt nut at the rear of the body bracket and spread the body bracket at the camber adjustment bolt area just enough to allow lateral movement of the arm when the adjusting bolt is turned. The bolt and eccentric are rotated clockwise from the high position to increase camber or counterclockwise to decrease camber.

After the caster and camber angles have been adjusted to the proper specifications, tighten the lower arm eccentric bolt nut and the strut front nut securely. Recheck the angles to be sure that they have remained within specifications.

### Toe-In 1975–80

Before checking and adjusting the toe-in, remove the alignment height spacers used in the caster and camber checks and adjustments. Toe-in should only be checked and adjusted when the caster and camber are within specifications. The toe-in is checked with the front wheels in the straight-ahead position. If the car is equipped with power steering, run the engine so that the power steering control valve will be in the center position. Measure the distance between the extreme front points of the front wheels, then compare this to the distance between the two extreme rear points. The difference between the distances is the amount of toe-in or toe-out of the front wheels. The front wheels should be toed-in (front measurement less than rear measurement) by $\frac{1}{16}$ inch to $\frac{5}{16}$ inch.

Adjustment of the toe-in and the steering wheel spoke position can be accomplished at the same time. When the front wheels are in the straight-ahead position, the steering wheel spokes should be horizontal. Loosen the two clamping bolts on each spindle connecting rod sleeve (see accompanying illustration). If the toe-in is incorrect and the steering wheel spokes are in the proper position, lengthen or shorten both rods equally until the correct toe-in is obtained. If the toe-in is incorrect and the steering wheel position is also incorrect, adjust the rods as necessary to obtain correct toe-in and steering wheel alignment. Check the toe-in and steering wheel position again. If the toe-in is correct, but the steering wheel position is incorrect, turn both connecting rod sleeves upward or downward the same number of turns in order to move the steering wheel to the proper position. When both the toe-in and the steering wheel position are correct, lubricate the clamps, bolts and nuts and tighten the clamping bolts on both sleeves to a torque of 9–15 ft. lb. Be sure that the sleeve position is not changed when the clamping

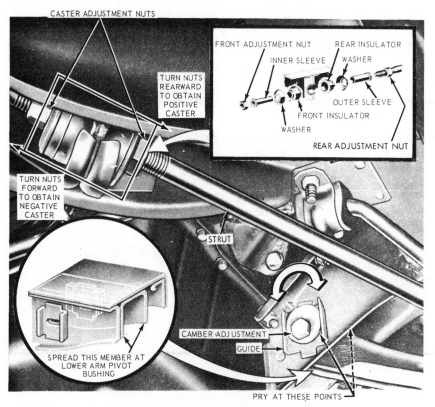

**Caster and camber adjustment procedures**

bolts are tightened. Recheck the toe-in and steering wheel position.

### Toe Adjustment 1981–82

Toe is the difference in width (distance), between the front and rear inside edges of the front tires.

1. Turn the steering wheel, from left to right, several times and center.

NOTE: *If car has power steering, start the engine before centering the steering wheel.*

2. Secure the centered steering wheel with a steering wheel holder, or any device that will keep it centered.

3. Release the tie-rod end bellows clamps so the bellows will not twist while adjustment is made. Loosen the jam nuts on the tie-rod ends. Adjust the left and right connector sleeves until each wheel has one-half of the desired toe setting.

4. After the adjustment has been made, tighten the jam nuts and secure the bellows clamps. Release the steering wheel lock and check for steering wheel center. Readjust, if necessary until steering wheel is centered and toe is within specs.

## REAR SUSPENSION 1975–80

These models employ a semieliptic leaf spring rear suspension. The axle housing is supported by a pair of conventional, longitudinally mounted leaf springs. The housing is secured to the center of the springs by two U-bolts, retaining plates, spring pads and nuts. Each spring is suspended from the underbody side rail by a hanger at the front and a shackle at the rear. The shock absorbers are mounted between the leaf spring retaining plates and brackets welded to the crossmember.

## Leaf Spring

### REMOVAL AND INSTALLATION

1. Raise the vehicle and place supports beneath the underbody and axle.

NOTE: *All used attaching components (nuts, bolts, etc.) must be discarded and replaced with new ones prior to assembly.*

2. Disconnect the lower end of the shock absorber from the spring clip plate and position it out of the way. Remove the supports from under the axle.

3. Remove the spring plate nuts from the U-bolt and remove the spring plate. With a jack, raise the rear axle just enough to remove the weight of the housing from the spring.

4. Remove the two rear shackle attaching nuts, the shackle bar, and the two inner bushings.

5. Remove the rear shackle assembly and the two outer bushings.

6. Remove the nut from the spring mounting bolt and tap the bolt out of the bushing at the front hanger. Lift out the spring assembly.

7. Position the leaf spring under the axle housing and insert the shackle assembly into the rear hanger bracket and the rear eye of the spring.

8. Install the shackle inner bushings, the shackle plate and the locknuts. Hand-tighten the locknuts.

9. Position the spring eye in the front hanger, slip the washer on the front hanger bolt and, from the inboard side, insert the bolt through the hanger and eye. Install the locknut on the hanger bolt finger-tight.

10. Lower the rear axle housing so that it rests on the spring. Place the spring plate on the U-bolt and tighten the nuts to 30–45 ft. lb.

11. Attach the lower end of the shock absorber to the spring plate, using a new nut.

12. Place jackstands under the rear axle. Lower the vehicle until the spring is in the approximate curb load position (normal riding height), and tighten the front hanger bolt to 80–120 ft. lb.

13. Tighten the rear shackle locknuts to 14–22 ft. lb. Close the hole in the inner rail with a body plug.

14. Remove the jackstands and lower the vehicle.

## REAR SUSPENSION 1981–82

The rear suspension is a four link coil spring design. The rear axle is suspended from the body by two upper arms which control side to side movement and two lower arms which control forward and rearward movement. Shock absorbers are located on each side. Each

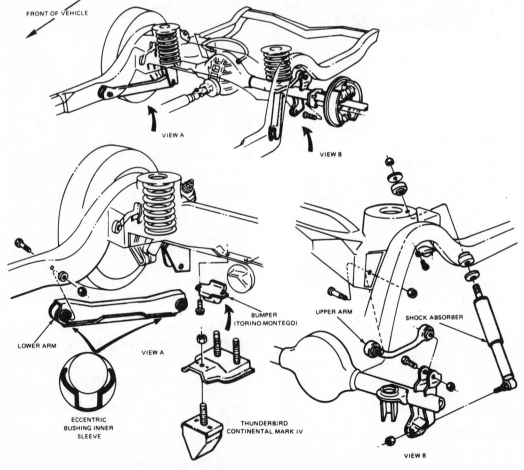

**Coil spring rear suspension assembly**

coil spring is mounted between an upper seat which is welded to the body and a lower seat which is part of the lower arm assembly. The shock absorbers are attached to an upper shock bracket which is welded to the rear axle tubes.

## Springs

NOTE: *Always use extreme caution when working with coil springs. Make sure the vehicle is supported sufficiently.*

### REMOVAL

NOTE: *Ford recommends that if one spring requires replacement the other spring should be replaced also.*

1. Raise the vehicle and support the body at the rear body crossmember.

2. Lower the hoist until the rear shocks are fully suspended.

NOTE: *The axle must be supported by the hoist, or a transmission jack, or jack stands.*

3. Place a transmission jack under the lower arm pivot bolt and remove the bolt and nut. Lower the transmission jack slowly until the coil spring load is relieved.

4. If the vehicle is equipped with a rear stabilizer bar remove the four retaining bolts and remove the stabilizer bar.

5. Remove the coil spring and insulators from the vehicle.

### INSTALLATION

1. Place the upper spring insulator into the spring seat in the body. Tape in place if necessary.

2. Place the lower spring insulator on the lower arm. Install the internal damper into the spring.

3. Position the coil spring on the lower arm spring seat. Slowly raise the transmission jack until the arm is in position. Insert a new rear pivot bolt and nut, with the nut facing outwards. Do not torque at this time.

4. Lower the transmission jack. Raise the axle to curb height. Torque the lower arm pivot bolt to 85 ft. lbs.

5. If the vehicle is equipped with a rear stabilizer bar, install it at this time. Torque the horizontal mount bolts to 35 ft. lbs. and the vertical mount bolts to 20 ft. lbs.

6. Remove the crossmember supports and lower the vehicle.

## Rear Shock Absorber

### REMOVAL AND INSTALLATION

1. Remove the lower end of the shockabsorber from the spring plate.

2. Remove the nut retaining the upper end

You'll have to hold the inner nut while you turn the outer one

of the shock absorber to the mounting bracket underneath the car.

3. Compress and remove the shock absorber.

NOTE: *All standard equipment shock absorbers are nonrefillable and cannot be repaired. Check the shock absorber by wiping it off and extending and compressing it several times. Severe leakage or weak damping action requires replacement. As a general rule, shock absorbers should be replaced in pairs (front and rear sets).*

4. Transfer the washers and bushings to the new shock absorber. Insert the upper stud through the mounting bracket, and install the attaching nut finger-tight.

5. Compress and install the shock absorber to the spring plate. Install the washers, bushings and attaching nuts.

6. Tighten the upper attaching nuts to 45–65 ft. lb. and the lower attaching nuts to 14–26 ft. lb.

## Shock Absorbers

### BOUNCE TEST

Each shock absorber can be tested by bouncing the corner of the vehicle until maximum up and down movement is obtained. Release the car. It should stop bouncing in one or two bounces. Compare both front corners or both rear corners but do not compare the front to the rear. If one corner bounces longer than the other it should be inspected for damage and possibly be replaced.

### REMOVAL

1. Open the trunk to gain access to the upper shock mounting.

2. Remove the rubber cap covering the shock absorber stud.

3. Remove the shock absorber attaching nut, and insulator.

4. Raise the vehicle and support the rear axle.

5. Compress the shock absorber to clear the hole in the upper shock tower.

6. Remove the lower shock absorber nut and washer from the shock mounting stud, and remove the shock absorber.

### INSTALLATION

1. Expel all air from the new shock absorber by extending the shock absorber fully in its right side up position then turning it upside down and fully compressing it. Follow this procedure at least three times to expel the air.

2. Compress the shock absorber and place the lower shock mounting eye over the lower mounting stud. Install the washer and new self locking attaching nut.

3. Place the inner washer and insulator on the upper shock stud.

4. Extend the shock absorber and position the upper stud into the mounting hole.

5. Lower the vehicle and install the insulator, outer washer and nut to the upper shock stud.

6. Install the rubber cap that covers the mounting stud.

## STEERING

## Steering Wheel

### REMOVAL AND INSTALLATION

1. Open the hood and disconnect the negative cable from the battery.

Tool T67L-3600-A

**Steering wheel removal using a puller**

2. On models with safety crash pads, remove the crash pad attaching screws from the underside of the steering wheel spoke and remove the pad. On all models equipped with a horn button, remove the horn button or ring by pressing down evenly and turning it counterclockwise approximately 20° and then lifting it from the steering wheel. On 1981–82 models, pull straight out on the hub cover. Disconnect the horn wires from the crash pad on models so equipped.

3. Remove and discard the nut from the end of the shaft. Install a steering wheel puller on the end of the shaft and remove the wheel.

CAUTION: *The use of a knock-off type steering wheel puller or the use of a hammer on the steering shaft will damage the collapsible column.*

4. Lubricate the upper surface of the steering shaft upper bushing with white grease. Transfer all serviceable parts to the new steering wheel.

5. Position the steering wheel on the shaft so that the alignment marks line up. Install a locknut and torque it to 30–40 ft. lbs. Connect the horn wires.

6. Install the horn button or ring by turning it clockwise or install the crash pad.

## Turn Signal and Hazard Flasher Switch Assembly

### REMOVAL AND INSTALLATION

#### Through 1979

1. Follow steps 1–4 under "Steering Wheel Removal and Installation."

2. Unscrew the turn signal switch lever from the steering column.

3. Remove the shroud from beneath the column.

4. Disconnect the steering column wiring connector plug from the bracket under the

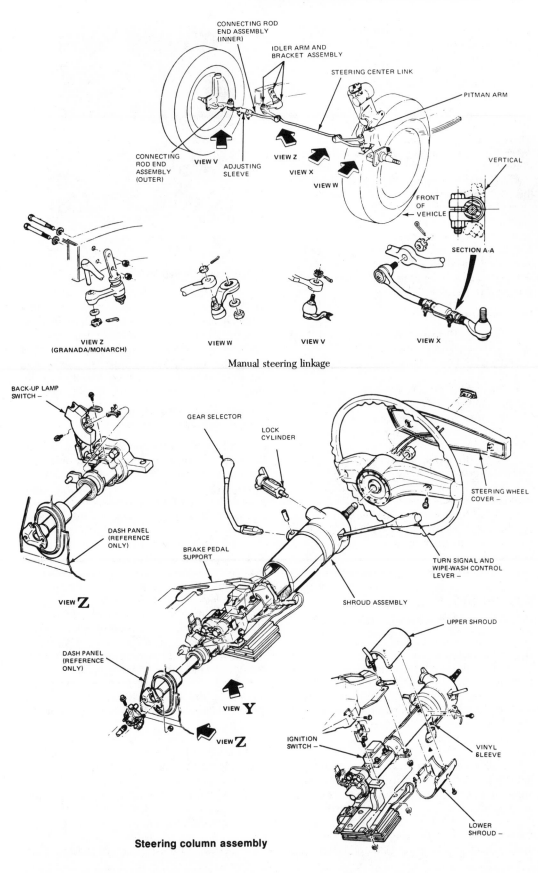

CONNECTING ROD
END ASSEMBLY
(INNER)

IDLER ARM AND
BRACKET ASSEMBLY

STEERING CENTER LINK

PITMAN ARM

CONNECTING
ROD END
ASSEMBLY
(OUTER)

VIEW V

ADJUSTING
SLEEVE

VIEW Z

VIEW X

VIEW W

VERTICAL

FRONT
OF
VEHICLE

SECTION A-A

VIEW Z
(GRANADA/MONARCH)

VIEW W

VIEW V

VIEW X

Manual steering linkage

BACK-UP LAMP
SWITCH –

GEAR SELECTOR

LOCK
CYLINDER

STEERING WHEEL
COVER –

DASH PANEL
(REFERENCE
ONLY)

BRAKE PEDAL
SUPPORT

TURN SIGNAL AND
WIPE-WASH CONTROL
LEVER –

SHROUD ASSEMBLY

VIEW Z

UPPER SHROUD

DASH PANEL
(REFERENCE
ONLY)

VIEW Y

VIEW Z

IGNITION
SWITCH –

VINYL
SLEEVE

LOWER
SHROUD –

**Steering column assembly**

dash above the steering column. Remove the screws retaining the turn signal/hazard flasher switch to the column.

5. Carefully pull the wires and connector plug up through the hole in the flange casting and remove the switch.

6. To install, route the wires and plug through the top of the column, so that they come out below the flange casting. Secure the swtich to the column with the three retaining screws.

7. Connect the plug to its mating plug at the lower end of the column.

8. Install the shroud and turn signal lever on the steering column.

9. Install the steering wheel as outlined under steps 6, 7 and 8 of "Steering Wheel Removal and Installation."

10. Test the operation of the turn signals and hazard flashers.

**1980 and Later**

1. Remove the steering column shroud attaching screws and remove the shroud.

2. Twist the turn signal lever and pull it out of the switch.

3. Pull back the foam shield from the switch and disconnect the two electrical connectors.

4. Remove the turn signal switch attaching screws and remove the switch.

To install:

1. Align the mounting holes and install the attaching screws.

2. Attach the switch wiring and put the foam shield back in place.

3. Install the lever into the switch by aligning the notch on the lever with the notch in the switch and pushing the lever in until it fully seats.

4. Install the steering column shroud.

# Manual Steering thru 1980
## STEERING GEAR INSPECTION

Before any steering gear adjustments are made, it is recommended that the front end of the car be raised and a thorough inspection be made for stiffness or lost motion in the steering gear, steering linkage, and front suspension. Worn or damaged parts should be replaced, since a satisfactory adjustment of the steering gear cannot be obtained if bent or badly worn parts exist.

It is also very important that the steering gear be properly aligned in the car. Misalignment of the gear places a stress on the steering worm shaft; therefore, a proper adjustment is impossible. To align the steering gear, loosen the mounting bolts to permit the gear to align itself. Check the steering gear mounting seat

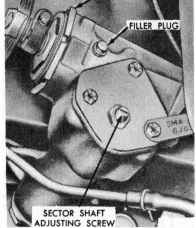

Steering gear adjustments

and, if there is a gap at any of the mounting bolts, proper alignment may be obtained by placing shims where excessive gap appears. Tighten the steering gear bolts. Alignment of the gear in the car is very important and should be done carefully so that a satisfactory, trouble-free gear adjustment may be obtained.

## WORM AND SECTOR GEAR ADJUSTMENTS THRU 1980

The ball nut assembly and the sector gear must be adjusted properly to maintain a minimum amount of steering shaft endplay and a minimum amount of backlash between the sector gear and the ball nut. There are only two adjustments that may be done on this steering gear and they should be done as follows:

1. Disconnect the pitman arm from the steering pitman-to-idler arm rod.

2. Loosen the locknut on the sector shaft adjustment screw and turn the adjusting screw counterclockwise until you feel it stop.

3. Measure the worm-bearing preload by attaching an in. lb. torque wrench to the steering wheel nut. With the steering wheel off center, note the reading required to rotate the input shaft about one and half turns to either side of center. If the torque reading is not 5–6 in. lbs. through 1977 or 2–4 in. lbs for 1978 and later, adjust the gear as given in the next step.

4. Loosen the steering shaft bearing adjuster locknut and tighten or back off the bearing adjusting screw until the preload is within the specified limits.

5. Tighten the steering shaft bearing adjuster locknut and recheck the preload torque.

6. Turn the steering wheel slowly to either stop. Turn *gently* against the stop to avoid possible damage to the ball return guides. Then

recenter the steering wheel by turning it exactly 2¾ turns on models through 1977 and exactly 2 turns on 1978 and later models.

7. Turn the sector adjusting screw clockwise until the proper torque (9–10 in. lb.) is obtained that is necessary to rotate the worm gear past its center (high spot).

8. While holding the sector adjusting screw, tighten the sector screw adjusting locknut to 32–40 ft. lb. and recheck the backlash adjustment.

9. Connect the pitman arm to the steering arm-to-idler arm rod.

## Power Steering thru 1980

### POWER STEERING SYSTEM ADJUSTMENTS

#### Control Valve Centering Spring Adjustment

1. Raise the car and install safety stands. Remove the spring cap attaching screws and the spring cap.

CAUTION: *Be very careful not to position the hoist adapters of two-post hoists under the suspension and/or steering components. Place the hoist adapters under the front suspension lower arms.*

2. Tighten the adjusting nut snugly (about 90–100 in. lb); then loosen the nut one-quarter turn (90°). Do not tighten the adjusting nut too tightly.

3. Place the spring cap on the valve housing. Lubricate and install the attaching screws and washers. Tighten the screws to 72–100 in. lb.

4. Lower the car and start the engine. Check the steering effort, using a spring scale attached to the steering wheel rim for a torque of more than 12 lb.

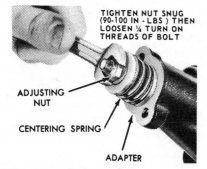

TIGHTEN NUT SNUG (90-100 IN -LBS) THEN LOOSEN ¼ TURN ON THREADS OF BOLT

ADJUSTING NUT

CENTERING SPRING

ADAPTER

**Adjusting the centering spring**

## Manual Steering, Rack and Pinion Type

### ADJUSTMENTS

The rack and pinion gear provides two means of service adjustment. The gear must be re-

moved from the vehicle to perform both adjustments.

### REMOVAL AND INSTALLATION

1. Disconnect the negative battery cable from the battery.

2. Remove the one bolt retaining the flexible coupling to the input shaft.

3. Leave the ignition key in the ON position, and raise the vehicle on a hoist.

4. Remove the two tie rod end retaining cotter pins and nuts. Separate the studs from the spindle arms, using the ball joint separator tool. Do not use a hammer or similar tool as this may damage spindle arms or rod studs.

5. Support the steering gear, and remove the two nuts, insulator washers, and bolts retaining the steering gear to the No. 2 crossmember.

6. Remove the steering gear assembly from the vehicle.

7. Insert the input shaft into the flexible coupling aligning the flats and position the steering gear to the No. 2 crossmember. Install the two bolts.

8. Connect the tie rod ends to the spindle arms, and install the two retaining nuts. Tighten the nuts to specifications, and install the two cotter pins.

9. Lower the vehicle, and install the one bolt retaining the flexible coupling to the input shaft. Tighten the bolt to specifications.

10. Turn the ignition key to the OFF position.

11. Connect the negative battery cable to the battery.

12. Check the toe, and reset if necessary.

### Support Yoke to Rack

1. Clean the exterior of the steering gear thoroughly and mount the gear by installing two long bolts and washers through the mounting boss bushings and attaching to Bench Mounted Holding Fixture, Tool T57L-500-B or equivalent.

2. Remove the yoke cover, gasket, shims, and yoke spring.

3. Clean the cover and housing flange areas thoroughly.

4. Reinstall the yoke and cover, omitting the gasket, shims, and the spring.

5. Tighten the cover bolts lightly until the cover just touches the yoke.

6. Measure the gap between the cover and the housing flange. With the gasket, add selected shims to give a combined pack thickness 0.13–0.15mm (.005–.006 inch) greater than the measured gap.

7. Remove the cover.

8. Assemble the gasket next to the hous-

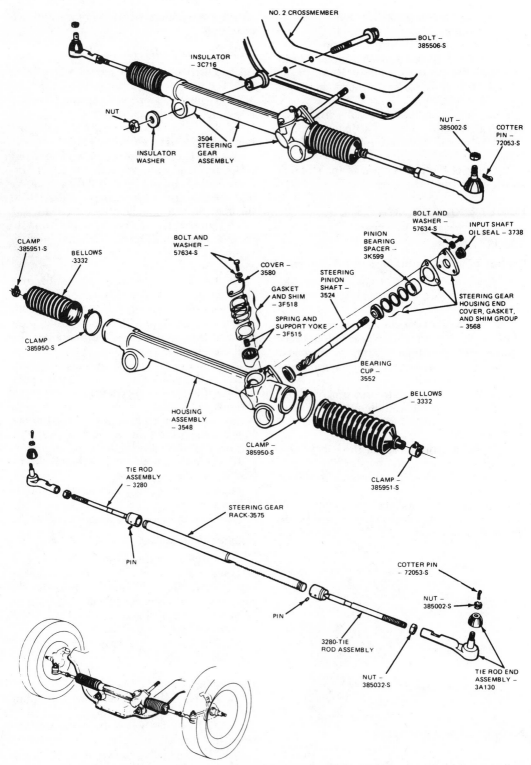

**Typical manual rack and pinion steering assembly**

ing flange, then the selected shims, spring, and cover.

9. Install cover bolts, sealing the threads with ESW-M46-132A or equivalent, and tighten.

10. Check to see that the gear operates smoothly without binding or slackness.

### Pinion Bearing Preload

1. Clean the exterior of the steering gear thoroughly and place the gear in the bench mounted holding fixture as outlined under Support Yoke to Rack Adjustment.

2. Loosen the bolts of the yoke cover to relieve spring pressure on the rack.

3. Remove the pinion cover and gasket. Clean the cover flange area thoroughly.

4. Remove the spacer and shims.

5. Install a new gasket, and fit shims between the upper bearing and the spacer until the top of the spacer is flush with the gasket. Check with a straightedge, using light pressure.

6. Add one 0.13mm (.005 inch) shim to the pack in order to preload the bearings. The spacer must be assembled next to the pinion cover.

7. Install the cover and bolts.

### Tie Rod Articulation Effort

1. Install hook end of pull scale through the hole in the tie rod end stud. Effort to move the tie rod should be 1–5 pounds. Do not damage tie rod neck.

2. Replace ball joint/tie rod assembly if effort falls outside this range. Save the tie rod end for use on the new tie rod assembly.

## Power Steering, Rack and Pinion Type

### ADJUSTMENTS

The power rack and pinion steering gear provides for only one service adjustment. The gear must be removed from the vehicle to perform this adjustment.

### REMOVAL AND INSTALLATION

1. Disconnect the negative battery cable from the battery.

2. Remove the one bolt retaining the flexible coupling to the input shaft.

3. Leave the ignition key in the On position, and raise the vehicle on a hoist.

4. Remove the two tie rod end retaining cotter pins and nuts. Separate the studs from the spindle arms, using the ball joint separator tool.

5. Support the steering gear, and remove the two nuts, insulator, washers, and bolts retaining the steering gear to the No. 2 crossmember. Lower the gear slightly to permit access to the pressure and return line fittings.

6. Disconnect the pressure and return lines from the steering gear valve housing. Plug the lines and parts in the valve housing to prevent entry of dirt.

7. Remove the steering gear assembly from the vehicle.

8. Support and position the steering gear, so that the pressure and return line fittings can be connected to the valve housing. Tighten the fittings to 15–20 ft. lb. The design allows the hoses to swivel when tightened properly. Do not attempt to eliminate looseness by overtightening, since this can cause damage to the fittings.

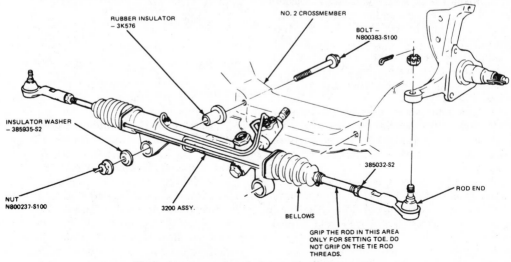

**Typical power rack and pinion steering assembly**

NOTE: *The rubber insulators must be pushed completely inside the gear housing before the installation of the gear housing on the No. 2 crossmember.*

9. No gap is allowed between the insulator and the face of the gear boss. A rubber lubricant should be used to facilitate proper installation of the insulators in the gear housing. Insert the input shaft into the flexible coupling, and position the steering gear to the No. 2 crossmember. Install the two bolts, insulator washers, and nuts. Tighten the two nuts to 80–100 ft. lb.

10. Connect the tie rod ends to the spindle arms, and install the two retaining nuts. Tighten the nuts to 35–45 ft. lb., then, after tightening to specification, tighten the nuts to their nearest cotter pin castellation, and install two new cotter pins.

11. Lower the vehicle, and install the one bolt retaining the flexible coupling to the input shaft. Tighten the bolt to 18–23 ft. lb.

12. Turn the ignition key to the Off position.

13. Connect the negative battery cable to the battery.

14. Remove the coil wire.

15. Fill the power steering pump reservoir.

16. Engage the starter, and cycle the steering wheel to distribute the fluid. Check the fluid level and add as required.

17. Install the coil wire, start the engine, and cycle the steering wheel. Check for fluid leaks.

18. If the tie rod ends were loosened, check the wheel alignment.

**Rack Yoke Plug Preload**

1. Clean the exterior of the steering gear thoroughly.

2. Install two long bolts and washers through the bushings, and attach to the bench mounted holding fixture, Tool T57L-500-B or equivalent.

3. Do not remove the external pressure lines, unless they are leaking or damaged. If these lines are removed, they must be replaced with new lines.

4. Drain the power steering fluid by rotating the input shaft lock-to-lock twice using Tool T74P-3504-R or equivalent. Cover ports on valve housing with shop cloth while draining gear.

5. Insert in. lb. torque wrench with maximum capacity of 30–60 in. lb. into the input shaft torque adapter, Tool T74P-3504-R or equivalent. Position the adapter and wrench on the input shaft splines.

6. Loosen the yoke plug locknut with wrench, Tool T78P-3504-H or equivalent.

7. Loosen yoke plug with a ¾ inch socket wrench.

8. With the rack at the center of travel, tighten the yoke plug to 45–50 in. lb. Clean the threads of the yoke plug prior to tightening to prevent a false reading.

9. Back off the yoke plug approximately ⅛ turn (44 degrees min. to 54 degrees max.) until the torque required to initiate and sustain rotation of the input shaft is 7–18 in. lb.

10. Place Tool T78P-3504-H or equivalent on the yoke plug locknut. While holding the yoke plug, tighten the locknut to 44–66 ft. lb. Do not allow the yoke plug to move while tightening or the preload will be affected. Recheck input shaft torque after tightening locknut.

11. If the external pressure lines were removed, they must be replaced with new service line. Remove the copper seals from the housing ports prior to installation of new lines.

## Tie Rod End

### REPLACEMENT

#### 1975–80

1. Raise and support the front end.

2. Remove and discard the cotter pin and nut from the rod end ball stud.

3. Disconnect the rod end from the spindle arm or center link.

4. Loosen the rod sleeve clamp bolts and turn the rod to remove. Count the exact number of turns required.

5. Install a new rod end using the exact number of turns it took to remove the old one.

6. Install all parts in reverse of removal. Torque stud to 40–43 ft. lbs. and clamp to 20–22 ft. lbs.

7. Check the toe-in.

#### 1981–82

1. Remove the cotter pin and nut at the spindle. Separate the tie rod end stud from the spindle with a puller.

2. Matchmark the position of the locknut with paint on the tie rod. Unscrew the locknut. Unscrew the tie end, counting the number of turns required to remove.

3. Install the new end the same number of turns. Attach the tie rod end stud to the spindle. Install the nut and torque to 35 ft. lbs., then continue to tighten until the cotter pin holes align. Install a new cotter pin. Check the toe and adjust if necessary, then torque the tie rod end locknut to 35 ft. lbs.

## Power Steering Pump
### REMOVAL AND INSTALLATION

1. Drain the fluid from the pump reservoir by disconnecting the fluid return hose at the pump. Then disconnect the pressure hose from the pump fitting. Do not remove it from the pump.

2. Remove the mounting bolts from the front of the pump. On eight-cylinder engines, there is a nut on the rear of the pump that must be removed. After removal, move the pump inward to loosen the belt tension and remove the belt from the pulley. Then, remove the pump from the car. Some newer models are equipped with a fixed pump. If this is the case, the pulley must be removed before the pump can be removed from the car. Simply loosen the pulley attaching nuts and remove the pulley.

3. To reinstall the pump, position it on the mounting bracket and loosely install the mounting bolts and nuts. Put the drive belt over the pulley and move the pump outward against the belt until the proper belt tension is obtained. Measure the belt tension with a belt tension gauge for the proper adjustment. Only in cases where a belt tension gauge is not available should the belt deflection method be used. If the belt deflection method is used, be sure to check with a belt tension gauge as soon as possible, since the deflection method is not accurate.

4. Tighten the mounting bolts and nuts to the specified torque.

5. Tighten the pressure hose fitting hex nut to 10–15 ft. lbs. Then connect the pressure hose to the pump and tighten the hose nut to 10–15 ft. lbs.

6. Connect the fluid return hose to the pump and tighten the clamp.

7. Fill the pump reservoir with power steering fluid and bleed the air bubbles from the system.

8. Check for leaks and recheck the fluid level. If necessary, add fluid to the proper level.

## Wheel Alignment

| Model | Caster Range (deg) | Caster Pref Setting (deg) | Camber Range (deg) | Camber Pref Setting (deg) | Toe-in (in.) | Steering Axis Inclination (deg) | Wheel Pivot Ratio (deg) Inner Wheel | Wheel Pivot Ratio (deg) Outer Wheel |
|---|---|---|---|---|---|---|---|---|
| 1975–80 | 1¼N to ¼P | ½N | ½N to 1P | ¼P | 0 to ¼ | 6¾ | 20 | 18⅓ ① |
| 1981–82 | ⅛P to 1⅞P ② | 1P | ⁵/₁₆N to 1³/₁₆P ② | ⁷/₁₆P | ¹/₁₆ to ⁵/₁₆ | 15¼ | 20 | 19.84 |

① Models with power steering—18⅛
② Caster and camber are preset and nonadjustable

# Brakes

## BRAKE SYSTEM

### *ADJUSTMENT*

Disc brakes are inherently self-adjusting, and no adjustment is possible or necessary. The rear drum brakes are also self-adjusting and all that is normally required to adjust them is to apply them moderately hard several times while backing the car up. However, if this doesn't work or if it proves necessary to readjust the brakes after replacing the linings or removing the drum, the following procedure may be used.

1. Block the front wheels, raise the car and support it with jackstands. Place the transmission in neutral and release the parking brake.

2. Remove the rubber plug from the adjusting slot in the backing plate.

3. Insert a brake adjusting spoon (a screwdriver will do if one is not available) into the slot and engage the lowest possible tooth on the starwheel. Move the end of the brake spoon downward to move the starwheel upward and expand the adjusting screw. Repeat this operation until the brakes lock the wheel.

4. Insert a small screwdriver into the adjusting slot and push the automatic adjuster lever out and free of the starwheel on the adjusting screw.

5. Holding the adjusting lever out of the way, engage the topmost tooth possible on the starwheel with a brake adjusting spoon. Move the end of the adjusting spoon upward to back off the adjusting screw. Back off the adjusting screw until the wheel spins freely with a minimum of drag. Keep track of the number of turns the starwheel is backed off.

6. Repeat this operation for the other side. The adjusting lever must be backed off the same number of turns to prevent side-to-side brake pull.

7. When the brakes are adjusted, make several stops, while backing the car, to equalize the wheels.

8. Road test the car.

## HYDRAULIC SYSTEM

All Granadas and Monarchs use a dual hydraulic brake circuit in accordance with federal safety regulations. Each circuit is independent of the other, incorporating a tandem master cylinder, a pressure differential warning valve and a proportioning valve. One circuit services the front brakes (rear of master cylinder) and the other the rear brakes (front of master cylinder). In case of a leak or other hydraulic system failure, one-half braking efficiency will be maintained. A brake system failure will decentralize the pressure differential warning valve, actuating a warning light on the dash. A proportioning valve located between the rear brake system inlet and outlet ports in the pressure differential warning valve serves to regulate the rear brake hydraulic pressure to prevent premature rear wheel lockup during hard braking.

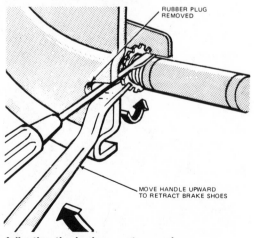

RUBBER PLUG REMOVED

MOVE HANDLE UPWARD TO RETRACT BRAKE SHOES

**Adjusting the brakes—cutaway view**

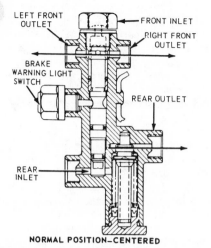

**NORMAL POSITION–CENTERED**
**Sectional view of the pressure differential valve**

## Master Cylinder
### REMOVAL AND INSTALLATION

#### Non-Power Brakes

1. Working from inside the car below the instrument panel, disconnect the master cylinder pushrod from the brake pedal assembly. The pushrod cannot be removed from the master cylinder.

2. Disconnect the stoplight switch wires at the connector. Remove the spring retainer.

Slide the stoplight switch off the brake pedal pin just far enough to clear the end of the pin, then lift and remove the switch from the pin. Take care not to damage the switch during removal.

3. Loosen the master cylinder attaching nuts from inside the engine compartment. Slide the master cylinder pushrod, nylon washers and bushings off the brake pedal pin.

4. Remove the brake tubes from the primary and secondary outlet ports of the master cylinder, and mark them for reassembly.

5. Remove the locknuts and lockwashers securing the master cylinder to the dash and lift the cylinder forward and upward from the car.

6. To install, position the rubber boot on the pushrod and secure the boot to the master cylinder. Carefully insert the boot through the dash panel opening and position the master cylinder and master cylinder mounting gasket (if so equipped) on the dash panel studs.

7. Install the attaching nuts and leave them loose.

8. Coat the nylon bushings with light (10W) engine oil. Install the nylon washer and bushing on the brake pedal pin.

9. Position the stoplight switch and pushrod on the brake pedal pin. Install the nylon bushing and washer and secure them in position with the spring retainer.

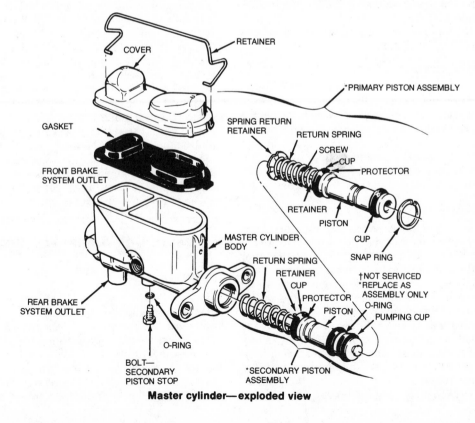

**Master cylinder—exploded view**

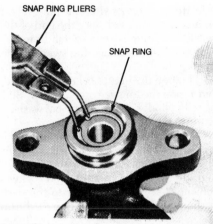

SNAP RING PLIERS

SNAP RING

**Master cylinder snap ring removal**

10. Connect the wires at the stoplight switch connector.

11. Tighten the master cylinder attaching nuts and connect the brake lines at the master cylinder.

12. Fill the master cylinder with brake fluid meeting SAE 70R3 or DOT-3 specifications to within ¼ inch of the top of the dual reservoirs.

13. Bleed the master cylinder and both the primary and secondary brake hydraulic systems, as outlined under "Hydraulic System Bleeding."

14. Centralize the pressure differential valve, as outlined under "Differential Valve Centering."

15. Operate the brakes several times and check for any leakage.

### Power Brakes

1. Remove the brake lines from the outlet ports on the master cylinder.

2. Remove the two nuts which attach the master cylinder to the brake booster assembly.

3. Remove the master cylinder by sliding it forward and upward.

4. Installation is in the reverse order.

## OVERHAUL

Referring to the accompanying exploded view of the dual master cylinder components, disassemble the unit as follows: Clean the exterior of the cylinder and remove the filler cover and diaphragm. Any brake fluid remaining in the cylinder should be poured out and discarded. Remove the secondary piston stop bolt from the bottom of the cylinder and remove the bleed screw, if required. With the primary piston depressed, remove the snap ring from its retaining groove at the rear of the cylinder bore. Withdraw the pushrod and the primary piston assembly from the bore.

NOTE: *Do not remove the screw that retains the primary return spring retainer, return spring, primary cup and protector on the primary piston. The assembly is adjusted at the factory and should not be disassembled.*

Remove the secondary piston assembly.

NOTE: *Do not remove the outlet tube seats, outlet check valves and outlet check valve springs from the cylinder body.*

All components should be cleaned in clean isopropyl alcohol or clean brake fluid and inspected for chipping, excessive wear and damage. Check to ensure that all recesses, openings and passageways are clear and free of foreign matter. Dirt and cleaning solvent may be removed by using compressed air. After cleaning, keep all parts on a clean surface. Inspect the cylinder bore for etching, pitting, scoring or rusting. If necessary, the cylinder bore may be honed to repair damage, but never to a diameter greater than the original diameter plus .003 inch.

During the assembly operation, be sure to use all parts supplied with the master cylinder repair kit. With the exception of the master cylinder body, submerge all parts in extra heavy duty brake fluid. Carefully insert the complete secondary piston and return spring assembly into the cylinder bore and install the primary piston assembly into the bore. With the primary piston depressed, install the snap ring into its groove in the cylinder bore. Install the pushrod, boot and retainer (if equipped), then install the pushrod assembly into the primary piston. Be sure that the retainer is properly seated and is holding the pushrod securely. Position the inner end of the pushrod boot (if equipped) in the master cylinder body retaining groove. Install the secondary piston stop bolt and O-ring at the bottom of the master cylinder body. Install the bleed screw (if equipped) and position the gasket on the master cylinder filler cover. Be sure that the gasket is securely seated. Install the cover and secure with the retainer.

## Pressure Differential Warning Valve

### CENTERING

Since the introduction of dual master cylinders to the hydraulic brake system, a pressure differential warning signal has been added. This signal consists of a warning light on the dashboard activated by a differential pressure switch located below the master cylinder. The signal indicates a hydraulic pressure differential between the front and rear brakes of 80—

150 psi, and should warn the driver that a hydraulic failure has occurred.

After repairing and bleeding any part of the hydraulic system, the warning light may remain on due to the pressure differential valve remaining in the off-center position. To centralize the valve a pressure difference must be created in the opposite branch of the hydraulic system that was repaired or bled last.

NOTE: *Front wheel balancing of cars equipped with disc brakes may also cause a pressure differential in the front branch of the system.*

To centralize the valve:

1. Turn the ignition to either the "acc" or "on" position.
2. Check the fluid level in the master cylinder reservoirs. Fill to within ¼ inch of the top if necessary.
3. Depress the brake pedal firmly. The valve will centralize itself, causing the brake warning light to go out.
4. Turn the ignition off.
5. Prior to driving the vehicle, check the operation of the brakes and obtain a firm pedal.

## Bleeding

The front and rear hydraulic systems are independent. If it is known that only one system has air in it, only that system has to be bled. Always bleed the brakes in a sequence that starts with the wheel cylinder farthest from the master cylinder and ends with the wheel cylinder or caliper closest to the master cylinder.

1. Fill the master cylinder with brake fluid.
2. Install a ⅜-inch box-end wrench to the bleeder screw on the right rear wheel.
3. Push a piece of small-diameter rubber tubing over the bleeder screw until it is flush against the wrench. Submerge the other end of the rubber tubing in a glass jar partially filled with clean brake fluid. Make sure the rubber tube fits on the bleeder screw snugly.

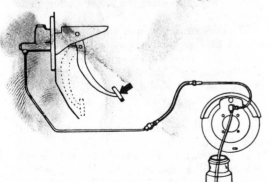

**Bleeding the brake system**

4. Have a friend apply pressure to the brake pedal. Open the bleeder screw and observe the bottle of brake fluid. If bubbles appear in the glass jar, there is air in the system. When your friend has pushed the pedal to the floor, immediately close the bleeder screw before he releases the pedal.
5. Repeat this procedure until no bubbles appear in the jar. Refill the master cylinder.
6. Repeat this procedure on the left rear, right front and left front wheels, in that order. Periodically refill the master cylinder with brand new brake fluid so it does not run dry. Never put old brake fluid back into the master cylinder.
7. Center the pressure differential warning valve, as outlined in the "Pressure Differential Warning Valve" section.

## FRONT DISC BRAKES

### Disc Pad
#### *REMOVAL AND INSTALLATION*
#### 1975-80

1. Remove approximately two-thirds of the fluid from the rear reservoir of the tandem master cylinder. Raise the vehicle, taking proper safety precautions. Install jackstands beneath the lower control arms.
2. Remove the wheel and tire assembly.
3. Remove the key retaining screw from the caliper retaining key.
4. Slide the retaining key and support spring either inward or outward from the anchor plate. To remove the key and spring, a hammer and drift may be used, taking care not to damage the key in the process.
5. Lift the caliper assembly away from the anchor plate by pushing the caliper downward against the anchor plate and rotating the upper end upward out of the anchor plate. Be careful not to stretch or twist the flexible brake hose. Safety wire the caliper to the suspension arm. *Don't let the caliper hang by the brake hose.*
6. Remove the inner shoe and lining assembly from the anchor plate. The inner shoe antirattle clip may become displaced at this time and should be repositioned on the anchor plate. Lightly tap on the outer shoe and lining assembly to free it from the caliper.
7. Clean the caliper, anchor plate, and disc assemblies, and inspect them for brake fluid leakage, excessive wear or signs of damage. Replace the pads if either of them are worn to within 1/32 inch of the rivet heads.
8. To install new pads, use a 4-inch C-clamp and a block of wood 1¾ x 1 inch and

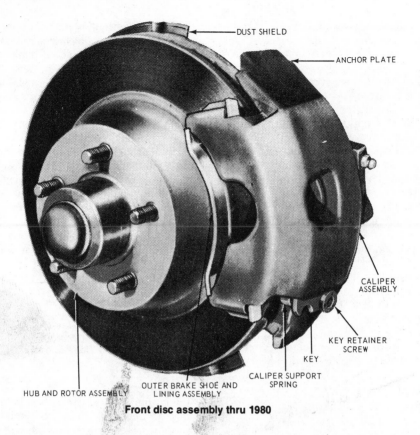

DUST SHIELD

ANCHOR PLATE

CALIPER
ASSEMBLY

KEY RETAINER
SCREW

KEY

CALIPER SUPPORT
SPRING

OUTER BRAKE SHOE AND
LINING ASSEMBLY

HUB AND ROTOR ASSEMBLY

**Front disc assembly thru 1980**

approximately ¾ inch thick to seat the caliper hydraulic piston in its bore. This must be done in order to provide clearance for the caliper to fit over the rotor when new linings are installed.

9. At this point, the antirattle clip should be in its place on the lower inner brake shoe support of the anchor plate with the pigtail of the clip toward the inside of the anchor plate. Position the inner brake shoe and lining assembly on the anchor plate with the pad toward the disc.

10. Install the outer brake shoe with the lower flange ends against the caliper leg abutments and the brake shoe upper flanges over the shoulders on the caliper legs. The shoe is installed correctly when its flanges fit snugly against the machined surfaces of the shoulders.

11. Remove the C-clamp used to seat the caliper piston in its bore. The piston will remain seated.

12. Position the caliper housing lower V-groove on the anchor plate lower abutment surface.

13. Pivot the caliper housing upward toward the disc until the outer edge of the piston dust boot is about ¼ inch from the upper edge of the inboard pad.

14. In order to prevent pinching of the dust boot between the piston and the inboard pad during installation of the caliper, place a clean piece of thin cardboard between the inboard pad and the lower half of the piston dust boot.

15. Rotate the caliper housing toward the disc until a slight resistance is felt. At this point, pull the cardboard downward toward the disc centerline while rotating the caliper over the disc. Then remove the cardboard and complete the rotation of the caliper down over the disc.

16. Slide the caliper up against the upper abutment surfaces of the anchor plate and center the caliper over the lower anchor plate abutment.

17. Position the caliper support spring and key in the key slot and slide them into the opening between the lower end of the caliper and the lower anchor plate abutment until the key semicircular slot is centered over the retaining screw threaded hole in the anchor plate.

18. Install the key retaining screw and torque to 12–16 ft. lb.

19. Check the fluid level in the master cylinder and fill as necessary. Install the reservoir cover. Depress the brake pedal several times to properly seat the caliper and pads. Check for leakage around the caliper and flexible brake hose.

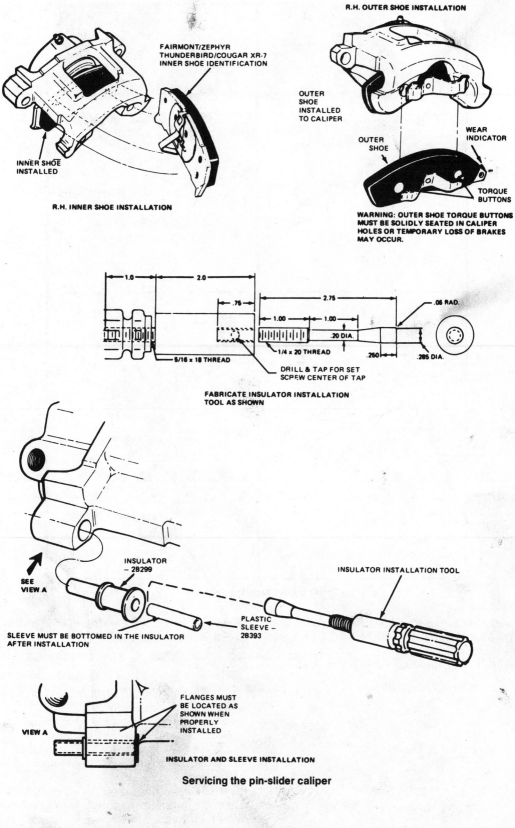

R.H. OUTER SHOE INSTALLATION

FAIRMONT/ZEPHYR
THUNDERBIRD/COUGAR XR-7
INNER SHOE IDENTIFICATION

OUTER
SHOE
INSTALLED
TO CALIPER

INNER SHOE
INSTALLED

OUTER
SHOE

WEAR
INDICATOR

TORQUE
BUTTONS

R.H. INNER SHOE INSTALLATION

WARNING: OUTER SHOE TORQUE BUTTONS
MUST BE SOLIDLY SEATED IN CALIPER
HOLES OR TEMPORARY LOSS OF BRAKES
MAY OCCUR.

1.0    2.0    .75    2.75    .06 RAD.

1.00    1.00

.20 DIA.

5/16 x 18 THREAD    1/4 x 20 THREAD

.250    .285 DIA.

DRILL & TAP FOR SET
SCREW CENTER OF TAP

FABRICATE INSULATOR INSTALLATION
TOOL AS SHOWN

INSULATOR
– 2B299

INSULATOR INSTALLATION TOOL

SEE
VIEW A

PLASTIC
SLEEVE –
2B393

SLEEVE MUST BE BOTTOMED IN THE INSULATOR
AFTER INSTALLATION

FLANGES MUST
BE LOCATED AS
SHOWN WHEN
PROPERLY
INSTALLED

VIEW A

INSULATOR AND SLEEVE INSTALLATION

**Servicing the pin-slider caliper**

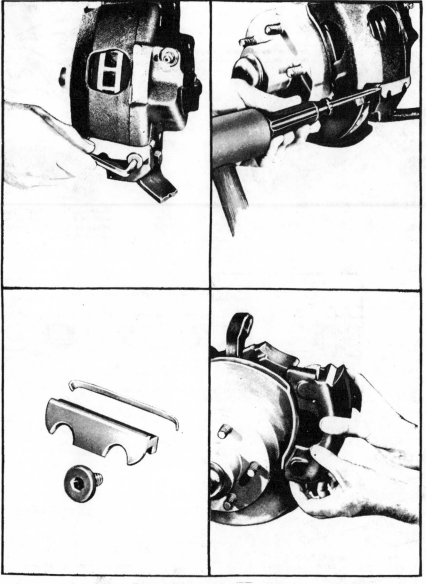

**Front caliper removal thru 1980**

20. Install the wheel and tire assembly and torque the nuts to 70–115 ft. lb. Install the wheel cover.

21. Lower the car. Make sure that you ob-

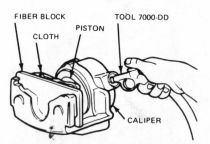

**Removing the piston from the front caliper**

tain a firm brake pedal and then road test the car for proper brake operation.

### 1981–82

1. Remove about half of the fluid from the master cylinder reservoir.

2. Loosen the lug nuts and raise and support the vehicle.

3. Remove the front wheel. Be careful to avoid damage to the caliper splash shield or bleed screw.

4. Remove the caliper locating pins. Remove the caliper assembly from the integral spindle anchor plate and rotor. Remove the outer shoe from the caliper.

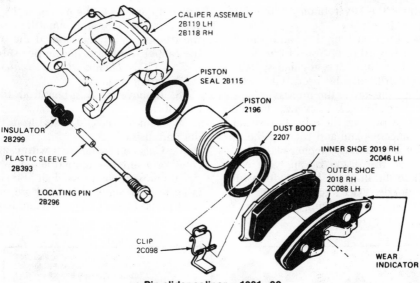

**Pin-slider caliper—1981–82**

5. Remove the inner shoe and inspect the rotor surfaces.

6. Secure the caliper assembly with a length of wire.

7. Remove and discard the plastic bushings inside the caliper locating pin insulators.

8. Remove and discard the plastic bushings inside the caliper locating pin insulators.

8. Remove and discard the locating insulators.

9. Using a 4 inch C-clamp and a 2¾ x 1 x ¼ in. piece of wood, seat the piston in its bore.

10. Install new insulators and sleeves in the caliper housing. Both insulator flanges must straddle the housing holes and the sleeves must bottom in the insulators as well as under the upper lip.

11. Inner shoes are marked left and right. Install the proper inner shoe in the caliper. Do not bend the clips too far or they will become distorted.

12. Outer shoes are marked left and right.

Install the proper outer shoe making sure that the clip and buttons are properly seated.

13. Refill the master cylinder.

14. Install the wheel, lower the car and test the brakes.

## Disc Caliper

### REMOVAL, OVERHAUL AND INSTALLATION

#### 1975–80

1. Raise the vehicle and place jackstands underneath the lower control arms.

2. Remove the wheel and tire assembly.

3. Disconnect the flexible brake hose from the caliper. To disconnect the hose, loosen the tube fitting which connects the end of the hose to the brake tube at its bracket on the frame. Remove the horseshoe clip from the hose and bracket, disengage the hose and plug the end. Then unscrew the entire hose assembly from the caliper.

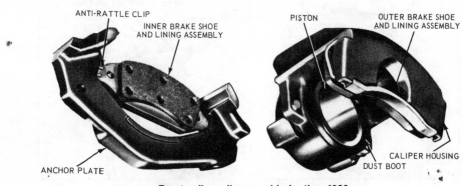

**Front caliper disassembled—thru 1980**

4. Remove the key retaining screw from the caliper retaining key.

5. Slide the retaining key and support spring either inward or outward from the anchor plate. To remove the key and spring, a hammer and drift may be used, taking care not to damage the key in the process.

6. Lift the caliper assembly away from the anchor plate by pushing the caliper downward against the anchor plate and rotating the upper end upward out of the anchor plate.

7. Remove the piston by applying compressed air to the fluid inlet port with a rubber-tipped nozzle. Place a towel or thick cloth over the piston before applying air pressure to prevent damage to the piston. If the piston is seized in the bore and cannot be forced from the caliper, lightly tap around the outside of the caliper while applying air pressure.

CAUTION: *Do not attempt to catch the piston with your hand.*

8. Remove the dust boot from the caliper assembly.

9. Remove the piston seal from the cylinder and discard it.

10. Clean all metal parts with isopropyl alcohol or a suitable nonpetroleum solvent and dry them with compressed air. Be sure there is no foreign material in the bore or component parts. Inspect the piston and bore for ex-

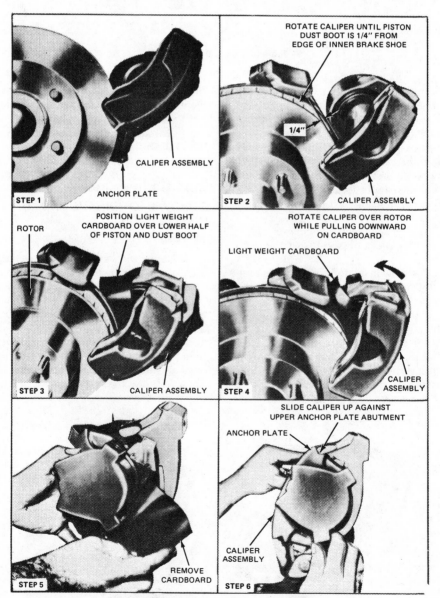

**Installing the front caliper—thru 1980**

cessive wear or damage. Replace the piston if it is pitted, scored, or if the chrome plating is wearing off.

11. Lubricate all new rubber parts in brake fluid. Install the piston seal in the cylinder groove, being careful not to twist it. Install the dust boot by setting the flange squarely in the outer groove of the bore.

12. Coat the piston with brake fluid and install it in the bore. Work the dust boot around the outside of the piston, making sure that the boot lip is seated in the piston groove.

13. Install the caliper as outlined in steps 12–18 in the sliding caliper "Disc Pad Removal and Installation" procedure.

14. Thread the flexible brake hose and gasket onto the caliper fitting. Torque the fitting to 12–22 ft. lbs. through 1978 and 20–30 ft. lbs. for 1979 and later. Place the upper end of the flexible brake hose in its bracket and install the horseshoe clip. Remove the plug from the brake tube and connect the tube to the hose. Torque the tube fitting nut to 10–15 ft. lb.

15. Bleed the brake system as outlined in the "Brake Bleeding" section.

16. Check the fluid level in the master cylinder and fill as necessary. Install the reservoir cover. Depress the brake pedal several times to properly seat the caliper and shoes. Check for leakage around the caliper and the flexible brake hose.

17. Install the wheel and tire assembly and torque the nuts to 70–115 ft. lb. Install the wheel cover.

18. Lower the car. Make sure that you obtain a firm brake pedal and then roadtest the car for proper brake operation.

### 1981–82

1. Loosen the front wheel lug nuts.

2. Raise and support the car.

3. Remove the front wheel taking care to avoid damage to the splash shield and bleeder screw.

4. Loosen the flexible brake hose-to-brake tube fitting at the frame and remove the horseshoe type retaining clip from the hose and bracket. Remove the hose from the bracket and unscrew it from the caliper. Plug the hose to avoid contaminants from entering the brake fluid.

NOTE: *If both calipers are being removed, mark them left and right.*

5. Remove the caliper locating pins.

6. Lift the caliper from the rotor.

7. Place a wadded cloth in front of the piston and apply compressed air at the hose hole.

*Never attempt to stop the piston with your hand. The piston can emerge from its bore with considerable force due to built-up air pressure.*

8. Remove the dust boot and piston seal.

9. Clean all metal parts in isopropyl alcohol. Dry all parts with compressed air.

10. Coat all parts with clean brake fluid before installing. Make certain that the seal does not become twisted, and that it is firmly seated in its groove.

11. Install a new dust boot and insert the piston in its bore. Spread the dust boot over the piston as it's installed.

12. Position the caliper over the rotor with the outer shoe against the rotor braking surface to prevent pinching the boot.

13. Connect the locating pins to the anchor plate and insulators. Be sure the locating pins are free of dirt, grease or oil.

14. Torque the locating pins to 30–40 ft. lbs.

15. Unplug the hose and install it into the caliper and torque it to 20–30 ft. lbs.

NOTE: *It is not necessary for the hose to be flush with the caliper when tightened; two or three threads may be visible when properly torqued. Do not overtorque.*

16. Connect the upper end of the hose. Tighten the fitting nut to 10–18 ft. lbs.

17. Bleed the system and center the differential valve. Fill the master cylinder to within ¼ in. of the top of the reservoir.

## Hub and Disc Assembly
### REMOVAL AND INSTALLATION

1. Raise the front of the vehicle and install jackstands beneath the lower control arms.

2. Remove the wheel and tire assembly.

3. Remove the caliper from its mount. Wire the caliper out of the way to the upper control arm, taking care not to twist or damage the flexible brake hose. Do not hang the caliper by the hose. Do not remove the anchor plate. Insert folded cardboard or wood between the brake pads to keep the piston seated.

4. Remove the grease cap from the hub. Remove the cotter pin, nut lock, and adjusting nut from the spindle.

5. Remove the outer wheel bearing and flat washer from the hub by first pulling the hub and disc assembly out far enough to loosen the bearing, then pushing it back in and removing the bearing and washer. Slide the hub and disc assembly off the spindle.

NOTE: *If a new disc is being installed, remove the protective coating with carburetor degreaser, and pack a new set of wheel bearings with wheel bearing grease. If the original disc is being installed, make sure that the grease in the hub is clean and adequate. Also make sure that the inner bearing and grease retainer is lubricated and in good condition, and that the disc braking surfaces are clean.*

6. Slide the hub and disc assembly onto the spindle. Install the outer wheel bearing and flat washer and adjusting nut on the spindle. Tighten the adjusting nut finger-tight, so that the hub and rotor may spin freely.

Inspect the disc (rotor) for scoring or corrosion. Minor scores or rust spots may be removed with a fine emery cloth. If the braking area is excessively scored or rusted the disc must be replaced. Check the disc for warpage (run-out). Tighten the wheel bearing adjusting nut so that the end-play is taken up. Make sure that the disc can still be rotated. Then, hand-spin the disc and check for wobbling or an out-of-round condition. Minor run-out may be corrected by machining. Maximum allowable runout is 0.003 inch. Readjust the wheel bearing to specifications.

7. Install the caliper to its mount as described under steps 12–18 of "Disc Pad Removal and Installation."

8. Install the wheel and tire assembly.

9. Adjust the wheel bearing as outlined under "Wheel Bearing Adjustment."

10. Remove the jack stands, lower the car, and tighten the wheel lug nuts to 70–115 ft. lb.

11. Apply the brakes several times to properly position the brake pads. Road test the car for proper brake operation.

## Wheel Bearings

### ADJUSTMENT

1. Raise the car and support it with jack-stands.

2. Remove the grease cap and the cotter pin and nut lock.

3. While rotating the wheel, tighten the adjusting nut to 17–25 ft. lb. in order to seat the bearings.

4. Back off the adjusting nut one-half turn, then retighten the adjusting nut to 10–15 in. lbs.

5. Reinstall the nut lock, cotter pin (use a new cotter pin) and grease cap.

6. Lower the car.

### REMOVAL AND INSTALLATION

1. Raise the front of the car and support it with safety stands.

2. Remove the front wheels.

NOTE: *In order to remove the rotor, the caliper and anchor plate must be removed from the car.*

3. Loosen, but do not remove, the upper

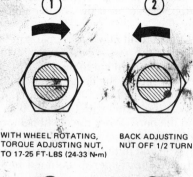

WITH WHEEL ROTATING, TORQUE ADJUSTING NUT, TO 17-25 FT-LBS (24-33 N·m)

BACK ADJUSTING NUT OFF 1/2 TURN

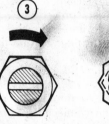

TIGHTEN ADJUSTING NUT TO 10-15 IN-LBS (1.2-1.6 N·m)

INSTALL THE LOCK AND A NEW COTTER PIN

**Wheel bearing adjustment**

anchor plate attaching bolt with a ¾-inch socket.

4. Using a ⅝-inch socket, remove the lower anchor plate attaching bolt.

NOTE: *When the caliper is removed from the car it must be wired out of the way of the rotor. Also, the brake pads will fall out of the caliper if they are not held in place when the caliper is removed. You will have to insert a small piece of wood or a folded piece of heavy cardboard between the shoes to hold them in place. Have a piece of wire and a piece of wood handy before you start the next step.*

5. Hold the caliper in place and remove the upper anchor plate attaching bolts.

6. Slide the caliper and anchor plate assembly off the rotor, inserting the block of wood between the brake pads as they become visible above the rotor.

7. When the anchor plate is clear of the rotor, wire it out of the way.

8. Remove the dust cap from the rotor hub by either prying it off with a screwdriver or pulling it off with a pair of channel-lock pliers.

9. Remove the cotter pin and the nut lock from the spindle.

10. Loosen the bearing adjusting nut until it is at the end of the spindle.

11. Grasp the rotor with a rag and pull it outward, push it inward.

12. Remove the adjusting nut and the outer bearing.

13. Remove the rotor from the spindle.

14. Place the rotor and tire on a clean, paper-covered surface with the wheel studs facing upward.

15. Working through the hole in the center of the wheel hub, tap the grease seal out of the rear hub with a screwdriver or drift.

NOTE: *Be careful not to damage the inner bearing while knocking out the grease seal.*

16. Remove the grease seal and bearing from under the rotor, and discard the grease seal.

17. Clean the inner and outer bearings and the wheel hub with a suitable solvent. Remove all old grease.

18. Thoroughly dry and wipe clean all components.

19. Clean all old grease from the spindle on the car.

20. Carefully check the bearings for any sign of scoring or other damage. If the roller bearings or bearing cages are damaged, the bearing and the corresponding bearing cup in the rotor hub must be replaced. The bearing cups must be driven out of the rotor hub to be removed. The outer bearing cup is driven out of the front of the rotor from the rear and vice versa for the inner bearing cup.

21. Whether you are reinstalling the old bearings or installing new ones, the bearings must be packed with wheel bearing grease. To do this, place a glob of grease in your left palm, then, holding one of the bearings in your right hand, drag the edge of the bearing heavily through the grease. This must be done to work as much grease as possible through the roller bearings and cage. Turn the bearing and continue to pull it through the grease until the grease is packed between the bearings and the cage all the way around the circumference of the bearing. Repeat this operation until all of the bearings are packed with grease.

22. Pack the inside of the rotor hub with a moderate amount of grease, between the bearing cups. Do not overload the hub with grease.

23. Apply a small amount of grease to the spindle.

24. Place the rotor, face down, on a protected surface and install the inner bearing.

25. Coat the lip of a new grease seal with a small amount of grease and position it on the rotor.

26. Place a block of wood on top of the grease seal and tap on the block with a hammer to install the seal. Turn the block of wood to different positions to seat it squarely in the hub.

27. Position the rotor on the spindle.

28. Install the outer bearing and washer on the spindle, inside the rotor hub.

29. Install the bearing adjusting nut and tighten it to 17–25 ft. lb. while spinning the rotor. This will seat the bearing.

30. Back off the adjusting nut one half turn.

31. Tighten the adjusting nut to 10–15 in. lb.

32. Install the nut lock on the adjusting nut so two of the slots align with the hole in the spindle.

33. Install a new cotter pin and bend the ends back so they will not interfere with the dust cap.

34. Install the dust cap.

35. Install the front tires if they were removed.

## REAR DISC BRAKES

### Disc Brake Caliper
#### REMOVAL AND INSTALLATION

1. Raise the car and install jackstands. Remove the rear wheels.

2. Remove the brake line from the caliper. Disconnect the hose bracket from the axle spring seat and remove the hollow retaining bolt used for connecting the hose fitting to the caliper, if so equipped. Unhook the parking brake cable.

3. Remove the retaining screw from the caliper retaining key.

4. Tap the retaining key and support spring from the caliper, using a hammer and a drift pin of some sort. Don't use excessive force. The key should slide out easily.

5. Rotate the caliper assembly up and away from the anchor plate and the rotor. It may be necessary to scrape away the rust buildup on the rotor edge in order to gain enough clearance to remove the caliper. Remove the caliper. If the caliper still cannot be removed, loosen the caliper end retainer one-half turn, after removing the retaining screw and caliper parking brake lever.

NOTE: *Turning the retainer more than one-half turn could cause internal fluid leaks in the caliper, which would make caliper rebuilding necessary.*

6. If the end retainer was loosened in order to remove the caliper, perform the following:

   a. Install the caliper on the anchor plate and secure it with the key, but do not install the pads.

   b. Torque the end retainer to 75–95 ft. lb.

   c. Install the caliper parking brake lever

**Rear disc caliper housing—sectional view**

with the arm pointing rearward and down. Tighten the lever retaining screw to 16–22 ft. lb. Check for free rotation of the lever.

d. Remove the caliper from the anchor plate.

7. Make sure that the antirattle clip is correctly positioned in the lower inner brake pad support and that the clip loop is facing the inside of the anchor plate.

8. Place the inner brake pad on the an-

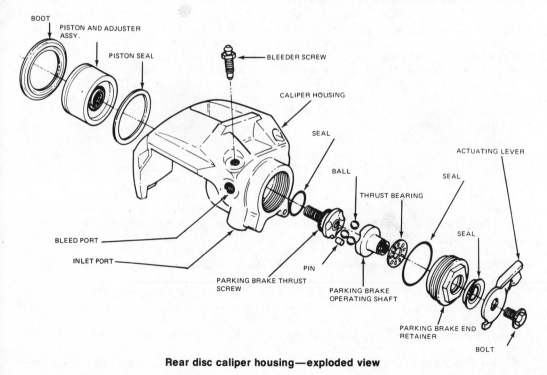

**Rear disc caliper housing—exploded view**

chor plate. Install the outer brake pad in the caliper.

9. Position the bottom of the caliper against the anchor plate lower abutment surface. Rotate the caliper housing until it is completely over the disc. Be careful not to damage the dust boot.

10. Slide the caliper outward until the inner pad is seated firmly against the disc. Measure the outer pad-to-disc clearance. It should be $1/16$ inch or less. If it is more, you will need a special tool (available from your Ford dealer) which is used to adjust the piston outward until the correct clearance is obtained.

11. Using the special tool, adjust the caliper piston outward if this needs to be done.

NOTE: *See the pad replacement section for instructions on how to use the special tool. Because of the parking brake assembly, pad-to-rotor clearance is critical. If piston clearance is more than $1/16$ inch, the adjuster may pull out of the piston when the brakes are applied, causing adjuster failure.*

12. Center the caliper over the anchor plate and install the retaining spring and key. Install the setscrew and tighten it to 12–16 ft. lb.

13. Attach the parking brake cable. Attach the brake line.

14. Bleed the brake system. Adjust the parking brake cable if necessary. Pump the brake a number of times to bring the pedal back up to normal.

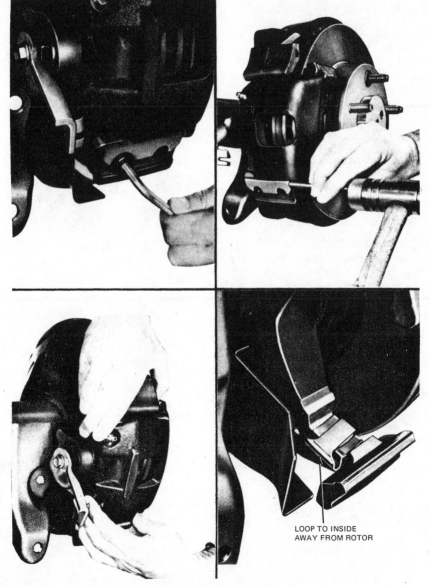

LOOP TO INSIDE
AWAY FROM ROTOR

**Rear caliper removal**

15. Reinstall the wheels and lower the car. Check the brake pedal to make sure it is firm, then road test the car.

## CALIPER OVERHAUL

1. Remove the caliper assembly from the car.

2. Remove the retaining screw, parking brake lever, and the caliper end retainer.

3. Pull out the operating shaft, thrust bearing and balls from the caliper. Using either a magnet or tweezers, extract the thrust screw antirotation pin.

4. Using a ¼-inch allen wrench, rotate the thrust screw counterclockwise to remove it.

5. Using the Ford special tool, push the piston adjuster assembly out of its bore from behind. Be careful not to scratch the caliper bore.

6. Remove and discard the piston seal, boot, thrust screw O-ring seal, and retainer O-ring and lip seal.

7. Clean all the metal parts in isopropyl alcohol, and dry them with either compressed air or a very clean soft cloth. Inspect the caliper bore to be sure it is clean and not pitted or scored.

8. If the piston is pitted, scored or the plating is worn off, replace the piston/adjuster as an assembly. The adjuster can must not be loose, high or damaged; if it is, replace the piston/adjuster assembly. If brake adjustment is incorrect, replace the piston/adjuster assembly.

NOTE: *The piston and adjuster must be replaced as an assembly. The adjuster is not repairable.*

9. To check adjuster operation, install the thrust screw in the piston/adjuster. Pull the two pieces apart by hand approximately ¼ inch and then release them. When the two pieces are pulled apart, the brass drive ring should remain stationary, causing the nut to turn. When the pieces are released, the nut should remain stationary and the drive ring should rotate. If the adjuster does not operate this way replace it.

10. Inspect all moving surfaces for wear or pitting. Replace any parts which seem worn. A polished appearance on ball paths or bearing surfaces is fine, so long as there is no sign of wear into the surface.

11. To assemble the caliper, first coat a new piston seal with clean brake fluid. Then seat the seal in the bore of the groove, making sure it is not twisted.

12. Seat the flange of a new dust boot in the caliper bore outer groove.

13. Coat the piston/adjuster assembly with clean brake fluid. Spread the dust boot over

**Checking the rear disc lining clearances**

**Checking adjuster operation**

**Bottoming the caliper piston**

the piston and install the piston. Seat the dust boot in the piston/adjuster groove.

14. Place the caliper assembly in a vise with the rear of the bore facing upward. Do not

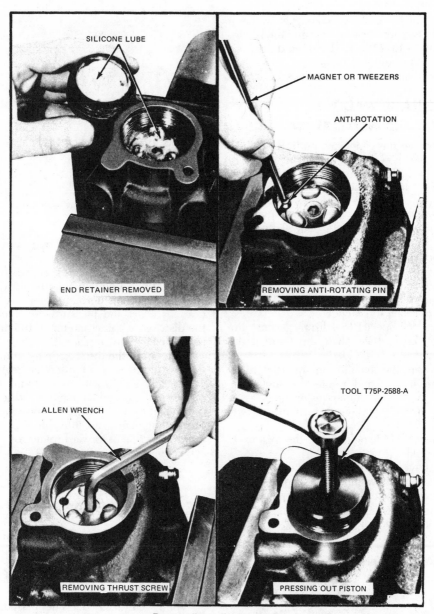

**Rear caliper disassembly**

tighten the vise or housing distortion will result. Fill the piston/adjuster assembly up to the bottom edge of the thrust screw bore with clean brake fluid.

15. Install a new O-ring in the thrust screw groove, after coating it with clean brake fluid. Using a 2-inch allen wrench, install the thrust screw in the adjuster assembly, until its top surface is flush with the bottom of the threaded bore. Align the notches on the thrust screw with those on the caliper housing. Install the antirotation pin.

16. Install one ball in each of the thrust screw pockets. Coat all the components of the parking brake system with a liberal amount of silicone grease.

17. Install the parking brake operating shaft over the balls. Coat the thrust bearing with silicone grease and fit it on the shaft.

18. Install a new lip seal and O-ring on the caliper end retainer. Coat both seals with a light film of silicone grease and install the end retainer on the caliper and tighten it to 75–90 ft. lb. Hold the operating shaft firmly seated against the internal mechanism while tightening the end retainer to prevent dislocating the balls. Reseat the lip seal if it is pushed out of position.

18. Install the parking brake lever so that it points down and rearward. Torque the retaining screw to 16–22 ft. lb. Check the lever for freedom of movement.

19. Bottom the piston using the special tool.

## DISC BRAKE PADS
### REMOVAL AND INSTALLATION

1. Remove the caliper as outlined earlier. In this case, however, it is not necessary to disconnect the brake line. Simply wire the caliper to the frame to prevent the brake line from breaking.

2. Remove the pads and inspect them. If they are worn to within ⅛ inch of the shoe surface, they must be replaced. Do not replace pads on just one side of the car. Uneven braking will result.

3. To install new pads, remove the disc and install the caliper without the pads. Use only the key to retain the caliper.

4. Seat the special tool firmly against the piston by holding the shaft and rotating the tool handle.

5. Loosen the handle one-quarter turn. Hold the handle and rotate the tool shaft clockwise until the caliper piston bottoms in the bore. It will continue to turn after it bottoms.

6. Rotate the handle until the piston is firmly seated.

7. Remove the caliper and install the disc.

8. Place the new inner brake pad on the anchor plate. Place the new outer pad in the caliper.

9. Reinstall the caliper according to the directions given earlier.

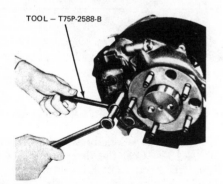

TOOL – T75P-2588-B

**Adjusting the piston depth**

## Brake Discs
### REMOVAL AND INSTALLATION

1. Raise the car and support it. Remove the wheels.

2. Remove the caliper, as outlined earlier.

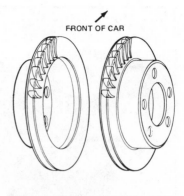

FRONT OF CAR

LEFT REAR ROTOR    RIGHT REAR ROTOR
**Rear rotors**

3. Remove the retaining bolts and remove the disc from the axle.

4. Inspect the disc for excessive rust, scoring or pitting. A certain amount of rust on the edge of the disc is normal. Refer to the specifications chart and measure the thickness of the disc, using a micrometer. If the disc is below specifications, replace it.

5. Reinstall the discs, keeping in mind that the two sides are not interchangeable. The words "left" and "right" are cast into the inner surface of the raised section of the disc. Proper reinstallation of the discs is important, since the cooling vanes cast into the disc must face in the direction of forward rotation.

6. Reinstall the caliper.

7. Install the wheels and lower the car.

## REAR DRUM BRAKES

The major components of the system are the drum, the brake shoes, the brake shoe return and hold-down springs, and the automatic adjuster assembly. The rear brakes also incorporate a parking brake mechanism.

When the brake pedal is depressed, and hydraulic pressure is delivered to the wheel cylinder, the wheel cylinder expands to force the shoes against the drum. The primary shoe moves first, contacting the drum and pivoting slightly on its hold-down spring mounting pin. As the top of the primary (front) shoe contacts the drum, the bottom of the shoe moves slightly away from the drum. This movement is transferred through the adjusting screw to the secondary brake shoe, where it aids the wheel cylinder in bringing the secondary shoe in contact with the drum. Friction between the brake shoes and the drum causes the car to slow down and stop. When the brake pedal is released, the brake shoe return springs move the brakes away from the drum. If the lining on the brakes becomes contaminated or if the

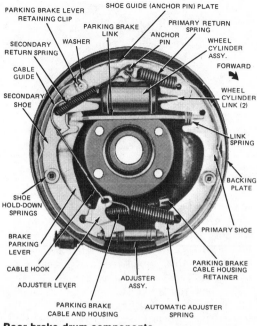

Rear brake drum components

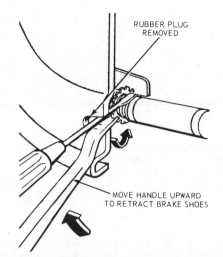

Drum brake adjustment

lining or drum becomes grooved, the engagement of the brakes and the drum will become very harsh causing the brakes to lock up and/or squeal. If the brake shoes on one wheel contact the drum before the same action occurs in the outer wheels, the brakes will pull to one side when applied.

The automatic adjuster assembly consists of a cable, cable guide, adjuster lever, automatic adjuster spring, and adjusting screw. The automatic adjuster operates only when the brakes are applied while the car is backing up. When the brakes are applied with the car moving rearward, the movement of the secondary (rear) brake shoe (the automatic adjuster is attached to this shoe) causes the adjuster cable to pull the adjusting lever upward. When the brakes are released, the automatic adjuster spring pulls the adjusting lever downward. As the lever moves downward, it contacts the star wheel on the adjusting screw and pushes it downward. This causes the adjusting screw to unscrew slightly (expand) and move the brake shoes closer to the drum. The adjusting lever then rests on the star wheel of the adjusting screw until the brakes are applied the next time the car backs up. If the brake adjustment is OK, the secondary shoe will not have to move very far to contact the drum. This limited shoe movement will not lift the adjusting lever off the star wheel, thus the brakes will not be adjusted.

The parking brake mechanism in the wheel consists of a parking brake link and lever. The link fits between the two brake shoes. The le-ver is attached to the parking brake cable and the secondary brake shoe. When the parking brake handle is pulled in the car, the rear brake shoes are moved into contact with the brake drums.

## INSPECTION

1. Raise the rear of the car and support the car with safety stands. Make sure the parking brake is not on.

2. To check the rear brakes, remove the lug nuts that attach the wheels to the axle shaft and remove the tires and wheels from the car. Pull the brake drum off the axle shaft. If the brakes are adjusted too tightly to remove the drum, see step three. If you can remove the drum, see step four.

3. If the brakes are too tight to remove the drum, get under the car (make sure you have safety stands under the car to support it) and remove the rubber plug from the bottom of the brake backing plate. Shine a flashlight into the slot in the plate. You will see the top of the adjusting screw star wheel and the adjusting lever for the automatic brake adjusting mechanism. To back off the adjusting screw, you must first insert a small, thin screwdriver or a piece of firm wire (coat hanger wire) into the adjusting slot and push the adjusting lever away from the adjusting screw. Insert a brake adjusting spoon into the slot and engage the top of the star wheel. Lift the bottom of the adjusting spoon to force the adjusting screw star wheel downward. Repeat this operation until the brake drum is free of the brake shoes and can be pulled off. See the brake adjustment procedure for an illustration.

4. Clean the brake shoes and the inside of the brake drum. There must be at least $1/32$ in. of brake lining above the heads of the brake

shoe attaching rivets. The lining should not be cracked or contaminated with grease or brake fluid. If there is grease or brake fluid on the lining, it must be replaced and the source of the leak must be found and corrected. Brake fluid on the lining means leaking wheel cylinders. Grease on the brake lining means a leaking grease retainer (front wheels) or axle seal (rear brakes). If the lining is slightly glazed but otherwise in good condition, it can be cleaned with medium sandpaper. Lift the bottom of the wheel cylinder boots and inspect the ends of the wheel cylinders. A small amount of fluid in the end of the cylinders should be considered normal. If fluid runs out of the cylinder when the boots are lifted, however, the wheel cylinder must be rebuilt or replaced. Examine the inside of the brake drum. It should have a smooth, dull finish. If excessive brake shoe wear has caused grooves to wear in the drum, it must be machined or replaced. If the inside of the drum is slightly glazed, but otherwise in good condition, it can be cleaned with medium sandpaper.

6. If no repairs are required, install the drum and wheel. If the brake adjustment was changed to remove the drum, adjust the brakes until the drum will just fit over the brakes. After the wheel is installed it will be necessary to complete the adjustment. See the brake adjustment procedure in this chapter. If a front wheel was removed, tighten the wheel bearing adjusting nut to 17–25 ft. lbs. while spinning the wheel. This will seat the bearing. Loosen the adjusting nut ½ turn, then retighten it to 10–15 in. lbs.

## Brake Shoe Removal

NOTE: *If you are not thoroughly familiar with the procedures involved in brake replacement, disassemble and assemble only one side at a time, leaving the other wheel intact as a reference.*

1. Remove the brake drum. See the above "Inspection" procedure.

2. Place the hollow end of a brake spring service tool (available at auto parts stores) on the brake shoe anchor pin and twist it to disengage one of the brake retracting springs. Repeat this operation to remove the other spring.

CAUTION: *Be careful the springs do not slip off the tool during removal, as they could cause personal injury.*

3. Reach behind the brake backing plate and place a finger on the end of one of the brake hold-down spring mounting pins. Using a pair of pliers grasp the washer on the top of the hold-down spring that corresponds to the pin

**Brake spring removal**

that you are holding. Push down on the pliers and turn them 90° to align the slot in the washer and with the head on the spring mounting pin. Remove the spring and washer and repeat this operation on the hold-down spring on the other brake shoe.

4. Place the tip of the screwdriver on the top of the brake adjusting screw and move the screwdriver upward to lift up on the brake adjusting lever. When there is enough slack in the automatic adjuster cable, disconnect the loop on the top of the cable from the anchor pin. Grasp the top of each brake shoe and move it outward to disengage it from the wheel cylinder (and parking brake link on the rear wheels). When the brake shoes are clear, lift them from the backing plate. Twist the shoes slightly and the automatic adjuster assembly will disassemble itself.

5. Grasp the end of the brake cable spring with a pair of pliers and, using the brake lever as a fulcrum, pull the end of the spring away from the lever. Disengage the cable from the brake lever.

## Wheel Cylinder Overhaul

Since the travel of the pistons in the wheel cylinder changes when new brake shoes are installed, it is possible for previously good wheel cylinders to start leaking after new brakes are installed. Therefore, to save yourself the expense of having to replace new brakes that become saturated with brake fluid and the aggravation of having to take everything apart again, it is strongly recommended that wheel cylinders be rebuilt every time new brake shoes are installed. This is especially true for cars with high mileage.

1. Remove the brakes.

2. Place a bucket or some old newspapers under the brake backing plate to catch the brake fluid that will run out of the wheel cylinder.

3. Remove the boots from the ends of the wheel cylinders.

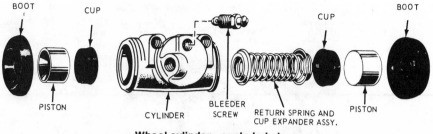

BOOT  CUP  CUP  BOOT

PISTON  PISTON

CYLINDER  BLEEDER  RETURN SPRING AND
SCREW  CUP EXPANDER ASSY.

**Wheel cylinder—exploded view**

4. Push one piston toward the center of the cylinder to force the opposite piston and cup out the other end of the cylinder. Reach in the open end of the cylinder and push the spring, cup, and piston out of the cylinder.

5. Remove the bleeder screw from the rear of the cylinder, on the back of the backing plate.

6. Inspect the inside of the wheel cylinder. If it is scored in any way, the cylinder must be honed with a wheel cylinder hone or fine emery paper, and finished with crocus cloth if emery paper is used. If the inside of the cylinder is excessively worn, the cylinder will have to be replaced, as only 0.003 in. of material can be removed from the cylinder walls. Whenever honing or cleaning wheel cylinders, keep a small amount of brake fluid in the cylinder to serve as a lubricant.

7. Clean any foreign matter from the pistons. The sides of the pistons must be smooth for the wheel cylinders to operate properly.

8. Clean the cylinder bore with alcohol and a lint-free rag. Pull the rag through the bore several times to remove all foreign matter and dry the cylinder.

9. Install the bleeder screw and the return spring in the cylinder.

10. Coat new cylinder cups with new brake fluid and install them in the cylinder. Make sure they are square in the bore or they will leak.

11. Install the pistons in the cylinder after coating them with new brake fluid.

12. Coat the insides of the boots with new brake fluid and install them on the cylinder. Install and bleed the brakes.

## Wheel Cylinder Replacement

1. Remove the brake shoes.

2. Loosen the brake line on the rear of the cylinder, but do not pull the line away from the cylinder or it may bend.

3. Remove the bolts and lockwashers that attach the wheel cylinder to the backing plate and remove the cylinder.

4. Position the new wheel cylinder on the backing plate and install the cylinder attaching bolts and lockwashers.

5. Attach the metal brake line.

6. Install the brakes and bleed the brake system.

## Brake Shoe Installation

1. The brake cable must be connected to the secondary brake shoe before the shoe is installed on the backing plate. To do this, first transfer the parking brake lever from the old secondary shoe to the new one. This is accomplished by spreading the bottom of the horseshoe clip and disengaging the lever. Position the lever on the new secondary shoe and install the spring washer and the horseshoe clip. Close the bottom of the clip after installing it. Grasp the metal tip on the parking brake cable with a pair of pliers. Position a pair of side cutters on the end of the cable coil spring and, using the pliers as a fulcrum, pull the coil spring back with the side cutters. Position the cable in the parking brake lever.

2. Apply a *light* coating of high-temperature grease to the brake shoe contact points on the backing plate. Position the primary brake shoe on the front of the backing plate and install the hold-down spring and washer over the mounting pin. Install the secondary shoe on the rear of the backing plate.

3. Install the parking brake link between the notch in the primary brake shoe and the notch in the parking brake lever.

4. Install the automatic adjuster cable loop end on the anchor pin. Make sure the crimped side of the loop faces the backing plate.

5. Install the return spring in the primary brake shoe and, using the tapered end of a brake spring service tool, slide the top of the spring onto the anchor pin.

CAUTION: *Be careful the spring does not slip off the tool during installation, as it could cause personal injury.*

6. Install the automatic adjuster cable guide in the secondary brake shoe, making sure the flared hole in the cable guide is inside the

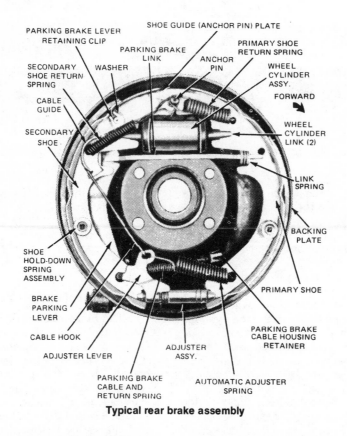

PARKING BRAKE LEVER
RETAINING CLIP

SHOE GUIDE (ANCHOR PIN) PLATE

PARKING BRAKE
LINK

PRIMARY SHOE
RETURN SPRING

SECONDARY
SHOE RETURN
SPRING

WASHER

ANCHOR
PIN

WHEEL
CYLINDER
ASSY.

CABLE
GUIDE

FORWARD

WHEEL
CYLINDER
LINK (2)

SECONDARY
SHOE

LINK
SPRING

BACKING
PLATE

SHOE
HOLD-DOWN
SPRING
ASSEMBLY

PRIMARY SHOE

BRAKE
PARKING
LEVER

CABLE HOOK

ADJUSTER LEVER

ADJUSTER
ASSY.

PARKING BRAKE
CABLE HOUSING
RETAINER

PARKING BRAKE
CABLE AND
RETURN SPRING

AUTOMATIC ADJUSTER
SPRING

**Typical rear brake assembly**

hole in the brake shoe. Fit the cable into the groove in the top of the cable guide.

7. Install the secondary shoe return spring through the hole in the cable guide and the brake shoe. Using the brake spring tool, slide the top of the spring onto the anchor pin.

8. Clean the threads on the adjusting screw and apply a light coating of high-temperature grease to the threads. Screw the adjuster closed, then open it one-half turn.

9. Install the adjusting screw between the brake shoes with the star wheel nearest to the secondary shoe. Make sure the star wheel is in a position that is accessible from the adjusting slot in the backing plate.

10. Install the short hooked end of the automatic adjuster spring in the proper hole in the primary brake shoe.

11. Connect the hooked end of the automatic adjuster cable and the free end of the automatic adjuster spring in the slot in the top of the automatic adjuster lever.

12. Pull the automatic adjuster lever (the lever will pull the cable and spring with it) downward and to the left and engage the pivot hook of the lever in the hole in the secondary brake shoe.

13. Check the entire brake assembly to make sure everything is installed properly. Make sure the shoes engage the wheel cylin-

der properly and are flush on the anchor pin. Make sure the automatic adjuster cable is flush on the anchor pin and in the slot on the back on cable guide. Make sure the adjusting lever rests on the adjusting screw star wheel. Pull upward on the adjusting cable until the adjusting lever is free of the star wheel, then release the cable. The adjusting lever should snap back into place on the adjusting screw star wheel and turn the wheel one tooth.

14. Expand the brake adjusting screw until the brake drum will just fit over the brake shoes.

15. Install the wheel and drum and adjust the brakes.

## Brake Adjustment

1. Raise the car and support it with safety stands.

2. Remove the rubber plug from the adjusting slot on the backing plate.

3. Insert a brake adjusting spoon into the slot and engage the lowest tooth on the star wheel possible. Move the end of the brake spoon downward to move the star wheel upward and expand the adjusting screw. Repeat this operation until the brakes lock the wheel.

4. Insert a small screwdriver or piece of firm wire (coat hanger wire) into the adjusting slot

and push the automatic adjuster lever out and free of the star wheel on the adjusting screw.

5. Holding the adjusting lever out of the way, engage the topmost tooth possible on the star wheel with a brake adjusting spoon. Move the end of the adjusting spoon upward to move the adjusting screw downward and contact the adjusting screw. Back the adjustment off until the wheel spins freely with a minimum of drag. Keep track of the number of turns the star wheel is backed off.

6. Repeat this operation on the other side of the car of the set (front or rear) of brakes that you are adjusting. When backing off the brakes on the other side, the star wheel must be backed off the same number of turns to prevent side-to-side brake pull.

7. Repeat this operation on the other set of brakes.

## PARKING BRAKE

The parking brake is operated by a locking foot pedal. Cables actuated by the pedal cause the rear brakes to contact the drums. The parking brake is released by pulling a T-handled control under the left side dash panel.

## Cable

### ADJUSTMENT

1. Release the parking brake and place the transmission control lever in the neutral position.

2. Raise the vehicle and support.

NOTE: *The rear axle must be supported so that there is weight on the rear springs.*

3. Tighten the adjusting nut against the cable equalizer (bracket that connects the cables running to the rear wheels with the front cable) until drag is felt while turning the rear wheels. Loosen the nut until all drag is released. Tighten the lock nut.

The arrow points to the adjuster nut. It's a good idea to spray the adjuster rod with penetrating oil

4. Check the operation of the parking brake, readjust if necessary.

### REMOVAL AND INSTALLATION

1. Release the parking brake and loosen the lock and adjusting nut.

2. Raise the vehicle and support it properly.

3. Remove the rear wheel parking brake cable from the equalizer.

4. Remove the hairpin clip that attaches the conduit to the conduit bracket, and remove the retaining clip that attaches the cable to the underbody.

5. Remove the rear wheels and tires then remove the brake drums.

6. Remove the self adjuster springs, and remove the adjuster springs from the backing plates.

7. Disconnect the ends of the cables from the parking brake levers on the secondary brake shoes.

8. Compress the cable retainer prongs, and pull the cable ends from the backing plates.

9. To install reverse the above procedure and adjust the parking brake as previously described.

## Brake Specifications
(All measurements are given in inches)

| Model | Master Cylinder Bore | Brake Disc | | | Brake Drum | |
| | | Minimum Thickness | Maximum Runout | Diameter | Inside Diameter | Maximum Runout |
|---|---|---|---|---|---|---|
| Front disc/ Rear drum | 0.938 ① | .810 | .003 | 11.03 ② | 10.00 ③ | .007 |
| Front disc/ Rear disc | 1.000 | .810 front/ .895 rear | .003 front/ .004 rear | 11.03 front/ 10.66 rear | — | — |

① 0.827: 1981–82    ③ 9.000 Sedans, 1981–82
② 10.08: 1981–82

# Troubleshooting

This section is designed to aid in the quick, accurate diagnosis of automotive problems. While automotive repairs can be made by many people, accurate troubleshooting is a rare skill for the amateur and professional alike.

In its simplest state, troubleshooting is an exercise in logic. It is essential to realize that an automobile is really composed of a series of systems. Some of these systems are interrelated; others are not. Automobiles operate within a framework of logical rules and physical laws, and the key to troubleshooting is a good understanding of all the automotive systems.

This section breaks the car or truck down into its component systems, allowing the problem to be isolated. The charts and diagnostic road maps list the most common problems and the most probable causes of trouble. Obviously it would be impossible to list every possible problem that could happen along with every possible cause, but it will locate MOST problems and eliminate a lot of unnecessary guesswork. The systematic format will locate problems within a given system, but, because many automotive systems are interrelated, the solution to your particular problem may be found in a number of systems on the car or truck.

## USING THE TROUBLESHOOTING CHARTS

This book contains all of the specific information that the average do-it-yourself mechanic needs to repair and maintain his or her car or truck. The troubleshooting charts are designed to be used in conjunction with the specific procedures and information in the text. For instance, troubleshooting a point-type ignition system is fairly standard for all models, but you may be directed to the text to find procedures for troubleshooting an individual type of electronic ignition. You will also have to refer to the specification charts throughout the book for specifications applicable to your car or truck.

## TOOLS AND EQUIPMENT

The tools illustrated in Chapter 1 (plus two more diagnostic pieces) will be adequate to troubleshoot most problems. The two other tools needed are a voltmeter and an ohmmeter. These can be purchased separately or in combination, known as a VOM meter.

In the event that other tools are required, they will be noted in the procedures.

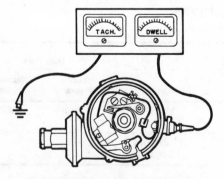

**Tach-dwell hooked-up to distributor**

# Troubleshooting Engine Problems

See Chapters 2, 3, 4 for more information and service procedures.

## Index to Systems

| System | To Test | Group |
|---|---|---|
| Battery | Engine need not be running | 1 |
| Starting system | Engine need not be running | 2 |
| Primary electrical system | Engine need not be running | 3 |
| Secondary electrical system | Engine need not be running | 4 |
| Fuel system | Engine need not be running | 5 |
| Engine compression | Engine need not be running | 6 |
| Engine vacuum | Engine must be running | 7 |
| Secondary electrical system | Engine must be running | 8 |
| Valve train | Engine must be running | 9 |
| Exhaust system | Engine must be running | 10 |
| Cooling system | Engine must be running | 11 |
| Engine lubrication | Engine must be running | 12 |

## Index to Problems

| Problem: Symptom | Begin at Specific Diagnosis, Number ____ |
|---|---|
| **Engine Won't Start:** | |
| Starter doesn't turn | 1.1, 2.1 |
| Starter turns, engine doesn't | 2.1 |
| Starter turns engine very slowly | 1.1, 2.4 |
| Starter turns engine normally | 3.1, 4.1 |
| Starter turns engine very quickly | 6.1 |
| Engine fires intermittently | 4.1 |
| Engine fires consistently | 5.1, 6.1 |
| **Engine Runs Poorly:** | |
| Hard starting | 3.1, 4.1, 5.1, 8.1 |
| Rough idle | 4.1, 5.1, 8.1 |
| Stalling | 3.1, 4.1, 5.1, 8.1 |
| Engine dies at high speeds | 4.1, 5.1 |
| Hesitation (on acceleration from standing stop) | 5.1, 8.1 |
| Poor pickup | 4.1, 5.1, 8.1 |
| Lack of power | 3.1, 4.1, 5.1, 8.1 |
| Backfire through the carburetor | 4.1, 8.1, 9.1 |
| Backfire through the exhaust | 4.1, 8.1, 9.1 |
| Blue exhaust gases | 6.1, 7.1 |
| Black exhaust gases | 5.1 |
| Running on (after the ignition is shut off) | 3.1, 8.1 |
| Susceptible to moisture | 4.1 |
| Engine misfires under load | 4.1, 7.1, 8.4, 9.1 |
| Engine misfires at speed | 4.1, 8.4 |
| Engine misfires at idle | 3.1, 4.1, 5.1, 7.1, 8.4 |

## Sample Section

| Test and Procedure | Results and Indications | Proceed to |
|---|---|---|
| **4.1**—Check for spark: Hold each spark plug wire approximately ¼″ from ground with gloves or a heavy, dry rag. Crank the engine and observe the spark. | → If no spark is evident: ——————— | →**4.2** |
| | → If spark is good in some cases: ——— | →**4.3** |
| | → If spark is good in all cases: ————— | →**4.6** |

## Specific Diagnosis

This section is arranged so that following each test, instructions are given to proceed to another, until a problem is diagnosed.

## Section 1—Battery

| Test and Procedure | Results and Indications | Proceed to |
|---|---|---|
| **1.1**—Inspect the battery visually for case condition (corrosion, cracks) and water level. | If case is cracked, replace battery: | **1.4** |
| | If the case is intact, remove corrosion with a solution of baking soda and water (**CAUTION**: *do not get the solution into the battery*), and fill with water: | **1.2** |

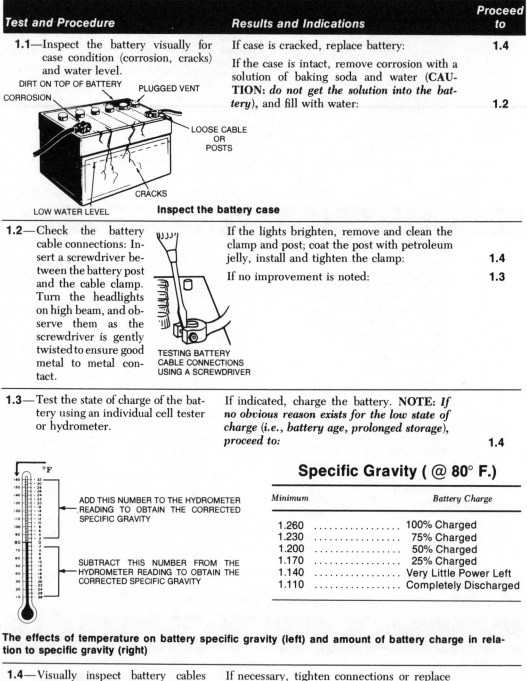

DIRT ON TOP OF BATTERY
PLUGGED VENT
CORROSION
LOOSE CABLE OR POSTS
CRACKS
LOW WATER LEVEL

**Inspect the battery case**

| | | |
|---|---|---|
| **1.2**—Check the battery cable connections: Insert a screwdriver between the battery post and the cable clamp. Turn the headlights on high beam, and observe them as the screwdriver is gently twisted to ensure good metal to metal contact. | If the lights brighten, remove and clean the clamp and post; coat the post with petroleum jelly, install and tighten the clamp: | **1.4** |
| | If no improvement is noted: | **1.3** |

TESTING BATTERY CABLE CONNECTIONS USING A SCREWDRIVER

| | | |
|---|---|---|
| **1.3**—Test the state of charge of the battery using an individual cell tester or hydrometer. | If indicated, charge the battery. **NOTE:** *If no obvious reason exists for the low state of charge (i.e., battery age, prolonged storage), proceed to:* | **1.4** |

°F

ADD THIS NUMBER TO THE HYDROMETER READING TO OBTAIN THE CORRECTED SPECIFIC GRAVITY

SUBTRACT THIS NUMBER FROM THE HYDROMETER READING TO OBTAIN THE CORRECTED SPECIFIC GRAVITY

## Specific Gravity ( @ 80° F.)

| Minimum | Battery Charge |
|---|---|
| 1.260 | ................. 100% Charged |
| 1.230 | ................. 75% Charged |
| 1.200 | ................. 50% Charged |
| 1.170 | ................. 25% Charged |
| 1.140 | ................. Very Little Power Left |
| 1.110 | ................. Completely Discharged |

**The effects of temperature on battery specific gravity (left) and amount of battery charge in relation to specific gravity (right)**

| | | |
|---|---|---|
| **1.4**—Visually inspect battery cables for cracking, bad connection to ground, or bad connection to starter. | If necessary, tighten connections or replace the cables: | |
| | | **2.1** |

## Section 2—Starting System
See Chapter 3 for service procedures

| Test and Procedure | Results and Indications | Proceed to |
|---|---|---|
| Note: Tests in Group 2 are performed with coil high tension lead disconnected to prevent accidental starting. | | |
| **2.1**—Test the starter motor and solenoid: Connect a jumper from the battery post of the solenoid (or relay) to the starter post of the solenoid (or relay). | If starter turns the engine normally: | 2.2 |
| | If the starter buzzes, or turns the engine very slowly: | 2.4 |
| | If no response, replace the solenoid (or relay). | 3.1 |
| | If the starter turns, but the engine doesn't, ensure that the flywheel ring gear is intact. If the gear is undamaged, replace the starter drive. | 3.1 |
| **2.2**—Determine whether ignition override switches are functioning properly (clutch start switch, neutral safety switch), by connecting a jumper across the switch(es), and turning the ignition switch to "start". | If starter operates, adjust or replace switch: | 3.1 |
| | If the starter doesn't operate: | 2.3 |
| **2.3**—Check the ignition switch "start" position: Connect a 12V test lamp or voltmeter between the starter post of the solenoid (or relay) and ground. Turn the ignition switch to the "start" position, and jiggle the key. | If the lamp doesn't light or the meter needle doesn't move when the switch is turned, check the ignition switch for loose connections, cracked insulation, or broken wires. Repair or replace as necessary: | 3.1 |
| | If the lamp flickers or needle moves when the key is jiggled, replace the ignition switch. | 3.3 |

**Checking the ignition switch "start" position**

**STARTER RELAY (IF EQUIPPED)**

| | | |
|---|---|---|
| **2.4**—Remove and bench test the starter, according to specifications in the engine electrical section. | If the starter does not meet specifications, repair or replace as needed: | 3.1 |
| | If the starter is operating properly: | 2.5 |
| **2.5**—Determine whether the engine can turn freely: Remove the spark plugs, and check for water in the cylinders. Check for water on the dipstick, or oil in the radiator. Attempt to turn the engine using an 18″ flex drive and socket on the crankshaft pulley nut or bolt. | If the engine will turn freely only with the spark plugs out, and hydrostatic lock (water in the cylinders) is ruled out, check valve timing: | 9.2 |
| | If engine will not turn freely, and it is known that the clutch and transmission are free, the engine must be disassembled for further evaluation: | Chapter 3 |

## Section 3—Primary Electrical System

| Test and Procedure | Results and Indications | Proceed to |
|---|---|---|
| **3.1**—Check the ignition switch "on" position: Connect a jumper wire between the distributor side of the coil and ground, and a 12V test lamp between the switch side of the coil and ground. Remove the high tension lead from the coil. Turn the ignition switch on and jiggle the key. | If the lamp lights: | **3.2** |
| | If the lamp flickers when the key is jiggled, replace the ignition switch: | **3.3** |
| | If the lamp doesn't light, check for loose or open connections. If none are found, remove the ignition switch and check for continuity. If the switch is faulty, replace it: | **3.3** |

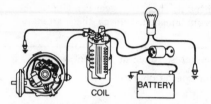

**Checking the ignition switch "on" position**

| | | |
|---|---|---|
| **3.2**—Check the ballast resistor or resistance wire for an open circuit, using an ohmmeter. See Chapter 3 for specific tests. | Replace the resistor or resistance wire if the resistance is zero. **NOTE:** *Some ignition systems have no ballast resistor.* | **3.3** |

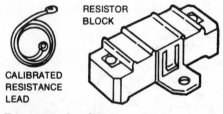

**Two types of resistors**

| | | |
|---|---|---|
| **3.3**—On point-type ignition systems, visually inspect the breaker points for burning, pitting or excessive wear. Gray coloring of the point contact surfaces is normal. Rotate the crankshaft until the contact heel rests on a high point of the distributor cam and adjust the point gap to specifications. On electronic ignition models, remove the distributor cap and visually inspect the armature. Ensure that the armature pin is in place, and that the armature is on tight and rotates when the engine is cranked. Make sure there are no cracks, chips or rounded edges on the armature. | If the breaker points are intact, clean the contact surfaces with fine emery cloth, and adjust the point gap to specifications. If the points are worn, replace them. On electronic systems, replace any parts which appear defective. If condition persists: | **3.4** |

| Test and Procedure | Results and Indications | Proceed to |
|---|---|---|
| **3.4**—On point-type ignition systems, connect a dwell-meter between the distributor primary lead and ground. Crank the engine and observe the point dwell angle. On electronic ignition systems, conduct a stator (magnetic pickup assembly) test. See Chapter 3. | On point-type systems, adjust the dwell angle if necessary. **NOTE: *Increasing the point gap decreases the dwell angle and vice-versa.*** | **3.6** |
| | If the dwell meter shows little or no reading; | **3.5** |
| | On electronic ignition systems, if the stator is bad, replace the stator. If the stator is good, proceed to the other tests in Chapter 3. | |

**Dwell is a function of point gap**

| | | |
|---|---|---|
| **3.5**—On the point-type ignition systems, check the condenser for short: connect an ohmeter across the condenser body and the pigtail lead. | If any reading other than infinite is noted, replace the condenser | **3.6** |

**Checking the condenser for short**

| | | |
|---|---|---|
| **3.6**—Test the coil primary resistance: On point-type ignition systems, connect an ohmmeter across the coil primary terminals, and read the resistance on the low scale. Note whether an external ballast resistor or resistance wire is used. On electronic ignition systems, test the coil primary resistance as in Chapter 3. | Point-type ignition coils utilizing ballast resistors or resistance wires should have approximately 1.0 ohms resistance. Coils with internal resistors should have approximately 4.0 ohms resistance. If values far from the above are noted, replace the coil. | **4.1** |

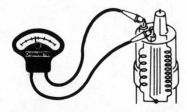

**Check the coil primary resistance**

## Section 4—Secondary Electrical System
See Chapters 2–3 for service procedures

| Test and Procedure | Results and Indications | Proceed to |
|---|---|---|
| **4.1**—Check for spark: Hold each spark plug wire approximately ¼" from ground with gloves or a heavy, dry rag. Crank the engine, and observe the spark. | If no spark is evident: | **4.2** |
| | If spark is good in some cylinders: | **4.3** |
| | If spark is good in all cylinders: | **4.6** |

**Check for spark at the plugs**

| | | |
|---|---|---|
| **4.2**—Check for spark at the coil high tension lead: Remove the coil high tension lead from the distributor and position it approximately ¼" from ground. Crank the engine and observe spark. **CAUTION:** *This test should not be performed on engines equipped with electronic ignition.* | If the spark is good and consistent: | **4.3** |
| | If the spark is good but intermittent, test the primary electrical system starting at 3.3: | **3.3** |
| | If the spark is weak or non-existent, replace the coil high tension lead, clean and tighten all connections and retest. If no improvement is noted: | **4.4** |
| **4.3**—Visually inspect the distributor cap and rotor for burned or corroded contacts, cracks, carbon tracks, or moisture. Also check the fit of the rotor on the distributor shaft (where applicable). | If moisture is present, dry thoroughly, and retest per 4.1: | **4.1** |
| | If burned or excessively corroded contacts, cracks, or carbon tracks are noted, replace the defective part(s) and retest per 4.1: | **4.1** |
| | If the rotor and cap appear intact, or are only slightly corroded, clean the contacts thoroughly (including the cap towers and spark plug wire ends) and retest per 4.1: | |
| | If the spark is good in all cases: | **4.6** |
| | If the spark is poor in all cases: | **4.5** |

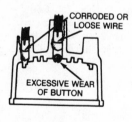

CORRODED OR LOOSE WIRE

EXCESSIVE WEAR OF BUTTON

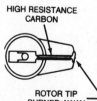

HIGH RESISTANCE CARBON

ROTOR TIP BURNED AWAY

**Inspect the distributor cap and rotor**

# CHILTON'S
# AUTO BODY REPAIR TIPS

**Tools and Materials • Step-by-Step Illustrated Procedures**
**How To Repair Dents, Scratches and Rust Holes**
**Spray Painting and Refinishing Tips**

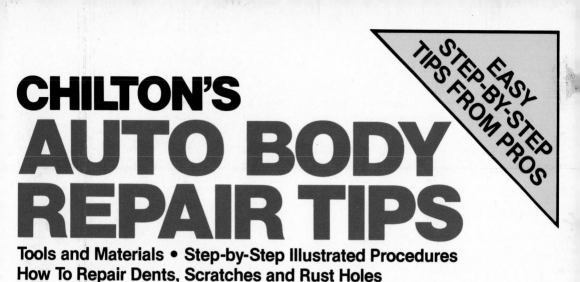

With a little practice, basic body repair procedures can be mastered by any do-it-yourself mechanic. The step-by-step repairs shown here can be applied to almost any type of auto body repair.

# TOOLS & MATERIALS

You may already have basic tools, such as hammers and electric drills. Other tools unique to body repair — body hammers, grinding attachments, sanding blocks, dent puller, half-round plastic file and plastic spreaders — are relatively inexpensive and can be obtained wherever auto parts or auto body repair parts are sold. Portable air compressors and paint spray guns can be purchased or rented.

## Auto Body Repair Kits

The best and most often used products are available to the do-it-yourselfer in kit form, from major manufacturers of auto body repair products. The same manufacturers also merchandise the individual products for use by pros.

Kits are available to make a wide variety of repairs, including holes, dents and scratches and fiberglass, and offer the advantage of buying the materials you'll need for the job. There is little waste or chance of materials going bad from not being used. Many kits may also contain basic body-working tools such as body files, sanding blocks and spreaders. Check the contents of the kit before buying your tools.

# BODY REPAIR TIPS

## Safety

Many of the products associated with auto body repair and refinishing contain toxic chemicals. Read all labels before opening containers and store them in a safe place and manner.

• Wear eye protection (safety goggles) when using power tools or when performing any operation that involves

the removal of any type of material.

• Wear lung protection (disposable mask or respirator) when grinding, sanding or painting.

## Sanding

**1** Sand off paint before using a dent puller. When using a non-adhesive sanding disc, cover the back of the disc with an overlapping layer or two of masking tape and trim the edges. The disc will last considerably longer.

**2** Use the circular motion of the sanding disc to grind *into* the edge of the repair. Grinding or sanding away from the jagged edge will only tear the sandpaper.

**3** Use the palm of your hand flat on the panel to detect high and low spots. Do not use your fingertips. Slide your hand slowly back and forth.

# WORKING WITH BODY FILLER

## Mixing The Filler

**C**leanliness and proper mixing and application are extremely important. Use a clean piece of plastic or glass or a disposable artist's palette to mix body filler.

**1** Allow plenty of time and follow directions. No useful purpose will be served by adding more hardener to make it cure (set-up) faster. Less hardener means more curing time, but the mixture dries harder; more hardener means less curing time but a softer mixture.

**2** Both the hardener and the filler should be thoroughly kneaded or stirred before mixing. Hardener should be a solid paste and dispense like thin toothpaste. Body filler should be smooth, and free of lumps or thick spots.

Getting the proper amount of hardener in the filler is the trickiest part of preparing the filler. Use the same amount of hardener in cold or warm weather. For contour filler (thick coats), a bead of hardener twice the diameter of the filler is about right. There's about a 15% margin on either side, but, if in doubt use less hardener.

**3** Mix the body filler and hardener by wiping across the mixing surface, picking the mixture up and wiping it again. Colder weather requires longer mixing times. Do not mix in a circular motion; this will trap air bubbles which will become holes in the cured filler.

## Applying The Filler

**1** For best results, filler should not be applied over 1/4" thick.

Apply the filler in several coats. Build it up to above the level of the repair surface so that it can be sanded or grated down.

The first coat of filler must be pressed on with a firm wiping motion.

Apply the filler in one direction only. Working the filler back and forth will either pull it off the metal or trap air bubbles.

# REPAIRING DENTS

**B**efore you start, take a few minutes to study the damaged area. Try to visualize the shape of the panel before it was damaged. If the damage is on the left fender, look at the right fender and use it as a guide. If there is access to the panel from behind, you can reshape it with a body hammer. If not, you'll have to use a dent puller. Go slowly and work the metal a little at a time. Get the panel as straight as possible before applying filler.

**1** This dent is typical of one that can be pulled out or hammered out from behind. Remove the headlight cover, headlight assembly and turn signal housing.

**2** Drill a series of holes ½ the size of the end of the dent puller along the stress line. Make some trial pulls and assess the results. If necessary, drill more holes and try again. Do not hurry.

**3** If possible, use a body hammer and block to shape the metal back to its original contours. Get the metal back as close to its original shape as possible. Don't depend on body filler to fill dents.

**4** Using an 80-grit grinding disc on an electric drill, grind the paint from the surrounding area down to bare metal. Use a new grinding pad to prevent heat buildup that will warp metal.

**5** The area should look like this when you're finished grinding. Knock the drill holes in and tape over small openings to keep plastic filler out.

**6** Mix the body filler (see Body Repair Tips). Spread the body filler evenly over the entire area (see Body Repair Tips). Be sure to cover the area completely.

**7** Let the body filler dry until the surface can just be scratched with your fingernail. Knock the high spots from the body filler with a body file ("Cheesegrater"). Check frequently with the palm of your hand for high and low spots.

**8** Check to be sure that trim pieces that will be installed later will fit exactly. Sand the area with 40-grit paper.

**9** If you wind up with low spots, you may have to apply another layer of filler.

**10** Knock the high spots off with 40-grit paper. When you are satisfied with the contours of the repair, apply a thin coat of filler to cover pin holes and scratches.

**11** Block sand the area with 40-grit paper to a smooth finish. Pay particular attention to body lines and ridges that must be well-defined.

**12** Sand the area with 400 paper and then finish with a scuff pad. The finished repair is ready for priming and painting (see Painting Tips).

Materials and photos courtesy of Ritt Jones Auto Body, Prospect Park, PA.

# REPAIRING RUST HOLES

There are many ways to repair rust holes. The fiberglass cloth kit shown here is one of the most cost efficient for the owner because it provides a strong repair that resists cracking and moisture and is relatively easy to use. It can be used on large and small holes (with or without backing) and can be applied over contoured areas. Remember, however, that short of replacing an entire panel, no repair is a guarantee that the rust will not return.

**1** Remove any trim that will be in the way. Clean away all loose debris. Cut away all the rusted metal. But be sure to leave enough metal to retain the contour or body shape.

**2** Grind away all traces of rust with a 24-grit grinding disc. Be sure to grind back 3-4 inches from the edge of the hole down to bare metal and be sure all traces of paint, primer and rust are removed.

**3** Block sand the area with 80 or 100 grit sandpaper to get a clear, shiny surface and feathered paint edge. Tap the edges of the hole inward with a ball peen hammer.

**4** If you are going to use release film, cut a piece about 2-3″ larger than the area you have sanded. Place the film over the repair and mark the sanded area on the film. Avoid any unnecessary wrinkling of the film.

**5** Cut 2 pieces of fiberglass matte to match the shape of the repair. One piece should be about 1″ smaller than the sanded area and the second piece should be 1″ smaller than the first. Mix enough filler and hardener to saturate the fiberglass material (see Body Repair Tips).

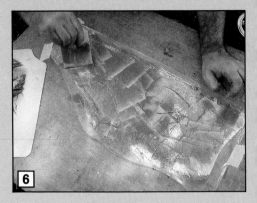

**6** Lay the release sheet on a flat surface and spread an even layer of filler, large enough to cover the repair. Lay the smaller piece of fiberglass cloth in the center of the sheet and spread another layer of filler over the fiberglass cloth. Repeat the operation for the larger piece of cloth.

**7** Place the repair material over the repair area, with the release film facing outward. Use a spreader and work from the center outward to smooth the material, following the body contours. Be sure to remove all air bubbles.

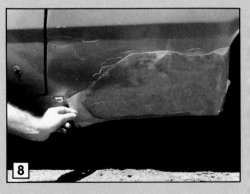

**8** Wait until the repair has dried tack-free and peel off the release sheet. The ideal working temperature is 60°-90° F. Cooler or warmer temperatures or high humidity may require additional curing time. Wait longer, if in doubt.

**9** Sand and feather-edge the entire area. The initial sanding can be done with a sanding disc on an electric drill if care is used. Finish the sanding with a block sander. Low spots can be filled with body filler; this may require several applications.

**10** When the filler can just be scratched with a fingernail, knock the high spots down with a body file and smooth the entire area with 80-grit. Feather the filled areas into the surrounding areas.

**11** When the area is sanded smooth, mix some topcoat and hardener and apply it directly with a spreader. This will give a smooth finish and prevent the glass matte from showing through the paint.

**12** Block sand the topcoat smooth with finishing sandpaper (200 grit), and 400 grit. The repair is ready for masking, priming and painting (see Painting Tips).

Materials and photos courtesy Marson Corporation, Chelsea, Massachusetts

# PAINTING TIPS

## Preparation

**1** SANDING — Use a 400 or 600 grit wet or dry sandpaper. Wet-sand the area with a 1/4 sheet of sandpaper soaked in clean water. Keep the paper wet while sanding. Sand the area until the repaired area tapers into the original finish.

**2** CLEANING — Wash the area to be painted thoroughly with water and a clean rag. Rinse it thoroughly and wipe the surface dry until you're sure it's completely free of dirt, dust, fingerprints, wax, detergent or other foreign matter.

**3** MASKING — Protect any areas you don't want to overspray by covering them with masking tape and newspaper. Be careful not get fingerprints on the area to be painted.

**4** PRIMING — All exposed metal should be primed before painting. Primer protects the metal and provides an excellent surface for paint adhesion. When the primer is dry, wet-sand the area again with 600 grit wet-sandpaper. Clean the area again after sanding.

## Painting Techniques

**P** aint applied from either a spray gun or a spray can (for small areas) will provide good results. Experiment on an old piece of metal to get the right combination before you begin painting.

**SPRAYING VISCOSITY (SPRAY GUN ONLY)** — Paint should be thinned to spraying viscosity according to the directions on the can. Use only the recommended thinner or reducer and the same amount of reduction regardless of temperature.

**AIR PRESSURE (SPRAY GUN ONLY)** — This is extremely important. Be sure you are using the proper recommended pressure.

**TEMPERATURE** — The surface to be painted should be approximately the same temperature as the surrounding air. Applying warm paint to a cold surface, or vice versa, will completely upset the paint characteristics.

**THICKNESS** — Spray with smooth strokes. In general, the thicker the coat of paint, the longer the drying time. Apply several thin coats about 30 seconds apart. The paint should remain wet long enough to flow out and no longer; heavier coats will only produce sags or wrinkles. Spray a light (fog) coat, followed by heavier color coats.

**DISTANCE** — The ideal spraying distance is 8″-12″ from the gun or can to the surface. Shorter distances will produce ripples, while greater distances will result in orange peel, dry film and poor color match and loss of material due to overspray.

**OVERLAPPING** — The gun or can should be kept at right angles to the surface at all times. Work to a wet edge at an even speed, using a 50% overlap and direct the center of the spray at the lower or nearest edge of the previous stroke.

**RUBBING OUT (BLENDING) FRESH PAINT** — Let the paint dry thoroughly. Runs or imperfections can be sanded out, primed and repainted.

Don't be in too big a hurry to remove the masking. This only produces paint ridges. When the finish has dried for at least a week, apply a small amount of fine grade rubbing compound with a clean, wet cloth. Use lots of water and blend the new paint with the surrounding area.

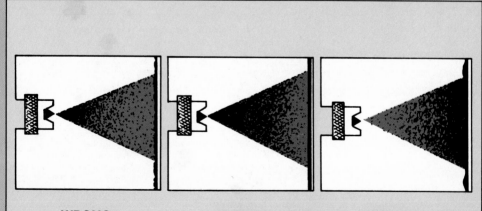

| WRONG | CORRECT | WRONG |
|---|---|---|
| Thin coat. Stroke too fast, not enough overlap, gun too far away. | Medium coat. Proper distance, good stroke, proper overlap. | Heavy coat. Stroke too slow, too much overlap, gun too close. |

| Test and Procedure | Results and Indications | Proceed to |
|---|---|---|

**4.4**—Check the coil secondary resistance: On point-type systems connect an ohmmeter across the distributor side of the coil and the coil tower. Read the resistance on the high scale of the ohmmeter. On electronic ignition systems, see Chapter 3 for specific tests.

The resistance of a satisfactory coil should be between 4,000 and 10,000 ohms. If resistance is considerably higher (i.e., 40,000 ohms) replace the coil and retest per 4.1. **NOTE: *This does not apply to high performance coils.***

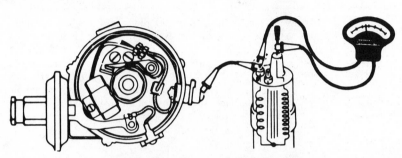

**Testing the coil secondary resistance**

**4.5**—Visually inspect the spark plug wires for cracking or brittleness. Ensure that no two wires are positioned so as to cause induction firing (adjacent and parallel). Remove each wire, one by one, and check resistance with an ohmmeter.

Replace any cracked or brittle wires. If any of the wires are defective, replace the entire set. Replace any wires with excessive resistance (over 8000 Ω per foot for suppression wire), and separate any wires that might cause induction firing.

**4.6**

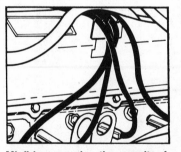

Misfiring can be the result of spark plug leads to adjacent, consecutively firing cylinders running parallel and too close together

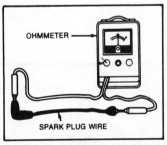

On point-type ignition systems, check the spark plug wires as shown. On electronic ignitions, do not remove the wire from the distributor cap terminal; instead, test through the cap

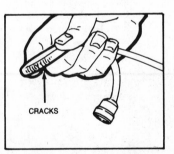

Spark plug wires can be checked visually by bending them in a loop over your finger. This will reveal any cracks, burned or broken insulation. Any wire with cracked insulation should be replaced

**4.6**—Remove the spark plugs, noting the cylinders from which they were removed, and evaluate according to the color photos in the middle of this book.

See following.

**See following.**

| Test and Procedure | Results and Indications | Proceed to |
|---|---|---|
| **4.7**—Examine the location of all the plugs. | The following diagrams illustrate some of the conditions that the location of plugs will reveal. | **4.8** |

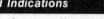

Two adjacent plugs are fouled in a 6-cylinder engine, 4-cylinder engine or either bank of a V-8. This is probably due to a blown head gasket between the two cylinders

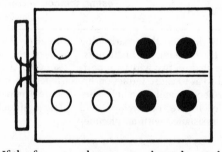

The two center plugs in a 6-cylinder engine are fouled. Raw fuel may be "boiled" out of the carburetor into the intake manifold after the engine is shut-off. Stop-start driving can also foul the center plugs, due to overly rich mixture. Proper float level, a new float needle and seat or use of an insulating spacer may help this problem

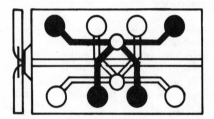

An unbalanced carburetor is indicated. Following the fuel flow on this particular design shows that the cylinders fed by the right-hand barrel are fouled from overly rich mixture, while the cylinders fed by the left-hand barrel are normal

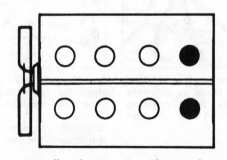

If the four rear plugs are overheated, a cooling system problem is suggested. A thorough cleaning of the cooling system may restore coolant circulation and cure the problem

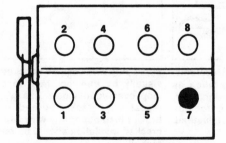

Finding one plug overheated may indicate an intake manifold leak near the affected cylinder. If the overheated plug is the second of two adjacent, consecutively firing plugs, it could be the result of ignition cross-firing. Separating the leads to these two plugs will eliminate cross-fire

Occasionally, the two rear plugs in large, lightly used V-8's will become oil fouled. High oil consumption and smoky exhaust may also be noticed. It is probably due to plugged oil drain holes in the rear of the cylinder head, causing oil to be sucked in around the valve stems. This usually occurs in the rear cylinders first, because the engine slants that way

| Test and Procedure | Results and Indications | Proceed to |
|---|---|---|
| **4.8**—Determine the static ignition timing. Using the crankshaft pulley timing marks as a guide, locate top dead center on the compression stroke of the number one cylinder. | The rotor should be pointing toward the No. 1 tower in the distributor cap, and, on electronic ignitions, the armature spoke for that cylinder should be lined up with the stator. | **4.8** |
| **4.9**—Check coil polarity: Connect a voltmeter negative lead to the coil high tension lead, and the positive lead to ground (**NOTE:** *Reverse the hook-up for positive ground systems*). Crank the engine momentarily. | If the voltmeter reads up-scale, the polarity is correct: | **5.1** |
| | If the voltmeter reads down-scale, reverse the coil polarity (switch the primary leads): | **5.1** |

**Checking coil polarity**

## Section 5—Fuel System
See Chapter 4 for service procedures

| Test and Procedure | Results and Indications | Proceed to |
|---|---|---|
| **5.1**—Determine that the air filter is functioning efficiently: Hold paper elements up to a strong light, and attempt to see light through the filter. | Clean permanent air filters in solvent (or manufacturer's recommendation), and allow to dry. Replace paper elements through which light cannot be seen: | **5.2** |
| **5.2**—Determine whether a flooding condition exists: Flooding is identified by a strong gasoline odor, and excessive gasoline present in the throttle bore(s) of the carburetor. | If flooding is not evident: | **5.3** |
| | If flooding is evident, permit the gasoline to dry for a few moments and restart. If flooding doesn't recur: | **5.7** |
| | If flooding is persistent: | **5.5** |

**If the engine floods repeatedly, check the choke butterfly flap**

| | | |
|---|---|---|
| **5.3**—Check that fuel is reaching the carburetor: Detach the fuel line at the carburetor inlet. Hold the end of the line in a cup (not styrofoam), and crank the engine. | If fuel flows smoothly: | **5.7** |
| | If fuel doesn't flow (**NOTE:** *Make sure that there is fuel in the tank*), or flows erratically: | **5.4** |

**Check the fuel pump by disconnecting the output line (fuel pump-to-carburetor) at the carburetor and operating the starter briefly**

| Test and Procedure | Results and Indications | Proceed to |
|---|---|---|
| **5.4**—Test the fuel pump: Disconnect all fuel lines from the fuel pump. Hold a finger over the input fitting, crank the engine (with electric pump, turn the ignition or pump on); and feel for suction. | If suction is evident, blow out the fuel line to the tank with low pressure compressed air until bubbling is heard from the fuel filler neck. Also blow out the carburetor fuel line (both ends disconnected): | **5.7** |
| | If no suction is evident, replace or repair the fuel pump: | **5.7** |
| | **NOTE:** *Repeated oil fouling of the spark plugs, or a no-start condition, could be the result of a ruptured vacuum booster pump diaphragm, through which oil or gasoline is being drawn into the intake manifold (where applicable).* | |
| **5.5**—Occasionally, small specks of dirt will clog the small jets and orifices in the carburetor. With the engine cold, hold a flat piece of wood or similar material over the carburetor, where possible, and crank the engine. | If the engine starts, but runs roughly the engine is probably not run enough. | |
| | If the engine won't start: | **5.9** |
| **5.6**—Check the needle and seat: Tap the carburetor in the area of the needle and seat. | If flooding stops, a gasoline additive (e.g., Gumout) will often cure the problem: | **5.7** |
| | If flooding continues, check the fuel pump for excessive pressure at the carburetor (according to specifications). If the pressure is normal, the needle and seat must be removed and checked, and/or the float level adjusted: | **5.7** |
| **5.7**—Test the accelerator pump by looking into the throttle bores while operating the throttle. | If the accelerator pump appears to be operating normally: | **5.8** |
| | If the accelerator pump is not operating, the pump must be reconditioned. Where possible, service the pump with the carburetor(s) installed on the engine. If necessary, remove the carburetor. Prior to removal: | **5.8** |

**Check for gas at the carburetor by looking down the carburetor throat while someone moves the accelerator**

| | | |
|---|---|---|
| **5.8**—Determine whether the carburetor main fuel system is functioning: Spray a commercial starting fluid into the carburetor while attempting to start the engine. | If the engine starts, runs for a few seconds, and dies: | **5.9** |
| | If the engine doesn't start: | **6.1** |

| Test and Procedure | Results and Indications | Proceed to |
|---|---|---|
| **5.9**—Uncommon fuel system malfunctions: See below: | If the problem is solved:<br><br>If the problem remains, remove and recondition the carburetor. | **6.1** |

| Condition | Indication | Test | Prevailing Weather Conditions | Remedy |
|---|---|---|---|---|
| Vapor lock | Engine will not restart shortly after running. | Cool the components of the fuel system until the engine starts. Vapor lock can be cured faster by draping a wet cloth over a mechanical fuel pump. | Hot to very hot | Ensure that the exhaust manifold heat control valve is operating. Check with the vehicle manufacturer for the recommended solution to vapor lock on the model in question. |
| Carburetor icing | Engine will not idle, stalls at low speeds. | Visually inspect the throttle plate area of the throttle bores for frost. | High humidity, 32–40° F. | Ensure that the exhaust manifold heat control valve is operating, and that the intake manifold heat riser is not blocked. |
| Water in the fuel | Engine sputters and stalls; may not start. | Pump a small amount of fuel into a glass jar. Allow to stand, and inspect for droplets or a layer of water. | High humidity, extreme temperature changes. | For droplets, use one or two cans of commercial gas line anti-freeze. For a layer of water, the tank must be drained, and the fuel lines blown out with compressed air. |

## Section 6—Engine Compression

See Chapter 3 for service procedures

| | | |
|---|---|---|
| **6.1**—Test engine compression: Remove all spark plugs. Block the throttle wide open. Insert a compression gauge into a spark plug port, crank the engine to obtain the maximum reading, and record. | If compression is within limits on all cylinders: | **7.1** |
| | If gauge reading is extremely low on all cylinders: | **6.2** |
| | If gauge reading is low on one or two cylinders: (If gauge readings are identical and low on two or more adjacent cylinders, the head gasket must be replaced.) | **6.2** |

**Checking compression**

| | | |
|---|---|---|
| **6.2**—Test engine compression (wet): Squirt approximately 30 cc. of engine oil into each cylinder, and retest per 6.1. | If the readings improve, worn or cracked rings or broken pistons are indicated: | **See Chapter 3** |
| | If the readings do not improve, burned or excessively carboned valves or a jumped timing chain are indicated:<br>**NOTE:** *A jumped timing chain is often indicated by difficult cranking.* | **7.1** |

## Section 7—Engine Vacuum
See Chapter 3 for service procedures

| Test and Procedure | Results and Indications | Proceed to |
|---|---|---|
| 7.1—Attach a vacuum gauge to the intake manifold beyond the throttle plate. Start the engine, and observe the action of the needle over the range of engine speeds. | See below. | See below |

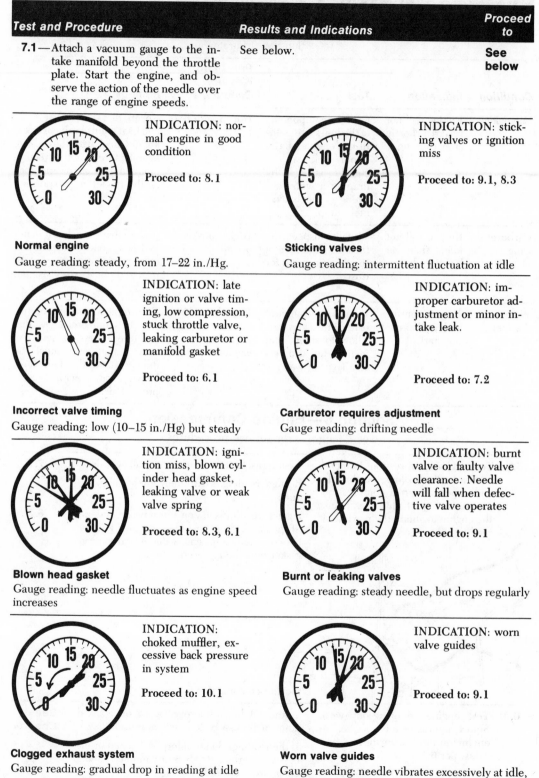

INDICATION: normal engine in good condition

Proceed to: 8.1

**Normal engine**
Gauge reading: steady, from 17–22 in./Hg.

INDICATION: sticking valves or ignition miss

Proceed to: 9.1, 8.3

**Sticking valves**
Gauge reading: intermittent fluctuation at idle

INDICATION: late ignition or valve timing, low compression, stuck throttle valve, leaking carburetor or manifold gasket

Proceed to: 6.1

**Incorrect valve timing**
Gauge reading: low (10–15 in./Hg) but steady

INDICATION: improper carburetor adjustment or minor intake leak.

Proceed to: 7.2

**Carburetor requires adjustment**
Gauge reading: drifting needle

INDICATION: ignition miss, blown cylinder head gasket, leaking valve or weak valve spring

Proceed to: 8.3, 6.1

**Blown head gasket**
Gauge reading: needle fluctuates as engine speed increases

INDICATION: burnt valve or faulty valve clearance. Needle will fall when defective valve operates

Proceed to: 9.1

**Burnt or leaking valves**
Gauge reading: steady needle, but drops regularly

INDICATION: choked muffler, excessive back pressure in system

Proceed to: 10.1

**Clogged exhaust system**
Gauge reading: gradual drop in reading at idle

INDICATION: worn valve guides

Proceed to: 9.1

**Worn valve guides**
Gauge reading: needle vibrates excessively at idle, but steadies as engine speed increases

White pointer = steady gauge hand

Black pointer = fluctuating gauge hand

| Test and Procedure | Results and Indications | Proceed to |
|---|---|---|
| **7.2**—Attach a vacuum gauge per 7.1, and test for an intake manifold leak. Squirt a small amount of oil around the intake manifold gaskets, carburetor gaskets, plugs and fittings. Observe the action of the vacuum gauge. | If the reading improves, replace the indicated gasket, or seal the indicated fitting or plug: <br><br> If the reading remains low: | **8.1** <br><br> **7.3** |
| **7.3**—Test all vacuum hoses and accessories for leaks as described in 7.2. Also check the carburetor body (dashpots, automatic choke mechanism, throttle shafts) for leaks in the same manner. | If the reading improves, service or replace the offending part(s): <br><br> If the reading remains low: | **8.1** <br><br> **6.1** |

## Section 8—Secondary Electrical System
### See Chapter 2 for service procedures

| Test and Procedure | Results and Indications | Proceed to |
|---|---|---|
| **8.1**—Remove the distributor cap and check to make sure that the rotor turns when the engine is cranked. Visually inspect the distributor components. | Clean, tighten or replace any components which appear defective. | **8.2** |
| **8.2**—Connect a timing light (per manufacturer's recommendation) and check the dynamic ignition timing. Disconnect and plug the vacuum hose(s) to the distributor if specified, start the engine, and observe the timing marks at the specified engine speed. | If the timing is not correct, adjust to specifications by rotating the distributor in the engine: (Advance timing by rotating distributor opposite normal direction of rotor rotation, retard timing by rotating distributor in same direction as rotor rotation.) | **8.3** |
| **8.3**—Check the operation of the distributor advance mechanism(s): To test the mechanical advance, disconnect the vacuum lines from the distributor advance unit and observe the timing marks with a timing light as the engine speed is increased from idle. If the mark moves smoothly, without hesitation, it may be assumed that the mechanical advance is functioning properly. To test vacuum advance and/or retard systems, alternately crimp and release the vacuum line, and observe the timing mark for movement. If movement is noted, the system is operating. | If the systems are functioning: <br><br> If the systems are not functioning, remove the distributor, and test on a distributor tester: | **8.4** <br><br><br> **8.4** |
| **8.4**—Locate an ignition miss: With the engine running, remove each spark plug wire, one at a time, until one is found that doesn't cause the engine to roughen and slow down. | When the missing cylinder is identified: | **4.1** |

## Section 9—Valve Train
See Chapter 3 for service procedures

| Test and Procedure | Results and Indications | Proceed to |
|---|---|---|
| **9.1**—Evaluate the valve train: Remove the valve cover, and ensure that the valves are adjusted to specifications. A mechanic's stethoscope may be used to aid in the diagnosis of the valve train. By pushing the probe on or near push rods or rockers, valve noise often can be isolated. A timing light also may be used to diagnose valve problems. Connect the light according to manufacturer's recommendations, and start the engine. Vary the firing moment of the light by increasing the engine speed (and therefore the ignition advance), and moving the trigger from cylinder to cylinder. Observe the movement of each valve. | Sticking valves or erratic valve train motion can be observed with the timing light. The cylinder head must be disassembled for repairs. | **See Chapter 3** |
| **9.2**—Check the valve timing: Locate top dead center of the No. 1 piston, and install a degree wheel or tape on the crankshaft pulley or damper with zero corresponding to an index mark on the engine. Rotate the crankshaft in its direction of rotation, and observe the opening of the No. 1 cylinder intake valve. The opening should correspond with the correct mark on the degree wheel according to specifications. | If the timing is not correct, the timing cover must be removed for further investigation. | **See Chapter 3** |

## Section 10—Exhaust System

| Test and Procedure | Results and Indications | Proceed to |
|---|---|---|
| **10.1**—Determine whether the exhaust manifold heat control valve is operating: Operate the valve by hand to determine whether it is free to move. If the valve is free, run the engine to operating temperature and observe the action of the valve, to ensure that it is opening. | If the valve sticks, spray it with a suitable solvent, open and close the valve to free it, and retest. If the valve functions properly: If the valve does not free, or does not operate, replace the valve: | **10.2** **10.2** |
| **10.2**—Ensure that there are no exhaust restrictions: Visually inspect the exhaust system for kinks, dents, or crushing. Also note that gases are flowing freely from the tailpipe at all engine speeds, indicating no restriction in the muffler or resonator. | Replace any damaged portion of the system: | **11.1** |

## Section 11—Cooling System
### See Chapter 3 for service procedures

| Test and Procedure | Results and Indications | Proceed to |
|---|---|---|
| **11.1**—Visually inspect the fan belt for glazing, cracks, and fraying, and replace if necessary. Tighten the belt so that the longest span has approximately ½″ play at its mid-point under thumb pressure (see Chapter 1). | Replace or tighten the fan belt as necessary: | **11.2** |

**Checking belt tension**

| Test and Procedure | Results and Indications | Proceed to |
|---|---|---|
| **11.2**—Check the fluid level of the cooling system. | If full or slightly low, fill as necessary: | **11.5** |
| | If extremely low: | **11.3** |
| **11.3**—Visually inspect the external portions of the cooling system (radiator, radiator hoses, thermostat elbow, water pump seals, heater hoses, etc.) for leaks. If none are found, pressurize the cooling system to 14–15 psi. | If cooling system holds the pressure: | **11.5** |
| | If cooling system loses pressure rapidly, reinspect external parts of the system for leaks under pressure. If none are found, check dipstick for coolant in crankcase. If no coolant is present, but pressure loss continues: | **11.4** |
| | If coolant is evident in crankcase, remove cylinder head(s), and check gasket(s). If gaskets are intact, block and cylinder head(s) should be checked for cracks or holes. | |
| | If the gasket(s) is blown, replace, and purge the crankcase of coolant: | **12.6** |
| | **NOTE:** *Occasionally, due to atmospheric and driving conditions, condensation of water can occur in the crankcase. This causes the oil to appear milky white. To remedy, run the engine until hot, and change the oil and oil filter.* | |
| **11.4**—Check for combustion leaks into the cooling system: Pressurize the cooling system as above. Start the engine, and observe the pressure gauge. If the needle fluctuates, remove each spark plug wire, one at a time, noting which cylinder(s) reduce or eliminate the fluctuation. | Cylinders which reduce or eliminate the fluctuation, when the spark plug wire is removed, are leaking into the cooling system. Replace the head gasket on the affected cylinder bank(s). | |

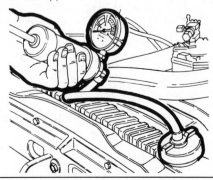

**Pressurizing the cooling system**

| Test and Procedure | Results and Indications | Proceed to |
|---|---|---|
| **11.5**—Check the radiator pressure cap: Attach a radiator pressure tester to the radiator cap (wet the seal prior to installation). Quickly pump up the pressure, noting the point at which the cap releases. | If the cap releases within ± 1 psi of the specified rating, it is operating properly:<br><br>If the cap releases at more than ± 1 psi of the specified rating, it should be replaced: | **11.6**<br><br>**11.6** |

**Checking radiator pressure cap**

| Test and Procedure | Results and Indications | Proceed to |
|---|---|---|
| **11.6**—Test the thermostat: Start the engine cold, remove the radiator cap, and insert a thermometer into the radiator. Allow the engine to idle. After a short while, there will be a sudden, rapid increase in coolant temperature. The temperature at which this sharp rise stops is the thermostat opening temperature. | If the thermostat opens at or about the specified temperature:<br><br>If the temperature doesn't increase: (If the temperature increases slowly and gradually, replace the thermostat.) | **11.7**<br><br>**11.7** |
| **11.7**—Check the water pump: Remove the thermostat elbow and the thermostat, disconnect the coil high tension lead (to prevent starting), and crank the engine momentarily. | If coolant flows, replace the thermostat and retest per 11.6:<br><br>If coolant doesn't flow, reverse flush the cooling system to alleviate any blockage that might exist. If system is not blocked, and coolant will not flow, replace the water pump. | **11.6** |

## Section 12—Lubrication
See Chapter 3 for service procedures

| Test and Procedure | Results and Indications | Proceed to |
|---|---|---|
| **12.1**—Check the oil pressure gauge or warning light: If the gauge shows low pressure, or the light is on for no obvious reason, remove the oil pressure sender. Install an accurate oil pressure gauge and run the engine momentarily. | If oil pressure builds normally, run engine for a few moments to determine that it is functioning normally, and replace the sender.<br><br>If the pressure remains low:<br>If the pressure surges:<br>If the oil pressure is zero: | —<br><br>**12.2**<br>**12.3**<br>**12.3** |
| **12.2**—Visually inspect the oil: If the oil is watery or very thin, milky, or foamy, replace the oil and oil filter. | If the oil is normal:<br><br>If after replacing oil the pressure remains low:<br><br>If after replacing oil the pressure becomes normal: | **12.3**<br><br>**12.3**<br><br>— |

| Test and Procedure | Results and Indications | Proceed to |
|---|---|---|
| **12.3**—Inspect the oil pressure relief valve and spring, to ensure that it is not sticking or stuck. Remove and thoroughly clean the valve, spring, and the valve body. | If the oil pressure improves:<br>If no improvement is noted: | —<br>**12.4** |
| **12.4**—Check to ensure that the oil pump is not cavitating (sucking air instead of oil): See that the crankcase is neither over nor underfull, and that the pickup in the sump is in the proper position and free from sludge. | Fill or drain the crankcase to the proper capacity, and clean the pickup screen in solvent if necessary. If no improvement is noted: | **12.5** |
| **12.5**—Inspect the oil pump drive and the oil pump: | If the pump drive or the oil pump appear to be defective, service as necessary and retest per 12.1:<br><br>If the pump drive and pump appear to be operating normally, the engine should be disassembled to determine where blockage exists: | **12.1**<br><br>**See Chapter 3** |
| **12.6**—Purge the engine of ethylene glycol coolant: Completely drain the crankcase and the oil filter. Obtain a commercial butyl cellosolve base solvent, designated for this purpose, and follow the instructions precisely. Following this, install a new oil filter and refill the crankcase with the proper weight oil. The next oil and filter change should follow shortly thereafter (1000 miles). | | |

# TROUBLESHOOTING EMISSION CONTROL SYSTEMS

See Chapter 4 for procedures applicable to individual emission control systems used on specific combinations of engine/transmission/model.

# TROUBLESHOOTING THE CARBURETOR

See Chapter 4 for service procedures

Carburetor problems cannot be effectively isolated unless all other engine systems (particularly ignition and emission) are functioning properly and the engine is properly tuned.

| Condition | Possible Cause |
|---|---|
| Engine cranks, but does not start | 1. Improper starting procedure<br>2. No fuel in tank<br>3. Clogged fuel line or filter<br>4. Defective fuel pump<br>5. Choke valve not closing properly<br>6. Engine flooded<br>7. Choke valve not unloading<br>8. Throttle linkage not making full travel<br>9. Stuck needle or float<br>10. Leaking float needle or seat<br>11. Improper float adjustment |
| Engine stalls | 1. Improperly adjusted idle speed or mixture<br>**Engine hot**<br>2. Improperly adjusted dashpot<br>3. Defective or improperly adjusted solenoid<br>4. Incorrect fuel level in fuel bowl<br>5. Fuel pump pressure too high<br>6. Leaking float needle seat<br>7. Secondary throttle valve stuck open<br>8. Air or fuel leaks<br>9. Idle air bleeds plugged or missing<br>10. Idle passages plugged<br>**Engine Cold**<br>11. Incorrectly adjusted choke<br>12. Improperly adjusted fast idle speed<br>13. Air leaks<br>14. Plugged idle or idle air passages<br>15. Stuck choke valve or binding linkage<br>16. Stuck secondary throttle valves<br>17. Engine flooding—high fuel level<br>18. Leaking or misaligned float |
| Engine hesitates on acceleration | 1. Clogged fuel filter<br>2. Leaking fuel pump diaphragm<br>3. Low fuel pump pressure<br>4. Secondary throttle valves stuck, bent or misadjusted<br>5. Sticking or binding air valve<br>6. Defective accelerator pump<br>7. Vacuum leaks<br>8. Clogged air filter<br>9. Incorrect choke adjustment (engine cold) |
| Engine feels sluggish or flat on acceleration | 1. Improperly adjusted idle speed or mixture<br>2. Clogged fuel filter<br>3. Defective accelerator pump<br>4. Dirty, plugged or incorrect main metering jets<br>5. Bent or sticking main metering rods<br>6. Sticking throttle valves<br>7. Stuck heat riser<br>8. Binding or stuck air valve<br>9. Dirty, plugged or incorrect secondary jets<br>10. Bent or sticking secondary metering rods.<br>11. Throttle body or manifold heat passages plugged<br>12. Improperly adjusted choke or choke vacuum break. |
| Carburetor floods | 1. Defective fuel pump. Pressure too high.<br>2. Stuck choke valve<br>3. Dirty, worn or damaged float or needle valve/seat<br>4. Incorrect float/fuel level<br>5. Leaking float bowl |

| Condition | Possible Cause |
|---|---|
| Engine idles roughly and stalls | 1. Incorrect idle speed<br>2. Clogged fuel filter<br>3. Dirt in fuel system or carburetor<br>4. Loose carburetor screws or attaching bolts<br>5. Broken carburetor gaskets<br>6. Air leaks<br>7. Dirty carburetor<br>8. Worn idle mixture needles<br>9. Throttle valves stuck open<br>10. Incorrectly adjusted float or fuel level<br>11. Clogged air filter |
| Engine runs unevenly or surges | 1. Defective fuel pump<br>2. Dirty or clogged fuel filter<br>3. Plugged, loose or incorrect main metering jets or rods<br>4. Air leaks<br>5. Bent or sticking main metering rods<br>6. Stuck power piston<br>7. Incorrect float adjustment<br>8. Incorrect idle speed or mixture<br>9. Dirty or plugged idle system passages<br>10. Hard, brittle or broken gaskets<br>11. Loose attaching or mounting screws<br>12. Stuck or misaligned secondary throttle valves |
| Poor fuel economy | 1. Poor driving habits<br>2. Stuck choke valve<br>3. Binding choke linkage<br>4. Stuck heat riser<br>5. Incorrect idle mixture<br>6. Defective accelerator pump<br>7. Air leaks<br>8. Plugged, loose or incorrect main metering jets<br>9. Improperly adjusted float or fuel level<br>10. Bent, misaligned or fuel-clogged float<br>11. Leaking float needle seat<br>12. Fuel leak<br>13. Accelerator pump discharge ball not seating properly<br>14. Incorrect main jets |
| Engine lacks high speed performance or power | 1. Incorrect throttle linkage adjustment<br>2. Stuck or binding power piston<br>3. Defective accelerator pump<br>4. Air leaks<br>5. Incorrect float setting or fuel level<br>6. Dirty, plugged, worn or incorrect main metering jets or rods<br>7. Binding or sticking air valve<br>8. Brittle or cracked gaskets<br>9. Bent, incorrect or improperly adjusted secondary metering rods<br>10. Clogged fuel filter<br>11. Clogged air filter<br>12. Defective fuel pump |

# TROUBLESHOOTING FUEL INJECTION PROBLEMS

Each fuel injection system has its own unique components and test procedures, for which it is impossible to generalize. Refer to Chapter 4 of this Repair & Tune-Up Guide for specific test and repair procedures, if the vehicle is equipped with fuel injection.

## TROUBLESHOOTING ELECTRICAL PROBLEMS

See Chapter 5 for service procedures

For any electrical system to operate, it must make a complete circuit. This simply means that the power flow from the battery must make a complete circle. When an electrical component is operating, power flows from the battery to the component, passes through the component causing it to perform its function (lighting a light bulb), and then returns to the battery through the ground of the circuit. This ground is usually (but not always) the metal part of the car or truck on which the electrical component is mounted.

Perhaps the easiest way to visualize this is to think of connecting a light bulb with two wires attached to it to the battery. If one of the two wires attached to the light bulb were attached to the negative post of the battery and the other were attached to the positive post of the battery, you would have a complete circuit. Current from the battery would flow to the light bulb, causing it to light, and return to the negative post of the battery.

The normal automotive circuit differs from this simple example in two ways. First, instead of having a return wire from the bulb to the battery, the light bulb returns the current to the battery through the chassis of the vehicle. Since the negative battery cable is attached to the chassis and the chassis is made of electrically conductive metal, the chassis of the vehicle can serve as a ground wire to complete the circuit. Secondly, most automotive circuits contain switches to turn components on and off as required.

*Every complete circuit from a power source must include a component which is using the power from the power source.* If you were to disconnect the light bulb from the wires and touch the two wires together (don't do this) the power supply wire to the component would be grounded before the normal ground connection for the circuit.

Because grounding a wire from a power source makes a complete circuit—less the required component to use the power—this phenomenon is called a short circuit. Common causes are: broken insulation (exposing the metal wire to a metal part of the car or truck), or a shorted switch.

Some electrical components which require a large amount of current to operate also have a relay in their circuit. Since these circuits carry a large amount of current, the thickness of the wire in the circuit (gauge size) is also greater. If this large wire were connected from the component to the control switch on the instrument panel, and then back to the component, a voltage drop would occur in the circuit. To prevent this potential drop in voltage, an electromagnetic switch (relay) is used. The large wires in the circuit are connected from the battery to one side of the relay, and from the opposite side of the relay to the component. The relay is normally open, preventing current from passing through the circuit. An additional, smaller, wire is connected from the relay to the control switch for the circuit. When the control switch is turned on, it grounds the smaller wire from the relay and completes the circuit. This closes the relay and allows current to flow from the battery to the component. The horn, headlight, and starter circuits are three which use relays.

It is possible for larger surges of current to pass through the electrical system of your car or truck. If this surge of current were to reach an electrical component, it could burn it out. To prevent this, fuses, circuit breakers or fusible links are connected into the current supply wires of most of the major electrical systems. When an electrical current of excessive power passes through the component's fuse, the fuse blows out and breaks the circuit, saving the component from destruction.

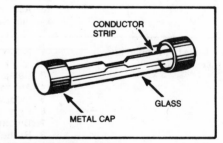

**Typical automotive fuse**

A circuit breaker is basically a self-repairing fuse. The circuit breaker opens the circuit the same way a fuse does. However, when either the short is removed from the circuit or the surge subsides, the circuit breaker resets itself and does not have to be replaced as a fuse does.

A fuse link is a wire that acts as a fuse. It is normally connected between the starter relay and the main wiring harness. This connection is usually under the hood. The fuse link (if installed) protects all the

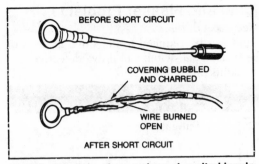

Most fusible links show a charred, melted insulation when they burn out

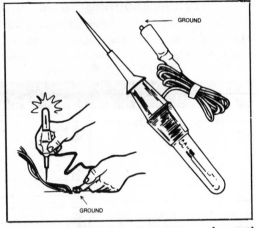

The test light will show the presence of current when touched to a hot wire and grounded at the other end

chassis electrical components, and is the probable cause of trouble when none of the electrical components function, unless the battery is disconnected or dead.

Electrical problems generally fall into one of three areas:

1. The component that is not functioning is not receiving current.

2. The component itself is not functioning.

3. The component is not properly grounded.

The electrical system can be checked with a test light and a jumper wire. A test light is a device that looks like a pointed screwdriver with a wire attached to it and has a light bulb in its handle. A jumper wire is a piece of insulated wire with an alligator clip attached to each end.

If a component is not working, you must follow a systematic plan to determine which of the three causes is the villain.

1. Turn on the switch that controls the inoperable component.

2. Disconnect the power supply wire from the component.

3. Attach the ground wire on the test light to a good metal ground.

4. Touch the probe end of the test light to the end of the power supply wire that was disconnected from the component. If the component is receiving current, the test light will go on.

**NOTE:** *Some components work only when the ignition switch is turned on.*

If the test light does not go on, then the problem is in the circuit between the battery and the component. This includes all the switches, fuses, and relays in the system. Follow the wire that runs back to the battery. The problem is an open circuit between the

battery and the component. If the fuse is blown and, when replaced, immediately blows again, there is a short circuit in the system which must be located and repaired. If there is a switch in the system, bypass it with a jumper wire. This is done by connecting one end of the jumper wire to the power supply wire into the switch and the other end of the jumper wire to the wire coming out of the switch. If the test light lights with the jumper wire installed, the switch or whatever was bypassed is defective.

**NOTE:** *Never substitute the jumper wire for the component, since it is required to use the power from the power source.*

5. If the bulb in the test light goes on, then the current is getting to the component that is not working. This eliminates the first of the three possible causes. Connect the power supply wire and connect a jumper wire from the component to a good metal ground. Do this with the switch which controls the component turned on, and also the ignition switch turned on if it is required for the component to work. If the component works with the jumper wire installed, then it has a bad ground. This is usually caused by the metal area on which the component mounts to the chassis being coated with some type of foreign matter.

6. If neither test located the source of the trouble, then the component itself is defective. Remember that for any electrical system to work, all connections must be clean and tight.

## Troubleshooting Basic Turn Signal and Flasher Problems

See Chapter 5 for service procedures

Most problems in the turn signals or flasher system can be reduced to defective flashers or bulbs, which are easily replaced. Occasionally, the turn signal switch will prove defective.

F = Front     R = Rear     ● = Lights off     ○ = Lights on

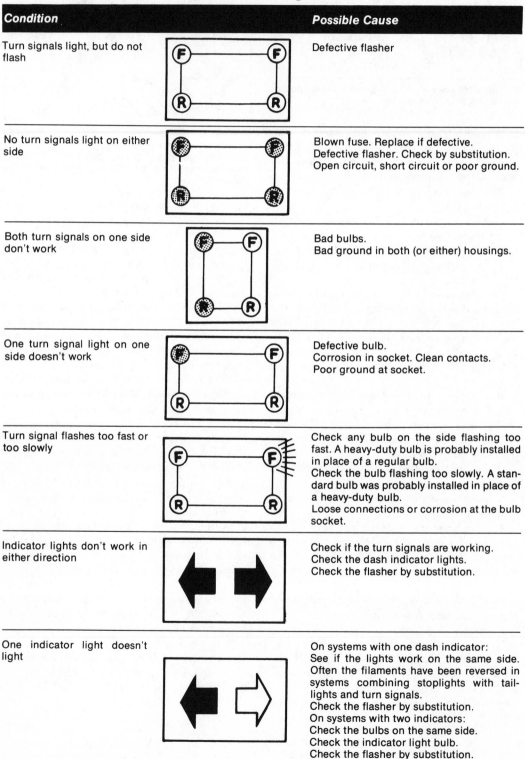

| Condition | Possible Cause |
| --- | --- |
| Turn signals light, but do not flash | Defective flasher |
| No turn signals light on either side | Blown fuse. Replace if defective.<br>Defective flasher. Check by substitution.<br>Open circuit, short circuit or poor ground. |
| Both turn signals on one side don't work | Bad bulbs.<br>Bad ground in both (or either) housings. |
| One turn signal light on one side doesn't work | Defective bulb.<br>Corrosion in socket. Clean contacts.<br>Poor ground at socket. |
| Turn signal flashes too fast or too slowly | Check any bulb on the side flashing too fast. A heavy-duty bulb is probably installed in place of a regular bulb.<br>Check the bulb flashing too slowly. A standard bulb was probably installed in place of a heavy-duty bulb.<br>Loose connections or corrosion at the bulb socket. |
| Indicator lights don't work in either direction | Check if the turn signals are working.<br>Check the dash indicator lights.<br>Check the flasher by substitution. |
| One indicator light doesn't light | On systems with one dash indicator:<br>See if the lights work on the same side. Often the filaments have been reversed in systems combining stoplights with taillights and turn signals.<br>Check the flasher by substitution.<br>On systems with two indicators:<br>Check the bulbs on the same side.<br>Check the indicator light bulb.<br>Check the flasher by substitution. |

## Troubleshooting Lighting Problems

See Chapter 5 for service procedures

| Condition | Possible Cause |
|---|---|
| One or more lights don't work, but others do | 1. Defective bulb(s)<br>2. Blown fuse(s)<br>3. Dirty fuse clips or light sockets<br>4. Poor ground circuit |
| Lights burn out quickly | 1. Incorrect voltage regulator setting or defective regulator<br>2. Poor battery/alternator connections |
| Lights go dim | 1. Low/discharged battery<br>2. Alternator not charging<br>3. Corroded sockets or connections<br>4. Low voltage output |
| Lights flicker | 1. Loose connection<br>2. Poor ground. (Run ground wire from light housing to frame)<br>3. Circuit breaker operating (short circuit) |
| Lights "flare"—Some flare is normal on acceleration—If excessive, see "Lights Burn Out Quickly" | High voltage setting |
| Lights glare—approaching drivers are blinded | 1. Lights adjusted too high<br>2. Rear springs or shocks sagging<br>3. Rear tires soft |

## Troubleshooting Dash Gauge Problems

Most problems can be traced to a defective sending unit or faulty wiring. Occasionally, the gauge itself is at fault. See Chapter 5 for service procedures.

| Condition | Possible Cause |
|---|---|

### COOLANT TEMPERATURE GAUGE

| | |
|---|---|
| Gauge reads erratically or not at all | 1. Loose or dirty connections<br>2. Defective sending unit.<br>3. Defective gauge. To test a bi-metal gauge, remove the wire from the sending unit. Ground the wire for an instant. If the gauge registers, replace the sending unit. To test a magnetic gauge, disconnect the wire at the sending unit. With ignition ON gauge should register COLD. Ground the wire; gauge should register HOT. |

### AMMETER GAUGE—TURN HEADLIGHTS ON (DO NOT START ENGINE). NOTE REACTION

| | |
|---|---|
| Ammeter shows charge<br>Ammeter shows discharge<br>Ammeter does not move | 1. Connections reversed on gauge<br>2. Ammeter is OK<br>3. Loose connections or faulty wiring<br>4. Defective gauge |

| Condition | Possible Cause |
|---|---|
| **OIL PRESSURE GAUGE** | |
| Gauge does not register or is inaccurate | 1. On mechanical gauge, Bourdon tube may be bent or kinked.<br>2. Low oil pressure. Remove sending unit. Idle the engine briefly. If no oil flows from sending unit hole, problem is in engine.<br>3. Defective gauge. Remove the wire from the sending unit and ground it for an instant with the ignition ON. A good gauge will go to the top of the scale.<br>4. Defective wiring. Check the wiring to the gauge. If it's OK and the gauge doesn't register when grounded, replace the gauge.<br>5. Defective sending unit. |
| **ALL GAUGES** | |
| All gauges do not operate<br><br>All gauges read low or erratically<br>All gauges pegged | 1. Blown fuse<br>2. Defective instrument regulator<br>3. Defective or dirty instrument voltage regulator<br>4. Loss of ground between instrument voltage regulator and frame<br>5. Defective instrument regulator |
| **WARNING LIGHTS** | |
| Light(s) do not come on when ignition is ON, but engine is not started<br><br><br>Light comes on with engine running | 1. Defective bulb<br>2. Defective wire<br>3. Defective sending unit. Disconnect the wire from the sending unit and ground it. Replace the sending unit if the light comes on with the ignition ON.<br>4. Problem in individual system<br>5. Defective sending unit |

## Troubleshooting Clutch Problems

It is false economy to replace individual clutch components. The pressure plate, clutch plate and throwout bearing should be replaced as a set, and the flywheel face inspected, whenever the clutch is overhauled. See Chapter 6 for service procedures.

| Condition | Possible Cause |
|---|---|
| Clutch chatter | 1. Grease on driven plate (disc) facing<br>2. Binding clutch linkage or cable<br>3. Loose, damaged facings on driven plate (disc)<br>4. Engine mounts loose<br>5. Incorrect height adjustment of pressure plate release levers<br>6. Clutch housing or housing to transmission adapter misalignment<br>7. Loose driven plate hub |
| Clutch grabbing | 1. Oil, grease on driven plate (disc) facing<br>2. Broken pressure plate<br>3. Warped or binding driven plate. Driven plate binding on clutch shaft |
| Clutch slips | 1. Lack of lubrication in clutch linkage or cable (linkage or cable binds, causes incomplete engagement)<br>2. Incorrect pedal, or linkage adjustment<br>3. Broken pressure plate springs<br>4. Weak pressure plate springs<br>5. Grease on driven plate facings (disc) |

## Troubleshooting Clutch Problems (cont.)

| Condition | Possible Cause |
|---|---|
| Incomplete clutch release | 1. Incorrect pedal or linkage adjustment or linkage or cable binding<br>2. Incorrect height adjustment on pressure plate release levers<br>3. Loose, broken facings on driven plate (disc)<br>4. Bent, dished, warped driven plate caused by overheating |
| Grinding, whirring grating noise when pedal is depressed | 1. Worn or defective throwout bearing<br>2. Starter drive teeth contacting flywheel ring gear teeth. Look for milled or polished teeth on ring gear. |
| Squeal, howl, trumpeting noise when pedal is being released (occurs during first inch to inch and one-half of pedal travel) | Pilot bushing worn or lack of lubricant. If bushing appears OK, polish bushing with emery cloth, soak lube wick in oil, lube bushing with oil, apply film of chassis grease to clutch shaft pilot hub, reassemble. NOTE: Bushing wear may be due to misalignment of clutch housing or housing to transmission adapter |
| Vibration or clutch pedal pulsation with clutch disengaged (pedal fully depressed) | 1. Worn or defective engine transmission mounts<br>2. Flywheel run out. (Flywheel run out at face not to exceed 0.005″)<br>3. Damaged or defective clutch components |

## Troubleshooting Manual Transmission Problems
### See Chapter 6 for service procedures

| Condition | Possible Cause |
|---|---|
| Transmission jumps out of gear | 1. Misalignment of transmission case or clutch housing.<br>2. Worn pilot bearing in crankshaft.<br>3. Bent transmission shaft.<br>4. Worn high speed sliding gear.<br>5. Worn teeth or end-play in clutch shaft.<br>6. Insufficient spring tension on shifter rail plunger.<br>7. Bent or loose shifter fork.<br>8. Gears not engaging completely.<br>9. Loose or worn bearings on clutch shaft or mainshaft.<br>10. Worn gear teeth.<br>11. Worn or damaged detent balls. |
| Transmission sticks in gear | 1. Clutch not releasing fully.<br>2. Burred or battered teeth on clutch shaft, or sliding sleeve.<br>3. Burred or battered transmission mainshaft.<br>4. Frozen synchronizing clutch.<br>5. Stuck shifter rail plunger.<br>6. Gearshift lever twisting and binding shifter rail.<br>7. Battered teeth on high speed sliding gear or on sleeve.<br>8. Improper lubrication, or lack of lubrication.<br>9. Corroded transmission parts.<br>10. Defective mainshaft pilot bearing.<br>11. Locked gear bearings will give same effect as stuck in gear. |
| Transmission gears will not synchronize | 1. Binding pilot bearing on mainshaft, will synchronize in high gear only.<br>2. Clutch not releasing fully.<br>3. Detent spring weak or broken.<br>4. Weak or broken springs under balls in sliding gear sleeve.<br>5. Binding bearing on clutch shaft, or binding countershaft.<br>6. Binding pilot bearing in crankshaft.<br>7. Badly worn gear teeth.<br>8. Improper lubrication.<br>9. Constant mesh gear not turning freely on transmission mainshaft. Will synchronize in that gear only. |

| Condition | Possible Cause |
|---|---|
| Gears spinning when shifting into gear from neutral | 1. Clutch not releasing fully.<br>2. In some cases an extremely light lubricant in transmission will cause gears to continue to spin for a short time after clutch is released.<br>3. Binding pilot bearing in crankshaft. |
| Transmission noisy in all gears | 1. Insufficient lubricant, or improper lubricant.<br>2. Worn countergear bearings.<br>3. Worn or damaged main drive gear or countergear.<br>4. Damaged main drive gear or mainshaft bearings.<br>5. Worn or damaged countergear anti-lash plate. |
| Transmission noisy in neutral only | 1. Damaged main drive gear bearing.<br>2. Damaged or loose mainshaft pilot bearing.<br>3. Worn or damaged countergear anti-lash plate.<br>4. Worn countergear bearings. |
| Transmission noisy in one gear only | 1. Damaged or worn constant mesh gears.<br>2. Worn or damaged countergear bearings.<br>3. Damaged or worn synchronizer. |
| Transmission noisy in reverse only | 1. Worn or damaged reverse idler gear or idler bushing.<br>2. Worn or damaged mainshaft reverse gear.<br>3. Worn or damaged reverse countergear.<br>4. Damaged shift mechanism. |

## TROUBLESHOOTING AUTOMATIC TRANSMISSION PROBLEMS

Keeping alert to changes in the operating characteristics of the transmission (changing shift points, noises, etc.) can prevent small problems from becoming large ones. If the problem cannot be traced to loose bolts, fluid level, misadjusted linkage, clogged filters or similar problems, you should probably seek professional service.

### Transmission Fluid Indications

The appearance and odor of the transmission fluid can give valuable clues to the overall condition of the transmission. Always note the appearance of the fluid when you check the fluid level or change the fluid. Rub a small amount of fluid between your fingers to feel for grit and smell the fluid on the dipstick.

| If the fluid appears: | It indicates: |
|---|---|
| Clear and red colored | Normal operation |
| Discolored (extremely dark red or brownish) or smells burned | Band or clutch pack failure, usually caused by an overheated transmission. Hauling very heavy loads with insufficient power or failure to change the fluid often result in overheating.<br>Do not confuse this appearance with newer fluids that have a darker red color and a strong odor (though not a burned odor). |
| Foamy or aerated (light in color and full of bubbles) | 1. The level is too high (gear train is churning oil)<br>2. An internal air leak (air is mixing with the fluid). Have the transmission checked professionally. |
| Solid residue in the fluid | Defective bands, clutch pack or bearings. Bits of band material or metal abrasives are clinging to the dipstick. Have the transmission checked professionally. |
| Varnish coating on the dipstick | The transmission fluid is overheating |

## TROUBLESHOOTING DRIVE AXLE PROBLEMS

First, determine when the noise is most noticeable.

Drive Noise: Produced under vehicle acceleration.

Coast Noise: Produced while coasting with a closed throttle.

Float Noise: Occurs while maintaining constant speed (just enough to keep speed constant) on a level road.

### External Noise Elimination

It is advisable to make a thorough road test to determine whether the noise originates in the rear axle or whether it originates from the tires, engine, transmission, wheel bearings or road surface. Noise originating from other places cannot be corrected by servicing the rear axle.

#### ROAD NOISE

Brick or rough surfaced concrete roads produce noises that seem to come from the rear axle. Road noise is usually identical in Drive or Coast and driving on a different type of road will tell whether the road is the problem.

#### TIRE NOISE

Tire noise can be mistaken as rear axle noise, even though the tires on the front are at fault. Snow tread and mud tread tires or tires worn unevenly will frequently cause vibrations which seem to originate elsewhere; *temporarily, and for test purposes only*, inflate the tires to 40–50 lbs. This will significantly alter the noise produced by the tires, but will not alter noise from the rear axle. Noises from the rear axle will normally cease at speeds below 30 mph on coast, while tire noise will continue at lower tone as speed is decreased. The rear axle noise will usually change from drive conditions to coast conditions, while tire noise will not. Do not forget to lower the tire pressure to normal after the test is complete.

#### ENGINE/TRANSMISSION NOISE

Determine at what speed the noise is most pronounced, then stop in a quiet place. With the transmission in Neutral, run the engine through speeds corresponding to road speeds where the noise was noticed. Noises produced with the vehicle standing still are coming from the engine or transmission.

#### FRONT WHEEL BEARINGS

Front wheel bearing noises, sometimes confused with rear axle noises, will not change when comparing drive and coast conditions. While holding the speed steady, lightly apply the footbrake. This will often cause wheel bearing noise to lessen, as some of the weight is taken off the bearing. Front wheel bearings are easily checked by jacking up the wheels and spinning the wheels. Shaking the wheels will also determine if the wheel bearings are excessively loose.

#### REAR AXLE NOISES

Eliminating other possible sources can narrow the cause to the rear axle, which normally produces noise from worn gears or bearings. Gear noises tend to peak in a narrow speed range, while bearing noises will usually vary in pitch with engine speeds.

## Noise Diagnosis

| The Noise Is: | Most Probably Produced By: |
| --- | --- |
| 1. Identical under Drive or Coast | Road surface, tires or front wheel bearings |
| 2. Different depending on road surface | Road surface or tires |
| 3. Lower as speed is lowered | Tires |
| 4. Similar when standing or moving | Engine or transmission |
| 5. A vibration | Unbalanced tires, rear wheel bearing, unbalanced driveshaft or worn U-joint |
| 6. A knock or click about every two tire revolutions | Rear wheel bearing |
| 7. Most pronounced on turns | Damaged differential gears |
| 8. A steady low-pitched whirring or scraping, starting at low speeds | Damaged or worn pinion bearing |
| 9. A chattering vibration on turns | Wrong differential lubricant or worn clutch plates (limited slip rear axle) |
| 10. Noticed only in Drive, Coast or Float conditions | Worn ring gear and/or pinion gear |

## Troubleshooting Steering & Suspension Problems

| Condition | Possible Cause |
| --- | --- |
| Hard steering (wheel is hard to turn) | 1. Improper tire pressure<br>2. Loose or glazed pump drive belt<br>3. Low or incorrect fluid<br>4. Loose, bent or poorly lubricated front end parts<br>5. Improper front end alignment (excessive caster)<br>6. Bind in steering column or linkage<br>7. Kinked hydraulic hose<br>8. Air in hydraulic system<br>9. Low pump output or leaks in system<br>10. Obstruction in lines<br>11. Pump valves sticking or out of adjustment<br>12. Incorrect wheel alignment |
| Loose steering (too much play in steering wheel) | 1. Loose wheel bearings<br>2. Faulty shocks<br>3. Worn linkage or suspension components<br>4. Loose steering gear mounting or linkage points<br>5. Steering mechanism worn or improperly adjusted<br>6. Valve spool improperly adjusted<br>7. Worn ball joints, tie-rod ends, etc. |
| Veers or wanders (pulls to one side with hands off steering wheel) | 1. Improper tire pressure<br>2. Improper front end alignment<br>3. Dragging or improperly adjusted brakes<br>4. Bent frame<br>5. Improper rear end alignment<br>6. Faulty shocks or springs<br>7. Loose or bent front end components<br>8. Play in Pitman arm<br>9. Steering gear mountings loose<br>10. Loose wheel bearings<br>11. Binding Pitman arm<br>12. Spool valve sticking or improperly adjusted<br>13. Worn ball joints |
| Wheel oscillation or vibration transmitted through steering wheel | 1. Low or uneven tire pressure<br>2. Loose wheel bearings<br>3. Improper front end alignment<br>4. Bent spindle<br>5. Worn, bent or broken front end components<br>6. Tires out of round or out of balance<br>7. Excessive lateral runout in disc brake rotor<br>8. Loose or bent shock absorber or strut |
| Noises (see also "Troubleshooting Drive Axle Problems") | 1. Loose belts<br>2. Low fluid, air in system<br>3. Foreign matter in system<br>4. Improper lubrication<br>5. Interference or chafing in linkage<br>6. Steering gear mountings loose<br>7. Incorrect adjustment or wear in gear box<br>8. Faulty valves or wear in pump<br>9. Kinked hydraulic lines<br>10. Worn wheel bearings |
| Poor return of steering | 1. Over-inflated tires<br>2. Improperly aligned front end (excessive caster)<br>3. Binding in steering column<br>4. No lubrication in front end<br>5. Steering gear adjusted too tight |
| Uneven tire wear (see "How To Read Tire Wear") | 1. Incorrect tire pressure<br>2. Improperly aligned front end<br>3. Tires out-of-balance<br>4. Bent or worn suspension parts |

# HOW TO READ TIRE WEAR

The way your tires wear is a good indicator of other parts of the suspension. Abnormal wear patterns are often caused by the need for simple tire maintenance, or for front end alignment.

Excessive wear at the center of the tread indicates that the air pressure in the tire is consistently too high. The tire is riding on the center of the tread and wearing it prematurely. Occasionally, this wear pattern can result from outrageously wide tires on narrow rims. The cure for this is to replace either the tires or the wheels.

This type of wear usually results from consistent under-inflation. When a tire is under-inflated, there is too much contact with the road by the outer treads, which wear prematurely. When this type of wear occurs, and the tire pressure is known to be consistently correct, a bent or worn steering component or the need for wheel alignment could be indicated.

Feathering is a condition when the edge of each tread rib develops a slightly rounded edge on one side and a sharp edge on the other. By running your hand over the tire, you can usually feel the sharper edges before you'll be able to see them. The most common causes of feathering are incorrect toe-in setting or deteriorated bushings in the front suspension.

When an inner or outer rib wears faster than the rest of the tire, the need for wheel alignment is indicated. There is excessive camber in the front suspension, causing the wheel to lean too much putting excessive load on one side of the tire. Misalignment could also be due to sagging springs, worn ball joints, or worn control arm bushings. Be sure the vehicle is loaded the way it's normally driven when you have the wheels aligned.

Cups or scalloped dips appearing around the edge of the tread almost always indicate worn (sometimes bent) suspension parts. Adjustment of wheel alignment alone will seldom cure the problem. Any worn component that connects the wheel to the suspension can cause this type of wear. Occasionally, wheels that are out of balance will wear like this, but wheel imbalance usually shows up as bald spots between the outside edges and center of the tread.

Second-rib wear is usually found only in radial tires, and appears where the steel belts end in relation to the tread. It can be kept to a minimum by paying careful attention to tire pressure and frequently rotating the tires. This is often considered normal wear but excessive amounts indicate that the tires are too wide for the wheels.

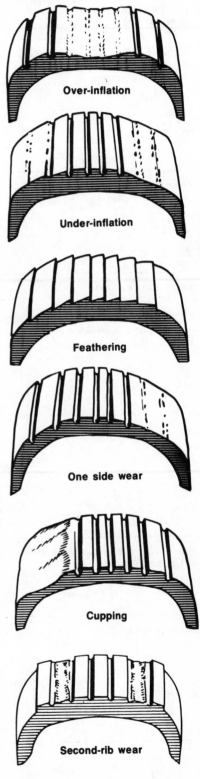

Over-inflation

Under-inflation

Feathering

One side wear

Cupping

Second-rib wear

## Troubleshooting Disc Brake Problems

| Condition | Possible Cause |
|---|---|
| Noise—groan—brake noise emanating when slowly releasing brakes (creep-groan) | Not detrimental to function of disc brakes—no corrective action required. (This noise may be eliminated by slightly increasing or decreasing brake pedal efforts.) |
| Rattle—brake noise or rattle emanating at low speeds on rough roads, (front wheels only). | 1. Shoe anti-rattle spring missing or not properly positioned. 2. Excessive clearance between shoe and caliper. 3. Soft or broken caliper seals. 4. Deformed or misaligned disc. 5. Loose caliper. |
| Scraping | 1. Mounting bolts too long. 2. Loose wheel bearings. 3. Bent, loose, or misaligned splash shield. |
| Front brakes heat up during driving and fail to release | 1. Operator riding brake pedal. 2. Stop light switch improperly adjusted. 3. Sticking pedal linkage. 4. Frozen or seized piston. 5. Residual pressure valve in master cylinder. 6. Power brake malfunction. 7. Proportioning valve malfunction. |
| Leaky brake caliper | 1. Damaged or worn caliper piston seal. 2. Scores or corrosion on surface of cylinder bore. |
| Grabbing or uneven brake action— Brakes pull to one side | 1. Causes listed under "Brakes Pull". 2. Power brake malfunction. 3. Low fluid level in master cylinder. 4. Air in hydraulic system. 5. Brake fluid, oil or grease on linings. 6. Unmatched linings. 7. Distorted brake pads. 8. Frozen or seized pistons. 9. Incorrect tire pressure. 10. Front end out of alignment. 11. Broken rear spring. 12. Brake caliper pistons sticking. 13. Restricted hose or line. 14. Caliper not in proper alignment to braking disc. 15. Stuck or malfunctioning metering valve. 16. Soft or broken caliper seals. 17. Loose caliper. |
| Brake pedal can be depressed without braking effect | 1. Air in hydraulic system or improper bleeding procedure. 2. Leak past primary cup in master cylinder. 3. Leak in system. 4. Rear brakes out of adjustment. 5. Bleeder screw open. |
| Excessive pedal travel | 1. Air, leak, or insufficient fluid in system or caliper. 2. Warped or excessively tapered shoe and lining assembly. 3. Excessive disc runout. 4. Rear brake adjustment required. 5. Loose wheel bearing adjustment. 6. Damaged caliper piston seal. 7. Improper brake fluid (boil). 8. Power brake malfunction. 9. Weak or soft hoses. |

## Troubleshooting Disc Brake Problems (cont.)

| Condition | Possible Cause |
|---|---|
| Brake roughness or chatter (pedal pumping) | 1. Excessive thickness variation of braking disc.<br>2. Excessive lateral runout of braking disc.<br>3. Rear brake drums out-of-round.<br>4. Excessive front bearing clearance. |
| Excessive pedal effort | 1. Brake fluid, oil or grease on linings.<br>2. Incorrect lining.<br>3. Frozen or seized pistons.<br>4. Power brake malfunction.<br>5. Kinked or collapsed hose or line.<br>6. Stuck metering valve.<br>7. Scored caliper or master cylinder bore.<br>8. Seized caliper pistons. |
| Brake pedal fades (pedal travel increases with foot on brake) | 1. Rough master cylinder or caliper bore.<br>2. Loose or broken hydraulic lines/connections.<br>3. Air in hydraulic system.<br>4. Fluid level low.<br>5. Weak or soft hoses.<br>6. Inferior quality brake shoes or fluid.<br>7. Worn master cylinder piston cups or seals. |

## Troubleshooting Drum Brakes

| Condition | Possible Cause |
|---|---|
| Pedal goes to floor | 1. Fluid low in reservoir.<br>2. Air in hydraulic system.<br>3. Improperly adjusted brake.<br>4. Leaking wheel cylinders.<br>5. Loose or broken brake lines.<br>6. Leaking or worn master cylinder.<br>7. Excessively worn brake lining. |
| Spongy brake pedal | 1. Air in hydraulic system.<br>2. Improper brake fluid (low boiling point).<br>3. Excessively worn or cracked brake drums.<br>4. Broken pedal pivot bushing. |
| Brakes pulling | 1. Contaminated lining.<br>2. Front end out of alignment.<br>3. Incorrect brake adjustment.<br>4. Unmatched brake lining.<br>5. Brake drums out of round.<br>6. Brake shoes distorted.<br>7. Restricted brake hose or line.<br>8. Broken rear spring.<br>9. Worn brake linings.<br>10. Uneven lining wear.<br>11. Glazed brake lining.<br>12. Excessive brake lining dust.<br>13. Heat spotted brake drums.<br>14. Weak brake return springs.<br>15. Faulty automatic adjusters.<br>16. Low or incorrect tire pressure. |

| Condition | Possible Cause |
|---|---|
| Squealing brakes | 1. Glazed brake lining.<br>2. Saturated brake lining.<br>3. Weak or broken brake shoe retaining spring.<br>4. Broken or weak brake shoe return spring.<br>5. Incorrect brake lining.<br>6. Distorted brake shoes.<br>7. Bent support plate.<br>8. Dust in brakes or scored brake drums.<br>9. Linings worn below limit.<br>10. Uneven brake lining wear.<br>11. Heat spotted brake drums. |
| Chirping brakes | 1. Out of round drum or eccentric axle flange pilot. |
| Dragging brakes | 1. Incorrect wheel or parking brake adjustment.<br>2. Parking brakes engaged or improperly adjusted.<br>3. Weak or broken brake shoe return spring.<br>4. Brake pedal binding.<br>5. Master cylinder cup sticking.<br>6. Obstructed master cylinder relief port.<br>7. Saturated brake lining.<br>8. Bent or out of round brake drum.<br>9. Contaminated or improper brake fluid.<br>10. Sticking wheel cylinder pistons.<br>11. Driver riding brake pedal.<br>12. Defective proportioning valve.<br>13. Insufficient brake shoe lubricant. |
| Hard pedal | 1. Brake booster inoperative.<br>2. Incorrect brake lining.<br>3. Restricted brake line or hose.<br>4. Frozen brake pedal linkage.<br>5. Stuck wheel cylinder.<br>6. Binding pedal linkage.<br>7. Faulty proportioning valve. |
| Wheel locks | 1. Contaminated brake lining.<br>2. Loose or torn brake lining.<br>3. Wheel cylinder cups sticking.<br>4. Incorrect wheel bearing adjustment.<br>5. Faulty proportioning valve. |
| Brakes fade (high speed) | 1. Incorrect lining.<br>2. Overheated brake drums.<br>3. Incorrect brake fluid (low boiling temperature).<br>4. Saturated brake lining.<br>5. Leak in hydraulic system.<br>6. Faulty automatic adjusters. |
| Pedal pulsates | 1. Bent or out of round brake drum. |
| Brake chatter and shoe knock | 1. Out of round brake drum.<br>2. Loose support plate.<br>3. Bent support plate.<br>4. Distorted brake shoes.<br>5. Machine grooves in contact face of brake drum (Shoe Knock).<br>6. Contaminated brake lining.<br>7. Missing or loose components.<br>8. Incorrect lining material.<br>9. Out-of-round brake drums.<br>10. Heat spotted or scored brake drums.<br>11. Out-of-balance wheels. |

## Troubleshooting Drum Brakes (cont.)

| Condition | Possible Cause |
|---|---|
| Brakes do not self adjust | 1. Adjuster screw frozen in thread.<br>2. Adjuster screw corroded at thrust washer.<br>3. Adjuster lever does not engage star wheel.<br>4. Adjuster installed on wrong wheel. |
| Brake light glows | 1. Leak in the hydraulic system.<br>2. Air in the system.<br>3. Improperly adjusted master cylinder pushrod.<br>4. Uneven lining wear.<br>5. Failure to center combination valve or proportioning valve. |

# Mechanic's Data

## General Conversion Table

| Multiply By | To Convert | To | |
|---|---|---|---|
| | | LENGTH | |
| 2.54 | Inches | Centimeters | .3937 |
| 25.4 | Inches | Millimeters | .03937 |
| 30.48 | Feet | Centimeters | .0328 |
| .304 | Feet | Meters | 3.28 |
| .914 | Yards | Meters | 1.094 |
| 1.609 | Miles | Kilometers | .621 |
| | | VOLUME | |
| .473 | Pints | Liters | 2.11 |
| .946 | Quarts | Liters | 1.06 |
| 3.785 | Gallons | Liters | .264 |
| .016 | Cubic inches | Liters | 61.02 |
| 16.39 | Cubic inches | Cubic cms. | .061 |
| 28.3 | Cubic feet | Liters | .0353 |
| | | MASS (Weight) | |
| 28.35 | Ounces | Grams | .035 |
| .4536 | Pounds | Kilograms | 2.20 |
| — | To obtain | From | Multiply by |

| Multiply By | To Convert | To | |
|---|---|---|---|
| | | AREA | |
| .645 | Square inches | Square cms. | .155 |
| .836 | Square yds. | Square meters | 1.196 |
| | | FORCE | |
| 4.448 | Pounds | Newtons | .225 |
| .138 | Ft./lbs. | Kilogram/meters | 7.23 |
| 1.36 | Ft./lbs. | Newton-meters | .737 |
| .112 | In./lbs. | Newton-meters | 8.844 |
| | | PRESSURE | |
| .068 | Psi | Atmospheres | 14.7 |
| 6.89 | Psi | Kilopascals | .145 |
| | | OTHER | |
| 1.104 | Horsepower (DIN) | Horsepower (SAE) | .9861 |
| .746 | Horsepower (SAE) | Kilowatts (KW) | 1.34 |
| 1.60 | Mph | Km/h | .625 |
| .425 | Mpg | Km/1 | 2.35 |
| — | To obtain | From | Multiply by |

## Tap Drill Sizes

### National Coarse or U.S.S.

| Screw & Tap Size | Threads Per Inch | Use Drill Number |
|---|---|---|
| No. 5 | 40 | .39 |
| No. 6 | 32 | .36 |
| No. 8 | 32 | .29 |
| No. 10 | 24 | .25 |
| No. 12 | 24 | .17 |
| 1/4 | 20 | 8 |
| 5/16 | 18 | .F |
| 3/8 | 16 | 5/16 |
| 7/16 | 14 | .U |
| 1/2 | 13 | 27/64 |
| 9/16 | 12 | 31/64 |
| 5/8 | 11 | 17/32 |
| 3/4 | 10 | 21/32 |
| 7/8 | 9 | 49/64 |

### National Coarse or U.S.S.

| Screw & Tap Size | Threads Per Inch | Use Drill Number |
|---|---|---|
| 1 | 8 | 7/8 |
| 1 1/8 | 7 | 63/64 |
| 1 1/4 | 7 | 1 7/64 |
| 1 1/2 | 6 | 1 11/32 |

### National Fine or S.A.E.

| Screw & Tap Size | Threads Per Inch | Use Drill Number |
|---|---|---|
| No. 5 | 44 | .37 |
| No. 6 | 40 | .33 |
| No. 8 | 36 | .29 |
| No. 10 | 32 | .21 |

### National Fine or S.A.E.

| Screw & Tap Size | Threads Per Inch | Use Drill Number |
|---|---|---|
| No. 12 | 28 | .15 |
| 1/4 | 28 | 3 |
| 6/16 | 24 | 1 |
| 3/8 | 24 | .Q |
| 7/16 | 20 | .W |
| 1/2 | 20 | 29/64 |
| 9/16 | 18 | 33/64 |
| 5/8 | 18 | 37/64 |
| 3/4 | 16 | 11/16 |
| 7/8 | 14 | 13/16 |
| 1 1/8 | 12 | 1 3/64 |
| 1 1/4 | 12 | 1 11/64 |
| 1 1/2 | 12 | 1 27/64 |

# Drill Sizes In Decimal Equivalents

| Inch | Decimal | Wire | mm | Inch | Decimal | Wire | mm | Inch | Decimal | Wire & Letter | mm | Inch | Decimal | Letter | mm | Inch | Decimal | mm |
|---|---|---|---|---|---|---|---|---|---|---|---|---|---|---|---|---|---|---|
| 1/64 | .0156 | | .39 | | .0730 | 49 | | | .1614 | | 4.1 | | .2717 | | 6.9 | | .4331 | 11.0 |
| | .0157 | | .4 | | .0748 | | 1.9 | | .1654 | | 4.2 | | .2720 | I | | 7/16 | .4375 | 11.11 |
| | .0160 | 78 | | | .0760 | 48 | | | .1660 | 19 | | | .2756 | | 7.0 | | .4528 | 11.5 |
| | .0165 | | .42 | 5/64 | .0768 | | 1.95 | | .1673 | | 4.25 | | .2770 | J | | 29/64 | .4531 | 11.51 |
| | .0173 | | .44 | | .0781 | | 1.98 | | .1693 | | 4.3 | | .2795 | | 7.1 | 15/32 | .4688 | 11.90 |
| | .0177 | | .45 | | .0785 | 47 | | | .1695 | 18 | | | .2810 | K | | | .4724 | 12.0 |
| | .0180 | 77 | | | .0787 | | 2.0 | 11/64 | .1719 | | 4.36 | 9/32 | .2812 | | 7.14 | 31/64 | .4844 | 12.30 |
| | .0181 | | .46 | | .0807 | | 2.05 | | .1730 | 17 | | | .2835 | | 7.2 | | .4921 | 12.5 |
| | .0189 | | .48 | | .0810 | 46 | | | .1732 | | 4.4 | | .2854 | | 7.25 | 1/2 | .5000 | 12.70 |
| | .0197 | | .5 | | .0820 | 45 | | | .1770 | 16 | | | .2874 | | 7.3 | | .5118 | 13.0 |
| | .0200 | 76 | | | .0827 | | 2.1 | | .1772 | | 4.5 | | .2900 | L | | 33/64 | .5156 | 13.09 |
| | .0210 | 75 | | | .0846 | | 2.15 | | .1800 | 15 | | | .2913 | | 7.4 | 17/32 | .5312 | 13.49 |
| | .0217 | | .55 | | .0860 | 44 | | | .1811 | | 4.6 | | .2950 | M | | | .5315 | 13.5 |
| | .0225 | 74 | | | .0866 | | 2.2 | | .1820 | 14 | | | .2953 | | 7.5 | 35/64 | .5469 | 13.89 |
| | .0236 | | .6 | | .0886 | | 2.25 | | .1850 | 13 | | 19/64 | .2969 | | 7.54 | | .5512 | 14.0 |
| | .0240 | 73 | | | .0890 | 43 | | | .1850 | | 4.7 | | .2992 | | 7.6 | 9/16 | .5625 | 14.28 |
| | .0250 | 72 | | | .0906 | | 2.3 | | .1870 | | 4.75 | | .3020 | N | | | .5709 | 14.5 |
| | .0256 | | .65 | | .0925 | | 2.35 | 3/16 | .1875 | | 4.76 | | .3031 | | 7.7 | 37/64 | .5781 | 14.68 |
| | .0260 | 71 | | | .0935 | 42 | | | .1890 | | 4.8 | | .3051 | | 7.75 | | .5906 | 15.0 |
| | .0276 | | .7 | 3/32 | .0938 | | 2.38 | | .1890 | 12 | | | .3071 | | 7.8 | 19/32 | .5938 | 15.08 |
| | .0280 | 70 | | | .0945 | | 2.4 | | .1910 | 11 | | | .3110 | | 7.9 | 39/64 | .6094 | 15.47 |
| | .0292 | 69 | | | .0960 | 41 | | | .1929 | | 4.9 | 5/16 | .3125 | | 7.93 | | .6102 | 15.5 |
| | .0295 | | .75 | | .0965 | | 2.45 | | .1935 | 10 | | | .3150 | | 8.0 | 5/8 | .6250 | 15.87 |
| | .0310 | 68 | | | .0980 | 40 | | | .1960 | 9 | | | .3160 | O | | | .6299 | 16.0 |
| 1/32 | .0312 | | .79 | | .0981 | | 2.5 | | .1969 | | 5.0 | | .3189 | | 8.1 | 41/64 | .6406 | 16.27 |
| | .0315 | | .8 | | .0995 | 39 | | | .1990 | 8 | | | .3228 | | 8.2 | | .6496 | 16.5 |
| | .0320 | 67 | | | .1015 | 38 | | | .2008 | | 5.1 | | .3230 | P | | 21/32 | .6562 | 16.66 |
| | .0330 | 66 | | | .1024 | | 2.6 | | .2010 | 7 | | | .3248 | | 8.25 | | .6693 | 17.0 |
| | .0335 | | .85 | | .1040 | 37 | | 13/64 | .2031 | | 5.16 | | .3268 | | 8.3 | 43/64 | .6719 | 17.06 |
| | .0350 | 65 | | | .1063 | | 2.7 | | .2040 | 6 | | 21/64 | .3281 | | 8.33 | 11/16 | .6875 | 17.46 |
| | .0354 | | .9 | | .1065 | 36 | | | .2047 | | 5.2 | | .3307 | | 8.4 | | .6890 | 17.5 |
| | .0360 | 64 | | | .1083 | | 2.75 | | .2055 | 5 | | | .3320 | Q | | 45/64 | .7031 | 17.85 |
| | .0370 | 63 | | 7/64 | .1094 | | 2.77 | | .2067 | | 5.25 | | .3346 | | 8.5 | | .7087 | 18.0 |
| | .0374 | | .95 | | .1100 | 35 | | | .2087 | | 5.3 | | .3386 | | 8.6 | 23/32 | .7188 | 18.25 |
| | .0380 | 62 | | | .1102 | | 2.8 | | .2090 | 4 | | | .3390 | R | | | .7283 | 18.5 |
| | .0390 | 61 | | | .1110 | 34 | | | .2126 | | 5.4 | | .3425 | | 8.7 | 47/64 | .7344 | 18.65 |
| | .0394 | | 1.0 | | .1130 | 33 | | | .2130 | 3 | | 11/32 | .3438 | | 8.73 | | .7480 | 19.0 |
| | .0400 | 60 | | | .1142 | | 2.9 | | .2165 | | 5.5 | | .3445 | | 8.75 | 3/4 | .7500 | 19.05 |
| | .0410 | 59 | | | .1160 | 32 | | 7/32 | .2188 | | 5.55 | | .3465 | | 8.8 | 49/64 | .7656 | 19.44 |
| | .0413 | | 1.05 | | .1181 | | 3.0 | | .2205 | | 5.6 | | .3480 | S | | | .7677 | 19.5 |
| | .0420 | 58 | | | .1200 | 31 | | | .2210 | 2 | | | .3504 | | 8.9 | 25/32 | .7812 | 19.84 |
| | .0430 | 57 | | | .1220 | | 3.1 | | .2244 | | 5.7 | | .3543 | | 9.0 | | .7874 | 20.0 |
| | .0433 | | 1.1 | 1/8 | .1250 | | 3.17 | | .2264 | | 5.75 | | .3580 | T | | 51/64 | .7969 | 20.24 |
| | .0453 | | 1.15 | | .1260 | | 3.2 | | .2280 | 1 | | | .3583 | | 9.1 | | .8071 | 20.5 |
| | .0465 | 56 | | | .1280 | | 3.25 | | .2283 | | 5.8 | 23/64 | .3594 | | 9.12 | 13/16 | .8125 | 20.63 |
| 3/64 | .0469 | | 1.19 | | .1285 | 30 | | | .2323 | | 5.9 | | .3622 | | 9.2 | | .8268 | 21.0 |
| | .0472 | | 1.2 | | .1299 | | 3.3 | | .2340 | A | | | .3642 | | 9.25 | 53/64 | .8281 | 21.03 |
| | .0492 | | 1.25 | | .1339 | | 3.4 | 15/64 | .2344 | | 5.95 | | .3661 | | 9.3 | 27/32 | .8438 | 21.43 |
| | .0512 | | 1.3 | | .1360 | 29 | | | .2362 | | 6.0 | | .3680 | U | | | .8465 | 21.5 |
| | .0520 | 55 | | | .1378 | | 3.5 | | .2380 | B | | | .3701 | | 9.4 | 55/64 | .8594 | 21.82 |
| | .0531 | | 1.35 | | .1405 | 28 | | | .2402 | | 6.1 | | .3740 | | 9.5 | | .8661 | 22.0 |
| | .0550 | 54 | | 9/64 | .1406 | | 3.57 | | .2420 | C | | 3/8 | .3750 | | 9.52 | 7/8 | .8750 | 22.22 |
| | .0551 | | 1.4 | | .1417 | | 3.6 | | .2441 | | 6.2 | | .3770 | V | | | .8858 | 22.5 |
| | .0571 | | 1.45 | | .1440 | 27 | | | .2460 | D | | | .3780 | | 9.6 | 57/64 | .8906 | 22.62 |
| | .0591 | | 1.5 | | .1457 | | 3.7 | | .2461 | | 6.25 | | .3819 | | 9.7 | | .9055 | 23.0 |
| | .0595 | 53 | | | .1470 | 26 | | | .2480 | | 6.3 | | .3839 | | 9.75 | 29/32 | .9062 | 23.01 |
| | .0610 | | 1.55 | | .1476 | | 3.75 | 1/4 | .2500 | E | 6.35 | | .3858 | | 9.8 | 59/64 | .9219 | 23.41 |
| 1/16 | .0625 | | 1.59 | | .1495 | 25 | | | .2520 | | 6. | | .3860 | W | | | .9252 | 23.5 |
| | .0630 | | 1.6 | | .1496 | | 3.8 | | .2559 | | 6.5 | | .3898 | | 9.9 | 15/16 | .9375 | 23.81 |
| | .0635 | 52 | | | .1520 | 24 | | | .2570 | F | | 25/64 | .3906 | | 9.92 | | .9449 | 24.0 |
| | .0650 | | 1.65 | | .1535 | | 3.9 | | .2598 | | 6.6 | | .3937 | | 10.0 | 61/64 | .9531 | 24.2 |
| | .0669 | | 1.7 | | .1540 | 23 | | | .2610 | G | | | .3970 | X | | | .9646 | 24.5 |
| | .0670 | 51 | | 5/32 | .1562 | | 3.96 | | .2638 | | 6.7 | | .4040 | Y | | 31/32 | .9688 | 24.6 |
| | .0689 | | 1.75 | | .1570 | 22 | | 17/64 | .2656 | | 6.74 | 13/32 | .4062 | | 10.31 | | .9843 | 25.0 |
| | .0700 | 50 | | | .1575 | | 4.0 | | .2657 | | 6.75 | | .4130 | Z | | 63/64 | .9844 | 25.0 |
| | .0709 | | 1.8 | | .1590 | 21 | | | .2660 | H | | | .4134 | | 10.5 | 1 | 1.0000 | 25.4 |
| | .0728 | | 1.85 | | .1610 | 20 | | | .2677 | | 6.8 | 27/64 | .4219 | | 10.71 | | | |

# Index